Jean Callaghan, Mathias Schönborn (Editors)

Warriors in Peacekeeping

George C. Marshall European Center
for Security Studies

LIT

Jean Callaghan, Mathias Schönborn (Editors)

Warriors in Peacekeeping

Points of Tension in Complex Cultural Encounters

A Comparative Study
Based on Experiences in Bosnia

LIT

Bibliographic information published by Die Deutsche Bibliothek
Die Deutsche Bibliothek lists this publication in the Deutsche
Nationalbibliografie; detailed bibliographic data are available in the
Internet at http://dnb.ddb.de.

ISBN 3-8258-5172-9

© LIT VERLAG Münster   2004
Grevener Str./Fresnostr. 2   48159 Münster
Tel. 0251-23 50 91   Fax 0251-23 19 72
e-Mail: lit@lit-verlag.de   http://www.lit-verlag.de

Distributed in North America by:

Transaction Publishers
New Brunswick (U.S.A.) and London (U.K.)

Transaction Publishers   Tel.: (732) 445 - 2280
Rutgers University   Fax: (732) 445 - 3138
35 Berrue Circle   for orders (U. S. only):
Piscataway, NJ 08854   toll free (888) 999 - 6778

CONTENTS

APPENDIX

PREFACE

This book is the result of a multinational, interdisciplinary research project organized and funded by the George C. Marshall European Center for Security Studies in Garmisch-Partenkirchen, Germany. Its authors have made an extraordinary contribution to broadening and deepening understanding of the complex range of relations in modern peacekeeping operations, including interactions between national contingents and their respective chains of command and their relations with other contingents in the field, as well as with regional authorities, scores of NGOs, and the media, the latter representing numerous countries of the world. Their findings help to identify "points of tension" in peacekeeping operations in Bosnia-Herzegovina, where, for the first time, contingents from more than 35 countries had to cooperate, each of which had their own, quite different constitutional, legal, cultural, social, and economic preconditions.

Through our courses, conferences, and research projects, we at the Marshall Center endeavor to bring together representatives of military and security establishments from the Atlantic to Eurasia to lay the foundation for an international environment of peace, stability, and economic growth. The Center advances George C. Marshall's vision of a prosperous and undivided Europe through its efforts to encourage open dialogue, partnerships, and cooperative relationships. The Marshall Center strives to develop shared values and common approaches to the diverse and complex challenges facing this community of nations. Conference and course participants contribute to the exchange of ideas by sharing their thoughts and experiences about relevant security and defense issues. In this way, the Marshall Center promotes awareness and mutual understanding as well as the opportunity to explore a range of potential solutions to the foreign and security problems our nations confront.

Like their colleagues in the College of International and Security Studies and the Conference Center, our Research Department reaches out to the region we serve by working with a variety of scholars, researchers, and academics in these countries' university and defense educational communities. For this project, the Research Department engaged 18 scholars from 15 countries in a research initiative. The particular value of this volume lies not only in the expertise of the authors and the thoroughness of the individual country studies, but also in its methodological approach. At the outset of their research and writing, project participants commonly developed an analytical framework, which all authors agreed to use in examining the agreed issues related to peacekeeping in Bosnia. The country case studies on the Russian and the Hungarian experiences, both of which concentrated on the political decision-making process leading up to participation in this multinational endeavor, were the only exceptions to this framework-based approach, but are nonetheless valuable contributions to the rest of our study.

An exceptional group of scholars and practitioners have contributed their expertise and experience to the production of this volume. Although the Cold War is now a decade behind us, the challenges of transition to new defense systems and institutional structures still confront us, both in international policy and domestic affairs. This volume should be required reading not only for interested academics. More importantly, politicians and decision-makers, as well as military and diplomatic staff officers and their civilian counterparts – no matter whether they act on the national, regional, or local level of responsibility – should read this book in order to better understand the range of complex interactions inherent in international peacekeeping operations.

Robert KENNEDY
Director
George C. Marshall European Center for Security Studies

Acknowledgements

We are indebted to our colleagues from other military, research, and diplomatic institutions for their assistance in developing this project. Over the last several years, we have had the benefit of numerous conversations and debates about peacekeeping operations with colleagues and friends from all over the Euro-Atlantic region. Organizations that merit special mention in this regard are the American Political Science Association (APSA), the European Research Group on Military and Society (ERGOMAS), the Inter-University Seminar on Armed Forces and Society (IUS), and Research Committee 01: Armed Forces and Conflict Resolution within the Framework of the International Sociological Association.

We would like to thank all of our friends and colleagues who have worked with us on this research project. In particular, we would like to thank the other founding members of this project: Franz Kernic, Donna Winslow, and Christopher Dandeker. The experience and commitment of all of our cooperating scholars, however, helped to bring an ambitious research project to a satisfactory conclusion.

Finally, without the generous support of the George C. Marshall European Center for Security Studies and its generous assistance in the areas of organization, personnel, and funding, this research project could never have been begun, much less carried to its conclusion. Therefore, all the scholars, colleagues, and friends who participated in this project join us in expressing their gratitude to the Marshall Center.

It goes without saying that the views expressed in this book are those of the authors and do not express the official policy or position of the George C. Marshall European Center for Security Studies, the U.S. Department of Defense, the German Ministry of Defense, or the U.S., German, or any other government.

INTRODUCTION

Jean CALLAGHAN and Mathias SCHÖNBORN

This volume is the result of a research project, initiated and executed by the Research Department of the George C. Marshall European Center for Security Studies, originally entitled *Warriors in Peacekeeping: Points of Tension in Complex Cultural Encounters – Comparing Experiences of National Contingents in Multinational Peace Operations in Bosnia-Herzegovina*. This volume is based upon country case studies, written according to a common research framework designed by the project participants. These authors are researchers, scholars, and military officers from 14 different countries, all of whom sent military contingents to participate in the peacekeeping operations in the former Yugoslavia in the aftermath of the Dayton Accords.

The work begins with a chapter designed to be used as the book's theoretical foundation. The authors, Christopher Dandeker and James Gow, discuss the changes that have taken place over the course of the 1990s in peacekeeping operations across the globe; in particular, they analyze the relatively rapid evolution from the "classical" peacekeeping operations that have been conducted under the auspices of the United Nations for the past 40 years to more recent operations, including those in the former Yugoslavia, which have required a much more robust response to conflict, characterized by the authors as "strategic peacekeeping." The bulk of this volume is composed of detailed country studies that investigate and evaluate the experience of more than a dozen national contingents participating in the peacekeeping operations in Bosnia-Herzegovina. The final chapter is an in-depth analysis of the experiences described by all the contributing authors, which discusses emerging trends, issues that deserve special attention, and lessons learned.

The Marshall Center initiated this project during the biannual meeting of the European Research Group on Military and Society (ERGOMAS), which was hosted by the Leadership Academy of the Swedish Armed Forces in Karlstad, Sweden. The majority of the contributors to this work were able to participate in this initial workshop, which launched this multinational, interdisciplinary, and – broadly speaking – comparative research project. During the workshop in Karlstad, the scholars collaboratively developed a common set of questions, which all agreed to use as the research framework of their individual country studies. [1]

This framework was developed over the course of several intensive discussion sessions, in which the research project participants considered what sort of project would prove most useful to scholars as well as policymakers and decisionmakers when planning future international peacekeeping and peace enforcement operations. Gradually it became clear to the project participants designing the framework that one potentially fruitful starting point would be to reflect on how the diverse backgrounds of all the organizations participating in the peacekeeping mission in the former Yugoslavia affect the implementation and success of the operation itself.

When considering the peacekeeping operation in Bosnia-Herzegovina, one must imagine a theater of operations where military contingents from more than 30 different countries work side by side, in a stressful, sometimes dangerous environment, with international organizations, parties in conflict, media representatives, and non-governmental agencies from all over the world. From a social science standpoint, it is logical in such an environment that one would discover tensions, as people from all of these different backgrounds come from diverse national, organizational, political, and professional cultures, and "do business" in very different ways.

This is not meant as criticism: each country's military establishment has strict rules and regulations based upon its individual security requirements, historical and economic background, and political alliances. Moreover, when one has worked for years within the hierarchical structure of one's own military, it can be difficult to accept that other militaries – not to mention media representatives, NGOs, and members of the former warring parties – do things differently and see problems differently. In a peacekeeping operation, which is of course, at least initially, primarily a military operation, the military – understandably – often sees the media, NGOs, and other non-military actors in the theater as getting in the way and complicating their work. These groups often have their own frustrations with the military, based upon different world views, goals, and work requirements. Therefore, it is not at all surprising that tensions occur, and have to be addressed in order to successfully conduct the peacekeeping mission.

It is important to note here that the mere existence of tensions should not lead one to assume that, in and of themselves, these tensions would lead to inefficiencies or disintegrative consequences; on the contrary, as in other areas of life, such tensions can produce innovative solutions and increased coopera-

---

[1]   For an overview of this framework and some of the key questions that the country study authors agreed to address, please turn to the Appendix to this book.

tion – in short, they can lead to synergies and symbiotic relationships that benefit all parties involved. The final framework resulting from these discussions was therefore designed with the intention of describing how each individual national contingent worked with and perceived the other organizations with which it came in contact, in particular other military contingents, international organizations, NGOs, the media, and the local population. Tensions arising from these complex cultural encounters, as well as means of addressing them, were also described and analyzed.

It was our intention that all case study authors follow this agreed framework, and most authors were able to do so. However, the working conditions for our contributors in the broad variety of countries covered in this book were, of course, very different indeed. Several of our authors, some with the support of their governments and home institutions, were able to design and conduct empirical studies, [2] but not all had this opportunity. Some country case studies could not cover the full range of our set of questions, e.g., the studies on Hungary and Russia, but both gave detailed descriptions of the political decision-making process preceding the decision to participate in the peacekeeping operation in Bosnia-Herzegovina. Despite these slight differences in format, however, we believe that the results of this research project provide rich and nuanced information that can be used for further study and applied to future international operations.

---

[2] The country studies for Austria, Bulgaria, Canada, Denmark, and Sweden all included empirical data of this sort.

PART I

CONCEPTUAL FRAMEWORK

1. MILITARY CULTURE AND STRATEGIC PEACEKEEPING

Christopher DANDEKER and James GOW

1. INTRODUCTION: NEW MISSIONS AND MILITARY CULTURE

Although the primary purpose of the armed forces is the preparation and conduct of war, the most likely future missions of the armed forces of the industrial democracies will not be war fighting but a variety of peace support missions. Consequently, military personnel have to face the conundrum encapsulated in the cliché that "peacekeeping is not a job for soldiers, but only soldiers can do it." This paper addresses some of the cultural aspects of this conundrum.

Many armed forces share the British view that it makes sense to train the armed forces for war fighting and then to "train down," as it were, to cater to the needs of missions in which a more restrained use of force is appropriate. The idea is based on the view that industrial democracies, such as those in Western Europe, have to prepare for war even if major interstate wars are the least likely scenarios that they will face in the future. It is prudent to prepare for the unlikely because it cannot be discounted entirely. Furthermore, the capacity to respond to the need for a war-fighting machine cannot be prepared over night. Such war-fighting preparation is required to buttress the conduct of the new age of more "muscular" peace support operations, in which peacekeepers face

11

a much more violent tempo of life than peacekeepers in classical peacekeeping operations are likely to encounter. Finally, with a downsized and ever cost-vigilant military, there is little scope for specialized peacekeepers even if such an option made strategic and military sense.

Yet questions remain. How must the culture of the war fighter be adjusted to meet the needs of a peacekeeping operation? What additional cultural problems arise for the war fighter in the new forms of muscular peacekeeping that have become more prominent during the past decade? This question is of particular concern in this paper, and it is addressed in the context of our collaborative work on the dynamics of strategic peacekeeping as this has developed in the region of the former Republic of Yugoslavia. [1]

1.1. THE UNIQUENESS OF MILITARY CULTURE

In general terms, culture comprises a set of ideas, beliefs, and symbols that provide a definition of the world for a group or organization and guides for action. [2] Organizations, by virtue of their status as *formal* organizations, normally possess both formal and informal cultures. The former include, in descending order of abstraction, first, the organization's vision as expressed in its mission statement, and second, policies as guides for action (such as equal opportunity policies) requiring application to specific circumstances. Third, more specific procedures would include such guides for action as, for example, the stricture in many countries not to talk to the media about failures of policy without reference first to the military chain of command or the command public affairs officer. Fourth, even more specific rules or prohibitions would include a requirement not to talk at all to the media except with the specific authorization of the higher command. Informal culture comprises those elements of shared values and beliefs (including more or less mythic statements about the history of the organization) that are not evident to or sanctioned by the formal culture. [3] As students of organizational culture are aware, one of the major difficulties in implementing organizational change is how to translate change in the formal culture – e.g., an organization's mission – into the informal culture and prac-

---

[1]   See Christopher Dandeker and James Gow, "The Future of Peace Support Operations: Strategic Peacekeeping and Success," *Armed Forces & Society* 23, No. 3, Spring 1997, pp. 327 – 348.

[2]   See Karen O. Dunivin, "Military Culture: Change and Continuity," *Armed Forces & Society*, Vol. 20, No. 4, Summer 1994, pp. 531 – 547; idem, "Military Culture: A Paradigm Shift," Air War College Maxwell Paper No. 10, Maxwell Air Force Base, Alabama, USA, February 1997.

[3]   This way of thinking is characteristic of the study of organizational culture in business schools. For a useful example of this, see David L. Sturges' course on Organizational Communication at the UT-Pan American College of Business Administration, http://www.baclass.panam.edu/courses/mana3335/culture.html.

tice of personnel on the ground. This is evident in such policy areas as equal opportunity. [4]

The culture of the military is unique. The functional imperatives of war and military operations ensure that the armed forces stand apart from civilian society. Of course, there are important ways in which the armed services are similar to civilian enterprises. For example, one can refer to the importance attached to teamwork, leadership, the idea of loyalty to the organization and its mission, and – of ever-increasing importance – the need to work with advanced technologies, particularly in the information field. Furthermore, the armed forces share with other "institutional organizations" (such as those in the field of education, health care, and religion) an approach to operations that is values-driven rather than market-driven. People carry out their tasks of educating, caring for the sick, and managing armed forces not primarily to make a profit but in order to carry forward the values that provide the overall purpose of the organization. In market-based organizations, the main driver is monitoring and adjusting to the demands of the market in order to make a profit on the capital invested. [5]

As institutional organizations, the armed forces also have their own unique culture and resulting contract with their personnel. Ensuring that service personnel are prepared to fight involves leadership, management, and motivation. For the military, the core values of military culture are subordination of the self to the group and the idea of sacrifice: the individual must be willing to subordinate himself or herself to the common good, i.e., the team and common task. Furthermore, there must be a willingness to sacrifice one's life for the team in peace and war; without this, an armed force will risk defeat. Ideally, as a result of leadership and training, these values will be upheld voluntarily as a result of conscience. However, if necessary, coercion may be required. This is what makes military discipline – an effective structure of command for the giving and receiving of orders – quite different from that of other organizations in terms of the demands it places upon personnel. The military is unique in the nature and extent of the demands it places upon its personnel. They are obliged to train to kill and to sacrifice self, to participate in a military community where one works, lives, and socializes with other service personnel and, when necessary, to respond to a 24-hour commitment with the risk of separation from family at short notice.

---

[4]   See Christopher Dandeker and Mady Wechsler Segal, "Gender Integration in Armed Forces: Recent Policy Developments in the United Kingdom," *Armed Forces & Society*, Fall 1996, pp. 29 – 47.

[5]   Henning Sorensen, "New Perspectives on the Military Profession: The I/O Model and Esprit de Corps Re-evaluated," *Armed Forces & Society*, Vol. 20, No. 4, Summer 1994, pp. 599 – 617.

Of course, individual services also have their own specific cultures. For example, combat units of different services have different military cultures, e.g., the army has a requirement to close with and kill the enemy, which contrasts with the greater "action at a distance" characteristic of other services. Especially in the teeth arms of the army, people are asked to perform a variety of tasks in a changing and hostile environment. In the navy, the ship and demands of the sea – in both peace and war – tie individuals into a cohesive unit; this is connected with the fact that non-duty personal life, away from ship, is of less concern to the navy than it is to the army. In the case of the British Army, for instance, this concern is particularly evident due to the peculiarly tribal nature of the regimental system.

Professional military culture is unlike other types of warrior cultures, including those that are likely to be encountered by muscular peacekeepers in future, notably the warlords that loom large in the complex emergencies associated with collapsing states.[6] As Ralph Peters has suggested (in many ways echoing Huntington's discussion of the modern military profession), the soldier-warrior should not be grouped together with other types of warrior, e.g., warrior bands produced by disintegrating states. Soldier-warriors serve the state. Their culture is rooted in concepts of honor, obedience, and sacrifice rather than the idea of booty or spoils. Through their linkage with the state, they are subjected to a bureaucratic chain of command. Consequently, they are characterized by an organizational rather than an individualistic orientation (although personal relations of loyalty play a key role in the performance of modern armed forces). The skills of soldier-warriors are focused on the instrumental problem of defeating the enemy soldier rather than on the intrinsic value of violence for its own sake. Soldier-warriors owe their allegiance to the state rather than to the person of a charismatic leader and have a clearly defined legal status as an agency authorized to use legitimate violence in pursuit of government objectives. Finally, Peters argues that the soldier-warrior uses legitimate violence as a means to restore order, whereas the warrior band is associated with the destruction of order and thus the continuation of the conditions of a failing state as a favorable material basis for maintaining their way of life.[7]

1.2. NEW MISSIONS AND MILITARY CULTURE

The new missions of the armed forces pose challenges to military culture. Many analysts have noticed this problem. A Swiss officer, General Däniker,

---

[6]   John Mackinlay, "Warlords," *RUSI Journal*, April 1998, pp. 24 – 32.
[7]   See Ralph Peters, "The New Warrior Class," *Parameters*, Summer 1994, 16 – 26. These distinctions are represented by Peters in Fig. 1, p. 18 of his article.

has provided a useful discussion. [8] He suggests that the core values of the military are to protect, help, and save. With regard to protection, armed forces need to be prepared to use force to deter aggression or to apply such force as may be required to achieve a political goal. However, new missions place armed forces in a war prevention or peacekeeping mode. This means that the military's role in shaping stability has important implications for the traditional culture and way of life of the armed forces.

In particular, the following characteristics become increasingly prominent:
- Pure fighting functions become of secondary importance.
- Military victory becomes a tactical goal. The strategic goal is to shape a positive basis for peace. As we shall see later, this notion corresponds closely with Morris Janowitz's constabulary concept. One component of this concept was the pragmatic idea that the goal of the military is viable international relations rather than the absolutist goal of victory.
- The ultimate goal of military doctrine is not to destroy the enemy but to punish or undermine the enemy's morale in order to neutralize the enemy.
- Consequently, plans for the use of force must be adequate for the goals desired. In particular, one must inflict the minimum number of casualties upon the enemy (or perhaps this idea should be refined to mean the minimum as perceived by one's own public opinion through the media). In any case, high "home-side" casualties are increasingly difficult to legitimize in today's conditions, especially when vital national territorial or other interests do not appear (at least to the public) to be involved in the conflict in which one's forces might be engaged. [9]
- Military leaders are no longer encouraged to think or act in terms of pure military categories; rather, they should think and act only in correspondence with the wider political goal of shaping peace.
- The capacity to be flexible and perform multiple missions is just as important as the power and ability to move rapidly on the battlefield.
- The tasks for the military in the 21st century are to protect, help, and save.

As will become clear later, there are important overlaps between these ideas and the concept of strategic peacekeeping. This concept has emerged from recent developments in peacekeeping practice and doctrine. There is

---

[8] These points arose in a discussion with Alise Weibull on Daniker's ideas, which have been delivered in a number of lectures.

[9] This point raises the question of the extent to which public opinion might be willing to accept significant casualties in pursuit of values far wider than national sovereignty or related interests such as the human values of compassion and whether it is easier for governments to sway public opinion if support for such humanitarian values can be couched in terms of national self-interest. For example, a concept of global peace and justice could be defended not only as a humanitarian value but also as a hard-headed objective that can promote national material well-being. See also later discussion and note 36.

a well-developed literature on how peacekeeping requires a change in the soldier-warrior's outlook. Let us focus on the British example. In the early 1990s, British military doctrine was formulated on the basis of a sharp division between peacekeeping and peace enforcement. This was clear in what became known as the "Dobbie doctrine." [10] Yet recent years have seen a doctrinal shift that is more in conformity with the themes developed by Daniker noted above and in the work of the present author with James Gow on the concept of "strategic peacekeeping."

Dobbie's basic thesis was that the international community has failed to adequately distinguish between peacekeeping and peace enforcement – two activities that require radically different conceptual approaches. [11] He argued that

> ... the conduct of peacekeeping depends on the presence of a workable modicum of in-theater consent and that such consent should determine the manner in which peacekeeping operations are planned, directed, and conducted at all levels – particularly with regard to the use of force. [12]

Further, peacekeeping is

> ... characterized by impartiality and minimum force. Peace enforcement, on the other hand, dispenses with consent and is conducted, in the main, in accordance with standard military principles predicated on the identification of an enemy. Peacekeeping and peace enforcement are thus separate and mutually exclusive activities that cannot be mixed, and which therefore need to be directed and handled in a consistent manner. Peacekeeping with consent, however, does not exclude significant applications of force. Indeed, the use of force is facilitated by consent and should not necessarily be equated to the non-consensual category of peace enforcement. [13]

The implication of this concept is that there are sharply differing systems of training appropriate for each logic. [14] It is useful to focus on two major issues here. First, with regard to the lower levels of command especially the young soldier or junior NCO operations of wider peacekeeping are

> ... likely to be complex, dangerous, and stressful, placing heavy demands on all individuals participating in field operations. The point of contact

---

[10] Charles Dobbie, "A Concept for Post-Cold War Peacekeeping," *Survival*, Vol. 36, Autumn 1994, pp. 121 – 148.

[11] Dobbie, *Ibid,* p. 121.

[12] *Ibid.*

[13] *Ibid.* In the next section of the paper, the idea of consent is used as a critical point of departure for developing the idea of strategic peacekeeping and its basis in legitimation.

[14] Dobbie develops this in some detail in the *Forsvarsstudier Monograph* 4/1994, especially Chapter 8, pp. 116 – 127.

between the belligerent parties and the wider peacekeeping force will frequently be the young soldier or non-commissioned officer. It is often at this level that crisis situations may be held in check or resolved. Alternatively, it is at this level that crisis situations can escalate and get out of control, thus threatening to destabilize the immediate environment – an effect that may easily spread to other areas. [15]

Second, one can focus on the issue of skill/competence and competency challenges (i.e., what is required for effective task performance and what one needs to bring to the task to perform effectively). Dobbie stressed the need for education to guide effective training because training derives from doctrine. The gulf between the logics of peacekeeping and peace enforcement leads to a related division between doctrines guiding the training programs for peacekeeping and peace enforcement.

> Rather than terminating conflict by force, the wider peacekeeper's task is to resolve conflict in the role of an impartial third party supervisor. This calls, above all, for an adjustment of the soldier's attitude and approach, which will differ markedly from what he would normally adopt in carrying out conventional operations. [16]

The peacekeeper will

> ... normally be a guest of the host nation, a representative of the UN, and a goodwill ambassador of his own nation. The demands of preserving a consensual framework for operations will require him to respect local culture, customs, and behavior. The principles of impartiality, minimum force, legitimacy, credibility, mutual respect, and transparency – the peacekeeping "ethos" – will govern his actions. [17]

All this will need to be explained to soldiers. However, Dobbie stressed that while one cannot "read off" peacekeeping from one set of basic military principles, successful peacekeeping operations require many of the skills and qualities required in conventional operations. Dobbie was careful to note that there were some clear overlaps between the skills and culture of the soldier-warrior and that of the peacekeeper; he listed these as

> ... professional competence, discipline, morale, leadership, initiative, flexibility, and alertness .... . Training for wider peacekeeping therefore re-

---

[15] *Ibid*, p. 116.

[16] *Ibid*, p. 117. By wider peacekeeping, Dobbie was referring to "the wider aspects of peacekeeping operations carried out with the consent of the belligerent parties but in an environment that may be highly volatile." Dobbie, "Concept for Post-Cold War Peacekeeping," p. 16. He was referring to the *Army Doctrine* publication of 14 December 1993.

[17] *Ibid*.

quires a thorough grounding in basic military skills including such things
as command control, communications, navigation, weapon handling, tactical skills, physical training, and administration. [18]

Despite these overlaps, the military cultures of different countries are more or
less compatible with the classical peacekeeping ethos. Certain types of soldier
do not make very good traditional peacekeepers. For example, in the British
case, the parachute regiment might not be the best suited for these duties, as
they are so focused on the sharper end of war fighting. The same might be
said of such hardened formations as the 82nd Airborne in the U.S. Army. The
deployment of Canadian paratroopers in Somalia in 1994 shows how serious
the consequences can be – for Somali society, the reputation of the Canadian
military, and Canadian civil–military relations – when a formation equipped
with an exaggerated war-fighting ethos is inserted into an operation in which
such an orientation is inappropriate. [19]

In contrast, certain societies find peacekeeping quite compatible with their
own military ethos, as for example in Sweden. Societies equipped with a pronounced war-fighting ethos such as the U.S. (especially the sharper end of their
formations) might find it difficult to adjust to the requirements of traditional
peacekeeping, as was the case with U.S. forces learning to operate together
with Scandinavian contingents in the preventive force in Macedonia. [20]

By the same token, forces used to traditional peacekeeping might encounter problems in dealing with the more muscular forms of peacekeeping
(in which there will be use of force beyond the requirements of self-protection)
that have emerged in recent years. The Swedish forces may be a case in point. [21]
Meanwhile, armed forces with long experience of not only war fighting but
also imperial and post-imperial policing may find this experience of use not
only in classic but also the more muscular peacekeeping of recent years.

If there are difficulties to be faced when adjusting warriors to the demands
of peacekeeping, then there are also, as we shall now observe, additional problems to be confronted by warriors engaged in the more muscular activities of
strategic peacekeeping.

---

[18] *Ibid.*
[19] See Donna M. Winslow, "The Canadian Airborne Regiment in Somalia: A Socio-Cultural
     Enquiry," Minister of Public Works and Government Services, Ottawa, Canada, 1997.
[20] See Dandeker and Gow, "The Future of Peace Support Operations".
[21] This point arose in discussions with Swedish personnel reflecting on how their service in
     Bosnia contrasted with previous deployments.

2. STRATEGIC PEACEKEEPING: A MILITARY OPERATION IN THE MIDDLE GROUND [22]

In general terms, "second-generation" or more muscular forms of peacekeeping have focused on a wider and more ambitious range of tasks than hitherto associated with classical forms of peacekeeping, including the separation and disarming of conflicting parties; the attempted restoration of peace between them; the protection of safe havens; the rebuilding of failed states; and military-assisted delivery of humanitarian aid. [23] The distinctive character of second-generation peacekeeping operations – and this is most pronounced in strategic peacekeeping – is that they occupy a place midway between traditional peacekeeping and forms of peace enforcement characteristic of operations such as DESERT STORM. This midway position is indicated by the way in which peacekeeping is likely to be associated with some enforcement measures. Such operations, conceptualized as strategic peacekeeping, will have the following characteristics. [24]

- First, they depend upon a degree of consent from the conflicting parties, but the level of such consent will be less than that to be expected in a traditional peacekeeping operation.
- Second, in contrast with both an enforcement operation, where there is a sharply defined political objective or end state to be achieved, and a traditional peacekeeping operation, where a political settlement has already been reached, here the situation is more fluid and opaque. The aim of the operation is to "hold the ring," i.e., to dampen the conflict and its negative humanitarian effects while diplomatic and political efforts seek to establish a momentum from which a settlement can be reached among the conflicting parties. [25]

---

[22] This section draws on previously published work by the author with James Gow.

[23] These activities include the "wider peacekeeping" that was the focus of Dobbie's analysis discussed earlier. One should be careful about adopting too chronological a view of second-generation peacekeeping. Thus, Hillen makes the observation that "The 'second generation' of peacekeeping missions all occurred after the Cold War, although they have a convincing historical antecedent in the Congo Operation of 1960–64." John Hillen, "The United Nations and the Use of Force," p. 20. For a similar point, see also Shashi Tharoor, "The Role of the United Nations," p. 56, Note 3.

[24] The following characterization draws on collaborative work with James Gow. See James Gow and Christopher Dandeker, "Peace Support Operations: The Problem of Legitimation," *World Today* 51, Issue 8/9, Aug/Sep 1995, pp. 171–175, and Christopher Dandeker and James Gow, "Strategic Peacekeeping," *Brassey's Defence Yearbook* 107, 1997, pp. 174–190.

[25] See James Gow, "Strategic Peacekeeping," p. 79; and Shashi Tharoor, "The Role of the United Nations," pp. 45–46.

- A third feature of a strategic peacekeeping operation is that it involves a mixture of coercive and non-coercive actions. In support of diplomatic and political efforts to generate a settlement to the conflict, peacekeepers might be involved not only in humanitarian aid activities, or in the guarding of weapons that have been given up by the parties, but also in more coercive action against those who have broken agreements or to spur their movement towards settling the dispute.
- Fourth, strategic peacekeeping involves the need for peacekeeping troops to be able to provide a response greater than that required for self-defense, although less than that required for a full enforcement operation. This will be reflected in the number of personnel employed and the capabilities of their equipment. [26]
- Fifth, these operations will be complex and multi-functional in character, requiring the military to cooperate with a variety of other professional and organizational bodies, including political entities, NGOs, the media, and of course the contingents of other contributing countries.
- Sixth, and finally, the pressures upon the force commander will be immense due to the functional complexity of the operation and the need to finely tune the competing demands upon it (for example, containing the intensity and spatial extent of the conflict; maintaining delivery of humanitarian aid; maintaining cooperation from the parties; using coercion to deal with those who persist in breaking agreements and/or to provide incentives for them to move towards a settlement of the dispute). Therefore, the commander's need for operational autonomy has to be respected. This can be expected to produce strains in civil–military relations if the commander is drawn from a democratic society in which the self-image (and public perception) of the military professional is that of the apolitical technician.

The distinctive features of strategic peacekeeping are presented in Figure 1.

In peace enforcement operations, the strategic initiative and the determination of the end state lie as much or more with the intervening powers than with the conflicting parties. With traditional peacekeeping, the conflicting parties determine both the strategic initiative and the end state. The peculiar dynamics (and tensions) of what we call strategic peacekeeping derive from the fact that the strategic initiative lies with the intervening parties (and not just the antagonists), yet the end state must be determined (albeit under pressure from the intervening powers) by the conflicting parties themselves. If this were not so, the end state would be hard to legitimize as one that the contending parties

---

[26] If armed forces are to prepare for more Bosnias than DESERT STORMs, then this has serious implications for future purchases of military equipment as well as force design and doctrine. See Michael Clarke, "The Framework of United Kingdom Defence Policy," *London Defence Studies* 30/31, November 1995, p.132.

Figure 1. Strategic peacekeeping

Classical Peacekeeping	Strategic Peacekeeping	Peace Enforcement > War
Initiative P	I	I
Solution P	P	I

                Consent line   Impartiality Line

had themselves reached (albeit under pressure from the intervening parties): a purely imposed settlement would have all the scant legitimacy of a modern form of colonialism.

3. STRATEGIC PEACEKEEPING AND MILITARY CULTURE

3.1. THE MILITARY AND LEGITIMATION

We are now in a position to analyze in more detail some of the tensions that will arise between traditional military culture and the practical realities of strategic peacekeeping. Two starting points are worth noting. First of all, the idea (at the heart of the "Dobbie doctrine") that strategic peacekeeping rests on consent – that is, of the conflicting parties – is an overly restrictive way of looking at this activity. Rather, strategic peacekeeping is a complex operation requiring legitimation. This process is construed in terms of (a) the legal and normative basis of the activity, (b) the support of various parties, including of course the protagonists but also a range of other bodies, including other groups in society as well as in the societies of the intervening powers, and (c) the extent to which effective performance of the activity generates support from the various parties and thus underpins the legal and normative basis of the action.[27] An armed force involved in this activity needs to have a concept of operations (and a military culture) attuned to these considerations.

A second starting point is to emphasize that the military plays a key role in the legitimation of a strategic peacekeeping operation. This is so in two ways. In the first place, it is itself one of the audiences that needs to be convinced about the purpose of the operation and its success (in addition to other audiences, including its own government and civil society, the wider world, the conflicting parties, and their constituencies). An additional consideration is that the military engaged in such a mission contributes to the legitimation of

---

[27] See Dandeker and Gow, "The Future of Peace Support Operations."

the mission through effective performance. Effectiveness not only sustains its own morale but can offset deficiencies in other aspects of legitimation for the operation – for example, a fragile or grudging support for the mission on the part of the conflicting parties or the civil society from which the participating military contingents are drawn. On the other hand, poor performance or lack of success can corrode the legitimacy of the operation in the eyes of various audiences and, in so far as it affects the morale of the participating troops, this will extend to the military itself.

3.2. PERFORMANCE, MOMENTUM, AND END STATES

In order to maximize the chances of effective performance, the commanders of an operation must (and must be able to) make the most of what has been called "defining moments." [28] This means that military commanders must seize to good effect those opportunities arising on the ground that can allow the momentum of the operation to be maintained. Consequently, space can be created for political initiatives to produce a settlement.

The ideas of momentum and defining moments raise problems for the values of victory and a clear end state in the traditional culture of the soldier-warrior. As discussed earlier, one of the key features of strategic peacekeeping is that the end state cannot be defined in advance by the intervening powers. Rather, it is their role to use force to edge the conflicting parties to a solution that is of their own making. In doing so, military commanders have to be able to make the most of a fluid and dynamic situation on the ground and to capitalize on defining moments.

This idea poses a sharp challenge to traditional military culture. In particular, it does not sit easily with the supposition that one should only use force if one knows in advance what the end state is, and that one has the necessary means to achieve it, together with knowledge of the time frame in which the operation will be concluded. The notion of operating without a predefined end state is perceived as particularly unhelpful if forces have to deploy in a volatile warlike environment. There is an understandable fear of the morale-corroding effects of stasis. This is why the next point about momentum is so important. [29]

---

[28] See Gow and Dandeker, "Legitimation of Strategic Peacekeeping."

[29] This discussion of end state echoes an earlier analysis made by Morris Janowitz in *The Professional Soldier: A Social And Political Portrait* (Glencoe, IL: Free Press, 1960). Janowitz referred to a constabulary force: one that was continuously prepared to act and focused on the minimum use of force and the pursuit of viable international relations rather than victory. We would suggest Janowitz would have been better served by using the term "measured" rather than "minimum" for it to be useful in illuminating the kind of operation that we are discussing here. Janowitz, however, was acutely aware of how these ideas challenged the values of the traditional military warrior or "heroic" leaders. They "tend to thwart the constabulary concept because of their desire to maintain conventional military doctrine and

The soldier feels the need for a clear purpose. In peace enforcement and war, this is relatively self-evident. In a strategic peacekeeping operation, given that the end state is not defined at the outset, it is critical that the sense of momentum is real – that the defining moments are seized – in order to sustain the morale of the soldier. Without this, the legitimacy of the operation amongst the troops becomes problematic. To be sure, setbacks or stasis can be resisted by the more professional formations, and tasks can be designed to maintain morale in the short term. [30] However, without progress on the ground and the sense that moves towards a settlement are being made, the legitimacy of the operation amongst the troops will be fragile. It would be unwise to underestimate the scale of this problem because, as events in Bosnia have shown, such operations have to be considered as long-term rather than rapid "quick fix" operations.

3.3. IMPARTIALITY AND NEUTRALITY

Another issue of military culture concerns the implications of strategic peacekeeping for the impartiality and neutrality of military forces. In a strategic peacekeeping operation, the force is not deployed as a "value-free," neutral agent. It is not confined to observing events and reporting back to the UN or some other sponsoring agency about what has occurred and focusing only on the protection of its own troops so far as is necessary to continue its observation role. Rather, it is charged and configured to use force to defend its mandate impartially. Its mandate can be expected to include Chapter VII components. The key point here is that, in an operation of this kind, an impartial application of the mandate may involve the military using force against one of the belligerent parties rather than another for a certain period because it so happens that it is this party that is not willing to conform to the terms of the mandate in question. In order for the legitimacy of the operation to be sustained, the mandate must be robustly enforced. The consequences of not doing so are a

---

their resistance to assessing the political consequences of limited military actions, which do not produce 'victory.'" Meanwhile, technologists tend to exaggerate the importance of high-intensity weapons and their importance in international relations. Janowitz pointed out that the task of the military manager (in conjunction with the actors at the political level) was to balance the role of technologists and heroes. Such ideas prefigure some of the reflections generated here on the use of force in strategic peacekeeping. See Janowitz, *Ibid*, pp. 424 – 425.

[30] This was the strongly held view of a number of French senior military personnel. Some British army officers feel that professional fighting forces should be able to forestall the onset of morale problems through, for example, the inventive use of exercises. This ability may well come easier to an armed force possessing a complex history of deployments ranging from conventional war fighting to varieties of imperial and post-imperial policing operations, as in the case of the British army. However, these officers admitted that without momentum on the ground, the process of maintaining morale becomes increasingly difficult.

corrosion of the morale and professional self-respect of the strategic peace-keepers. In addition, there will be a weakening of the credibility of the UN and of the other international bodies that states belong to and believe in, both as the basis of international order as well as useful vehicles for the pursuit of their own interests.

3.4. INTERACTION BETWEEN MILITARY AND POLITICAL ACTORS

Strategic peacekeeping adds further momentum to the process of blurring the differences in roles of military and political actors, which was observed by Janowitz nearly 40 years ago. This blurring involves a process of politicization of the military through a fusion of civilian, political, and military actors. Any possibility of a sharp division between military means and political ends, and thus a clear division of labor between military and civilian political respon-sibilities, has been eroded first by the emergence of nuclear weapons, second by the evolution of the electronic media, and third by the emergence of new missions for the armed forces. [31] Nuclear weapons ensured that, with the future of civilization at stake, senior military officers and civilian politicians were drawn closer together in thinking through the problem of how to threaten and, if necessary, use force in such a way as not to lead to nuclear Armageddon. The electronic media have made civilian politicians more nervous about the political consequences of military action. This can tempt them into the micro-management of operations or at least into an intensification of the process of political-military consultation in what are, for technological reasons, increas-ingly complex and fast-moving operations. These latter features are especially evident in complex peace support missions of the kind under discussion here.

As a result of operations in Bosnia-Herzegovina, some have spoken of the need for improvement in the quantity and quality of the military input into the "what" (the political objective), the "how" (military means and objectives), and the "means" (force composition). Generally, this has been associated with

---

[31] These points have been rehearsed in the interesting discussion by Bernard Boëne in his "How 'Unique' Should the Military Be?" *European Journal of Sociology*, Vol. 31, 1990, pp. 3–59. As Boëne, drawing on Janowitz, argues, despite Huntington's desire (at least in 1957) for a military profession under political direction but serving as an apolitical agent through a sharp division of labor between means (military expertise) and ends (political objectives), historical trends were undermining this position even as it was being developed. In any case, such a position, even if only a theoretical possibility, involves a questionable reading of Clausewitz. Hew Strachan has suggested Clausewitz recognized both the dangers of reading the formulation of military plans as purely military matters isolated from political considerations, as well as the idea that politicians should, when thinking of using armed force, ask their military officers only for purely military advice. As Strachan puts it, on this reading, "Politicians need to be militarily informed, and soldiers – more controversially – need to be politically integrated." Hew Strachan, *The Politics of the British Army* (Oxford: Clarendon Press, 1997), p. 2.

a call for the military to be involved earlier in the design of operations and for this to be considered in the overall UN context. [32] With regard to the first of these observations – setting the political objective – as discussed above, without a predefined end state, military commanders will necessarily be involved in the ongoing political assessment of the effects of limited military actions on the momentum of the operation.

In classical peacekeeping, because the strategic initiative and the solution/end state are in the hands of the protagonists, the military provides a service that is then used by these actors. With peace enforcement, the military is set in motion by an end state declared by civilian politicians and is asked to produce a result for politicians. (Even here, as argued above, there is a process of blurring.) However, the material point is that, in strategic peacekeeping, the blurring is even more pronounced. Here there are no clear "political filters" established by a pre-defined end state; this is a challenge for the military, as they have to be involved in the calculation of the political results of military acts much more than in either of the other two scenarios. [33] In strategic peacekeeping, we find – in an operational context – Charles Moskos' "soldier statesman," while in the area of doctrine and development that underpins such operations, we find the "soldier-scholar." [34]

Such pressures must be resisted by strategic peacekeepers in the application of the mandate, despite the understandable political pressures for micromanagement of these operations (for example, the fear of casualties and the concern that small-scale military actions can have larger-scale political consequences). It is essential that the military personnel involved have sufficient autonomy to take the initiative in applying the mandate. Without the scope for and presence of such initiative, creative opportunities may well be lost, contributing to a loss of momentum in the operation and thus a deterioration of the legitimacy and credibility of the force.

This initiative is not confined to the more senior levels of the military hierarchy but applies to unit commanders and lower levels in the chain of command, as well. In operations of this kind, the tendency is for authority to be dispersed to lower levels of command. Through their actions, quite junior personnel, such as NCOs, can make a major contribution to the success or failure of a mission. One operational similarity between strategic peacekeeping and the role of troops in the Troubles in Northern Ireland is that both can be re-

---

[32] Views of officers from UK armed forces in interviews with the authors.

[33] I owe the idea of "political filters" as used in this context to discussions with Professor Michael Clarke of the Center for Defense Studies, University of London.

[34] See Charles Moskos and James Burke, "The Post-Modern Military," in James Burke (Ed.), *The Military in New Times: Adjusting Armed Forces to a Turbulent World* (Boulder: Westview Press, 1994).

garded as "corporals' wars." The need for greater sensitivity to the political context of military acts thus applies to force planners, the theater commanders, local commanders, and lower-level NCOs.

3.5. MILITARY AND OTHER NON-MILITARY ACTORS

As with other kinds of second-generation peacekeeping operations, strategic peacekeeping takes place in a complex multi-functional environment, which involves a complex set of arrangements among a mixture of military and civilian agencies, including NGOs, the media, and regional political organizations. The media, in particular, provide a glare of publicity that exposes the successes and flaws of such operations. Whether leading or led by public opinion, the media can complicate the security policymaking process by placing pressure upon political elites to mount operations as well as to withdraw from them if the casualties amongst peacekeepers appear to be unacceptable. [35] In this environment, military culture has to be attuned to ensure effective working relations with non-military components. The need for greater professional military sensitivity to the requirements of the media is clearly recognized in contemporary armed forces; it is reflected in professional education and training and is, indeed, a key dimension of the role of the soldier-statesman.

In addition, there is the problem of coming to terms with traditional cultural divisions between soldiers as war fighters and "takers of life" and, for example, the self-perceptions of members of relief organizations as "savers of lives." As Laura Miller has argued,

> Peacekeeping operations in the 1990s … have called for military goals to align with those of relief agencies. Because of this shift, relief workers have become pro-military intervention, but remained essentially anti-military. These workers have experienced the need for armed intervention in their regions, and have seen the concrete benefits of military deployments. Nevertheless, aid workers have not developed a favorable view of soldiers. This seeming paradox is explained by the concept of "dirty work:" relief workers view armed tasks as necessary for reaching their goals, but they would not carry out these tasks themselves and they still disdain the use of weapons. [36]

---

[35] There are complex issues here. The capacity of the media to lead opinion in peacekeeping or other military operations may well have been overstated, and the same can be said for the supposed irrationality of public opinion in giving or withholding its support for such operations. That said, judging from interview material derived from the UNPROFOR operation, it seems that political elites often perceive that the public is sensitive to casualties and emotionally unpredictable in its responses to events. Some of these issues are rehearsed in Christopher Dandeker, "Review Essay: Public Opinion and the Gulf War," *Armed Forces & Society*, 1996. See also note 9 of this paper.

[36] See Laura L. Miller, "Relief Workers' Attitudes Toward the U.S. Military in Peacekeeping

Meanwhile, it has to be said, military personnel can be frustrated by NGOs' reluctance to recognize the importance of military command and control in areas of deployment, and irritated by the disdain for their armed but "dirty" work, as noted by Miller. [37]

4. CONCLUSION

This paper has explored some of the implications of strategic peacekeeping operations for military culture. It has suggested that, in order to conduct these operations successfully, certain elements of traditional military culture need to be modified. These flow from the central idea that, in operations of this kind, there can be no sharp, pre-defined end state. Consequently, to be successful in strategic peacekeeping, the military culture of the armed forces must become less resistant to what Janowitz called the "constabulary concept" and the corresponding need to "assess the political consequences of limited military actions that do not produce victory." [38] This will require not only changes in military culture but also changes in wider civil–military relations, not least in the political authorization allowing force commanders to seize the strategic initiative in an operation in order to maintain its momentum and chances of success. Some societies and their armed forces can be expected to find participating in such missions more difficult than others depending upon their national experience and military ethos. Given that such missions are likely to be increasingly multinational in the future, it will be important to ensure that the lessons learned in such operations are shared as widely as possible.

Operations," Paper presented at the Biennial Conference of the Inter-University Seminar on Armed Forces and Society (IUS), Baltimore, MD, October 24–26, 1997.

[37] That these barriers will not be easy to overcome is confirmed by the difficulties experienced recently (at least in the UK) by those seeking to bring NGO and military representatives together in peacekeeping workshops. This has emerged in recent discussions with British military officers

[38] Janowitz, *Ibid*, 424–425.

PART II

COUNTRY CASE STUDIES

2. PEACEKEEPING IN BOSNIA-HERZEGOVINA THE AUSTRIAN EXPERIENCE: A CASE STUDY

Franz KERNIC

Outline:

This chapter focuses on the Austrian peacekeeping experience in Bosnia in 1996 and 1997. The analysis is based upon empirical data derived from surveys carried out among Austrian soldiers participating in the Implementation Force (IFOR) operation before and during their deployment in the former Yugoslavia. The Austrian contribution to IFOR consisted of one transport and logistics contingent (a reinforced company of 294 men), which we approached for our study. The Austrian contingent was integrated into the so-called Corps Support Group "BELUGA" (which stands for Belgium, Luxembourg, Greece, and Austria).

1. INTRODUCTION

1.1. AUSTRIA AND UN PEACEKEEPING

Austria has been a member of the United Nations since December 14, 1955. Since that time, the country has always lent its active support to UN efforts to maintain world peace. For decades, the country's security policy has demonstrated Austria's deep commitment to the primary role of the UN in the maintenance of international peace and security and its core function of UN peacekeeping operations. Since 1960, more than 40 years, the country has contributed more than 40,000 soldiers to many UN peacekeeping missions.

Austria has always been one of the leading troop contributors to UN operations; nearly 900 Austrians serve abroad at any given time, all of them volunteers. In the 1980s, Austria's total troop commitment was among the largest of all the national contingents involved in UN peacekeeping operations. Currently some 1,200 Austrians – troop contingents, military observers, civilian police, and civilians – are serving in a number of UN missions and in the Stabilization Force (SFOR) in Bosnia and Herzegovina. The country also took part in establishing the UN Stand-by Forces High Readiness Brigade in December 1996, which was created to build a capacity for quick preventive action and crisis response. Currently, Austria intends to intensify its participation in new peacekeeping operations all over the world.

1.2. AUSTRIA'S PARTICIPATION IN IFOR

In December 1995, the Austrian government declared its readiness to contribute to the Bosnia Implementation Force (IFOR) by dispatching a transportation contingent to the area. One month later, the Austrian transportation unit was deployed to Visoko, 15 miles northwest of Sarajevo. For the first time since World War II, Austrian soldiers served within the framework of NATO. The contingent's major task was to secure supplies for all the peacekeeping forces in this sector of the country.

It must be mentioned that Austria's participation in IFOR had become possible through a new orientation (the idea of "European solidarity") in the country's foreign and security policy. When Austria acceded to the European Union in 1995, the country also accepted, in principle, the probable future of a common European security and defense policy. All major political parties agreed to participate in European activities in the area of crisis management based on an interaction between the European Union and NATO or the WEU. In addition, the Partnership for Peace program (PfP) brought Austria closer to NATO. For Austria (still a neutral country!), participation in the IFOR operation seemed to offer a unique chance to begin military activities with the U.S. and many other NATO member states and, for the first time in history, to serve with a peacekeeping force under NATO command in Bosnia. Undoubtedly, some Austrian politicians even considered this emerging international military cooperation to be Austria's first step toward NATO membership and the abolition of the country's neutrality.

When comparing UNPROFOR (United Nations Protection Force, March 1992 – December 1995) and IFOR, we can say that IFOR was more heavily armed and better prepared for the mission in Bosnia than UNPROFOR.[1] Since the very beginning, this mission was generally considered to be an operation authorized to use military resources beyond the traditional concept of self-defense and was empowered to implement the agreement by force. But IFOR turned out to be a relatively safe operation. As a result, the soldiers' task shifted to a humanitarian one. The most dangerous aspect of the soldiers' work remained the ever-present mines in the mission area.

Austria faced several new experiences due to its contribution to IFOR. These experiences included:

- Austria participated for the first time within the framework of a "regional arrangement" according to Chapter VIII of the UN Charter.
- Austria participated in an operation explicitly mandated under Chapter VII with consent of the parties and guided by the principles of impartiality and the minimum use of force.
- Also for the first time, Austria participated in a peacekeeping operation in cooperation with NATO (with certain legal and political restrictions in the application of the IFOR Rules of Engagement).[2]
- Finally, Austrian forces were operationally integrated into a multinational, battalion-sized, mission-tailored command structure under the leadership of a non-Austrian commanding officer together with other NATO contingents.

1.3. EMPIRICAL DATA AND METHODOLOGY

The main purpose of this chapter is to analyze the Austrian peacekeeping experience during the IFOR mission in 1996 and 1997. The main issues to be addressed are:

- An analysis of the motives for Austrian soldiers to volunteer for the IFOR mission.
- Analysis and discussion of points of tensions that were internal to the Austrian contingent (particularly the new understanding of the "peacekeeping

---

[1]   Compare Evan Potter, "Peacekeeping and Peacemaking: Former Yugoslavia." *http://www.cfp-pec.gc.ca/english/P4_7.htm* (May 1999). See also Wolfgang Biermann and Martin Vadset, *UN Peacekeeping in Trouble: Lessons Learned from the Former Yugoslavia* (Aldershot, UK: Ashgate, 1998).

[2]   It must be mentioned that Austria's participation in IFOR was restricted to a "self-defense-only policy."

task" and the problems associated with perceptions of the soldier's role in a peacekeeping operation that became obvious at the very beginning of Austria's participation in IFOR).
- Points of tension between different national military contingents during the operation from an Austrian point of view.
- An analysis of the experience of the Austrian soldiers in the new cultural environment of Bosnia and the importance of constructive civil–military relations for a successful outcome of peacekeeping operations. [3]

This chapter refers primarily to two comprehensive studies, which have been published recently under the titles *Zur Soziologie von UN-Peacekeeping-Einsätzen* (On the Sociology of UN Peacekeeping) and *Warriors for Peace: A Sociological Study on the Austrian UN Peacekeeping Experience.* [4] Both books are based on the *Austrian Peacekeeping Study* conducted among Austrian peacekeeping troops in 1996 and 1997. This comprehensive investigation was conducted both as a quantitative study based on several surveys (using questionnaires and interview techniques) and a field research study (daily observation). [5]

In detail, this chapter's analysis is based on the following empirical data:

- *IFOR survey* (using questionnaires) among Austrian IFOR soldiers prior to their departure to Bosnia (February 1996; N=188).
  - This survey *IFOR* was conducted a few days before the first Austrian IFOR contingent left for Bosnia. 188 soldiers completed the questionnaire, which means that about 64% of the contingent (294 men) responded. This response rate must be considered very high since, at the time of the survey, an advance party was already on its way to Bosnia.
- *Field research* including research diary, documentation, and personal interviews among UNDOF (United Nations Disengagement Observer Force, Golan Heights) and IFOR soldiers (January 1996 – June 1997).

---

[3]   Compare also Franz Kernic, "'Peace Angels' versus 'Warriors for Peace?' The Austrian Experience in Preparing Soldiers for UN Peacekeeping Missions," paper presented to the International Sociological Association, Research Committee 01, Montreal, July 1998.

[4]   Harald Haas and Franz Kernic, *Zur Soziologie von UN-Peacekeeping-Einsätzen. Ergebnisse sozialempirischer Erhebungen bei österreichischen UN-Kontingenten* (Baden-Baden: Nomos, 1998); Franz Kernic and Harald Haas, *Warriors for Peace: A Sociological Study on the Austrian Peacekeeping Experience* (Frankfurt-New York-Vienna: Peter Lang, 1999).

[5]   This chapter also refers to a research report of the Austrian Military Psychological Service dealing with specific social and psychological problems reported by Austrian UN soldiers deployed in Bosnia in 1996. In addition, it also takes into account the official NATO/PfP paper on the Austrian experiences and concrete lessons learned in IFOR Operation JOINT ENDEAVOR presented by the Austrian Ministry of Defense, "Austrian Experiences and Concrete Lessons Learned in IFOR Operation JOINT ENDEAVOR" (Vienna, October 1996).

– The field research included face-to-face interviews with Austrian soldiers before, during, and after their UN service/peacekeeping. Part of this field research was conducted by a team of psychologists (Austrian Military Psychological Service) in Visoko, Bosnia, in June 1996.

1.4. SOCIAL PROFILE OF THE AUSTRIAN UN CONTINGENT IN BOSNIA

UN service is voluntary in Austria. Conscripts may volunteer to take part in peacekeeping missions after completing their regular six months basic training. Both professional and militia (reserve) soldiers have the right to volunteer for peacekeeping operations. In addition to basic military training, every peacekeeper undergoes special training varying from two to eight weeks, depending on his position and function within the unit. In general, emphasis is placed on both military and civilian skills. There is no predominance of one specific military service among the Austrian peacekeeping force (generally known as "Austrian UN force" or "blue helmets") because all units are set up only for peacekeeping purposes as so-called "peacekeeping contingents," which can be joined by soldiers from all military services and branches.

More than two thirds of the Austrian IFOR personnel were under 30 years of age (Table 1). Approximately the same percentage of soldiers stated that they were single (Table 2); only one out of four reported having children. Taking into account their relatively young age, it is surprising that many have already taken part in UN peacekeeping missions. The share of soldiers with earlier peacekeeping experience (41.5%) must be considered high (Table 3).

Table 1: Age Distribution

Under 20	2.1 %
20–25	38.8 %
26–30	29.8 %
31–35	18.1 %
36–40	5.9 %
41–45	2.7 %
Above 45	1.1 %
No answer	1.6 %

Source: Harald Haas and Franz Kernic, *UN Study 1998*, IFOR (N=188).

As far as the soldiers' educational background is concerned, the number of those with higher education is relatively small. Only a few hold a university degree (approximately 2%) or graduated from high school (approximately 10%). Most soldiers (approximately 80%) had just attended secondary school

Table 2: Marital Status

Single	61.7 %
Married/long-term relationship	26.1 %
Divorced/permanently separated	9.6 %
Widowed	0
No answer	2.7 %

Source: Harald Haas and Franz Kernic, *UN Study 1998*, IFOR (N=188).

Table 3: Participation in earlier UN Missions
Question: Have you already participated in previous UN missions?

Yes	*41.5 %*
Less than one year	23.9 %
One to three years	12.8 %
Longer than three years	3.7 %
No answer	1.1 %
No	*58.5 %*

Source: Harald Haas and Franz Kernic, *UN Study 1998*, IFOR (N=188).

followed by an apprenticeship with part-time schooling or intermediate vocational training. The unemployment rate among UN soldiers also seems to be relatively high. Almost 20% of Austrian IFOR soldiers reported that they were unemployed before their peacekeeping service.

2. INTERNAL MILITARY DIMENSION

This section focuses on the motives which prompted Austrian IFOR soldiers to volunteer for the Bosnian peacekeeping operation, and the major points of tension that were internal to the Austrian contingents. It must also be mentioned that the interviews conducted among Austrian IFOR soldiers in 1996 showed that the soldiers' perceptions of the meaning, value, and effectiveness of the mission, as well as of the adequacy of material, human, and organizational resources allotted to the peacekeeping operation hardly differed between contingents and units.

2.1. SOLDIERS' MOTIVES TO VOLUNTEER FOR THE PEACEKEEPING MISSION IN BOSNIA-HERZEGOVINA

One major purpose of the *Austrian Peacekeeping Study* was to elicit reasons and motives for the individual's application for UN service/peacekeeping (Table 4). In this respect, the results of two comparative surveys (UNDOF/Golan

Heights and IFOR/Bosnia) show a broad spectrum of reasons and motives, ranging from the wish to experience something new and exciting (adventure) to the chance to earn and save some money. Of course, strong arguments for UN service/peacekeeping are the relatively high pay (clearly the top motivating factor), the wish to experience something new and exciting, to experience friendship and military comradeship, and to develop as a person. In some cases, serving with the UN or IFOR seems to be a better alternative to being unemployed. More and more, regular officers find that international service is becoming an advantage for their careers. [6]

In addition, interviews with soldiers and selected family members show that the peacekeeping mission also constitutes an escape route for soldiers facing various personal problems at home. These problems include a range of issues from problems with the family or the job to divorce and unemployment. Volunteering for UN service/peacekeeping seems to be related to the hope of finding a solution for these problems through a longer distance or absence. From a socio-psychological point of view, signing up for peacekeeping missions is often an attempt to gain at least some physical distance from certain problems, events, and developments that are considered uncomfortable.

2.2. POTENTIAL POINT OF TENSION: PEACEKEEPERS AS "WARRIORS FOR PEACE"

A comparison of the results among Austrian IFOR soldiers with those of the Austrian UNDOF contingent (Golan Heights) showed many similarities with respect to the soldiers' motivation for volunteering for UN peacekeeping. But there were also two major differences in the soldiers' responses we should be aware of. First, IFOR soldiers showed radically less interest in their region (the Balkans) than did UNDOF soldiers with regard to the Middle East. Second, IFOR soldiers stated far more often than UNDOF soldiers that it was important for them to gain military experience, i.e., "to practice my military skills." Furthermore, IFOR soldiers obviously felt more attracted to experiencing "the way soldiers live" than UNDOF personnel did.

In many respects, the available empirical data prove that, at the time of the survey, Austrian IFOR soldiers showed a clear tendency toward a stronger military orientation. They considered themselves "soldiers" and they acted like soldiers. Undoubtedly, the military motivation for applying for peacekeeping service was stronger among the IFOR soldiers than among UNDOF soldiers.

---

[6] See also Franz Kernic, "Freiwillig in den UN-Einsatz – warum? Die Ergebnisse einer empirischen Erhebung" (Volunteer for a UN Deployment? Why? Results of an Empirical Inquiry), *Truppendienst* 1, 1998, pp. 20–24; Franz Kernic, "The Soldier and the Task: Austria's Experience of Preparing Peacekeepers," *International Peacekeeping* 6, No. 3 (Autumn, 1999), pp. 113–128.

Table 4: Motivation for UN Service
Question: How important do you consider the following motives for your application for UN service?

	Very Impor- tant	Impor- tant	Unim- portant	Absolutely Unim- portant	No Answer
To leave behind a boring life at home	17.0	24.5	25.0	26.6	6.9
To save some money	62.2	29.8	4.3	1.6	2.1
To escape unemployment	3.7	9.0	6.4	73.9	6.9
To experience something exciting	22.9	46.8	16.5	7.4	6.4
To contribute to worldwide peace efforts	35.6	45.2	11.7	3.7	3.7
To gain additional skills for the future	55.9	27.7	11.7	1.6	3.2
To prove myself in dangerous situations	23.9	39.4	26.1	5.9	4.8
To learn foreign languages	37.8	38.8	17.6	3.2	2.7
I'm attracted by the way soldiers live	33.5	30.3	21.8	8.5	5.9
To have regular employment	5.9	18.6	25.5	42.6	7.4
High salary	53.2	32.4	8.5	2.1	3.7
To practice my military skills	49.5	29.3	11.7	5.9	3.7
To see if I can accomplish my tasks	48.4	37.8	7.4	2.1	4.3
To have a more interesting job than in Austria	35.1	38.8	11.7	8.0	6.4
Interest in the Balkans	11.7	28.7	34.0	19.7	5.9
To be able to pay off my debts	12.8	16.0	19.1	46.8	5.3
To get to know a foreign country	45.7	39.4	8.5	4.3	2.1

Source: Harald Haas and Franz Kernic, *UN Study 1998*, IFOR (N=188).

On the one hand, they showed no real interest in the culture and language of the country or region where they were going to be deployed. On the other hand, they rated their own military skills (including use of weapons) very highly.

A new image of a peacekeeper's task came to prevail among Austrian IFOR soldiers, leading to specific expectations of their tour of duty. Of course, most soldiers look for some excitement and risk. They do not want to expect a boring life; they volunteered for service in order to leave this behind as soon as possible. But the results of the surveys and interviews show that not only did a risky and dangerous environment attract Austrian IFOR soldiers, but they found the idea of experiencing war far more important and wanted the feeling of being a "real combat soldier."

Furthermore, Austria's IFOR soldiers really wanted to be seen as soldiers or warriors. To most of them, the term *Friedensengel* (peace soldier) seemed to be a contradiction in terms, although soldiers generally admitted that the aim of their mission was to enforce "peace." According to their point of view, however, to be a "real soldier" meant not only being exposed to risky and dangerous situations, it primarily meant both having at least a minimum chance of being involved in fighting as well as experiencing a war-like environment.

This observation leads us to an important lesson that can be learned from the Bosnian case: Soldiers generally consider "peace operations" in a peaceful environment boring and meaningless. Soldiers who consider themselves warriors obviously expect at least a touch of war or combat and some fighting among the conflicting parties from time to time. The so-called "T-shirt scandal" of 1996 (Austrian IFOR soldiers wearing T-shirts with racist slogans in public) is just one example to be mentioned in this context. We could also observe that, in a "boring" environment, soldiers frequently showed a surprisingly high level of aggression against animals, which sometimes led to the organized killing of dogs and cats. Coping with a "status of peace" is probably the most difficult task for this type of soldier to imagine.

2.3. TRAINING FOR PEACEKEEPING

This section focuses on the selection process and the preparation of Austrian UN soldiers for peace operations in Bosnia. The analysis is based on a sociological point of view and therefore differs in some respects from other statements based on an organizational military theory. An emphasis is put upon the capability of Austrian UN soldiers to contribute to peace efforts in a complex cultural encounter. Of course, training for peacekeeping is crucial for the outcome of the missions. Although Austria has established two major training centers for peacekeepers,[7] one for military and the other for civilian peacekeepers (which is itself an interesting development that might be called into question), the Bosnian experience clearly showed that new concepts of preparing soldiers for their missions are necessary.

Austria's selection of personnel for the Bosnia operation was based on Austria's prior experience with UN troops. The only difference from earlier selection processes was that this time, medical, psychological, and fitness examinations were applied more rigorously. Due to threat assessments and the hard conditions anticipated at the start of IFOR, as well as the likelihood of

---

[7] The military training center was originally located at Stammersdorf and moved in 1999 to Goetzendorf; the civilian peacekeeping courses are offered at Schlaining.

using military force, emphasis was put on military skills and military readiness. This led to a higher dropout rate, putting strains on the availability of personnel. From a purely military point of view, these selection criteria proved effective for the contingent in the mission area. On the other hand, this also resulted in the establishment of a typical combat unit with less cultural understanding and lower intellectual capabilities.

IFOR soldiers had more or less the same pre-mission training as UNDOF soldiers. According to the official Ministry of Defense report on Austrian experiences and concrete lessons learned in IFOR,

> ... emphasis was laid on training with regard to the national ROE [rules of engagement], driving skills, and technical expertise in maintenance, escort missions, and mine awareness. The contingent was prepared by field exercises simulating the anticipated threat, tasks, and constraints of the harsh weather conditions and terrain. This training contributed to a high operational standard, discipline, and motivation of the soldiers, and a low accident rate.[8]

For additional information, soldiers were given briefings about the latest political developments and the history of the conflict in the former Yugoslavia.

All in all, selection and preparation of UN personnel met exclusively military needs. The military establishment (in particular the Austrian Ministry of Defense) put a clear emphasis on military skills. So-called "civilian" skills such as foreign language or negotiation skills, the ability to conduct intercultural communication, etc., were seen as additional skills rather than as an advantage or a necessity. The military establishment deemed the Bosnian peacekeeping operations to be an exclusively military operation.[9]

Because of this type of preparation, most Austrian IFOR soldiers believed their task in Bosnia was clear: they had to act as soldiers. Through their former UN experiences, many soldiers were familiar with all technical and operational requirements. About 50% of the soldiers considered themselves to be well prepared for the deployment in Bosnia. The only problem that soldiers and the Ministry of Defense seemed to discuss was whether they were adequately armed and equipped for the task (helmets, weapons, etc.). The majority of Austrian IFOR soldiers felt confident that they would do a "good job." Prior to their deployment, most soldiers believed that cultural concerns as well as negotiation skills were "none of their business." Many officers agreed with this assessment.

---

[8]   Austrian Ministry of Defense, *Austrian Experiences*, p. 9.
[9]   In this context, see Appendix C ("Training") in Department of the Army/Headquarters, *FM 100–23 Peace Operations* (Washington DC, 1994), pp. 86–89.

There is evidence that good preparation and pre-mission training are crucial for a sense of well-being during the tour of duty. In their study, Vogelaar et al. showed that good preparation improves the soldiers' belief in the meaningfulness of the mission and increases their feelings of satisfaction with their job. [10] The quality of preparation also positively influences general well being and alleviates feelings of fear (including depression) for prolonged periods of time. There is no doubt that good preparation for UN service has positive effects on the UN mission because it not only helps the soldiers to feel better and more comfortable in their environment, but also enables the soldiers to accomplish their tasks in a more efficient way.

During the study, soldiers did not complain about their pre-mission training. Most of them considered it necessary, although some soldiers, especially those with previous UN experience, tried to figure out a way to circumvent this training because they considered it too boring. Before their departure to the mission area, the soldiers' general opinion of training and preparation was that it was sufficient to provide them with all they had to know. Nobody asked for better or longer military training. On the other hand, there was a relatively high demand for better preparation concerning the "human aspects" of peacekeeping, such as intercultural communication and cultural appreciation. Soldiers were least certain about how to deal with the local population and its authorities. Most of them showed very little knowledge about the culture, political system, language, and religion that they were going to encounter. In this respect, the study clearly indicates deficiencies in the pre-mission training. Many soldiers requested better and more intensive language training. A high percentage of soldiers had the general impression that even their English should be better. It also became obvious that there was a lack of basic knowledge in other foreign languages that played a major role in the mission area (such as French in the BELUGA group). [11]

3. MILITARY-MILITARY RELATIONS

This section focuses on the Austrian experience with military-military relations in the peacekeeping operation in Bosnia. In general, all Austrian soldiers reported that they were very satisfied with regard to their interaction with soldiers of other nationalities. Most of them even stated that the international cooperation between different national contingents made their work

---

[10]   Ad Vogelaar, Joseph Soeters, and Hans Born, "Working and Living in Bosnia: Experiences of Dutch IFOR Soldiers," paper presented to the IUS conference (Baltimore, October 1997), p. 12.

[11]   Cf. Georg Aminoff, "Experiences for a Multinational HQ," paper presented to Lessons Learned from the Nordic Polish Brigade seminar held at SWEDINT (December 1997), p. 44.

more challenging and satisfying. No major problems were reported with respect to military-military relations in the IFOR mission.

Austrian soldiers were, of course, aware of the differences among militaries with respect to organization, task, values, and the differing abilities to influence the mission. On the one hand, everybody knew that the task of the Austrian transportation unit was of minor importance within the entire framework of the mission. The military role of the Austrian contingent was directly related to the country's level of participation in the operation. On the other hand, soldiers had the general feeling that they were not left alone in such a position. All other countries of the BELUGA group shared with Austria the experience of being a "small-state troop contributor." Hence, the "big power game" in the IFOR peacekeeping operation did not affect the Austrian soldiers' perception of their country's role in international peacekeeping operations. Nobody, for example, expected a stronger Austrian influence in the decision-making process. The Austrian military seemed to be satisfied with the "Olympic idea" that it is more important to take part than to win.

Furthermore, cooperation with NATO countries made Austrian soldiers more self-confident. Among Austrian IFOR soldiers, most NATO and particularly all former Warsaw Pact countries lost their high military prestige within a couple of days. Austrian soldiers quickly realized that soldiers from both NATO and former Warsaw Pact countries were not different from anybody else. This made it easier for Austrian soldiers to cooperate with other national contingents. Comparing their own language skills (particularly their command of English) with the communication capabilities of soldiers from Greece, Belgium, or other Eastern European countries gave Austrian soldiers additional self-confidence.

In this context, it must be mentioned that Austrian soldiers noticed differences with respect to military culture among the different contingents insofar as soldiers from countries with professional armies showed a different "professional ethic." In general, soldiers from the professional armies had not been asked whether or not they wanted to join the peacekeeping mission in Bosnia. For most of them, "peacekeeping" was a job they had to carry out. They did not have the choice of whether or not they could drop out. They considered themselves "professional soldiers" and not "peacekeepers." From an Austrian perspective, this different identity made it difficult to develop a common peacekeeper identity or, at least, a common view of peacekeeping.

Summing up, we may conclude that the multi-dimensional nature of the Bosnian peacekeeping operation and the necessity to cooperate with different national military contingents posed new challenges to the Austrian peacekeeper in the field. Hence, one important lesson Austria learned in the course of the IFOR mission was that peacekeeping today encompasses not only military tasks, but also a variety of other functions, such as civilian police activities; humanitarian assistance; demobilization and reintegration of former combatants; enhancing and monitoring respect for human rights; and, last but not least, public information. Moreover, in the course of the Bosnian operation, Austrian soldiers soon realized that the key to success could be found in smooth interactions and constructive relationships between the military and non-military actors in the field.

4. CIVIL–MILITARY RELATIONS

4.1. PEACEKEEPING AS A COMPLEX CULTURAL ENCOUNTER

During their mission, Austrian soldiers encountered a reality that included almost everything from boredom to real stress, from daily military routine to sudden "civilian" demands. But most important is the fact that the Austrian IFOR soldiers did not find themselves in a military theater of operations. There was no battle going on in Bosnia, so soldiers had to act in both a civilian and a military way, but never as warriors. The Austrian IFOR soldiers thus encountered a complex cultural environment that was quite new and demanding for them. It was not the war-like situation many soldiers had expected. As a result, this environment challenged the soldiers' self-esteem as warriors. Suddenly there was a need for an "intelligent" soldier, for somebody who was trained not only to use force, but also to use human communication skills. There was no demand for Rambo-type soldiers in Bosnia, so some Austrian soldiers were, of course, rather disappointed. IFOR turned out to be an operation with the same peacekeeping requirements as previous UN missions. As such, it provided a challenge to the prevailing military warrior culture. [12]

IFOR demanded interactions not only among various national contingents but also between military and non-military organizations. Instead of the expected warrior culture in Bosnia, Austrian soldiers had to deal with a peacebuilding process that, in fact, excluded the use of military force. Thus, most soldiers had to learn an important lesson: any peacekeeping or peace support-

---

[12]   Cf. Zentrum Innere Führung (Ed.), *Entscheiden und Verantworten – Konfliktsituationen in UN-Einsätzen* (Decisions and Responsibilities – Conflict Situations in UN Deployments), Working Paper 1, 1996 (Koblenz, 1996); Zentrum Innere Führung (Ed.), *Erfahrungen der Bundeswehr aus UN-Einsätzen auf dem Gebiet der Inneren Führung* (*Bundeswehr* Experiences from UN Deployments in the Area of *Innere Führung*), Working Paper 4, 1994 (Koblenz, 1994); Hans-Christian Beck, "Angst, Tod, Verwundung – nichts mehr ist tabu. Führungsausbildung für den Einsatz des deutschen Kontingents im ehemaligen Jugoslawien am Zentrum Innere Führung" (Fear, Death, and Injury – Nothing is Taboo Anymore: Leadership Training for the Deployment of German Troop Contingents to the Former Yugoslavia at the Center for *Innere Führung*), *Truppenpraxis/Wehrausbildung* 6, 1996, pp. 570–572.

ing operation must be seen as civil–military cooperation, as an interaction between the military and other organizations with a common aim. This view also indicates that it is always necessary to take civil–military cooperation and coordination into consideration. Peace operations are not purely military operations.

In Bosnia, soldiers had to cooperate with a variety of non-military social actors whose views of the purpose of the mission and how business should be conducted differed substantially from their own point of view. [13] Certainly, the success or failure of peace operations depends on the way military and non-military actors cooperate and resolve the tensions arising from these different perspectives on how to accomplish the mission.

In this respect, field research showed that the peaceful environment in Bosnia disappointed some IFOR soldiers. The lack of risky and dangerous situations actually led to attempts among them to constitute a more dangerous and risky environment. In this context, the systematic killing of dogs and cats must be mentioned again, as well as all attempts to intensify combat training due to a fictitious "external threat." Soldiers who had major difficulties with their new "humanitarian" role (which was, of course, considered a "non-military task") tried to revert to the so-called "real military culture." [14] Resistance to missions that diverge from the primary goal of fighting or "enforcing peace" became obvious among many military personnel.

4.2. PEACEKEEPING AND THE "WAR/PEACE DILEMMA"

This tendency toward the establishment of a strong "military culture" within peacekeeping or peace supporting operations reveals a general dilemma: as soon as there is "peace" (i.e., no fighting) in the mission area, soldiers become uncertain about their role and begin to question the meaningfulness of their mission. Generally speaking, a "peaceful setting" puzzles the soldier more than a "combat-like" situation because it calls into question his basic view of a soldier's role.

By addressing this dilemma, this chapter highlights the problem that, very often, soldiers hardly understand peacekeeping tasks because they are not really trained for "peace." As long as there is at least some fighting, the soldier can feel "at home" and can identify with the (traditional) role of a soldier. With the achievement of peace, this role becomes obsolete. He can no longer consider himself a "warrior" without at the same time contradicting his peace-

---

[13] In this context, cf. Charles C. Moskos, "Memorandum for Gen. Dennis J. Reimer and LTG Theodore G. Stroup, Preliminary Report Task Force Eagle," Northwestern University, Evanston, IL (July 20, 1996), p. 7.

[14] Cf. Laura L. Miller, "Do Soldiers Hate Peacekeeping? The Case of Preventive Diplomacy Operations in Macedonia," *Armed Forces and Society* 3, 1997, pp. 415–450.

keeping task. He can only identify with the new role of "peacekeeper," which is in contrast with that of a "soldier" or "warrior."

The dilemma sheds light again on the gap between the traditional understanding of peacekeeping on the one hand, and the idea of strategic peacekeeping or peace enforcement – which by definition includes at least the possibility of using force – on the other. Whereas the first concept tries to overcome the dilemma by defining the peacekeeper's role primarily as a civilian (non-military) task, the second idea puts the emphasis again on the military task and the so-called "traditional role" of soldiers as warriors.

The two faces of peacekeeping – as we might call this gap between those two major concepts of peacekeeping – correlate with two different ideas of the type of soldier needed to accomplish the mission successfully. The first concept, which we already described as traditional UN peacekeeping (no use of force, only self-defense, general agreement among conflicting parties about the peacekeeping operation), favors an understanding of the soldier's task as one of a diplomat in uniform who negotiates between conflicting parties without using force. The second concept (strategic peacekeeping or peace supporting operations) responds more to the traditional military image of a soldier and sees peacekeeping primarily as an "enforcement" task carried out by an international military force. This military task can be compared with a police force's task on the state level. It requires men who are willing to use force when necessary. We describe this type of soldier either as a "global policeman" or as a "warrior for peace." An in-depth analysis of the empirical data shows that it is mainly the second type of soldier who could be found in the newly established Austrian contingent for the IFOR (and SFOR) mission in Bosnia.

4.3. INTERNATIONAL COOPERATION

Another important lesson learned from the Bosnian experience is that, up to now, the UN generally has been able to provide a solid infrastructure for more traditional peacekeeping missions, whereas in enforcement operations (e.g., IFOR in Bosnia), institutions such as NATO have proved much better suited to act. For political reasons it might, of course, still be useful to have a mandate of the UN Security Council for operations involving the use of force. Among Austrian soldiers, the switch of the Bosnia mission from UNPROFOR to the NATOled IFOR was generally seen as an important step forward in the process of achieving peace in the area. Furthermore, most Austrian soldiers considered NATO the only guarantor for success in the peacekeeping operation.

Another phenomenon of the peacekeeping operation in the former Yugoslavia was that more and more regional organizations became involved in efforts to reach a peaceful solution to the conflict. For example, in mid1991, the European Community (later European Union) contributed effectively to defusing the situation in Slovenia; a European Community Monitor Mission (EC/MM) has since been active in the Balkan conflict, gathering information and mediating on a local level. Within the framework provided by the Conference (now Organization) of Security and Cooperation in Europe (OSCE), several observer missions have been sent to the former Yugoslavia. In the early 1990s, the OSCE started to play a major role in the former Yugoslavia with respect to crisis management, conflict resolution, and the protection of minorities. Although Austrians were involved in most of these OSCE and EU missions, there was almost no interaction between representatives of these organizations and the Austrian IFOR contingent. Military or civilian observers in the field usually acted on their own, without any closer contact to the Austrian peacekeeping unit.

Analyzing the relationship between the Austrian military transportation unit and the variety of non-governmental organizations (NGOs), private voluntary organizations (PVOs), and media acting in the field, we can briefly draw the following conclusions:

- Due to the differences between the military and NGOs and PVOs with regard to the tasks they had to accomplish, relations between the Austrian military contingent and NGOs were limited to a minimum of cooperation. In general, Austrian soldiers considered NGOs to be "obstacles" with respect to the accomplishment of the peacekeeping mission. Since all these different types of organizations were outside the military hierarchy (the military chain of command), they were seen as a potential threat to the military rather than as a partner.
- Soon, however, soldiers realized the importance of smooth and positive civil–military relations for the successful outcome of the peacekeeping operation. This perception caused the military to focus on the work of liaison officers in order to exchange information and coordinate actions. In the course of the mission, the military was forced to intensify its relationship with NGOs and PVOs. For example, periodic meetings between representatives of PVOs and NGOs and the leaders of the military contingent had to be conducted in the area.
- Military leaders also realized the importance of good relations with the media. Since the media affect public opinion, it became obvious to military commanders in the field that a positive image is a key to success in terms of public acceptance of military actions and to maintaining soldiers' motivation.

4.4. PUBLIC AND FAMILY SUPPORT

Undoubtedly, public support for Austria's participation in IFOR was a crucial issue. Since the mid-1960s there has always been a high acceptance of UN peacekeeping among the Austrian population. One crucial question in a February 1996 opinion poll (the "Market" survey) [15] addressed the issue of Austrian military participation in the IFOR mission in Bosnia. This study showed that 63% of all interviewees were in favor of deploying Austrian soldiers in Bosnia, stating the following reasons: "Everyone should help," "feeling of duty to assist neighboring countries" (*Nachbarschaftshilfe*), and "maintenance of peace." Those who were against Austrian participation (37%) were mainly of the opinion that the mission in Bosnia "was none of our business," and that Austria "had enough problems of its own." (Table 5).

Table 5: Public Opinion toward Austria's Peacekeeping Engagement
The Case of Austrian Soldiers in Bosnia
Question: The UN and NATO are making concerted efforts to secure peace in Bosnia. Are you in favor of Austrian soldiers helping to secure peace in Bosnia or are you against this?

	In Favor	*Against*
Total population (age 18+)	**63%**	**37%**
Men	70%	30%
Women	58%	42%

Source: "Market" study 1996.

Although there is high public support for Austria's participation in peace operations, only a small number of men actually express an interest in volunteering for UN service/peacekeeping. Most people support peacekeeping operations in general but are not willing to contribute individually to such political activities. That leads to the problem that only a small number of men are ready to volunteer for UN service. Hence, the Austrian Ministry of Defense has a very small reservoir of potential UN soldiers from which it can draw volunteers.

In this context, other important questions must be raised: Do Austrian UN soldiers get enough support from their families? How do their relatives and friends view their personal decision to volunteer for UN service/peacekeeping? In general terms, the survey's results show that most Austrian soldiers had their

---

[15] Study of Austrian attitudes toward peace enforcement measures (*Die Einstellung der Österreicher zu friedensstiftenden Maßnahmen*, Linz, 1996) performed by the "Market" Institute in February 1996. This survey was based on a telephone sample with a total of 804 Austrians.

families' support for joining peacekeeping forces. With regard to the Austrian situation, it must also be noted that the proportion of family members who were firmly against participation was larger with the IFOR contingent than with UNDOF (Table 6). One reason for the reduced support for this mission among the families of IFOR soldiers may have been the fact that the IFOR soldiers who were questioned were members of a so-called "first mission" (i.e., the first Austrian contingent taking part in this mission) and that, at the time of their departure, Bosnia was generally seen as an area where soldiers could easily get involved in fighting.

Table 6: Families' Views Regarding Participation in UN Service
Comparison between AUSBATT/UNDOF and the Austrian IFOR Contingent
Question: What is your family's view of your participation in UN service?

	UNDOF	*IFOR*
Full support and acceptance	39.0%	20.7%
General acceptance	41.9%	35.5%
Some reservations and objections	16.6%	40.4%
Strong reservations and objections	1.5%	3.4%
No answer	1.2%	–

Source: Harald Haas and Franz Kernic, *UN Study 1998*, UNDOF (N=172) and IFOR (N=188).

5. SUMMARY

The available empirical data from the *Austrian Peacekeeping Study* also shed light on the fact that, with the beginning of Austria's participation in IFOR and SFOR, radical political and military changes came into play.

- First, the image of UN soldiers as warriors for peace has gained more and more acceptance since the mid-1990s. This IFOR contingent can be considered the first Austrian military unit with a strong military and combat emphasis participating in an international peace supporting mission.
- Second, selection and training for new peace operations reflect this new view that soldiers must be better prepared for military requirements than was the case with the traditional blue helmet concept. In addition, it must be mentioned that there is only a small reservoir of potential peacekeepers in Austria; therefore the Austrian Ministry of Defense is currently forced to accept almost all applicants who apply for the peacekeeping force.
- Third, many Austrian UN soldiers tend to see the peacekeeping job as a military profession. Taking into account the soldiers' young age, it is very surprising that the share of soldiers with earlier UN experience is so high.

A total of 48.8% among UNDOF and 41.5% among IFOR soldiers reported that they had already served with the UN, some of them even longer than three years. Many Austrian UN soldiers consider themselves professional soldiers serving in an "All-Volunteer Force" – the "Austrian All-Volunteer Peacekeeping Force," as we might call it.

An in-depth analysis of the available empirical data concerning the social profile of the Austrian peacekeeper provides us with a rough picture of the "type of soldier" Austrian peacekeepers represent. A comparison of these data with those of other European states supports, in general terms, this point of view. In the Austrian experience, UN peacekeeping service attracts a specific type of person, i.e., a human being with limited social ties, who is weakly rooted in Austrian society. In general, this person has no particular problem with military hierarchy and obedience or with the soldier's Spartan way of life. Trends seem to indicate that the potential Austrian peacekeeper is, of course, not reluctant to earn money rapidly because he usually does not come from a wealthy home or from the upper social class.

From a sociological point of view it is important to note that the soldiers' primary concern is not "peace" in the region where they are going to serve with the peacekeeping force. Far more important is their job as soldiers acting in a different cultural environment. According to the soldiers' view, "peacekeeping" is considered a job for soldiers because only soldiers have the capability and power to "enforce" peace and to supervise cease-fires. Many soldiers see the military (or military culture) as the only guarantee for ensuring the possibility of building peace, establishing stable political conditions in an area of conflict, and enforcing law and order.

This leads us again to a contradiction, itself rooted in the concept of peacekeeping, which has been precisely expressed in the famous quote that "peacekeeping is not a job for soldiers – but only soldiers can do it." [16] Keeping this general dilemma of peacekeeping in mind helps us to be aware of the dangers of a peace operation carried out by soldiers who consider themselves warriors. It also reminds us that, in the end, a peace-building process can never be achieved by soldiers alone.

With respect to future peacekeeping operations and Austria's participation in such missions, we can conclude that these recent developments within

---

[16] Cf. Charles C. Moskos, *Peace Soldiers: The Sociology of a United Nations Military Force* (Chicago-London, 1976); Charles C. Moskos, "UN Peacekeepers," *Armed Forces & Society* 1, 1975, pp. 388–401; Mauritz S. Mortensen, "The UN Peace-Keeper – A New Type of Soldier?" paper presented to the American Sociological Association Convention (Washington, D.C., August 11–15, 1990); Mauritz S. Mortensen, "Peace-keeping/-making – Soldiers Alone Cannot Do It," paper presented at the International Sociological Association Convention (Bielefeld, July 18–23, 1994).

the Austrian peacekeeping force also include a potential threat. As soon as the peacekeeping job is considered only a military job to be carried out by warriors, soldiers begin to develop a new military identity and to constitute a specific military culture that must be seen as a contradiction to the aim of peacekeeping.

3. CANADIAN WARRIORS IN PEACEKEEPING

Donna WINSLOW

Outline:

1. Introduction
2. Canadian Participation in Peace Operations
3. Force Structure, Preparation, and Training
4. Military Tensions in Theater
5. Military Relationships with the Local Population
6. Military Relationships with International Relief Agencies and NGOs
7. Military Relationships with the Media
8. Conclusions

1. INTRODUCTION [1]

Canada has a long tradition of participation in peace operations. The first true UN peacekeeping force was conceived by Lester B. Pearson, then Canadian Secretary of State for External Affairs and later Prime Minister of Canada. He received the Nobel Peace Prize for proposing the creation of a multinational force, which would place itself between the warring factions in support of a cease-fire agreement in the Suez Crisis. As a result, the first official peace-keeping force was deployed to the Sinai under Canadian command in 1956. [2] During the Cold War period, Canada participated in every UN peacekeeping mission, in addition to several non-UN missions, such as the Multinational

---

[1]   Funding for some of this research was received from the Defence and Civil Institute of Environmental Medicine [DCIEM], Canadian Department of Defence. I wish to thank particularly Ross Pigeau for his support of this project. I also wish to thank my research assistants, Jason Dunn and Glenn Gilmour, for their good humor and hard work on this project.

[2]   According to official histories of the UN, the first peacekeeping mission was the UN Truce Supervision Organization (UNTSO), established in 1948. Canada began participating in this organization only in 1954. However, Canada was involved in UN efforts beginning as early as 1949 in an observer mission in India and Pakistan. Allen G. Sens, "The Decline of the Committed Peacekeeper," in Allen G. Sens (Ed.), *Canadian Security and Defence Policy: Strategies and Debates at the Beginning of the 21st Century* (Vancouver: University of British Columbia Press, 2000), p. 2.

Force and Observers in the Sinai. According to Huldt, [3] Canada has rightfully earned the title "old peacekeeper" by virtue of being part of all 13 operations that constituted the first generation of peace operations.

> These states have rightfully earned the honorific label the "UN fire brigade" though there is obviously no such monopoly anymore. They have been directly involved in the laying of the ground rules for traditional peacekeeping, based on "consent" of the parties involved (and certainly of the host country or countries) and on "impartiality." [4]

Even in the second generation of peace operations, Canada is still prominently at the top of the list of participants in peacekeeping operations. In terms of the number of troops actually contributed to UN operations, Canada is in third place, after France and the United Kingdom. [5] In addition to ground forces, Canada supplies naval and air support to peace operations around the world. For example, Canada provides for the airlift of humanitarian supplies for the United Nations High Commissioner for Refugees (UNHCR) and participates in joint NATO naval deployments and air strikes. In this chapter, however, we will focus upon the activities of the Canadian Army in the former Yugoslavia.

Canada was among the first countries to commit troops to this region. [6] In March 1992, a battle group (from the First Battalion, Royal 22e Regiment) was deployed to the Western Slavonia region of Croatia. In addition, Canadians conducted cordon and search operations and set up roadblocks and checkpoints. Canada also provided the force engineer contingent to the United Nations Protection Force (UNPROFOR) and temporarily deployed to Sarajevo Airport to open the airport and provide security for the delivery of humanitarian aid. [7] In addition, in March 1993, the commander of UNPROFOR in Bosnia-Herzegovina asked the Canadians to temporarily assure the territorial integrity of Srebrenica; consequently, the Second Battalion of the Royal Cana-

---

[3]   Bo Huldt, "Working Multilaterally: The Old Peacekeepers' Viewpoint," in Donald Daniel and Bradd Hayes (Eds.), *Beyond Traditional Peacekeeping* (London: MacMillan Press, 1995), p. 105.

[4]   *Ibid,* p. 105.

[5]   *Ibid,* p. 107.

[6]   Canada also participated in the European Community Monitor Mission, a non-United Nations mission throughout the former Yugoslavia and the neighboring states of Albania, Bulgaria, and Hungary from September 1991 – August 1994. The mission monitored and reported upon elements of the cease-fire agreements, performed humanitarian assistance, and participated in confidence-building measures.

[7]   Dunne, MAJ Tim, "United Nations and Coalition Operations in the Former Yugoslavia," from http://www.lfaahq.hlfx.dnd.ca/fyi/yugo_hist.htm; accessed 4 October 1999.

dian Regiment deployed 300 troops to the area. [8] The Canadians occupied eight observation posts around the enclave in addition to escorting convoys, protecting civilians, and confiscating weapons. [9] Until April 1994, Canada also supplied manpower to the UN Commission of Experts set up to report on human rights violations.

Thus, during UNPROFOR, Canadians were placed in a number of dangerous and difficult circumstances. By January 1995, 10 Canadian soldiers had been killed and more than 40 had been seriously injured. [10] There were moments of despair when Canadians were taken hostage, [11] moments of glory when Canadians distinguished themselves, [12] and moments of shame when Canadians were involved in breakdowns of discipline. [13] The number of Canadian troops in the region reached a peak of 2,600 until reductions began in September 1995. UNPROFOR alone accounted for 2,080 Canadian peacekeepers, based on two major units, a logistics battalion, UN military observers, and personnel in the various headquarters. Canada also provided a Major General, who served as the Deputy Force Commander. With the signing of the Dayton Accords in 1995, Canada deployed a battle group in the NATO-led Implementation Force (IFOR). IFOR's mandate was limited to 12 months; the Canadian contribution consisted of a Multinational Brigade headquarters with units totaling 1,200 troops.

---

[8]   For details, see Leonard J. Cohen and Alexander Moens, "Learning the Lessons of UNPROFOR: Canadian Peacekeeping in the Former Yugoslavia," *Canadian Foreign Policy* 6, No. 2 (Winter, 1999), pp. 85–101.

[9]   Following the Second Battalion of the Royal Canadian Regiment, the Second Battalion, Royal 22e Regiment took over the task from May to October 1993. From November 1993 to March 1994, the protection of the enclave was assured by 156 men and women from the 12e Régiment Blindé du Canada, until they were replaced by forces from the Netherlands. See Dunne, "United Nations and Coalition Operations in the Former Yugoslavia," from http://www.lfaahq.hlfx.dnd.ca/fyi/yugo_hist.htm.

[10]   See Cohen and Moens, *Ibid*, p. 94.

[11]   In November 1994, 55 Canadians were among approximately 500 UN soldiers taken hostage following NATO air strikes against Serb positions. Canadians were also taken hostage in several other incidents. See Cohen and Moens, *Ibid*, pp. 91–92.

[12]   In the Medak Pocket Incident of September 1993, Canadian troops attempted to interpose themselves between the Serb and Croat front lines in order to maintain a cease-fire agreement. The Croatian side opened fire on the Canadians and a number of gun battles took place. Eventually the Croatians fell back. In addition, Canadians observed ethnic cleansing by Croat troops and were able to assist some Serbs in escaping. See Cohen and Moens, *Ibid*, pp. 91–92; David Hewitt, *From Ottawa to Sarajevo: Canadian Peacekeepers in the Balkans* (Kingston, Ontario: Center for International Relations, 1998), pp. 62–66.

[13]   In 1994, Canadian Soldiers from the 12th Armored Regiment were involved in incidents in Bacovici Hospital ranging from drunkenness to sexual assault of mental patients. See Donna Winslow, "The Role of Culture in the Breakdown of Discipline during Peace Operations," *Canadian Review of Sociology and Anthropology (Special Issue: Organizational Crisis)* 35, No. 3 (August 1998), pp. 345–368.

Following its contribution to IFOR, the Canadian government announced that in December 1996 it would contribute a well-equipped force to the NATO-led Stabilization Force (SFOR). Operation PALLADIUM was Canada's largest peace commitment, with approximately 1,300 persons. It consisted of an infantry battalion battle group deployed throughout an area in the western part of Bosnia-Herzegovina near the Croatian border. The Canadians were responsible for one of the largest (183,108 square kilometers) and most active areas of responsibility (AORs) found in the South West Division. In fact, it is the same size as one of our Canadian provinces: Prince Edward Island. The administrative headquarters were in Velika Kladusa, about two hours from Zagreb, while the battle group headquarters were further south in Coralici. Other principal centers in the Canadian AOR are Cazin, Bihac, Bosanski Petrova, Zgon, and Drvar. The Canadian contribution during the time I was there can roughly be broken down as follows:

- About 900 troops form the battle group, which is made up of armored, engineer, and strong infantry elements based in Coralici, Drvar, and Zgon.
- About 250 troops from service support units that form the National Support Element are stationed in Velika Kladusa.
- A tactical helicopter detachment of three CH-146 GRIFFON helicopters with about 50 personnel is stationed in Velika Kladusa.
- Other smaller elements, including military police and headquarters staff, serve in Velika Kladusa at the Canadian Contingent's National Command Element; others fill positions in NATO's SFOR headquarters in Sarajevo.

In addition to documentary sources, research for this chapter was carried out in the archives of the Canadian Department of National Defence Headquarters. The bulk of our information, however, came from unstructured interviews and focus groups carried out with Canadian soldiers in Bosnia. In October 1998, I conducted fieldwork in the Canadian AOR. [14] During my visit, I traveled from one end of the AOR to the other, participating in mounted and foot patrols. I slept and ate in platoon houses and was even able to closely observe a live fire exercise.

Another important source of information was a study conducted by the Canadian forces in 1988. This project was based on a survey of ethical risks in peacekeeping and comments on handling these risks. [15] Many of the comments

---

[14] I wish to thank the Canadian Department of National Defence and the soldiers and officers of the 3rd Battalion of the Royal Canadian Regiment Battle Group deployed in Bosnia for taking care of me. I am well aware that such a trip requires time and energy to organize and I am extremely appreciative of the support and information given to me during the trip.

[15] Paul Maillet (Ed.), *Canadian Forces Ethics and Peacekeeping Survey Report* (Ottawa: National Defence Headquarters, Defence Ethics Program, 1998), henceforth called the *Ethics Survey*.

by the 62 respondents, who ranged in rank from general officer to corporal, are relevant to our subject. The interviews were semi-structured and open-ended so that there is little quantitative data. It is important to note, however, when the respondents were asked what they felt were the greatest ethical risks that they have experienced in peacekeeping, "cultural differences" topped the list. For example, 45 respondents cited "applying our cultural norms" as an ethical issue encountered in their peace operation experience. The respondents had a variety of peacekeeping experiences; however, it was possible to find some references to deployments in Bosnia-Herzegovina. We have quoted from those interviews as illustrations of attitudes towards cultural differences in peace operations below.

This chapter is organized into seven sections, each examining a particular dimension of the Canadian deployment in the former Yugoslavia. The first section addresses the political dimensions of the deployment and the decision to commit Canadian forces to UNPROFOR, IFOR, and SFOR. We discuss how participation in peace operations is compatible with Canada's national security agenda and peacekeeping's popularity with the Canadian public, since it appeals to the Canadian value of helping others. In addition, participation brings credit to Canada internationally and allows Canada to have a voice in international organizations. The next section examines how the SFOR operation is organized and how training and previous experience prepare Canadians for the mission. We also examine the attitudes that Canadian peacekeepers have towards the mission. In the following section, we go on to discuss the relationships that Canadians have with other national contingents and how our NATO experience affects our ability to work with other military contingents in SFOR. The next section examines how Canadians organize and maintain relationships with the local population. The final two sections examine relationships that Canadian military personnel have with other organizations in theater, particularly international and voluntary relief agencies and the media.

2. CANADIAN PARTICIPATION IN PEACE OPERATIONS

Canada participates in peace operations for a variety of reasons. Certainly the peacekeeping image appeals to Canadian popular self-images and sentiments of altruism and generosity, doing good to help others who are suffering, etc. In many ways, peacekeeping contributed to the formation of a Canadian identity in the international arena. Peacekeeping represented Canadian multiculturalism, tolerance, and respect for the rule of law. "Peacekeeping had become a mirror, reflecting the finest qualities Canadians ascribed to their own society and national character." [16] There are, however, other more self-motivated rea-

---

[16] Sens, *Ibid*, p. 7.

sons for participation in peace operations. During the Cold War, there were
Canadian security matters to consider. As Sens points out, international security and national security became intertwined:

> Canada's paramount strategic concern during the Cold War was an esca-
> lation of superpower hostilities in Europe or elsewhere into a global con-
> frontation, which would threaten Canadian territory. As it became evident
> that the United States and the Soviet Union could clash in various regional
> conflicts, Canada acquired an interest in the prevention, control, or contain-
> ment of hostilities in areas of tension around the world. [17]

This theme appears in Canada's Defence White Papers of that period. Indeed,
in 1986, a Special Joint Committee of the Canadian Senate and House of Commons stated, "the threat to Canada is one and the same with the threat to international stability and peace." [18]

In the post-Cold War period, peacekeeping meshes well with Canadian foreign policy conceptions of Canada as a "middle power." [19] According to General Michel Maisonneuve, former Chief of Operations in UNPROFOR headquarters, "Canada was able to carve out an independent role within the western
world. By demonstrating initiative, Canada was able to find practical solutions
to problems not easily solved by the big powers." [20] It is also interesting to
note that, according to some observers, Canada's initiative in the Balkans was,
to some extent, influenced by then Prime Minister Brian Mulroney's special
sensitivity to the Balkan region, "owing both to his wife's Serbian ethnic background and also to Canada's large South Slavic immigrant community." [21]

As a middle power, Canada relies on a cooperative approach to security issues and a stable environment for international trade. Peacekeeping was seen as
a contribution to multilateralism and to the UN. According to Wiseman, peacekeeping "enhanced Canada's reputation as a middle power [and contributed] to
Canada's stature and influence in the UN." [22] Participation in peace operations

---

[17] Sens, *Ibid,* p. 5.
[18] Canada, A Special Joint Committee of the Senate and House of Commons on Canada's
      International Relations, *Independence and Internationalism* (Ottawa, June 1986), p. 34.
[19] The term "middle power" is commonly used to refer to the role of states like Canada, Swe-
      den, Ireland, and Austria in the context of UN peacekeeping operations.
[20] Michel Maisonneuve, "Practical Aspects of the Use of Force in Peace Operations," in Alex
      Morrison, Douglas Fraser, and James Kiras (Eds.), *Peacekeeping with Muscle: The Use
      of Force in International Conflict Resolution* (Cornwallis Park, NS: Canadian Peacekeeping
      Press, 1997), p. 144. See also "Speaking Notes for an Address by Prime Minister Brian Mul-
      roney on the Occasion of the Centennial Anniversary Convocation," Stanford University, 29
      September 1991.
[21] Cohen and Moens, *Ibid*, p. 87.
[22] Henry Wiseman, "United Nations Peacekeeping and Canadian Policy: A Reassessment,"
      Canadian Foreign Policy 1, No. 3 (Fall, 1993) p. 138.

also gave Canada some leverage in international forums. According to Sens, "By contributing contingents to ventures such as peacekeeping, Canada hoped to gain a seat at the table, a voice, and therefore some input into decision-making forums." [23] Thus, foreign policy, as well as public and elite opinion, favored an internationalist approach and active Canadian participation in international security.

The Canadian military has argued that it is still primarily a combat force. Over the years, however, peace operations have become the military's primary function. During the Cold War, peacekeeping was seen as secondary to issues of collective defense; later, however, peacekeeping became a key element in the military's battle for both government and public support of defense budgets. In addition, peace operations did provide the military with some form of operational experience. [24] Jockel has noted that, during this time, Canada evolved from a reluctant peacekeeper into a committed peacekeeper. [25]

In the post-Cold War period and particularly in the 1990s, Canada supported the more robust forms of peace operations and humanitarian intervention. Then Prime Minister Brian Mulroney talked about the necessity of "rethinking the limits of national sovereignty" in a world of intra-state and transnational problems. This coincided with a surge in peace operations by Canadians. [26] These new forms of operations were considerably different from those of the past. For example, the UNPROFOR mission proved risky and dangerous to Canadian troops. Between 1991 and 1994, Canadians suffered casualties, kidnappings, and hostage-taking. This did not go over well with the Canadian public. A January 1994 Angus Reid-Southam News Poll found that 57% of Canadians surveyed wanted Canada to withdraw from Bosnia when its contribution was slated to end. [27]

The Canadian government also became concerned about the financial and human costs of the more robust forms of peace operations. Nevertheless, support for peace operations continued. According to Sens, these operations were still in Canada's national interests in the post-Cold War period. Peace operations "contributed to the resolution or containment of conflicts, which could threaten international or regional peace and stability." Contributions to peace operations continued to be expressions of Canada's commitment to the UN

---

[23]   Sens, *Ibid*, p. 6.

[24]   Sens, *Ibid*, p. 7.

[25]   Joseph T. Jockel, *Canada and International Peacekeeping*, Canada Series 16 (Washington, D.C.: Center for Strategic and International Studies and Toronto: Canadian Institute for Strategic Studies, 1994), p. 11.

[26]   For details, see Sens, *Ibid*.

[27]   See Doug Fischer, "Poll Indicates Most Want Peacekeepers out of Bosnia," *Ottawa Citizen*, 25 January 1994, p. A1.

and to regional organizations. This "remained an important outlet for Canadian diplomacy on a wide range of issues." Sens goes on to tell us, "the desire to be both represented and consulted on international affairs continued to be an important driving force behind Canadian foreign policy ... peacekeeping helped maintain Canada's profile and influence as an independent sovereign actor in the world." Finally, participation in the operations in the former Yugoslavia was an expression of Canada's ongoing commitment to European security and to NATO. [28]

This said, the latest trend in Canadian foreign policy is towards "soft power," [29] that is, the belief that "knowledge and information confer international influence." [30] The current Canadian Foreign Affairs Minister, Lloyd Axworthy, has described "soft power" as "[p]unching above your weight. In Canada's case ... ideas, values, persuasion, skill, [and] technique." [31] What this essentially means "is affecting and influencing behavior by information, by values, and by forms of non-intrusive intervention." [32]

This emphasis on "soft power" has coincided with considerable reductions in the defense budget [33] and a resulting loss of "hard power" capabilities. The new buzzword is "peacebuilding" (i.e., efforts to identify and support structures [that] will tend to strengthen and solidify peace in order to avoid a relapse into conflict). [34] This has led to support for "human security," a concept also championed by Lloyd Axworthy:

> The concept of human security recognizes that human rights and fundamental freedoms, the rule of law, good governance, sustainable development, and social equality are as important to global peace as are arms con-

---

[28]   Sens, *Ibid,* p. 14.

[29]   For a review of the debate surrounding soft power in Canada, see Dr. Dean Oliver, "Soft Power and Canadian Defence," *Strategic Datalinks*, No. 76 (Toronto: Canadian Institute of Strategic Studies, February 1999).

[30]   Canada, Department of Foreign Affairs and International Trade, "Foreign Policy in the Information Age," Policy Statement 96/53 (Ottawa: December 1996).

[31]   Lloyd Axworthy, Minister of Foreign Affairs, quoted in "We're Doing Things Nobody Else Could Do," *Ottawa Citizen,* 5 April 1998, p. A7.

[32]   Lloyd Axworthy, quoted in Mike Trickey, "Canada, Norway Change Their Ways,"*Ottawa Citizen,* 28 May 1998, p. A18.

[33]   The Canadian defense budget fell from $CDN12 billion in 1994 to $CDN 9.25 billion in 1999. This represents a 25% reduction in fiscal outlays, which have resulted in force reduction. Between 1989 and 1999, there was a 30% force reduction. The Canadian forces have decreased from 126,000 in 1962 and 100,000 in 1968 to 80,000 in 1975; in 1999, there were 60,600. The Land Forces now total 20,900 with seven battalions. (Sens, *Ibid,* p. 19.)

[34]   Boutros Boutros-Ghali, *An Agenda for Peace: Preventive Diplomacy, Peacemaking and Peacekeeping. Report of the Secretary General Pursuant to the Statement Adopted by the Summit Meeting of the Security Council on 31 January 1992* (New York: United Nations, 1992), p. 32.

trol and disarmament. It follows therefore that, to restore and sustain peace in countries affected by conflict, human security must be guaranteed just as military security must. This is where peacebuilding comes in: as a package of measures to strengthen and solidify peace by building a sustainable infrastructure of human security. Peacebuilding aims to put in place the minimal conditions under which a country can take charge of its destiny, and social, political, and economic development become possible. [35]

If Canada is going to support this package of measures to solidify peace, then civil–military cooperation will be an even more important component of peace operations in the future. Non-governmental organizations (NGOs), humanitarian agencies, local representatives, and the military will all have to collaborate closely in future efforts to restore and maintain global peace.

3. FORCE STRUCTURE, PREPARATION, AND TRAINING

Canada rotates whole battle groups into the AOR for six months at a time. [36] These groups are drawn from Canadian Army regiments. The group that was in the AOR during my visit was the 3rd Battalion of the Royal Canadian Regiment (3RCR). It was the second group (or "roto") from the Royal Canadian Regiment to be in Bosnia and was replaced by another battle group from the Royal Canadian Regiment. As of this writing, the following three rotations of six months each were scheduled to be from the Royal 22e Regiment, etc. In this way, continuity of operations would be assured, since members of the Royal Canadian Regiment who handed off their rotation to the next group knew that group's members, were used to working with them, and shared the same standard operating procedures.

The battle group carried out NATO's SFOR tasks in accordance with Canadian strategic direction. Headquarters in Velika Kladusa interpreted these directions and conveyed them to the troops. I was told that the mission of the 3RCR battle group was to "conduct operations to prevent hostilities within the AOR, implementing the military tasks of the General Framework Agreement for Peace (GFAP) and supporting civil development, in order to achieve

---

[35] Lloyd Axworthy, "Building Peace to Last: Establishing a Canadian Peacebuilding Initiative," Notes for an Address by the Honorable Lloyd Axworthy, Minister of Foreign Affairs, York University, 30 October 1996, p. 2.

[36] Within the AOR, there are different rotation methods. In Bihac, for example, approximately 40 people rotated from Coralici about every two months. The rotation of units into Bihac on a regular basis was seen as a good leadership opportunity. Also, troops are less likely to become bored and no one becomes "king of the roost." The down side is the loss of institutional memory, which can be gathered over an extended period of six months. The parachute company there had no rotation. The group stayed the whole six months in their platoon house. In this way, "you get recognition from the locals."

a secure environment, adequate for the continued consolidation of the peace without further need for NATO-led military forces in BH." [37] The military aspects include liaison, cantonment site/GOF [38] inspections, monitoring of the entities (Serb, Croatian, and Bosnian military forces), mine monitoring, and visible SFOR training. [39]

The overall operational focus is to ensure that Entity Armed Forces [40] (EAF) become political forces. Therefore, there is a need to ensure EAF compliance. As one officer commented, "There is a general lack of respect here for the rule of law, [so] we need to encourage civil development in a secure environment where the rule of law prevails. The SFOR commander has established that 'rule of law' is our center of gravity." In order to do so, the Canadians monitor the potential for violence in the Muslim/northern part of the AOR and maintain force protection in Drvar. A recent "roto" was surprised by riots that took place in Drvar over the return of displaced persons. These soldiers now do more wheeled patrols in rural areas and more foot patrols in the built-up areas. This increases contact with the locals in the hope that these measures will prevent further "surprises."

Securing the environment is the "bread and butter" of the mission; however, civilian aspects are becoming more and more important. The civilian aspects are the SFOR campaign pillars: economic recovery; demining; police services; displaced persons, refugees, and evacuees (DPRE); elections; arms control; and "common institutions" (which is a minor activity consisting mainly of monitoring license plates). These civilian aspects of the mission mean new tasks for the Canadian forces.

As in other peace operations, decision-making is pushed downwards. One interviewee noted: "In wars, a battle group has a predetermined task and dealing with displaced persons, etc., was handled much higher up the chain. Here it is the battle group commander who now has to deal with these matters." Similarly, another officer stated: "Now, in UN ops, the brigade aspect is missing; formerly, the brigade and national HQ dealt with the international aspects. Now, the battle group deals with international aspects. So in a UN tour, captains are getting experience because decision-making is pushed down lower."

Some soldiers are not happy with the increasing emphasis on the civilian aspects of the mission. They do not like doing these civilian tasks because they

---

[37]   BH is Bosnia-Herzegovina. Unless otherwise noted, all quotations from soldiers, NCOs, and officers come from my interviews.

[38]   GOF refers to ordnance depots.

[39]   While in the AOR, I was able to participate in a live-fire exercise that took place right beside an Entity military camp.

[40]   There are only two forces in the Canadian AOR: the Army of Bosnia and Herzegovina and the Croatian Home Defense Council.

were "not what we trained for, which was green." For the most part, however, Canadian soldiers see the value of their presence in Bosnia. For example, the 1999 elections held there went off without a hitch. The military goes out on patrol over the whole region in order to show an SFOR presence. Freedom of movement is now increasing. One young soldier told me that we should do more humanitarian aid and said he thinks that we should stay because, if we leave, the Entities will start "duking it out again." One veteran of many tours described the impact of their presence over the three missions: "In UN-PROFOR, they were shooting at us and children were throwing rocks at us. In IFOR, we were taking the guns away from the big guys. In SFOR, we see people coming back; children are waving at us." According to the men in one mounted patrol, this mission is better than the others because of better food, improved living quarters, and hot showers. They also told me that the financial incentive they receive for peace operations is very important: "It can help you get out of debt, pay [for] a car, or make the down payment on a house." Nevertheless, they believe strongly that their presence keeps the peace.

There were 1,314 people (including 277 local civilians) working in the Canadian camps during the time I was there. 3RCR contributes 883 people (seven subunits). The administration company in Velika Kladusa has 150 people. According to 3RCR's battle group commander: "From Canada, information is filtered through Velika Kladusa, mainly because most business is financial. They interface with Canada on the administrative stuff and we focus on the AOR. I don't need guidance from them. The battle group focuses on the AOR and the HQ on administration, so I don't have to be thinking about that."

The administration section includes the chaplains, medical services, supply organization, cooks, maintenance, and communications. The chaplains are in Velika Kladusa and Zgon – the two extremes of the AOR. Velika Kladusa covers Coralici and Zgon covers Drvar. Chaplains play an important role in terms of morale. There is also a military psychologist deployed with the unit, who is stationed in Coralici. This person reports directly to the commander of the battle group and administers unit climate surveys that are intended to monitor unit morale. The advanced surgical team (AST) and the military police (MPs) are separate and technically part of the Canadian Contingent Stabilization Force (CCSFOR).

Soon after I left the AOR, GRIFFON helicopters came in. This meant an additional 50 people joined the contingent. I was told that there was some tension arising from the control of the GRIFFON resources. There was some controversy over who would control the tasks of the helicopters. "SFOR thinks the helicopters are here to serve SFOR; the Canadians say they are here primarily for the Canadians." In addition to the GRIFFONs, the Canadians expect to receive other force multipliers, like the COYOTE reconnaissance vehicle. [41] When this occurs, during the Royal 22e Regiment's series of rotations, the number of personnel in Bosnia can be reduced. This is important, since Canada has other important commitments in the Balkans, having sent over 1,000 soldiers to Kosovo.

Of the 883 members of the battle group, 520 had been working together since the summer of 1997. The other 250 came in December 1997 or January 1998. The other people in the battle group (regular service, reservists, and augmentees) came in only a few weeks before deployment. Normally, reservists come from the Queen's Own Rifles but, since they could not meet all the manpower demands, the battle group got reservists from all over Canada. I was told: "Having people working together over a longer period (than just a few weeks prior to deployment) is better." This said, the companies with a large number of reservists were working well. Those groups which, like the engineers, had young reservists, were dealing with these reservists by seeing that they were supervised by senior personnel: "There are 13 reservists who are very young (18 – 19 years old), who are supervised by more experienced personnel. So, for example, one field section is made up of nine people with one sergeant (12 – 15 years' time in); one master corporal (8 – 12 years), and seven sapper corporals (mixed – very young and old)." Similarly, for most of the non-commissioned officers (NCOs), the rotation I observed was their second to fourth tour. This is important since the platoon commanders are all young officers who are, for the most part, on their first tour.

Another important factor in the Canadian context is the advantage of being a small army. [42] At the higher levels, I was told, "We know each other ... we are comfortable with each other." The brigade commander, the battle group commander, and the colonel in Velika Kladusa all know each other. "We know and trust each other; thus we work on the assumption that they know what is best for the battle group. This makes for a smooth operation." Another officer told me:

> The Army is a small organization; the command and staff element knew each other from working together in Petawawa. We all have a feel for each other. Knowing each other is a big benefit. The unfortunate thing is that it is not always possible. It is best to take a unit and a HQ that are used to

---

[41] This will be a big improvement, since the vehicles that the Canadians are using are extremely old. Some soldiers are driving vehicles that are older than they are. These vehicles were refitted with ceramic and Kevlar, which made them too heavy, so the suspension, wheel drums, etc. need constant work. This affects morale. Other equipment is sorely in need of repair. For example, the demining machine was not functional at all when I was there.

[42] As stated above, almost 21,000 people serve in the Canadian Army, of which 5,000 are in the combat arms.

working together and deploy them together. One example is the Dragoons, who usually work with 2RCRJ artillery that trains with them. As Officer Commanding (OC) of the unit, we took a captain who was used to working with us rather than a major who did not know us.

The commander of the battle group echoed this: "The group has a history of working together. It was a seamless transition to 'YUGO,' a well-oiled team. *Ad hoc* groupings are inferior. At least you need a critical mass of people who are used to working with each other – 75 – 80% at least. Thus, everyone is a known quantity." Therefore, it seems that whether a person is a good soldier is not as important as how well one knows the soldier and, therefore, can anticipate what to expect from him or her. Also, shared experience working together means that everyone is familiar with the same procedures.

The down side of having such a small army, however, is that the high operational tempo can deleteriously affect its members. A member of the Canadian Army can expect to face many deployments during his or her military career. This takes a high toll on family and personal life. There is "burn-out" not only from the stress of the job, but also from the stress of constant deployment.

This is more true for some trades than for others. A group of NCOs said, "The smaller the trade gets, the more times you are sent away." Some of the soldiers I met had done three rotations in seven years: "It's good for the money and hard on family life. There is lots of marital burn-out. Some marriages are stronger but not many. Releases [i.e., leaving the service] go up after a tour." Constant rotations can also affect the ability of a soldier to perform well in-theater. As one soldier quoted in the Ethics Survey put it: "[W]hen a member is exposed to more than one mission, I feel that the risks increase and mission focus diminishes." [43]

In terms of training, we saw above that most people assigned to the battle group began training for a mission six months prior to deployment. This training was organized at the battle group level and included mainly combat exercises, mine awareness, and the like; however, training sessions on cultural awareness and orientation to the AOR were also included. There was a pre-deployment exercise in Arkansas. There was also training in-theater, including monthly rules of engagement training, general-purpose combat training, live-fire training and scenario training (such as dealing with a car accident in the AOR). "These in-theater combat exercises are necessary to secure the environment in that they demonstrate that we have good combat capabilities." Everyone down to the privates must know the pillars of the mission. They all receive memo cards setting out the mission; furthermore, the pillars are posted around camp and even in platoon house latrines.

---

[43]   Maillet, *Ibid*, p. 29/34.

It is particularly interesting to note that almost all of the people with whom
I talked during my tour of the AOR, from soldier to commanding officer, were
in agreement that another event – an ice storm – had been more significant in
terms of preparation for Bosnia than the pre-deployment training they received
from the military. In the winter of 1997 – 1998, a severe ice storm struck Eastern Canada. Power was knocked out in some regions for as long as three weeks.
It was declared a national disaster and the military was called in. Many of the
people on the rotation had participated in the ice storm disaster relief. This
event not only gave them experience in working together, it also gave them
experience in dealing with many situations similar to those encountered in
Bosnia. According to one officer, "The training nut is a hard one to crack. The
January 1998 ice storm was a great training event. It meant dealing with daily
life when life is upside down. We derived great benefit from the experience,
especially the liaison staff, who had to work with local mayors, etc. We all
worked in that ice storm." As one NCO commented, "The ice storm prepared
us more for the operation than pre-deployment training." Another added:

> The ice storm was a better preparation dealing with people arguing over
> wood, taking food for themselves, but most of all the "do it for me attitude."
> In the ice storm, people were waiting for the Army to clear their driveway
> for them. Big, healthy men were waiting for us to come and do it for them.
> Families here in Bosnia also wait for the Army to come and build their roof
> or house for them instead of moving into town or doing it for themselves.

Of course, Canadian soldiers recognize that training will never exactly mirror
conditions in-theater. "This was a very challenging experience, which Canada
did try to prepare me for; however, reality is always the harshest teacher." [44]
UNPROFOR was particularly challenging: "Regardless of any experiences
you had prior to participating in a mission, nothing can prepare oneself for
the atrocities of war." [45]

Nonetheless, deficiencies in training do exist. One of the most important
aspects of training noted in the Ethics Survey was the need for more detailed
cultural awareness training:

- "We need programs in world history, international affairs, international law,
  international development, etc." [46]
- "It is most important for peacekeepers to be made aware of customs/patterns
  of behavior in the area of operations." [47]

---

[44] Maillet, *Ibid*, p. 34/34.
[45] Maillet, *Ibid*, p. 33/34.
[46] Maillet, *Ibid*, p. 26/34.
[47] Maillet, *Ibid*, p. 25/35.

- "We need cross-cultural awareness/political/social [training] in relation to the mission area. Sadly, most Canadians are ignorant and make mistakes because of this lack of "soft" knowledge." [48]
- "When I did my tour, there was little/no in-brief; and after a year of civil war, I had virtually no out-brief. Preparation via education in what lies ahead on a foreign tour is essential, I believe." [49]
- "Better preparation in regards to the background, and background and beliefs of the local populations, is called for. A better informed soldier will be better equipped to make the right decision and will be less likely to find himself in a tempting or compromising position." [50]
- "Better prepare our people for UN tours – advise them on cultural differences." [51]

Rules of engagement (ROE) pose a particular training challenge. The Ethics Survey shows that Canadian soldiers were critical of the training they received on ROE and the limits imposed on the use of force by soldiers in-theater.

- "We need continuous in-theater training [on the ROE/use of force] to ensure troops do not "defend" materiel too vigorously." [52]
- "I found my ROE to be very frustrating. I essentially had to wait until I was fired upon before I could draw my weapon! My personal safety was jeopardized. As well, as a peace officer, I found it frustrating that I couldn't use anything but lethal force (i.e., no intermediate weapons)." [53]

General Maisonneuve gives one example where the limits on use of force placed soldiers in a position in which they had to use more, not less, force:

- "Riot control agents cannot be used against belligerents. Thus, during the riots of April 1996, the Czech battalion, under the operational control of [Canadian] Brigadier General Jeffries, was forced to fire warning shots." [54]

The Ethics Survey also pointed to problems arising from different sets of ROE.

- "We need to [b]e very specific on our ROE, and our responsibilities towards non-combatants and combatants." [55]

---

[48]   Maillet, *Ibid*, p. 24/34.
[49]   Maillet, *Ibid*, p. 24/34.
[50]   Maillet, *Ibid*, p. 23/34.
[51]   Maillet, *Ibid*, p. 23/34.
[52]   Maillet, *Ibid*, p. 27/34.
[53]   Maillet, *Ibid*, p. 34/34.
[54]   Michel Maisonneuve, "Practical Aspects of the Use of Force in Peace Operations," in *Peacekeeping with Muscle: The Use of Force in International Conflict Resolution*, p. 151.
[55]   Maillet, *Ibid*, p. 24/34.

- "In UNPF [United Nations Peace Forces], Canadians had two sets of ROE, one for Bosnia, one for Croatia; this was especially difficult for soldiers who worked in both countries." [56]
- "Developing ROE for IFOR seemed to be problematic. Canadian ROE were different than those of the Division we worked for." [57]
- "We didn't maintain the same status quo within participating nations, i.e., ROE." [58]

4. MILITARY TENSIONS IN-THEATER

Once the national decision was taken to commit Canadian troops to UNPRO-FOR, the logical choice was to send Canada's NATO brigade, since they were already at a high state of readiness, well-equipped, and only hours away by train. The first tension arose with the UN, which did not think that sending a fully mechanized brigade "fit" with the image of a peacekeeping force. Civilian considerations and military security issues clashed. According to Major-General Robert Gaudreau, the Canadian division commander at that time:

> The UN bureaucrats, mainly concerned with costs, would have preferred to limit armored vehicles to one company per unit. Our national concerns [were] the physical security of our troops and the recognition, based on experience, that a show of force not only provides immediate safety but also critical flexibility should the situation deteriorate. [59]

Canada eventually sent a fully mechanized battalion (CANBAT) with its integral support weapons and a mechanized engineer regiment. According to Major-General Gaudreau, the first consequence was that the force commander realized that the Canadians were the only troops able to give him some operational flexibility. The Canadians were identified as the sole source for a force reserve. This led to difficulties for the contingent commander:

> Canada's national policy is that Canadian command should not be divided and [that] operational missions need to be directly related to the mandate agreed to on deployment. This means that the contingent commander needs to get national approval for in-theater changes to the deployment, grouping, or mission as accepted. This national restriction ... goes against UN

---

[56] Maillet, *Ibid,* p. 21/34.
[57] Maillet, *Ibid,* p. 21/34.
[58] Maillet,*Ibid,* p. 20/34.
[59] Major-General Gaudreau, "Would a United Nations Fighting Force Have Changed Events in Croatia in 1992?" in *Peacekeeping with Muscle: The Use of Force in International Conflict Resolution,* p. 140.

thinking, which sees troops deployed under full operational command as opposed to operational control.[60]

The participation of the Great Powers, and particularly of the United States, in recent peace operations in the Balkans will probably serve to marginalize Canadian input. "Canada cannot expect to have the same level of input or voice into collective decision-making or operational planning and execution as it did in the era of traditional peacekeeping."[61] Moreover, Canada's declining defense budget means that there are less military resources and capabilities available. Dwindling land force capacity will affect Canada's ability to sustain prolonged substantial commitments abroad. This may also have an effect on Canada's ability to influence peace operations in the Balkans. According to the executive director of the Canadian Institute of International Affairs, "Our rhetoric will start to ring hollow unless it is backed up by resources. ... There has been minimal investment in our international commitments."[62] There was already an indication of this when Canada's position in opposition to air strikes was overridden. In 1994, Canada was excluded from the Contact Group, which became the primary mechanism for policy on the Balkans. According to Sens, "Canada's allies were dissatisfied with Canada's contribution to IFOR."[63]

Under SFOR, the Canadians operate within a multinational force that includes battalions from the Czech Republic and Belgium/Luxembourg, a battle group from the Netherlands, and two from the United Kingdom (UK). The Canadian commander has limited contact with commanders of other contingents and there is little contact with other national units on his flanks. Little time is spent "liaising" with flanking units, since he spends most of the time in his own AOR. There is some contact with Multinational Headquarters (HQ) in Banja Luka. Multinational HQ had Dutch, Belgian, and three Canadian representatives, but was mainly staffed by the UK during the time I was there.

The Canadians have a long tradition of working with the UK and share standard operating procedures. When the Canadians were stationed in Germany, they were also attached to the UK. Since the Canadians pulled out of Germany, there has been less opportunity to train in a multinational environment. In the long term, this may affect Canada's interoperability.

- "One of the things we lost when we pulled out of Germany was the opportunity to train in a multinational environment; the commanders here have experience from Germany."

---

[60] Gaudreau, *Ibid,* p. 140.
[61] Sens, *Ibid,* p. 18.
[62] Daryl Copeland quoted in Marcus Gee, "World's Poor Overlooked as Foreign Aid Stays Low," *The Globe and Mail,* 18 February 1999, p. A20.
[63] Sens, *Ibid,* p. 21.

- "We have begun to drift away since we left Germany. We are losing touch with the SOPs [Standard Operating Procedures], etc."
- "My experience in Germany was invaluable – we were open then to new ways of doing things. It's a shame that folks coming up don't get that experience. They get low-level exchanges, and that is not the same as training at the corps level in integrated forces as we did in Germany. It is not as intense as it was in Germany. We try to get together with exchanges; e.g., we exchange people with the Brits and the Czechs, but the mission is busy so we don't have time to play around with professional development. The focus is on the AOR."

According to General Maisonneuve, "[In IFOR] problems of interoperability are lessened by the fact that most of the troops are from NATO."[64] Under IFOR, there were 14 non-NATO nations (13 Partnership for Peace member states and one other). The vast majority of the major troop-contributing nations, however, belonged to NATO. It is also important to note that the Partnership for Peace program promotes interoperability among the participants. The general described this interoperability as "common doctrine and procedures, as well as interoperable equipment. The method of 'certification' conducted by the alliance for the non-NATO members ensured all contributors were able to employ their full capabilities and understood the rules of engagement."[65] In addition, the common values and shared military cultures of NATO nations such as Canada make for better communication and common standards in the application of the mandate.[66]

Canadians also promote interoperability through exchanges. In Coralici, there were British, American, and Dutch intelligence officers at the battle group headquarters when I visited. Since IFOR, Canadians have commanded Czech Republic troops. There were also exchanges among the armored units, where Canada exchanged troops with the British. (For example, Canada sent one crew of three people for one-week exchanges). While I was in Coralici, I observed joint training in a traffic accident scenario. The Czechs played non-English-speaking participants in the drama (they were really hamming it up and having a lot of fun being difficult for the Canadians who were training to "do crowd control"), while the British liaison team was running the scenario and observing how the Canadians handled the situation. "They – the Brits – are fully integrated participants in our team," commented an officer. This was

---

[64] Maisonneuve, *Ibid,* p. 149.

[65] Maisonneuve, *Ibid,* p. 151.

[66] For further information on cultural interoperability, see Donna Winslow and Peer Everts, "Cultural Interoperability for NATO: UNPROFOR and SFOR Compared," in Gustav Schmidt (Ed.), *NATO: The First Fifty Years* (London: Macmillan, 2000).

an example of inter-military cooperation and building good relations between the three groups.

I observed much camaraderie between the three groups. I was told that the Canadians respect the Czechs, who are "serious" soldiers with a lot of fire-power. I was also told the other contingents think that Canadians are soft because they give their people three weeks leave and extra money for deploying overseas. The British who came from Germany actually lost money by coming to the former Yugoslavia.

Although there appears to be a common military culture that promotes effective coordination among NATO countries, significant differences arise when the Canadian military works with some non-NATO countries. The Ethics Survey reveals that cultural tensions are prevalent in multinational deployments. These included differences between Canadian and some other UN forces on substantive ethical issues, such as participating in the black market.

- "Other [problems] involved some contingents' views of officer status vs. that of soldiers. Specifically, taking the rations provided by the UN, feeding the contingent members at different standards based on rank, and selling the remainder on the black market." [67]

- "There were also different degrees of compliance with host nation rules and regulations (e.g., with respect to money-changing on the "black market"). Canadians would be sent home [if proven guilty of infractions] whereas other contingents freely and actively participated – up to the Commanding Officer level." [68]

- "It was clear that neighboring nations were black marketing fuel, yet, due to the "political" considerations, this went unchallenged." [69]

- "UN troops [were] involved in black marketeering at the expense of the war-torn area. UN troops [were also] involved in providing prostitutes for other UN troops. If these had been Canadian troops, I could have *enforced* Canadian law; but they came from other countries and all I could do was report incidents to their contingents." [70]

- "It does … become an ethical dilemma when dealing with other UN forces who do not adhere to the ethical standards … . We must have the ethical backbone to call our 'allies' to task when we see, or believe, they are acting beyond the bounds, for example, [by engaging in] black marketeering. Offending a foreign national unit by telling the *truth* should not be the driving force that puts the lid on events." [71]

---

[67] Maillet, *Ibid,* p. 17/34.
[68] Maillet, *Ibid,* p. 15/34.
[69] Maillet, *Ibid,* p. 15/34.
[70] Maillet, *Ibid,* p. 12/34.
[71] Maillet, *Ibid,* pp. 32/34 – 33/34.

- "Some UN officials were caught stealing hotel silverware and using UN-procured material for their personal benefit." [72]
- "Ukrainian and Russian UN employees purchased huge quantities of staples required for Bosnia, i.e., fuel, potatoes, cabbage, etc., and then moved into other areas to sell them for profit. This was reported to the Ukrainian and Russian contingents, yet no action was taken." [73]
- "I believe that there is a risk that coalition forces' resources may be inappropriately "donated" to non-CF agencies or persons. Examples include fuel, food, materiel, and supplies that may be given to NGOs, other forces, or local persons." [74]

Other problems arose from differences in value systems among the contingents.

- "I have observed that the different cultural values, not only within different groups in the host country, but also among the components of a multinational deployment, appear [to be] the most prevalent in causing stress." [75]
- "There is a big difference in standards between the countries that take part in UN missions because of their own cultures." [76]
- "There are big differences between ethical standards of host nations and *especially* between other contingents who may have different value systems (especially with respect to harassment, gender integration, etc.)" [77]
- "There is a difference in standard[s] between the various contingents, and the level of authority and discipline over the troops/members." [78]
- "We did ... face major problems in dealing with the cultural differences between UN civilians and other countries' views of ethics." [79]

When I asked about working with non-NATO and non-Warsaw Pact countries, I was told that this "would be very difficult because of the differences in military culture and basic cultural differences. There are significant differences in the way things are done between militaries, e.g., the relationship between officers and senior NCOs or officers and soldiers." General Maisonneuve specifically critiques the participation of troops from developing countries:

> Today Third World nations see UN participation as a way of improving
> their cash flows. In many cases, conditions in the home nations of these

[72] Maillet, *Ibid,* p. 21/34.
[73] Maillet, *Ibid,* p. 21/34.
[74] Maillet, *Ibid,* p. 13/34.
[75] Maillet, *Ibid,* p. 20/34.
[76] Maillet, *Ibid,* p. 20/34.
[77] Maillet, *Ibid,* p. 10/34.
[78] Maillet, *Ibid,* p. 12/34.
[79] Maillet, *Ibid,* p. 29/34.

forces are little better than those in which they are deployed; consequently, their perceptions, attitudes, and actions will reflect this. [80]

Maisonneuve adds:

> The equipment, personnel, and training of the military forces of Third World nations may not be adequate for the peacekeeping role they are assigned. Countries that may not be familiar with the use of force, are not equipped properly, and have not received adequate training in the use of force, may have problems applying the required force. In fact, when the need is there, they may be more of a hindrance than a help. As an example, during the first attack of sector South by Croatian forces in January 1993, some nations' forces reacted well, and were prepared to use force. Other forces cowered in their bunkers and were just one more problem for the UN commander to solve. [81]

Thus, it appears that Canadian soldiers perceived NATO forces to be more professionally competent than UN forces. As one soldier from the Ethics Survey stated: "I was initially very bothered by the incompetence of the UN, but realized that the UN also recognized this by ultimately handing [the mission] over to NATO." [82]

5. MILITARY RELATIONSHIPS WITH THE LOCAL POPULATION

In the SFOR rotation I observed, the Canadian military conducted a variety of liaison activities with municipal and cantonment officials, particularly the Ministry of Reconstruction. It also had to remain neutral while dealing with ethnic conflict within local governments. For example, I was told, "We have to deal with Serbs and Croats. For example, the deputy mayor is Croat, as is the acting mayor, since the Serb mayor is not here. However, the Serb reps on the town council are stonewalling the Croat. The Serbs are also fighting amongst themselves. They can't agree on anything. We treat everyone as equal." The military also met with the local police force weekly and provided security if the UN civilian police were not able to be there. According to one officer, "the IPTF [UN International Police Task Force] is ineffective. We have to monitor the monitors. We were the ones who had to get the local police going." And a warrant officer mentioned: "The IPTF can be from different countries and not always from the best country to set the example of good policing (e.g., Malaysians, Ghanaians, and Pakistanis)."

---

[80] Maisonneuve, *Ibid,* p. 147.
[81] Maisonneuve, *Ibid,* p. 148.
[82] Maillet, *Ibid,* p. 34.

The local community saw SFOR and the Canadians as friends and partners, as the emphasis of the mission became more one of hearts and minds. "We are not an occupying force. We have a lot of eyes and ears on the ground." The Canadians did not buy food locally (they did not want to create a false and dependent economy), and therefore their food came from Denmark.[83] They did not buy local fuel either, but they did buy some construction material. Of course, soldiers spent some money locally, but I do not think it was significant since the Canadian camps were very much like prisons. Soldiers were not allowed to go into town except when they stopped to have coffee while on patrol. The goal of the coffee stops was to have a very visible presence and to gather information.

The Canadians also operated a radio show and distributed pamphlets about their mission. "We try to influence the local population via radio, leaflets, etc. The goal is to infect them with Canadian western values plus give them information." Gathering and disseminating information was another important aspect of the Canadian mission in Bosnia. The military was not a coordinator of humanitarian effort so much as a conduit of information; when contacted, they gave information (e.g., Community X needs Y and Z). The SFOR soldiers also collected census data on those who had returned to the villages, as well as information on any unexploded ordnance that villagers or others in the area had discovered. Platoons collected information on each returnee and passed it on to the next "roto." During my visit, the Canadians were developing a Displaced Persons and Refugees database, which they updated monthly with results from the civil–military cooperation teams' canvassing of the area. Also, information was passed onto NGOs so that they would know, for example, that there were families in isolated area "X" that had returned and were in need of food and perhaps a roof on their house before the onset of winter.

Local people worked for the Canadians, as well. For example, in Camp Holopina, 70 civilians had to be paid and supervised. Canadians even transported them to and from work. The civilians worked in the kitchen, as well as in sanitation and laundry sections, grounds maintenance, etc. In addition, the Canadians used local contractors for various jobs. This seems to have been a source of tension.

> We are having trouble with the Bosnian contractors who still have the old communist regime mentality of getting paid even if they don't do the work. Therefore, everything is put off until tomorrow. Our translator helps. She's Croatian with no ties to the local contractors or businessmen. Therefore she can be effective.

---

[83]   At this time, food for the group cost about $CDN 2 million per month. This amount of money would have had a large impact on the local economy.

The translators were an important link to the local population and accompanied many patrols.

The commander of the battle group determined the goals for the humanitarian thrust of the rotation (for example, the group I observed was concerned with medical infrastructure: they established a dental clinic and rebuilt the psychiatric wing of the Bihac hospital). The Canadians also got DM 1,000 per company to provide humanitarian relief. Thus, one group was refurbishing a dental clinic. They obtained the equipment from Canada. A local Canadian politician – a friend from the ice storm – sent about $6,000 of dental equipment. As the battle group commander remarked, "It is out of the Canadians' specific mandate, but soldiers enjoy volunteering for this stuff." To keep up their skills, the doctors also provided humanitarian assistance twice a week at Bihac hospital. This hospital was in the line of fire and was left in very poor condition. It was severely damaged in the bombing, but the Canadians have rebuilt it and helped to provision it. A medical officer stated: "When our medicines are in the window of six months' expiry date, we give them to the hospital."

Another group had two "Hearts-and-Minds" projects, one of which was to rebuild a footbridge along local waterfalls in a Serbian area. Sometimes there is competition with the NGOs for projects. For example, one group wanted to put a woodshed in a school in the Republika Srpska. An aid agency beat them to it, so they had to identify another school for their woodshed. Canadians also took on families and dropped off goods/aid. "We have six families that we provide aid for." (They are Serbian, Bosnian, and Croatian.) These families "were handed off to us by our predecessors." Through this relationship, these families became dependent on the group and now the Canadians cannot cut the umbilical cord. Another group dropped off food and water to isolated families. With the onset of winter, the Canadians planned to start chopping wood for local families so that they might heat their homes. The Canadians coordinated this with the NGOs: the NGOs dropped off the wood, and the Canadian military later came and chopped it. Some soldiers resented this work: "I hate cutting wood for people who can cut their own." This reminded them of the problems they had in the ice storm when "lazy" Canadians expected soldiers to shovel their driveways for them.

But the work done by Canadian personnel in-theater was only part of a very complex relationship between the military and the local population. Canadian forces personnel, when contacting the local population, encountered many forms of cultural tension. In particular, they faced ethical dilemmas about how to treat impoverished locals, how to remain neutral in a conflict-ridden society, and how to deal with pervasive corruption. The Ethics Survey illustrates this cultural tension. The list of difficulties included:

- "Dealing with an uneducated and poor populace in a condescending and intrusive way." [84]
- "Those accepting the company of and sexual favors from young girls and women who naively look for a ticket out of their country, and promising such help in return for their company." [85]
- "Allowing oneself to be sucked into an economy where bribery and black market dealings are rampant." [86]
- "Not recognizing that a belligerent party who is being nice or friendly and who provides gifts, foods, alcohol, etc., at times, is doing so to compromise you. An offering of gifts and friendship was often for ulterior motives. Unless you recognized the issue, you became biased or favored one side/party over the other." [87]
- "During Operation HARMONY, our unit was garrisoned on the Krajina side of the zone of separation. Living on the Serbian side (or any single side) created ethical dilemmas, in that there is a tendency to see the conflict through the eyes of the people you live with (children, hospitals, human rights, etc.) and thus the potential to become prejudiced became great, particularly as seen through the soldiers' eyes. Ensuring that operations are carried out without these prejudices is an ethical challenge." [88]
- "Bribery attempts range from what is locally accepted business practice to illegal activity. An example of the former would include gifts and cash to the unit supply officer to cement a local procurement contract." [89]
- "We saw lots of criminal activity by local police, including beatings and graft. How do you work with them when they behave this way and you need to maintain their trust? At what point to you step in and say enough is enough?" [90]

The Ethics Survey pointed out that bribery and attempted bribery by locals (for example, by contractors in order to get work) was the second most cited ethical dilemma identified by respondents. [91]

---

[84]   Maillet, *Ibid,* p. 20/34.
[85]   Maillet, *Ibid,* p. 20/34.
[86]   Maillet, *Ibid,* p. 20/34.
[87]   Maillet, *Ibid,* p. 19/34.
[88]   Maillet, *Ibid,* p. 19/34.
[89]   Maillet, *Ibid,* p. 17/34.
[90]   Maillet, *Ibid,* p. 17/34.
[91]   Maillet, *Ibid,* p. 3/34.

6. MILITARY RELATIONSHIPS WITH INTERNATIONAL RELIEF AGENCIES AND NGOS

In this section, we will look at the international agencies, with which Canadian forces worked in-theater. We will also examine points of tension that can arise from organizational differences concerning goals and tasks and ways of accomplishing them. The Canadian International Development Agency (CIDA) funded a number of projects. According to one CIMIC officer, "CIDA had given DM 250,000 and the Brits have pumped a lot in. Other agencies are ECHO (EU), World Bank, OXFAM (British – worked on the elections in Drvar), and CESVI (Italian – built 350 houses)." Canadians worked closely with the UNHCR. I was told that the demands are small compared to 1994 – 1995, when the UNHCR used Canadian military vehicles. When they first arrived, the NGOs wanted the members of 3RCR to deliver goods and cattle for them. The military refused but did share information with NGOs through the population survey conducted by CIMIC. Canadian military personnel monitored returning refugees; as mentioned above, they also sometimes cut and dropped off wood for the NGOs.

Another form of cooperation was medical. Once a month, the Head of Medical Unit had a meeting with the World Health Organization; (s)he also kept in contact with other medical staff in the area (for example, *Médecins Sans Frontières* / Doctors Without Borders) about the main medical problems in the region. These were mainly tuberculosis, AIDS, communicable skin diseases, oral hygiene, and cancer.

The Canadian military also cooperated with the UN Mine Action Center. The UN requested that someone work in the Center. While I was there, the military had seconded a major to Bihac to work as the Center coordinator. This major checked safety, techniques used to actually clear mines, and hiring procedures.

Canadian officers also managed projects for the Canada Fund, CIDA, and the British Overseas Development Agency. The army liaison officer put together projects. CIDA and the Canadian Department of Foreign Affairs and International Trade (DFAIT) reviewed the proposals and recommended those that they most wanted to fund. These small projects included the distribution of small farm equipment. The military was not, however, involved with humanitarian decisions at a very high level. In the AOR, "we are just the execution aspect of the operation."

The number of NGOs in areas of conflict has increased dramatically in the post-Cold War period and so has their impact on these crises. They are often the first to enter and the last to leave. While I was there, there were literally hundreds of NGOs operating in Bosnia. They encompassed a wide variety of organizations, often with varying tasks, goals, competence, types of personnel, etc., which could make liaison with them at times difficult for the military. There were large organizations, such as CARE Canada, which were active in the Canadian AOR. The Canadian Cooperation Fund also contributed grants for a number of initiatives. CARE International had a program of home visits for isolated elderly people. The Danish Mobile Hospital had a container clinic program. *Terre des Hommes*, a Swiss charity, opened up youth centers in Prijrdor, Bosanska Krupa, and Banja Luka. Conflict Resolution Catalysts had a program to train teachers to deal with aggression in 11 – 17 year olds and a peer mediation training program that worked in cooperation with youth centers established by *Terre des Hommes*. The Spanish charity, *Moviemento por la paz, el desarme, y la libertad* (MODL), supported youth sports and social activities for refugees in collective centers. [92]

An important aspect of the NGO-military relationship is related to security. All NGOs understand the need for security. This is particularly important since some NGOs were targeted in riots in Drvar in the Canadian AOR. The Canadian military was thus there to assure security should tensions arise. For example, during an emergency, NGOs could use the Canadian military's radio net. With the Kosovo crisis and the threat – however remote – of evacuation, NGOs started showing up more often and checking in. Each person working for an NGO was issued a number, which they could use when calling in. In this way, the military knew where each person was, so that everyone could be evacuated, should the need arise. I was also told cynically that civilian agencies came to the platoon houses for a free meal. This became such a habit that the camp in Drvar began charging NGO personnel for their meals.

Although the UNHCR regional office in Banja Luka provided a forum for the coordination of NGO programs and assets, it was CIMIC coordination centers that permitted detailed cooperation among the many NGOs and local authorities. The Canadian military tried to facilitate information-sharing and to promote coordination among the NGOs in-theater. The CIMIC liaison section in the battle group I visited consisted of 18 people; their role was to assist international organizations in the AOR (e.g., the International Committee of the Red Cross [ICRC], the UNHCR, and their partners). The CIMIC liaison section also assisted the municipal and cantonment authorities in their efforts to implement the civil aspects of the Dayton Accords. For example, they coordinated with the UNHCR to help the DPREs. CIMIC also had the task of conducting liaison efforts with international organizations, such as the UNHCR and the IPTF, who were the Dayton Accord's implementing partners.

---

[92] David M. Last, "Defeating Fear and Hatred through Peacebuilding: Multiplying the Impact of a Military Contribution," *Canadian Foreign Policy* 5, No. 2 (Winter, 1998), p. 162.

CIMIC units also dealt with smaller NGOs in the AOR. One of the problems these civilian organizations faced was their size. They must be small to keep their overhead down and be capable of direct action. However, because they are small, they often lack access to current information and cannot coordinate with other organizations. According to one CIMIC officer, "Smaller NGOs have [a] more narrow focus. They want the most 'bang' for their money. It's an *ad hoc* situation. They just show up at the microcredit meeting." Another problem was that NGOs sometimes used locals to carry out their activities: "Our interaction is primarily with the local population. When we run across an NGO administrator we try to get as much information from him as possible. But often they are just local contractors working on projects and they know nothing."

The Canadian military organized regular meetings plus *ad hoc* information-sharing. One of the mechanisms for this was the called the Principals Group. The Principals Group of NGOs met in the Canadian camp in Coralici. The military facilitated the meeting and produced the agenda. The military tried to be sensitive to the NGOs. They did not want to appear heavy-handed, so they tried to arrive at a consensus and to develop and coordinate NGO strategy because the military leadership believed it was important to show consistency of effort. This can be difficult, since some NGOs do not like the military and some do not like other NGOs. For example, the NGOs that were targeted during the Drvar riots believed that they were targeted because of their contacts with SFOR. As a result, they have cut all contacts with the military since that time.

The Canadian military had to carefully maintain objectivity and credibility with the locals and other NGOs, since there was sometimes conflict between various NGOs in-theater. Sometimes local politicians tried the "divide and conquer" strategy with the international organizations and NGOs to foster their own ends. The inability of NGOs to work with each other was often cited as a problem during my trip to Bosnia. I was told, "NGOs are a business, each with their own agendas, and sometimes their own agendas don't coincide with other NGO activities. Sometimes NGOs don't want to talk to each other." For example, UNHCR wanted to return refugees (Serbs) while another international agency was interested in getting the (Croat) Council going. This caused some difficulties; as one soldier remarked, "They have different mandates so they get into conflict with each other."

One of the characteristics of peace operations is that lower levels of command (that is, the major level or below) must sometimes deal with differences between humanitarian agencies. It is also important to note that officers and NCOs experienced more contact with non-military persons than enlisted soldiers did. [93] The officers who were deployed when I visited did, however, have experience in facing these difficulties because of their past participation in domestic disaster relief. As one of them remarked, "Aid agencies don't cooperate with each other. During the ice storm it was the same way. In fact there are a lot of similarities. The NGOs here seem to be working at cross-purposes to each other, just like at home."

Questions of age, gender, and race can exacerbate the gap between NGOs and the military. The military is a conservative organization in comparison with NGOs, which tend to attract young, socially conscious individuals, many of whom are female. For example, UN agencies such as the UNHCR recruit women on a positive-discrimination basis, which means that half of the staff of UN agencies and NGOs operating in Bosnia is female. [94] Female UNHCR officials and the UNHCR's multinational staff presented problems for some officers, who are accustomed to dealing only or largely with men. [95] The brevity of military tours (usually six months) can also cause tension with NGOs. "Once familiarized with local conditions, officers have little time left to establish solid working relationships with their civilian counterparts, or [to] acclimatize themselves to local values, culture, and politics. ... By contrast, it is unusual for civilians to serve for less than 12 months. ... It was not unusual for civilians with UNPROFOR to be in their posts for three years." [96]

The UNHCR is one of the most important UN agencies involved in peace operations since it often takes the lead. Although the military and the UNHCR are developing better ways of working together, difficulties still remain. According to Colonel Bob Stewart, the commander of the first British deployment to Bosnia in 1992: "The military are hierarchical, authoritarian, centralized, large, and robust, while UNHCR is flat, consensus-based, with highly decentralized field offices." [97] According to Williams, the UNHCR's perceived lack of structure and tendency to delegate decision-making to people of a much

---

[93]   In a survey of 1,200 members of the Canadian forces who participated in UNPROFOR, enlisted soldiers reported working with interpreters and having social interactions with the locals as their major contact experience. NCOs also had that profile; in addition, they had to negotiate with non-military individuals and groups. All the officers had been interviewed by the media in addition to working with interpreters, and had negotiating experience with a wide variety of both military and non-military people. David Last, *Theory, Doctrine and Practice of Conflict De-Escalation in Peacekeeping Operations* (Cornwallis, Nova Scotia: Pearson Peacekeeping Centre, 1997), p. 80.

[94]   Michael Williams, *Civil Military Relations and Peacekeeping*, Adelphi Paper 321 (London: International Institute for Strategic Studies, 1998), p. 34.

[95]   Williams, *Ibid*, p. 37.

[96]   Williams, *Ibid*, p. 36.

[97]   Williams, *Ibid*, p. 36.

younger age than the military were additional sources of frustration. [98] From the UNHCR's point of view, the presence of the military can compromise their work. For example, while UNPROFOR convoy escorts provided protection and deterred attack, their presence in some cases heightened local hostility. [99]

Many NGOs regard the military as out of touch with both the values and the members of the society they seek to protect. In contrast, NGOs are flexible and anti-bureaucratic. "These organizations form the nucleus of an international civil society whose *esprit de corps* distrusts national military structures. They therefore tend to resist attempts by the security-conscious military to coordinate their activities in the field." [100] As the Canadian Chief of Defence Staff, General Maurice Baril, has remarked, "Humanitarian agencies and non-governmental organizations seemed to be in every area of conflict but remained independent and reluctant to modify their approach and agree to coordinate their efforts with the military force." [101]

Many in the military, on the other hand, perceive NGOs as being undisciplined "non-guided organizations," as one military person remarked to me. David Owen found the military in Bosnia "bitter in their denunciation of some of the NGOs, who to them were a pestilential nuisance, resisting all attempts at coordination and then complaining that they were not properly protected." [102] Canadians were equally cynical concerning NGOs, saying that the NGOs wanted nothing to do with the military until there was a perceived security threat. Then they started showing up to make sure that they could be evacuated or protected by the military.

Nonetheless, there appears to be a growing recognition by the Canadian forces of the value of working with NGOs.

> The Canadian military, in collaboration with the NGO community, has developed a Disaster Assistance Response Team. This helps each community to view the other as equally professional and committed to common objectives. After one military–NGO exercise, a Canadian Defence Ministry official noted that some NGO workers had more battlefield experience than most Canadian Forces personnel did. [103]

In order to improve relations with NGOs, the Canadian armed forces began an exchange with the NGO CARE in 1996, in which an officer is attached to the organization on a six-month basis.

---

[98] Williams, *Ibid*, p. 37.

[99] Williams, *Ibid*, p. 40.

[100] Williams, *Ibid*, p. 39.

[101] Maurice Baril, "Peacekeeping and Force," in *Peacekeeping with Muscle: The Use of Force in International Conflict Resolution*, p. 119.

[102] David Owen, *Balkan Odyssey* (London: Victor Gollancz, 1995), p. 208.

[103] Cited in Williams, *Ibid*, p. 41.

7. MILITARY RELATIONSHIPS WITH THE MEDIA

The Canadian military is suffering from a "Somalia hangover"[104] and, as a result, has tremendous mistrust and antipathy towards the media. The tension between the media and the military is described by General Maisonneuve:

> With the advent of instant information, the public may know, faster than the chain of command, that an accident has occurred. The media interpret and analyze the event and "fact" is formed. The effect of this instant information is that our contingent commanders must compete with the media to ensure the rapid transmission of accurate information to decisionmakers, both military and political. The Commander must also be able to counter misinformation in such a manner that his force is seen as the credible source. Used effectively, the media is a tool, which provides a valuable alternative to the use of force. Under certain circumstances, the belligerents could attempt to use the media as a tool to force certain behaviors from peace forces. On the other hand, media presence may influence the belligerents into performing certain actions, which might avoid our use of force. The media then becomes our tool. [105]

Maisonneuve went on to give an example from IFOR: "After a local agreement was made with a former warring faction, the opening of a checkpoint was only accomplished after the arrival of the media. The belligerents did not want to appear to be uncooperative." [106]

The Canadian public information officer promotes SFOR to the local population, while the public affairs officer promotes the battle group to Canada. I asked who had visited the battle group and was told "mainly small-town people doing features." I was told that the military sees the visits of these "hometown" media people as more positive; they are, therefore, not so heavy-handed with this type of media. In general, media representatives could go where they liked, but they had to stay in the Canadian AOR.

Nevertheless, soldiers and officers were often very critical of the media: "The media feel themselves the self-appointed reps of the Canadian people." Another example: "The media is gender-focused, so [they] ignore 90–95% of what we are doing here." People were resentful of the media who, on visiting the camp, focused on gender issues, which interfered with the work of female soldiers. I was told, "They were supposed to be doing research on how

---

[104] From 1995 to 1997, there was a public inquiry into the activities of Canadian peacekeepers in Somalia. The media did a very public vivisection of the Canadian forces during this time, and the relationship between the Canadian forces and the media suffered. For details, see Donna Winslow and Christ Klep, "Learning Lessons the Hard Way: Somalia and Srebrenica Compared," *Small Wars and Insurgencies*, Vol. 10 (2), pp. 93 – 137.

[105] Maisonneuve, *Ibid*, p. 146.

[106] Maisonneuve, *Ibid*, p. 150.

Canadians were dealing with ethnic conflict. Then the article came out and it trivialized the work of the female soldiers. This depressed everyone since it was a sophomoric profile of the issue of the woman soldier. Therefore people feel burned and will be more careful next time."

Even though soldiers were sometimes upset with journalists, one person emphasized strongly that "It's okay just as long as THEY GET IT RIGHT." The people I interviewed believed that the journalists trivialize or over-dramatize things and get details wrong. "Journalists never send anything back to be checked for accuracy." One officer commented that he was angry because the journalist who wrote an article on what his company did for the dental clinic got the name of the company wrong. He also said, "Canadian soldiers overseas are not news like the U.S. military. We are mostly forgotten." Other soldiers were more explicit: "The media are muckrakers."

8. CONCLUSIONS

During the post-Cold War period, a qualitative change has taken place in the types of peace operations that Canadians are asked to participate in. Mandates are now wider and more ambiguous and the tasks more multi-dimensional and multi-functional. More and more, missions are tasked with facilitating humanitarian relief, social reconstruction, and protecting civilians in areas where there is no peace to keep. In these chaotic environments it becomes increasingly difficult for Canadian soldiers to respect Canadian cultural norms (honesty, integrity, responsibility, self-discipline, and respect for law and legitimate authority) while dealing with cultural differences, particularly unethical behavior either by belligerents (bribery, fraud, abuse, criminal activity, etc.), international aid workers (theft), or other national contingents (inequality, theft, black marketeering, etc.).

In the new forms of peace operations, there are larger numbers of civilians involved, whether they work within the mission (the UN and its agencies), on the fringes of the mission (NGOs), or outside the mission (the local population). According to Williams, "civil–military relations in peacekeeping, peace-enforcing, or peace-building operations are fundamentally different from those that pertain in 'normal' conditions of peace or war." [107] The military are now asked to broker deals; shelter the displaced; protect human rights; supervise the return of refugees; organize and monitor elections; and support civilian reconstruction. [108] In these circumstances, civilian and military cooperation is called for and an effective interface for civil–military cooperation becomes essential. In theater, CIMIC coordination centers permit detailed cooperation between

---

[107] Williams, *Ibid*, p. 15.
[108] Williams, *Ibid*, p. 14.

the military and the civilians with whom they must work. CIMIC operations need to be finely tuned and staffed with competent people. Of course, for a military professional, a career in civil–military relations may not mean the same chances for professional advancement as is possible for those involved in the core business of combat. There is thus a need for clear tracks of professional advancement in order to encourage participation in these functions.

Canada now has a number of initiatives under way to improve civil–military relations. There is the Pearson Peacekeeping Center, which runs classes for Canadians and international participants – military and NGO alike – on a variety of peace-related issues from ethics to culture. As already noted, the Canadian forces have also established links to the NGO community by sending an officer to an NGO for six months to learn more about the way it operates. Working together helps each community to view the other as equally professional and committed to common objectives. These efforts seem to be producing results. Flora MacDonald, Canadian Secretary of State for External Affairs, who went with NGOs to both Somalia and Rwanda, said there were about 200 NGOs operating at that time and "the confusion was total." However, MacDonald stated that Kosovo was different due to the tremendous integration in the work being done by the Canadian military and the NGOs there – integration she had not seen elsewhere. [109]

---

[109] Cited in Jennifer Ross, "Human Security in Peace Operations," paper presented to the Canadian War Museum, 2 June 2000, p. 4.

4. DANISH SENIOR OFFICERS' EXPERIENCES FROM IFOR/SFOR

Henning SØRENSEN

Outline:

1. BACKGROUND [1]

1.1. DANISH POLITICAL MOTIVATION FOR AND MILITARY EXPE-
RIENCE IN PEACEKEEPING OPERATIONS (PKOS)

Denmark represents an interesting case as a peacekeeper nation for a number
of reasons. It has dramatically changed its foreign policy from a low-profile
NATO member during the Cold War period to a highly active agent in Peace
Support Operations (PSOs) since the Gulf War of 1991. It has had almost no
scandals abroad. Its UNPROFOR and IFOR/SFOR soldiers are a mix of former conscripts who contracted with the Danish Reaction Brigade (DIB) for a
three-year period, during which they may be deployed twice (63%), [2] and professionals, i.e., non-commissioned officers (NCOs) and commissioned officers
(37%). Finally, it has integrated military units from the three Baltic countries in
the Danish battalion (DANBN) under the Nordic-Polish Brigade (NORDPOL
BDE).

A basic reason for the increase in multinational PKOs is a foreign policy
shift among Western countries from "collective" to "selective" security. This
shift is illustrated by a model of the presence/absence of enemies or allies, in
which any country can be placed in one of four security positions:

- A country with neither enemies nor allies is in an *independent security* position.
- A nation with enemies but no allies is in an *isolated security* position.
- A country with enemies and allies at the same time is in a *collective security*
  position.
- Finally, a country with no enemies that also has allies is in the best of all
  possible security positions: *selective security*.

Figure 1 shows how the NATO and former Warsaw Pact countries have
moved from collective to selective security and how the neutral Western countries (such as Austria, Finland, Ireland, and Sweden) have shifted from iso-

---

[1] Acknowledgement: The Danish Institute of International Relations has contributed finan-
     cially to this project, which would never have been completed without this support. For this,
     I am most grateful. I would also like to express my gratitude to the Danish Defense Ministry,
     Army Operational Command, the Royal Library of the Armed Forces, Center for Manage-
     ment, and, last but not least, all the Danish officers interviewed, without whom this report
     would never have had the qualities it now may have. I am, however, solely responsible for
     any shortcomings.
[2] Denmark had originally planned to use 80% former conscripts on this deployment.

Figure 1: The Four National Security Positions

Enemies

		−	+
+		Independent Security	Isolated Security
Allies		Selective Security	Collective Security
−			

lated to selective security. This new selective security position has improved the ability of smaller nations within an alliance to intervene in world politics, particularly in incidents such as famine, natural catastrophes, riots, population displacement (refugees), civil wars with ethnic cleansing, etc. Today, even smaller nations can make a difference and play a role in world politics through the individual selections they make among a number of possible foreign policy options. For instance, Denmark was asked by the UN to deploy soldiers to Bosnia and did so, but declined the UN invitation to do the same in Somalia, while Germany did exactly the opposite. Both Denmark and Germany now see their military participation in such missions as a moral obligation and a security investment. They may sacrifice the lives of some of their soldiers by deploying them "out of area," but do so for a higher moral cause and a more stable world.

This increase in military interventions since the end of the Cold War can be found for most Western countries. "Over the last few years, U.S. forces have participated in more than 20 non-combat operations."[3] The United States has, moreover, headed many war operations, such as DESERT STORM in Iraq in January through March 1991; the air attack in Bosnia from August through September 1995 resulting in the Dayton Agreement; the multinational air strike against Iraq since November 1998; the air campaign against Serbia from March through June 1999; and finally the IFOR/SFOR deployment in Bosnia since 1995.

Even if Denmark has shifted its foreign policy since the end of the Cold War, its strong UN commitment has been a fact for half a century. Since 1948, 50,000 Danish soldiers have taken part in about half of all UN military missions around the world,[4] but mostly as UN military observers. Recent Danish

---

[3]   Volker C. Franke, *Learning Peace: Attitudes of Future Officers towards the Security Requirements of the Post-Cold War World*, Working Paper No. 9 (Cambridge, MA: The John M. Olin Institute for Strategic Studies, Harvard University, January 1997), p. 3.

[4]   HQ Chief of Defense, *Facts about Denmark. The Armed Forces. 1998*, Vedbæk 1998, pamphlet.

military engagement abroad can be documented by the number of soldiers deployed in missions under the auspices of the UN, NATO, EU, or OSCE for more than three months. From April 1992 to December 1997, 3,902 soldiers from the Army, 572 from the Navy, and 214 from the Air Force have served abroad. Divided into personnel categories, this represents 715 officers, 1,059 enlisted men/NCOs, and 2,128 conscripts. Therefore, 35% of all Army officers, 44% of NCOs, and 7 – 10% of all conscripts have been deployed. For the Navy, the participation rate is 10%, 12%, and 13%, respectively; for the Air Force, the participation rate is 7%, 6%, and 3%.[5]

Other indicators of a strong relationship with the UN include the establishment of Denmark's Reaction Brigade (DIB) for use in UN, NATO, OSCE, or national missions, as well as the establishment of both a special UN stand-by force maintained in cooperation with the other Nordic countries and of a Multinational UN Stand-By High Readiness Brigade (SHIRBRIG) for Peace-keeping Operations. Finally, it can be mentioned that today Denmark is the world's foremost contributing nation per capita to the Less Developed Countries. Currently, Denmark contributes 1% of its Gross National Product (GNP), compared to Norway (0.9%), the Netherlands (0.8%), most other EU countries (approximately 0.3%), and the U.S. (0.1%).[6]

1.2. RESEARCH METHODS AND MAIN FOCUS

The data presented here on the experiences of the Danish Army in IFOR/SFOR missions in Bosnia from January 1996 through late 1999 are based upon four major sources. First, from February through July 1999, I conducted in-depth, face-to-face interviews with 30 senior officers (i.e., lieutenant colonels [LTCs] to brigadier generals), out of a total of 33 Danish senior officers who served there. The 30 Danish senior officers interviewed for this study normally served for six months (from January/February 1996 to July/August 1999) and were deployed as follows: 6 in the National Logistic Support Unit (NSE)/Nordic Support Group (NSG), 11 in the Danish battalion (DANBN), 10 in NORD-POL BDE, and 6 in the NATO-led "Allied Command Europe Rapid Reaction Corps" (ARRC) in Sarajevo or the U.S. Army-dominated Multinational Division (North) in Tuzla [MND (N)]. The total number of senior officers here reaches 33, but three officers had double functions in either NSE/NORDPOL BDE or in NORDPOL BDE/MND (N).

Their profile is as follows:

• Rank: 19 were LTCs, 10 colonels (COLs), and 1 was a brigadier general.

---

[5]   Forsvarsministeriet, *Opgørelse over udsendt dansk personel 1992– 1997*, Copenhagen 1998b. A record of Danish soldiers deployed from April 1992–December 1997.
[6]   *Berlingske Tidende*, 6 July 1999.

- Age at time of deployment: 3 were 40 years old or below; 10 were between 41–45; 8 were between 46–50; 7 were between 51–55; and 2 were over 55.
- Occupational responsibility: 57% "staff," 53% "operations," 23% "logistics," and 7% CIMIC. Here again, several officers stated that they had served in two or more main occupational areas.
- Multinational military peace supporting experience: 53% had no experience at all, while 23% had less than one year; only 23% had more than one year. It must, however, be remembered that the deployment of Danish soldiers to Bosnia was a relatively new phenomenon, so an increasing Danish participation rate for officers is unavoidable.

Second, I used information from and interviews with soldiers during my last visit in March 1999 to the two Danish camps, Valhalla and Dannevirke, which house the Danish battalion in Bosnia. Third, my research included an investigation of Danish literature on Danish UNPROFOR and IFOR/SFOR participation, including regimental leaflets; "FOV-nyhedsbrev"; the "UNPROFOR-DANBAT" books; the seven contingents' "End of Tour Reports" for the Danish IFOR/SFOR missions; Danish Defense data on the internet; newspaper articles; official reports; and civil and military material. Finally, I included information from the debriefing on 26 February 1999 of the SFOR Tour 7, where all officers, having just ended their turn in Bosnia, met with the officers and civilians from Denmark who had supported them.

The main aim of this project has concentrated on observing the multinational cooperation among contingents sent to Bosnia, which are different in many aspects. They come from a great number of countries with different political and military cultures. These different cultures influence behavior and ways of doing business, which can lead to tensions in practical cooperation on the ground in multinational military deployments.

To conclude, the improved national security situation of the Western world, in which we have neither enemies nor military threats but more combat areas around the world, has fundamentally influenced the armed forces. Today, the job of a soldier has become less violent and more varied, involves the participation of more nations for new reasons, and is characterized by faster intervention. [7]

Politically, soldiers play a more active and exposed role in society than they once did because they are perceived as ambassadors for their country when deployed abroad, and because their decisions may have foreign political content and consequences. Economically, the armed forces are now paid as

---

[7] Henning Sørensen, "NATO and Its New Military Security Position," *European Security* 7, Spring 1998: 75–79.

much for their performance in low-level conflicts and humanitarian missions
as they are for national defense operations. Actually, many Western European
armed forces receive heavy weaponry and air/sea lift materiel more easily for
their interventions in humanitarian missions than they do for traditional national defense missions. Militarily, Western armed forces cannot rely only on
their combat capabilities, but must also reconcile contrasting objectives and
situations: alleviation and violence; the presence of international and national
actors; military and humanitarian objectives; speedy intervention and deliberate non-commitment. All this demonstrates the expansion of Western military
functions. The old discussion of "guns or butter" is now a "butter for guns"
debate.

2. INTERNAL MILITARY DIMENSION

2.1. DEFENSE OBJECTIVES

The new national security situation for Western societies after the end of the
Cold War has changed the size and composition of their armed forces dramatically. Regiments and garrisons have been downsized; military budgets reduced; military equipment scrapped; the number of soldiers cut and personnel
redistributed, with fewer conscripts and civilians; acceptance of homosexuals;
female conscription (at least in Scandinavia); [8] women in combat positions,
etc. Denmark is no exception to the rule, as demonstrated in the Defense Act
of 1999. But at the same time as resources have diminished, objectives have
increased. During the Cold War period, Denmark had two main military aims:
national and collective (NATO) defense. Today, we have four: national defense, NATO defense, strengthened cooperation in Europe, and participation
in PSOs. [9]

2.2. PERSONNEL AND MATERIEL IN BOSNIA/HUNGARY

The size of the local Danish force in IFOR/SFOR missions in Bosnia/Hungary
since 1996 amounted to 850 soldiers, mainly distributed across three different
military organizations: [10]
- 40 soldiers in NSE/NSG in Pecs, Hungary, gradually reduced to 15 since
  1996;
- 545 soldiers in the DANBN in Bosnia;
- 253 soldiers in the NORDPOL BDE, including the headquarters company,
  and 10 MP soldiers.

---

[8]   Henning Sørensen, "Conscription in Scandinavia," *Armed Forces & Society*, January 2000.
[9]   *FOV nyhedsbrev.* 21.1999, special issue.
[10] HOK,TTJ UDV.096. 240/ORG, October 1998.

A few Danish officers were assigned to MND (N), the American division "Task Force Eagle" in Tuzla, or to the ARRC Headquarters in Sarajevo responsible for the implementation of IFOR/SFOR. The selection of Danish soldiers was – as mentioned above – a mix: 63% were former self-selected conscripts who signed a contract with the DIB, while 37% were professionals ordered to duty in the Balkans. In contrast, all Norwegian officers and soldiers were volunteers.

DANBN was placed near Doboj in Bosnia and divided into two camps, Valhalla (in Muslim territory) and Dannevirke (in Serbian territory), making Denmark one of the few peacekeeper nations with a garrison on both sides; the Netherlands is another. The DANBN mission area was 530 square kilometers,[11] including a Zone of Separation (ZOS) 150 kilometers long and 4 kilometers wide. DANBN, along with battalions from Finland, Norway, Poland, and Sweden, formed the Nordic Polish Brigade (NORDPOL BDE), bringing the number of soldiers up to 5,000. NORDPOL BDE was part of MND (N), headed by the U.S. Army, including three other brigades from Turkey, Russia, and the United States. The latter, however, with its staff, were directly placed within that of the MND (N).

Some observations are in order with respect to the local Danish force structure in Bosnia. First, both in the battalion and in NORDPOL BDE, the multinational element is evident. Approximately 100 U.S. soldiers from an artillery unit and a radar unit were deployed in the Danish battalion. In addition, military contingents from all three Baltic nations served in DANBN. At first, the Baltics were represented by mixed units made up of soldiers and officers from all three Baltic nations, with each country simultaneously contributing a platoon of 30 soldiers, resulting in one joint unit with some 100 soldiers. Later on, the three countries started a new system, where each in turn rotated one complete single-nation company-sized unit into Bosnia at a time. On top of that, interpreters from all three ethnic groups (Croats, Serbs, and Muslims) worked for and, in some cases, even lived in the Camp. In NORDPOL BDE, the multinational component was even more visible, with nine countries and groups working together: Denmark, Norway, Sweden, Finland, Poland, the U.S., and the three ethnic groups. Second, both the staffs of DANBN and NORDPOL BDE were larger than normal. In Denmark, a normal battalion has 10 staff officers; in Bosnia, DANBN had 25 officers as it had more functions to perform, i.e., civil–military cooperation (CIMIC) and logistics. In the same way, while a normal brigade in Denmark would have had 25 officers, in Bosnia, the NORD-

---

[11] "The Voice from Bosnia," *Danske Livregiment* 6 (1996): 3 – 5; *Musketten* 5 (1997): 13 – 15, here p 13. This article, "Newsletter from the 1st Squadron," describes daily work routines and resettlement problems. English translations of article titles are by the author.

POL BDE had between 63 and 115 officers. Third, in the MND (N) staff, the U.S. presence was significant, as 98% were American soldiers. Therefore, in staff representation, number of soldiers, and equipment, the U.S. Army dominated.

2.3. THE PKO SCENARIO IN GENERAL

A basic change in international politics after the end of the Cold War is more peace among nations. Many indicators support the impression of a more peaceful world. Today, we have almost 200 nations in the world; a generation ago we had around 160. In spite of this 20% increase in the number of nations, the number of wars between them has not risen accordingly. Moreover, many of the 30 internal wars during the Cold War period were conflicts brought about by the ideological confrontation between the East and the West. These civil wars have now largely come to an end; consequently, most countries feel less threatened today than they once did.

However, the number of combat areas around the world has increased from around 30 to 60. [12] These "wars" are now waged more for ethnic and religious reasons than for political-ideological causes. They are fought by some four million men, who are often neighbors, loosely organized in armed gangs that occasionally shoot at one another. In addition, "there are, by one count, forty-two private armies of the world." [13] Therefore, we are far from the large classic battles between well-defined enemies, as in World Wars I and II. The change in industrial production from mass production to flexible specialization is reflected in the change in warfare from mass production warfare to "demassified warfare." [14]

But the negative impression of more combat areas has to be seen in light of the growing ethnic and cultural self-consciousness among the more than 2,000 different cultural and ethnic groups of the world. These groups are organized into 200 countries, but only 5 – 10% of all countries are nation-states, in which language, culture, religion, and border coincide, such as in Scandinavia.

The many more combat areas should, moreover, be compared with the increased democratization of around 30 former dictatorships since 1979, in particular in Latin America and Eastern Europe. These more than 30 nations have become democracies almost without the use of violence and through peaceful democratic means such as words, demonstrations, boycotts, strikes, etc. Thus,

---

[12]   Larry Seaquist (Ed.), *The Venice Deliberations. Transformations in the Meaning of Security: Practical Steps toward a New Security Culture* (Paris: UNESCO, 1996), p. 20.

[13]   Seaquist, p. 25.

[14]   Alvin and Heidi Toffler, *War and Anti-War: Survival at the Dawn of the 21st Century* (Boston: Little, Brown and Company, 1993).

citizens of these countries have demonstrated the potential for peaceful political improvements.

This changed combat situation – characterized by local combat between neighbors, who occasionally fight each other, sometimes using unorthodox weapons, causing outrageous violence against one another, and denying Western military "rules of the game" – does, of course, influence the work of Western soldiers deployed in such combat areas. The extent to which Danish senior officers envisage points of tension within their own military unit in Bosnia will now be explored by focusing on their motivation, time consumption, risk environment, and role perception.

2.4. MOTIVATION

Danish senior officers are not that motivated to ask for deployment abroad. They are ordered to go and left with only two answers, either "Yes, Sir" or "Thank you, Sir." For that reason motives such as "higher salary" and "avoiding unemployment" are excluded. However, the study shows not only the kind of motives but also their intensity by asking: "How important are the following motives for your serving in IFOR/SFOR missions?" at three levels: "very," "somewhat," and "less/unimportant." Here, only the "very" important motives are represented:

- "Gain additional skills for the future" was chosen by 60% of all officers;
- "Practice my military skills" by 57%;
- "See if I can accomplish my tasks" by 50%;
- "Contribute to world peace" by 43%;
- "Other" and "experience something exciting" received 33% each; and
- "Improve career possibilities," "interest in the Balkans," "get to know a foreign country," and "prove myself in dangerous situations" were selected by 10% or less of Danish senior officers.

The motives for Danish senior officers are therefore professionally oriented (i.e., related to exercising skills and performing tasks), whereas ideological motives ("contribute to world peace") and personal ones ("prove myself," "interest in the Balkans," "get to know a foreign country") play a minor role. Here, the professional senior officers distinguished themselves from former Danish conscripts, whose most frequently mentioned motive for joining the DIB, cited by 38% of respondents, was "to get exciting experiences." [15] A difference in motivations between officers and regulars might indicate some tensions; however, this is not the case. First, in civil and military hierarchies, in general, management and employees have different motives. Second, studies

---

[15] Marianne Bache, *DIB-soldat eller ej?* (Copenhagen: FCL, March 1998) (This publication discussed the results of a study of 5,451 Danish conscripts and their reasons for joining the DIB for a three-year contract period). The study went on through 2000.

of regimental leaflets found no evidence of dissatisfied comments from regulars during this period. Third, the professional motives do not exclude personal enthusiasm and even gratitude for having served for six months in IFOR/SFOR missions in Bosnia. Many Danish senior officers defined it as the best experience of their entire military careers and enjoyed working closely with their soldiers for a good cause.

2.5. TIME CONSUMPTION

The Danish senior officers were asked to "Distribute your actual time consumption (100%) in IFOR/SFOR" according to the options: "internal military," "external military," and "local politics." After calculating their time consumption among each of the three areas, the 30 officers reported spending 56% of their time on internal military issues (i.e., within their own military organizations, such as the NSE, DANBN, NORDPOL BDE, or MND (N)/ARRC), 33% of their time on external military liaison (i.e., with other military organizations within IFOR/SFOR), and 10% on local politics, although large differences from one officer to another were evident.

Of course, more caveats should be made here: planning of operations/patrolling in mission area is calculated as time spent on internal military matters, but might also be characterized as local politics; many staff officers are by definition mostly engaged in "internal military" issues. Over their six months of service, many officers experienced a shift from "internal military" time consumption toward more "external" and "local" time consumption, because in the beginning they had to focus on making their own soldiers "fit to fight" outside the garrison. Finally, more senior officers reported that the modest results from negotiations with local authorities made them reduce the time spent on these efforts. [16]

The time consumption of Danish senior officers in Bosnia (56% on internal military, 33% on external military, and 10% on local politics) differs from that of Danish Army senior officers in Denmark, who, in 1983, spent 83% of their time on internal military issues (i.e., subordinates, conscripts, and close superiors), 12% on external military issues (i.e., other commands and services), and only 5% on politicians, the media, officers' trade unions, etc. [17] In short, the reduced time spent on internal military issues in Bosnia is instead used on other military contingents.

This change results in only minor tensions. First, 83% of all Danish senior officers were content with the actual distribution of time in the three areas: in-

---

[16] "So HQ COY Works in Bosnia," *Musketten* 1 (1998): 14–15, "After around one month, everybody was 100% familiar with their tasks … "

[17] Henning Sørensen, *Den danske officer* (Copenhagen: Nyt fra Samfundsvidenskaberne, 1988), p. 139, table 24a.

ternal and external military and local politics. Second, in spite of the combat scenario in Bosnia, Danish senior officers spent the majority of their time on their own military forces, which is business as usual in Denmark. This was highly appropriate in the initial phase of the implementation of DANBN/IFOR beginning in January 1996 [18] and in the first month after deployment. [19] Third, the increased external time consumption has been used on other IFOR/SFOR military contingents, not on local authorities or populations. This indicates a tension, as only 10% of Danish senior officers' time was spent on local politics, even if "local authorities and local population have caused Danish officers considerable problems" and even though they were actually the reason for their deployment abroad. If Danish senior officers did want to increase their local contacts, however, they could easily do so just by arranging more meetings with local authorities or more patrolling in the area. So, time consumption in itself is not a source of tension even if relations between Danish senior officers and local authorities could be problematic, as shown below.

2.6. RISK ENVIRONMENT

The danger of the environment for IFOR/SFOR soldiers, NGOs, and locals was tested by asking: "To what extent have you reported the following incidents/problems during your tour of duty?" The officers were provided with three options: "often" (i.e., six or more times during the service period of six months), "sometimes" (2 – 6 times), and "seldom/never" (0 – 1 time). The formulation "reported," meaning that the senior officer himself wrote about it, excluded hearsay information. The seriousness of incidents was divided into three categories: death/injury, dangerous situations, and problems such as "harassment," "involvement in conflicts," and "conflicts." Only seven Danish senior officers reported the "death or injury of [an] IFOR/SFOR soldier, NGO worker, or local citizen;" 13 officers reported "dangerous situations for [an] IFOR/SFOR soldier, NGO worker, or local citizen;" and 15 officers reported "conflicts with the local population;" 10 officers did not report any incident at all.

The risk environment in the Danish mission area, as was the case all over Bosnia, was low. [20] In the beginning of the IFOR/SFOR mission, however, casualties were rather high. In the first period, from January–August 1996, the deaths of four IFOR soldiers were reported in the mission area, and in February

---

[18] "The Soldier is Danish, the Food is French, and the Boss is American," *Gyldenløve* 2 (1996): 22ff, which describes the difficulties establishing the Danish camp from almost the ground up.

[19] See "So HQ COY Works in Bosnia."

[20] "Peace Redeemers," *Danske Livregiment* 5 (1996): 6 – 7; "Extract of Newsletter," *Musketten* 2 (1996): 5.

1996, mine explosions killed 15 local citizens from Doboj. In the same period, monthly reports of mine explosions killing locals, of confrontations between locals, and of the disarmament of locals were issued. For instance, 500 Muslims and 1,500 Serbs aggressively stood against one another at Bridge Zulu 09 connecting Serb and Federation (Muslim and Croat) territory. [21] From August 1996–February 1997, reports of two dead IFOR soldiers were made, a Danish tank was overturned, and Bridge Zulu 09 was damaged by a bomb. But casualties did drop over time. From February–August 1997, no casualties were reported, even though a Danish tank was ambushed and then attacked by Molotov cocktails, and even though NATO decided on 9 August 1997 to disarm the Serbian special police force for having acted violently toward its own population, an action implemented on 10 November 1997. [22] In the greater NORD-POL BDE mission area, casualties were, of course, higher, including suicides among U.S. soldiers from February 1997, and, in the period from February to August 1998, when two Polish soldiers were killed after hitting a mine. In general, however, the risk environment for Danish soldiers was low and tensions in the IFOR period faded away over time.

2.7. ROLE PERCEPTION

Western soldiers have faced a fundamental change in recent years with regard to new roles. Based on the presence/absence of combat missions and formal armed enemies, a nation can identify four ideal types of roles for its military personnel deployed in conflicts around the world: humanitarian worker, peacekeeper, war preventer, and warrior (see Figure 2 below).

Figure 2: The Roles of Western Soldiers

Formal Armed Enemies

	-	+
Combat Missions -	Humanitarian Worker	War Preventer
Combat Missions +	Peacekeeper	Warrior

The four roles in Figure 2 can be exemplified by U.S. military interventions in the previous decade. The U.S. deployed soldiers in the Andrew relief operation and UNOSOM in Somalia, bringing food from Mogadishu to the starving rural population in 1992 – 1993. Here, U.S. soldiers served as humanitarian

---

[21] "Letter from Bosnia," *Danske Livregiment* 8 (1996): 12.
[22] For a brief description, see *Musketten* 5 (1997), p. 14.

workers. The U.S. contribution to the IFOR/SFOR missions in Bosnia illustrates the role of a peacekeeper. This role includes the most different kinds of work from operations against terrorism and drugs to intervention in civil wars, i.e., "the thin blue line" of the UN between local combatants. By definition, peace still prevails, as no external national organized enemy or threat is identified; combat or shooting incidents may, however, still occur. The third role is war prevention, i.e., keeping the formal armed forces of one or more countries from using violence against either their own population or other nations by threats or the use of military force. The U.S. deployment of armed forces in Europe in the Cold War period to stop any USSR/Warsaw Pact aggression is an example of this type of military role. Other examples include the U.S. military presence in Macedonia and Albania; the air attacks on the Bosnian Serbs in August–September 1995 resulting in the Dayton Agreement; the air strike against Iraq in November 1998; and the air strike campaign against Serbia from March to June 1999. Such security situations are, by definition, more dangerous than that of peacekeeping, as the armed forces of two or more countries confront one another. The fourth role is warrior. Here, the armed forces of two or more countries formally meet in combat on the battlefield as in operation DESERT STORM against Iraq in January–March 1991, where U.S. soldiers served as warriors.

A basic reason for this expansion of the soldier's role is not only the new type of PSO, but also a new attitude toward war and violence, which is now perceived as uncivilized conduct. Less than a century ago, in World War I, war was a goal in itself. It was argued that war would strengthen morale in the armed forces and educate young men, who would later serve their country. Since World War II, however, the waging of war has needed a cause and new "rules" have been introduced. Today, PSOs have to be justified not only by their humanitarian cause but also by how they are performed. It means that Western soldiers are prohibited from going beyond certain limits of violence, even in the case of stopping human suffering caused by reckless political leaders. Moreover, the removal of politicians is not a PSO option. A third rule is to use as little violence as possible. This was seen in the Gulf War of 1991, when the U.S. and its allies withdrew their troops instead of taking advantage of the situation and destroying Saddam Hussein's political system and his armed forces. In short, justification of multinational military intervention is based on two pillars: a good cause and a minimal use of violence.

This strategy was performed by the NATO air campaign against Serbia from March to June 1999. It was a military success for three reasons: NATO had no casualties; NATO tried to avoid civilian casualties among the Serbs; and NATO made Muslim resettlement possible. Nevertheless, it was less than a military or political success as the destruction of Serbian military targets was far from accomplished and president Milosevic remained in office.

If this overall role shift is correct, Danish senior officers may be expected to have changed their role perception, as well. The role perception of Danish senior officers was tested by asking them to "characterize the four most important roles in your military organization (DANBN, NORDPOL BDE, MND (N), ARRC, HQ IFOR Army)" with the following options: "professional soldier, citizen soldier, mediator, ambassador, humanitarian worker, social worker, other." All Danish officers answered "professional soldier"; 80% mentioned "mediator" and "ambassador"; and 53% stated "humanitarian worker."

This distribution can explain the lack of tension for a number of reasons. Danish senior officers have a very broad role perception, ranging from professional soldier (i.e., warrior) to humanitarian worker. The inclusion of the role of "humanitarian worker" among the four most important roles is not only new (a decade ago, no Danish senior officers would ever have dreamed of that self-identification), but is also extremely necessary in PSOs, as Danish soldiers are used to reestablish water facilities, electricity, and gas pipelines; assist in local/regional elections; monitor the local population living in or visiting (former) hostile territories; distribute aid, etc. This civil–military cooperation is highly valued, as the increased contact with locals can improve the force protection of Danish soldiers.

As described above, tensions among Danish soldiers in DANBN were at a minimum and the general atmosphere seemed good. [23] This is confirmed by the regimental leaflets, in which regulars, NCOs, and officers described their time and service in Bosnia; hardly any criticism was brought forward. [24]

On the other hand, examples of "individual tensions" can be found by looking into the number of repatriated soldiers. For the tour from August 1998 – February 1999, only 23 of 900 soldiers were repatriated and 52 sanctioned. [25] Even officers have been repatriated. Although one could argue that any such figure is too high, they are comparably low.

Some reasons for the low rate of sanctions and tensions could be a humane personnel policy; a liberal attitude toward alcohol; acceptance of homosexuality; many welfare arrangements; more free trips to Denmark and elsewhere for

---

[23] "Leopard (Tanks) in Service of Peace," *Prinsens* 2 (1997): 5; see also "The Soldier is Danish, the Food is French, and the Boss is American," p. 26; "The Mechanics in Valhalla Are Thrown into the Cold," *Danske Livregiment* 9 (1997): 19.

[24] Only one of all the regimental leaflets expressed criticism of the education and experience of Danish soldiers. See "Tank Squadron in the IFOR Mission," *Kentaur* 3 (1997): 8 – 10 ("One year's experience as tank commander ought to be an absolute minimum .... A tank platoon ought to have nine months of time together before deployment").

[25] *End of Tour Report*, June 1999. DANBN: p. 8, HQCOY: p. 10ff., NSE: p. 2.

rest and relaxation, including those given to stressed and overworked soldiers to the lively Pecs, Hungary (location of the Danish National Logistic Support Unit), etc. Actually, nine welfare tours for 350 soldiers around Bosnia, Croatia, and Hungary were arranged, and 900 free trips back home were conducted, as well as 150 trips elsewhere. [26]

To conclude, Danish senior officers had a clear and positive attitude toward the PSO in Bosnia and, for that and other reasons, little tension was found to be caused by internal military factors. For example, Danish senior officers are professionally, and not personally, motivated to serve there. These officers spend the majority of their time working with their own soldiers to improve their effectiveness (much as they would at home in Denmark). The risk environment in this PSO is currently low, and the officers' role perception is broad, including both professional and humanitarian roles. They are confident about their own performance and the lack of tension and lack of a feeling of relative deprivation within the Danish contingent; the regimental leaflets confirm this perception. This is not to say that everything within the Danish armed forces in Bosnia is, and in particular was, just fine. Actually, in the UNPROFOR mission from 1992–1995, Danish soldiers criticized their country's compliant character and the lack of education/materiel within the Danish Army. [27] Nevertheless, as a bottom line, Danish soldiers in DANBN on the IFOR/SFOR mission served at all levels and within all branches without encountering or engendering much tension.

3. MILITARY TO MILITARY RELATIONS

After having analyzed "internal" military issues, our study focused on Danish senior officers' external relations toward other military contingents by asking three questions:

- "Please rate the extent to which you have been in professional contact with the following political/ military/humanitarian authorities."
- "Please identify where you personally consider improvements absolutely necessary to facilitate your work."
- "Please rate the extent to which you have had professional problems with the same political/military/humanitarian authorities."

As seen from the formulations, the external relations of Danish senior officers included not only other military actors, but also 19 different military/political/humanitarian authorities:

- Peace Implementation Council (PIC)

---

[26] See, e.g., *End of Tour Report*, June 1999, DANBN: p. 22.

[27] Henning Sørensen and Anders Svendsen, *Civil kontrol med militæret i Danmark* (Copenhagen: ISFs Forlag, 1995), p. 38ff.

- NATO (SHAPE)
- OSCE
- Office of the High Representative (OHR)
- Office of the UN High Commissioner for Refugees (UNHCR)
- United Nations Missions in Bosnia-Herzegovina (UNMIBH)
- Danish Defense Ministry (MoD)
- Danish Defense Command (DC)
- Army Operational Command (HOK)
- *Danske Livregiment* (DLR, the regiment responsible for supporting DANBN)
- National Logistic Support Unit (NSE)
- DANBN
- NORDPOL BDE
- MND (N)
- Red Cross (or other NGOs)
- UN International Police Task Force (IPTF)
- Republika Srpska authorities
- Federation authorities
- Media
- Other

The results show that Danish soldiers in Bosnia (and those Danish military officers and soldiers supporting them in Hungary) are mainly in contact with four military authorities:

- MND (N) staff of the American Division "Task Force Eagle" in Tuzla, Bosnia;
- NORDPOL BDE in Doboj, Bosnia and in NSG in Pecs, Hungary;
- Baltic military units in DANBN;
- Danish military units: HOK, DLR serving DANBN and NORDPOL BDE from Denmark, of which a few were identified as problematic.

Figure 3 shows that NORDPOL BDE was the key contact unit for 87% of Danish senior officers, followed by DANBN (77%) and HOK (40%).

When asked to evaluate other military organizations and identify which unit caused the most working tensions, the U.S. Army-headed MND (N) was identified by 40% of all Danish senior officers as the most problematic, followed by DLR (37%) and NORDPOL BDE (27%). We shall explore the figures for the four most contacted military authorities and try to explain criticisms by distinguishing between three different sources of tension:

- National values and organizational principles;
- Rules of command and control;
- Daily working relations.

Figure 3: The Three Most Contacted, Most in Need of Improvement, and Most Problematic Military Authorities (1999)
(in percent)

	The three most contacted authorities	Improvement in this authority necessary to facilitate your job	Problematic authorities
MND (N)	30	*47 (1)*	*40 (1)*
NORPOL BDE	*87 (1)*	27 (2)	27 (3)
DANBN	77 (2)	7	3
HOK	40 (3)	13	7
DLR	3	27 (2)	37 (2)

3.1. MULTINATIONAL DIVISION (NORTH)

Tensions in multinational/international staffs consisting of "1,600 U.S. Army soldiers, four Danish, and some twenty other European soldiers, a great (but to me unknown) number of locals, and one single Canadian captain" [28] are to be expected. Thus, it may be interesting to study the causes of these tensions. We will start with differences in military values and organizations.

3.1.1 MILITARY VALUES AND ORGANIZATIONAL PRINCIPLES

The military values of an officer are defined here by four terms: ethics, morale, law, and norms. Behind each of the four terms we find a different actor: the individual soldier, the military organization, politicians, and societies, i.e., citizens/the officer corps.

Ethics are individually determined. They involve self-imposed behavior. Morale is an overall code for all members to follow in situations within a well-defined context, often an organization. Moral values include loyalty, trust, brotherhood, tradition, and honor. Law is a set of specific messages issued by politicians to be followed in a precise situation. Norms are decided by a group/society and tell all potential members how to behave.

The key word for military values is morale. This will normally refer to three important aspects of a soldier's life: job (job satisfaction, self-esteem, self-image, motivation), unit (platoon relations, buddy system, group cohesion, *esprit de corps*), and branch/service (its legitimacy, civil–military relations). Moreover, morale is important because it is an instrument with which the military organization imposes uniform behavior. Sometimes, however, we find contrasting moral values, for instance between those of the platoon and

---

[28]   "The Mud Camp, a Piece of the USA," *Prinsens* 4 (1997): 8.

those of the military organization. Such dilemmas are more seldom seen in laws and norms. Figure 4 offers a framework for understanding the four military values regulating soldiers' behavior and the sanctions imposed if they are disobeyed or violated.

The dotted lines in Figure 4 illustrate Danish perceptions of the reduced influence of morale and law and the increased influence of the ethics of the individual officer/soldier. This is not to say that morale and law play a more minor role in Danish than in U.S. military units. It means, though, that Danish soldiers are given the right to influence military orders and that unit morale in Denmark has increased at the cost of the higher formal military system. This is supported by three observations.

Figure 4
The Values of Military Leadership

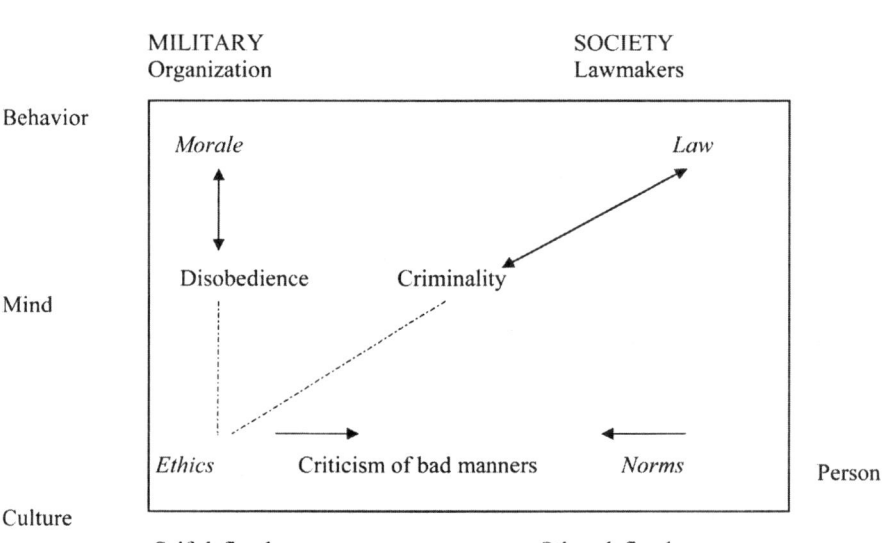

Figure 4: The Values of Military Leadership

First, as the armed forces have become more civilized, the need for a specific military sanction system has, in general, been reduced. In Denmark, for instance, capital punishment has been abandoned, and the relevance of a specific Danish Military Law for uniformed personnel is currently being discussed. The number of arbitrary military disciplinary sanctions has dropped: from over 4,000 in 1994 to 3,800 in 1995; there were 3,250 in 1996 and around 3,000 in 1997. [29]

---

[29] *Søndagsavisen*, 5 April, 1999: 6.

Second, Danish senior officers were asked: "Please describe the concept of 'good military leadership.'" They did so by referring to civil factors and relations with soldiers, such as "get results," "cooperate with others," and "responsibility for soldiers." Traditional military qualities usually accentuate personal characteristics such as bravery, honor, charisma, and tradition. Danish officers, however, seldom mentioned these values. Here is a contradiction: Danish senior officers define "military leadership" through the prism of civilian values but include military values when they define themselves as professional soldiers. Of course, military leadership is a complex concept. But it is even more so in complex alleviation actions and in PSOs. Here, we mostly find "*ad hoc* leadership" in which the specific "military" elements of leadership are strongly reduced. This perception is confirmed when one reviews the Danish manual for all soldiers, [30] in which only two pages (of the more than 70 pages devoted to "military leadership") are used to explain *military* leadership, while the major part of the chapter deals with leadership in general.

The reason for this is that "... no major differences seem in principle to exist between the social-psychological and group dynamic factors in civil and military organizations." [31] In short, military leadership values in Denmark are team-oriented and accept the involvement and participation of the individual soldier in defining the intended goal, allowing him to influence how it is accomplished, and letting him have a say when the success of the task has to be evaluated. [32]

Third, the expansion of personal ethics at the cost of morale and law is shown in the answers of Danish senior officers when asked: "Which are the qualities of Danish soldiers (contracted and enlisted personnel)?" The answers can be divided into the following four categories, which are accompanied by sample explanations:

• Orientation toward results: "Danish soldiers feel responsible for the accomplishment of a task."

• Social behavior: "Danish soldiers perceive themselves as human beings," "I know that my soldiers may question my orders, so I have to anticipate the potential reactions and questions of my subordinates and thereby improve my orders," and "Danish soldiers act in a socially responsible manner, taking into account the situations of others."

• Social/educational background: "Danish soldiers are rather well-educated, starting in elementary school," and "Due to conscription, we still get soldiers with a good social background."

---

[30] Forsvarskommandoen, *Ledelse og Uddannelse. En grundbog* (Copenhagen, 1998), pp. 310–379.

[31] Forsvarskommandoen, *Ledelse og Uddannelse,* 1998, p. 343.

[32] "With the Social Worker in the Former Yugoslavia," *Danske Livregiment* 3 (1998): 13.

- Decentralized military structure: "There are only a few steps from the soldier on the ground to his commander (LTC/COL)," and "Easy for any soldier to get in touch with his superior."

This Danish military culture is quite different from that of the U.S. Army. In part, this is because the normal qualities of Danish regulars are not defined by phrases like "obey orders," and "always refer to and abide by rules, laws, and military regulations." [33] Second, the distance between soldier and superior is much more pronounced in the U.S. than in the Danish Army. I was quite surprised by the open and critical remarks that young officers made to their senior and higher ranking colleagues during debriefing meetings, where issues such as a lack of fire extinguishing equipment in Bosnia, problems with budgeting systems, etc., were placed on the agenda by the younger officers, with the expectation that the responsible senior officers would respond to their needs and requests.

This culture of close relations is taught and established in a number of ways. All Danish army officers are educated together across regiments and branches (infantry, cavalry, artillery, etc.) at least twice, at the Military Academy and at the Staff Officer course (VUT I), before they meet for the third time at the General Staff course (VUT II). While the first time a U.S. Army officer will generally meet functionally with colleagues from other branches is at the General Staff course, Danish officers are often asked to work across branch lines. They know each other's function and the corporate culture within each of the services and branches, even if differences in culture exist among the three Danish services. [34]

There are other differences between U.S. and Danish/European army organizations with respect to manning a staff, using specialists, and promoting a career. As said earlier, the MND (N) staff was dominated by U.S. Army soldiers, who made up 98% of the organization, while in the two other European divisions, a more equal representation was found. [35] In the U.S. Army, specialists are used more often than in Europe, where a commissioned officer normally is a generalist. One problem with using specialists up to the level of LTC is that, when they deliver information, they unintentionally interpret this information in a narrow, "specialist" way. Often, a generalist can better analyze

---

[33] U.S. officers normally refer to the law or military regulations when giving orders. Adhering to the letter of the law appears to be more important than coming up with the most humane solution to a difficult situation. In Denmark, officers can sometimes bend the rules to alleviate hardship to their soldiers or to protect people in danger in peacekeeping operations. Danish officers have the flexibility to adapt to situations, which it seems U.S. officers do not have or do not believe they have.

[34] Michael H. Clemmesen, *Værnskulturerne og forsvarspolitikken* (*The Cultures of the Services and Defense Policy*) (Århus: Politica, 1986).

[35] See, e.g., "The Mud Camp, a Piece of the USA," p.8.

a situation and suggest the best course of action. Because the U.S. system, up to the rank of LTC, is run by officers who usually specialize in a single narrow field, less senior officers often fail to take a broad enough perspective when recommending changes or courses of action.

This awkward situation is reinforced by the U.S. military career system, described by Danish senior officers as an "up-or-out" system. This means that an officer's performance in his present position is the basis for his evaluation, and for his potential for promotion. One bad remark on the record of an officer can stop his career. Therefore, he is more vulnerable to criticism than a Danish officer, whose total career pattern, from Military Academy via General Staff courses to his present position, is taken into consideration.

3.1.2 Command and Control

A major reason for tension is different rules of command and control. In a direct sense, the U.S. Army uses its own standards in Bosnia, while all other Western nations adapt to the "NATO Major Command: Doctrines for Peace Support Operations." An example: a division never issues "orders;" rather, it gives "directives" to its brigades. This normal procedure between divisions and brigades is violated by the U.S. Army officers who give *orders* to the NORDPOL BDE.

In an indirect – but unavoidable – sense, tensions will arise when two opposing perceptions of the rules of command and control are implemented. According to the U.S. Army, leadership is an Officer A (platoon leader to general/admiral) ordering his Soldier B to do y; it means that the leader A causes B to perform y instead of z, as B would have done had it not been for the influence of A. In other words, the outcome y is related to the qualities of A, e.g., his socio-educational background, charisma, and present performance, and only A decides if/how B has succeeded.

More problems can be identified with this type of command system or leadership style. First, it perceives orders as a one-way relationship between A and B. B is the passive recipient of an order from A and is unable to think or act on his own. Therefore, B's behavior demands the presence and/or influence of A. Second, this model presupposes clear orders, objectives, and methods, which are impossible to foresee, in particular, in complex alleviation missions and PSOs such as the one in Bosnia. Third, A is often hiding the intended goal for B instead of sharing or defining it together with B. Fourth, the potential of B is overlooked. [36] Fifth, it is difficult to prove that A caused B to do y; maybe B would have done y on his own initiative. Sixth, according to the model, A

---

[36] When evaluating success, failure, or the potential for achievement, the entire situation must be considered; for example, an officer defending a post with only 10 soldiers against 1,000 for two hours is most certainly a better leader than the officer who wins that battle.

is not influenced by B, even if we all know that A will normally adapt x to anticipate the reaction of B.

The Danish command and control model incorporates and addresses most of these criticisms and expands on the U.S. leadership process. Figure 5 illustrates these two command and control models; the U.S. model is depicted by solid lines, while the Danish model includes the dotted lines, as well.

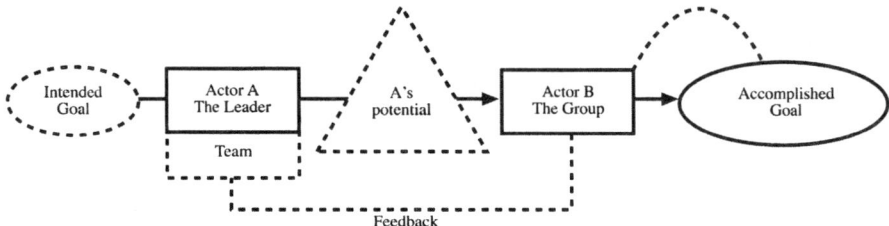

Figure 5: The Process of Command and Control

Figure 5 shows the Danish command and control process *in toto*, starting with a common understanding of and agreement on the intended goal between A and B. Next, military leadership is seen as a team effort, not a "one man show." Then, the potential of A and the influence of B on A is included. [37] Any leader will adapt his order x to B depending on the present status of B. The new model, moreover, accepts B's influence on how to accomplish the intended goal. Finally, feedback is integrated and so is the mutual evaluation of the degree of success.

Therefore, the Danish model moves away from an individual, consensual, and instrumental leadership perception toward a "collective" (i.e., symbiotic) relationship between leaders and followers. Relations characterized by dissent (i.e., conflicts) are included; otherwise, we are trapped in a false utopian dream. Danish officers are trained to employ a "causative" style of leadership, i.e., one in which leaders can invent and create ideas, institutions, and memories that can empower followers to satisfy their needs. [38] In short, the American leadership model says: "An officer, A, commands Private B to do y" while a

---

[37]   "Back from Tuzla," *Kentaur* 3 (1996): 3 ("The second [leadership characteristic] is a solid knowledge of and acceptance of all the persons you have to work with. This goes for the [attitude of the] leader toward his crew and as much as it goes for the [attitude of the] crew toward their leader").

[38]   James MacGregor Burns, *Leadership* (New York: Harper and Row, 1978). Burns focuses here on "causative leadership." The causative style of leadership is not a one-way relationship; rather, leaders engage their subordinates, inspire them to follow a common plan, and strengthen their belief in what they are doing.

Danish/Northern European model suggests: "Leadership is a process where A agrees with B about how to accomplish a task." [39]

The different command and control model is reflected in the answers to the following question put to Danish senior officers: "An incident with a local woman and her child caught in a car in a crossfire situation between local soldiers. Describe the reaction of soldiers from Denmark, Norway, Sweden, Finland, Poland, Estonia, Latvia, Lithuania, UK, and the USA" with four options: "Interfere," "Call for help," "Call for instructions," and "Ignore." The answers indicate a decline in activity for the platoon from "interfere" to "ignore." The difference between "call for help" and "call for instructions" is that in the first case the platoon has already defined the situation as one where back-up is needed, while soldiers in the latter situation expect their superiors to do so. It was understood that the platoon had no officer to command it.

Even though some of the Danish senior officers hesitated before answering, 93% agreed that a Danish platoon will "interfere." 87% expected soldiers from the UK to do the same, while 70% expected this behavior of soldiers from Norway. 63% believed soldiers from Finland would react in this manner, and 57% expected this of soldiers from Sweden. It is interesting to note that 90% of Swedish senior officers expected U.S. soldiers to "call for help/instructions." U.S. soldiers were therefore considered significantly more likely to call for help/instructions before acting than were Scandinavian soldiers or even soldiers from the former Warsaw Pact countries (67% for Polish soldiers, and 40% for Baltic soldiers).

The different answers illustrate many possible reactions to the same incident due to unforeseeable elements in alleviation missions/PSOs and military experiences. Thus, it is obvious that U.S. doctrine states that one should never enter a potential conflict without sufficient back-up; this was a lesson learned from Lebanon in 1982 and Somalia in 1994. Therefore, when the U.S. Army-led MND (N) applied one set of command and control rules and the Nordic battalions another, it was not surprising that tensions could arise.

3.1.3 BEFEHLSTAKTIK VERSUS AUFTRAGSTAKTIK

Another reason whereby rules of command and control can create tension is a different understanding of tactics. American soldiers are taught *Befehlstaktik;* Danish soldiers are taught *Auftragstaktik. Befehlstaktik* means that the officer dictates to the soldiers not only what job to do, but moreover how to do it, which way to go, for how long a time, what tool to use, etc. *Auftragstaktik* defines for the soldiers only the task that must be accomplished. Thereafter,

---

[39] Kim Schmidt, "FN- og NATO-tjeneste i Kroatien og Bosnien – en kompagnichefs erfaringer," *Militært Tidsskrift* 2 (1996), pp. 100 – 104 (issue on "Lessons from the Former Yugoslavia").

the platoon is expected to know what to do. The instruction of Danish soldiers in *Auftragstaktik* increases their sense of responsibility, self-esteem, etc., and makes them more engaged in doing their jobs. This criticism of the American way is not, *per se*, a rejection of *Befehlstaktik*. It depends on the type of mission. In clear battlefield operations, *Befehlstaktik* might be the better doctrine. But in an IFOR/SFOR type of mission with low risks, high uncertainty, a lack of predictability, and broad functionality, *Auftragstaktik* is called for. In short, the problem is simply to relate tactics to tasks.

3.1.4 AREA OF RESPONSIBILITY (AOR)

A third command and control area ripe for tensions is the different understanding of responsibility. A U.S. soldier, even up to the rank of LTC, has a restricted AOR, which is confined to a specific order. A Danish soldier has an overall responsibility for any task, including its accomplishment, cost-effectiveness, etc.

One consequence of the U.S. Army principle of limited responsibility is that American soldiers are not expected to mentally decline or break down, while "the Danish concept is based on the understanding that stress symptoms are normal reactions to abnormal situations." [40] Another is that the U.S. Army wastes a lot of time pushing failures around instead of learning from or fixing them; in Denmark, this game is called: "Who's got the monkey?" In turn, it means that officers in the U.S. Army are seldom ready to take even minor risks.

3.1.5 DAILY WORK RELATIONS

But perhaps the most difficult things for Danish senior officers to deal with in interactions with U.S. personnel are daily routines and working frictions. Many examples can be mentioned. First, minor problems in the U.S. Army are often elevated to the level of colonel/general, where in Denmark, such problems would be for the platoon leader to decide. For example, a Danish soldier took a photo of a Serbian T-34 Tank, which was forbidden. This misdemeanor was inflated to the status of a major criminal act and an American general even became involved in deliberations over what to do about this "crime" before the discussions were stopped through Danish intervention. A Danish senior officer, having worked closely with the Americans, describes this upward pressure on the decision-making system as a "push-up system," referring to younger women using "push-up bras" to make their breasts look bigger. Whatever it looks like, however, there is no doubt that inflation of problems haunts the U.S. Army decision-making process and results in an indecisive military orga-

---

[40]   Steen Martini, "Peacekeepers Facing the Horrors of Civil-like Conflict: Danish Lessons Learned in Preparing and Taking Care of Soldiers" in Wolfgang Biermann and Martin Vadset (Eds.), *UN in Trouble: Lessons Learned from the Former Yugoslavia,*" Part V (Sidney: Ashgate, 1998).

nization, which creates an additional problem for other brigades to deal with, as well.

Second, U.S. Army soldiers sometimes seem unwilling to listen to and learn from other soldiers. For example, according to a Danish major serving as a United Nations Military Observer (UNMO), "... the English and French IFOR staffs were very satisfied with their cooperation with the UNMO organization, while it was very difficult for these colleagues when briefing the Americans. They would not listen, but 'knew the total situation after just four days in the field." These UNMO colleagues and personnel from ECMM had risked their lives to get this information over the course of the previous three years; some had even died trying to get as many pieces of good information as possible. [41]

Third, if, for example, a U.S. soldier wants to go for a pizza, he will need four armored vehicles manned with 16 armed soldiers (four in each car) to drive to the pizza tavern. After having reached it, they will descend, with two soldiers in front and two in back to guard the expedition, while two privates go inside to order the pizza. Danish soldiers in Bosnia would use a jeep with two soldiers to do the same job. One reason for this heavy back-up for two U.S. Army soldiers buying a pizza is, of course, force protection, because they are more exposed than a Danish soldier. Another is that no U.S. Army officer wants to be seen as responsible for taking too few precautions, even in a low-threat situation, in case any casualty should happen.

Behind the different behavior of U.S. and Danish/European soldiers lies a different perception of the importance of force protection. In Bosnia, force protection is a main objective for the U.S. Army, whereas it is just one consideration among others for European soldiers. Yet another reason is that the U.S. and Danish armies perceive the environment in which they work very differently. American soldiers behave like warriors in a situation they believe has high risks and where they see combat as normal. Danish soldiers, on the other hand, act like mediators or supervisors in a civil conflict.

A fourth area of criticism is the rigid treatment by U.S. Army officers of their personnel. Many indicators point in this direction. For instance, there were two to three suicides per month among U.S. privates in the period from January–May 1997; American soldiers told me that they referred to MND (N), whose official designation was "Task Force Eagle," as "Task Force Evil." In another example, a U.S. private assigned to the Danish section of NORDPOL BDE had arranged for his wife to go to Zagreb to meet him there, but was afterwards forbidden to go there by his American superior. A senior Danish officer circumvented the decision by sending him on a "special assignment" for

---

[41] "A UN Monitor's Changeable Life," *Prinsens* 2 (1996): 17.

three days – to Zagreb! In another case, a U.S. general ordered all NORDPOL BDE senior officers to come to a meeting, but then the general arrived a full hour late. As a rule, the U.S. Army officers start with very rigid discipline, after which they loosen up. A Danish officer will try to keep the same level of discipline throughout the whole mission period.

A fifth area of criticism is the U.S. Army's attitude toward Civil–Military Affairs (CIMIC). CIMIC is a new organization built on the UN idea of establishing cooperation between the UNHCR and NGOs on the one hand and armed forces on the other. CIMIC had been tested elsewhere for two years before being implemented in Bosnia. The U.S. Army downplayed the importance of this work in Bosnia, contributing only 36 of the 500 CIMIC soldiers in the whole MND (N) area, and only two of the 100 officers in NORDPOL BDE. Danish soldiers, on the other hand, believe that CIMIC operations contribute to their force protection, not only because 70% of all information in Bosnia now comes from CIMIC work and only 30% from the well-established intelligence effort, but also because it is hoped that conflicts can be stopped before they break out if soldiers are directly engaged in local affairs. [42]

Perhaps the best indicator of tensions is the fact that Denmark had to turn a normal NORDPOL BDE officer job into a part-time job at MND (N) in order to filter out the problematic decisions of the MND (N). Later on, the job was expanded, requiring billets for two officers, one full time, with one officer serving at MND (N) and the other at NORDPOL BDE to influence the decisions of the U.S. Army officers (and sometimes even have them changed) to make them acceptable to the brigades.

The examples could go on and on. Each is like a pearl. Each pearl unto itself does not comprise a necklace, but one by one, these pearls add up and become a less than flattering pearl necklace.

3.2. Nordic-Polish Brigade (NORDPOL BDE)

The NORDPOL BDE consists of five battalions from the four Nordic countries and Poland. They were organized according to the NATO G-system of functions, with each nation responsible for a specific area: for example, Sweden was responsible for personnel (G1), Norway for intelligence (G2), Denmark for operations (G3), and so on, including Logistics (G4), CIMIC (G5), and Communications (G6). From January 1996 to July 1997, the NORDPOL BDE staff was made up of 63 persons; from July 1997 onwards, 115 people served on this staff.

To assist NORDPOL BDE with respect to logistics, a Nordic Logistical Support Group (NSG) – responsible for coordinating supplies for the five bat-

---

[42] "Distribution of Aid," *Prinsens* 4 (1998): 5.

talions – was established on top of each nation's Logistical Support Units (NSE). It was located far away in Pecs, Hungary, due to the NATO logistical principles of storing goods in the closest secure country next to the battlefield, which stands in contrast to the UN logistical principle of deploying resources directly in the area where needed.

Within NORDPOL BDE, Denmark played a leading role. This stems from a number of factors, including the facts that Denmark initiated the NORDPOL BDE, had been in charge of the G3 operation, was responsible (through its headquarters company) for the whole NORDPOL BDE Camp, and, as an active NATO member, was expected to have good relations with the U.S. Army in MND (N). This leading role was reflected in the fact that Denmark provided the first and third brigadier general to lead NORDPOL BDE.

For the reasons listed below, 27% of all Danish senior officers defined NORDPOL BDE as the third most problematic military organization with which they had to work in Bosnia (see Figure 3), saying that "improvements [to this unit] were absolutely necessary to facilitate work" and that this unit was one that caused them "professional problems."

3.2.1 MILITARY VALUES AND ORGANIZATIONAL PRINCIPLES

It seems fair to say that, in spite of different values in the armed forces of the Nordic countries and Poland, these differences caused no major tensions. The following organizational principles, however, might cause tensions:

1. Deployment period: Poland's contingents serve 12 months, while Denmark's serve only six. This means that, to some extent, any new Danish team will have to start all over, even if the debriefing of the returning contingent is effective.
2. Criteria for serving: Norwegian officers volunteer, while Danish officers are ordered to serve in Bosnia.
3. Language skills: some (Polish) officers had less command of the English language than did officers from other countries.
4. Command procedures: Sweden has a 22-point command system; Denmark and Norway applied the 5-point NATO Standard Procedure.
5. Relationship to NATO: Denmark and Norway, as members of NATO, have greater influence upon and receive more information from the U.S. Army-dominated MND (N) than do Sweden, Finland, and in particular Poland.
6. Recruitment background: Norway has more reservist soldiers than any of the other four nations.
7. Living conditions: officers from Sweden and Finland brought their wives with them to Pecs, while Danish officers were forbidden to do the same. Norwegian officers were the most highly paid, received the greatest tax reductions, and had the most free trips back home. The Finnish soldiers were

very well equipped with personal computers, while Polish soldiers were the least well equipped.

3.2.2 INTERNAL NORDPOL BDE RULES OF COMMAND AND CONTROL

Tensions with and within NORDPOL BDE caused by different command and control rules were unavoidable for the simple reason that, even though NORD-POL BDE may have been overstaffed, its competence was more limited than that of a normal brigade. NORDPOL BDE had only operational control of its battalions. It could never in reality command its five battalions to exercise. It was required to do so only theoretically, through command post exercises. Moreover, the brigade could never order any battalion to transfer any of its troops to another unit; the brigade was only allowed to combine two or more complete battalions. It could not change the composition of any of the units by extracting components of one battalion and placing them into another already existing battalion. In practice, it was then arranged that a whole battalion must be subordinated to another if even a single platoon from one battalion had to join another. Some of the Danish officers characterized NORDPOL BDE as being "in command of nothing." Others modified this evaluation and said that if a battalion had problems (with the locals, for example), it could turn to the brigade for assistance (from other battalions, for instance); under these circumstances, the battalions liked working with NORDPOL BDE.

3.2.3 DAILY WORK RELATIONS

Tensions stemming from daily work relations were mutual. Sweden and Finland tended to give extremely detailed orders (i.e., micro-management), and Sweden had more regulations than any of the other four countries. Sweden supplied the Swedish NGO "Verket" with vehicles, unheard of in the other battalions. Norway's main directive toward locals was "Stay out." Denmark's was "Act fast." According to some Danish senior officers, half of the NORDPOL BDE did not work and the other half was ineffective due to lack of means and competence. There was much better cooperation on the level of the battalions. One illustration of this is that the Nordic battalions worked together instead of, as would have been the normal procedure, contacting the NORDPOL BDE to take the initiative in leading cooperation between the battalions.

Economics, of course, will always cause frictions. In general, the two NATO nations, Denmark and Norway, held the most discussions; Sweden and Finland had fewer, and Poland had the least. Denmark was criticized for its unwillingness to pay for fire extinguisher materials, as it was responsible for the headquarters company, but Denmark argued that the NORDPOL BDE camp expenses were mutual, and, for that reason, expenses for fire-fighting material should also be mutual. Norway, on the other hand, in the first half of 1997, tried to have the other participants in NORDPOL BDE pay for the transfer of its NSE unit out of Pecs.

3.2.4 DANISH MILITARY ORGANIZATIONS ABROAD AND AT HOME

DANBN was, as shown in Figure 3, the second most contacted military authority, according to 77% of all Danish senior officers. HOK was the third most contacted authority, with 40%. However, when it came to problematic military authorities, the *Danske Livregiment*, DLR was a clear number two or three, competing with regional/local authorities for that position. [43] One may wonder how a Danish military organization providing logistical support to DANBN and NORDPOL BDE received such a poor rating, where 27% found "improvements of DLR absolutely necessary to facilitate Danish senior officers' work" and 37% identified DLR as "the military authority with which you have had professional problems."

One explanation is that the accusations against DLR were unjust. Others argue, in contrast, that there were more problems with DLR values:

* Lack of engagement/organization: DLR suffered from a lack of personnel, an excess of unqualified staff members, and the lack of a logistics specialist. In fact, DLR was just an office for a specific regiment.
* Rules of command and control: DLR was only the messenger trying to get materiel from Hærens Materiel Kommando (HMAK), which is the agency responsible for materiel.
* Daily work relations: For DLR, working hours were from 8:00 a.m.– 4:00 p.m., while DANBN and NORDPOL BDE worked 24 hours a day.

Whatever the reason, DLR caused deployed Danish officers problems; its services were therefore brought to an end with the establishment of a new international Army center for logistics.

3.3. DANBN–BALTIC COOPERATION

The composition of Baltic units in DANBN has shifted over time. In the first two IFOR/SFOR missions, from February 1996 to February 1997, the three Baltic countries deployed a joint unit of 100 soldiers, with each country's contingent of approximately 30 soldiers headed by one platoon leader from that country. From February 1997 onwards, the individual Baltic countries, in rotation, deployed one company of 100 soldiers headed by a major. The reason for the new arrangement was that a company headed by a major is more operational than three minor units with only a platoon leader in command. Of course, under this new rotational system of single-country units, mutual cooperation among Baltic soldiers was put aside.

---

[43] Please refer to the section on "Military to Regional/Local Authorities and Populations," below.

The Danish senior officers were asked to "evaluate the Danish-Baltic military cooperation" with respect to "cultural differences," "treatment of soldiers," "tensions between Danish and Baltic soldiers," "achievements," and "improvement."

3.3.1 MILITARY VALUES AND ORGANIZATIONAL PRINCIPLES

Different "cultural" values did cause tensions, particularly in the beginning. One of these "values" involved what the Danish soldiers saw as over-consumption of food and alcohol by Baltic soldiers. The basic difference, however, is the relationship between privates and their NCOs/officers. A Danish officer expects his soldiers to tell him if something is wrong. A Baltic soldier would never dare to do so. He is used to robot-like discipline. Besides, Baltic soldiers are very unfamiliar with the Danish *Talsmandssystem* (job steward system). It will take Denmark a lot of effort over a long period of time to improve this situation. In an actual conflict in Viborg, Denmark, between a Baltic officer and his soldiers, a whole weekend (normally spent enjoying recreation) was spent discussing with such a conflict, in order to have the problem thoroughly understood and dealt with. It was quite a new experience for Baltic soldiers to go through this process of conflict management.

3.3.2 RULES OF COMMAND AND CONTROL

The rules of command and control create no problems, as Baltic military units join the Danish battalion to learn NATO standard procedures. [44] The same goes for the education of Baltic soldiers. It begins in Viborg, where each Baltic company is given a 6 – 10 week preparation course before deployment to one of the two Danish camps in Bosnia. This training goes on during their stay, where they live and work with Danish soldiers. This education ends (for officers) with Staff Officers/General Staff courses at the multinational Baltic Defense College, established to serve all three Baltic nations, headed by a Danish brigadier general and staffed by instructors from 12 nations. [45]

3.3.3 DAILY WORK RELATIONS

In their daily work, Baltic soldiers are hardworking, robust, and experienced (having been deployed 3 – 4 times), but the Danish officers interviewed thought they lacked initiative and openness, and were made less effective because of widespread lack of English language skills (although they often speak Russian and therefore serve as shadow interpreters when DANBN soldiers communicate with the Serbs). They do as they are told but have no tradition of discussing problems, for instance if they don't understand an order or if something is broken. Therefore, they are given neither the poorest nor the best jobs.

---

[44]   See, e.g., "Danish is Sweet Music to the Ears," *Gyldenløve* 1 (1998): 8ff.

[45]   Michael H. Clemmesen, "De baltiske forsvars nye hjernevugge," *Udenrigs* 1 (1999): 1 – 8.

What is in this for Denmark? We are convinced that we are doing the right thing; teaching them about our northern European military leadership style and NATO procedures improves their chances for successful membership in NATO by spreading our culture throughout their military educational system. But we learn a lot, as well. In particular, we are reminded of how poorly Danish officers once treated their own soldiers.

To conclude, Danish senior officers' relationships with other military contingents clearly showed that MND (N), headed by the U.S. Army, was without doubt the most criticized external organization; 47% of our senior officers said "improvements were absolutely necessary to facilitate their work in Bosnia" while another 40% referred to having "professional problems" with MND (N). The second most problematic military organization was DLR, with 27% and 37% of senior officers registering concerns with this unit according to these two categories. Finally, NORDPOL BDE was the third most problematic organization, with 27% of senior officers answering in the affirmative to both categories. In contrast, DANBN, other battalions, and Danish national military institutions such as MoD, DC, and HOK enjoyed general respect. It is important to note that criticism of the U.S. Army, in particular, was aimed at its senior officers, not at its regulars, and that this criticism was not only described, it was explained as well, focusing on all three aspects: U.S. Army values and organizational principles, rules of command and control, and daily work behavior.

The bottom line, however, is that criticism should be neither excused nor silenced, but rather dealt with constructively in order to diminish tensions and improve cooperation between the many military contingents committed to fight for the same good cause.

4. MILITARY RELATIONS WITH INTERNATIONAL POLITICAL AND HUMANITARIAN ORGANIZATIONS (NGOs)

The contact between Danish senior officers and international political authorities (PIC, OSCE, OHR, UNHCR,[46] UNMIB, humanitarian agencies, and NGOs) is rather modest, as shown in Figure 6.

Figure 6 shows no tensions between Danish senior officers and international or governmental political authorities. Nevertheless, 27% of Danish officers mentioned NGOs/PVOs as problematic organizations, saying, "improvements were absolutely necessary to facilitate their work in Bosnia." Danish senior officers argued that NGOs often withheld information on where, when,

---

[46] "1,000 Teddy Bears or Gunpowder and Bullets," *Slesvigeren* 7 (1996): 6–7.

Figure 6: The Three Political and Humanitarian Authorities Most Contacted, Most in Need of Improvements, and Most Problematic (1999) (in percent)

	The three most contacted authorities	Improvement in this authority necessary to facilitate your job	Problematic authorities
PIC, OSCE, UNHCR, OHR	13	7	13
NGOs/PVOs	0	27 (3)	7
Regional/local authorities	10	33 (2)	27 (3)
Local population	–	3	0

and how to work, partly because they did not want to share information with other NGOs for competitive reasons and partly because they did not want to coordinate with the Danish armed forces in supplying aid. [47] The problem for the Danish armed forces was that, in cases of emergency, they could not rescue NGO representatives. [48]

To conclude, international political organizations caused no tensions, and NGOs did so only because Danish officers felt responsible for NGO representatives' lives and wanted to coordinate their aid work with that of NGOs.

5. MILITARY RELATIONS WITH REGIONAL/LOCAL AUTHORITIES AND POPULATION

5.1. REGIONAL/LOCAL AUTHORITIES

Regional/local authorities represent a broad segment of the local power elite in Bosnia, i.e., military officers, civilian mayors, local police forces, etc., within all three ethnic groups. Danish officers in charge of negotiations with local representatives describe these talks as peaceful but delicate. [49] Nevertheless,

---

[47]   For a short description of DANBN's aid to the local population, see "Distribution of Aid;" "The Rebuilding of Bosnia," *Danske Livregiment* 7 (1998): 19ff.

[48]   "1,000 Teddy Bears or Gunpowder and Bullets" notes the unwillingness of NGOs to "assist an 'aggressor' in spite of the fact that civilian Serbian families suffer at least as much as those on the Federation side."

[49]   See "Last News from C-Squadron in Camp Dannevirke," *Musketten* 1 (1998): 7–8 ("Our cooperation with the Bosnian Serb and Croatian military authorities still takes place without any big problems. The [only] problems there have been with the local police"); "Experiences

as shown in Figure 6 above, 33% of Danish senior officers mentioned that "improvements [in dealing with local authorities] were absolutely necessary to facilitate their work in Bosnia;" 27% had "professional problems" with both Republika Srpska and Federation authorities.

Thus, there is no doubt that local authorities created tensions for Danish senior officers. [50] But such tensions were expected and they disappeared after some time. [51] Local authorities are a kind of counterpart to Danish senior officers in negotiations on disarmament and creating peace in Bosnia. [52]

Therefore, the real question is not whether local authorities caused tensions but how Danish senior officers coped with them. Actually, most Danish senior officers argued that they were on a good footing with all sides and that they tried to remain so for a number of reasons. First, DANBN was located in both sectors; accordingly, its officers could play a more impartial role by balancing their time, aid, and control over the population equally. Second, they urged the three ethnic groups to sit around the same table and negotiate. For instance, in the beginning, when the Danish battalion chief asked Serbian, Muslim, and Croatian military commanders for a meeting, the local authorities did not even communicate with one another; their communications were only with the Danish officers. After more meetings, however, conversations between all three ethnic groups emerged. Third, Danish senior officers have extensive experience in negotiating with local Danish mayors, other county/municipal politicians, trade union representatives, and other civilian officials. Fourth, Danish senior officers strove not to act in "too military" a manner. [53] Of course, they were not equal partners because the Danes could always order the local authorities to do as they wanted. From time to time, though, Danish senior officers had to demonstrate their military muscle, e.g., during the disarmament of the Serbian special police force, and when the Danes had to control 1,500 Serbs and 500 Muslims who stood in hostile gatherings on each bank of the Sava River. Danish senior officers always tried to use as little military power as possible, in contrast to U.S. Army officers who, during the same actions, employed all their heavy gear.

In short, the explanation for the rather low and few tensions between Dan-

---

as an Intelligence Officer," *Kentaur* 4 (1997): 8 – 10.

[50] "The Bull's Roar from the South," *Gyldenløve* 6 (1996): 6 – 9.

[51] "So HQ COY Works in Bosnia," pp. 14 – 15.

[52] For a description of negotiations with local authorities, see "Experiences as an Intelligence Officer."

[53] "Back from Tuzla" describes a tense situation in which a calm Swedish regular walked towards Muslim soldiers blocking the road to let a four-star U.S. Army general pass a checkpoint.

ish senior officers and local authorities is that the former are used to dealing
with local authorities using as little military might as possible.

5.2. LOCAL POPULATION

In contrast to the tensions between Danish senior officers and local authorities,
no tensions were found between the officers and the local population (see Figure 6 below). [54] On the other hand, the type of incidents most often reported
were "problems with the local population" (50%) and "problems with local
civil and military authorities" (43%). Therefore, according to Danish senior
officers, the locals create problems but not tensions. [55]

One explanation is the Danish soldiers' impartiality toward the local population. This was tested when asking the Danish senior officers: "What is your
general attitude toward the local population in your mission area?" Officers
were given three possible options: "Positive," "Neutral," or "Negative" for each
of the three ethnic groups: "Croats," "Serbs," and "Muslims." 57% of all Danish senior officers had the same (either positive, neutral, or negative) attitude
toward all three groups; the number of officers with negative attitudes toward
Croats and Muslims were balanced out by the same number having positive
attitudes. This opinion balance was a little more negative toward the Serbs,
as only one Danish officer had a positive attitude toward Serbs while six had
negative attitudes.

All Danish senior officers were aware, however, that almost all Western
aid (95%) went to the Federation, Croats, and Muslims, and only 5% went to
the Serbs. In Bosnia, there were some 250 NGOs, of which only 18 supported
the Serbs. Therefore, Danish soldiers deliberately tried to balance this biased
distribution by supplying the Serbian sector with clothes, food rations, etc.,
in particular because the federal populations declined the simple aid, as they
did not need it. For instance, an old but still functional dental clinic from the
Danish armed forces was given to the Serbian Doboj hospital.

The positive evaluation of the Danish PKO effort in the IFOR/SFOR mission shown in this report, which was based on Danish senior officers' statements, could lead one to the assumption that Danish senior officers strongly
believed in what they were doing in Bosnia. However, this is far from being
the case. When asked: "What is the most essential impact of the presence of

---

[54] For a description of the distribution of the three ethnic groups in the mission area, see
"Greetings from Valhalla," *Danske Livregiment* 8 (1998): 3–4.

[55] See "With IFOR in Bosnia," *Slesvigeren* 5 (1996): 7 ("The population is very friendly towards us and waves when we pass, which, we hope, will last"); "Leopard (Tanks) in the Service of Peace," *Prinsens* 2 (1997): 5; "Peace Redeemers," p. 6 ("We do not experience much
hostility. Mostly children and old people wave at us"); "So HQ COY Works in Bosnia,"
p. 14 ("There is no detectable discontent with the SFOR presence in either Serbian or Muslim areas").

the Danish armed forces in Bosnia?" 90% of Danish senior officers answered: "military" (i.e., they keep the peace). When asked, however, "In your opinion, what is the solution for peace in Bosnia?" 43% saw no solution under the Dayton Agreement while 53% believed that peace is possible, provided that the area receives economic aid, war crimes trials take place, educational efforts are undertaken, etc. Thus, although Danish soldiers are doing a good job in Bosnia, they do so as professionals, not as idealists.

6. CONCLUSION

Per capita, Denmark is in a vanguard position with regard to PKOs. During the Cold War period, Denmark was militarily active only with UN Military Observer missions around the world. After the end of the Cold War, and due to the shift from collective to selective security, Denmark has increased its military engagement and, more decisively, has moved from a verbal to a violent foreign policy. [56] Reductions in military spending have been lower than in most other Western countries. With the Defense Act of 1999, passive military spending (regiments, garrisons) has shifted toward active expenses (weapons, sea- and airlift materiel) to improve the effectiveness of Danish PSOs, especially the DIB. Danish officers are professionally motivated and are doing a good job for professional reasons, not as convinced idealists.

Tensions were not found within DANBN. In contrast, Danish Army personnel experienced tension in particular with U.S. Army personnel, DLR, and NORDPOL BDE (see Figure 3 for exact statistics). Therefore, it seems clear that external military organizations were the main creators of tension. These tensions are reflected in the time consumption of Danish officers, having moved from "internal" in national military positions to more "external" in this multinational mission. More of Danish senior officers' time in Bosnia was spent dealing with other military contingents than with local politics, indicating that multinational relations were more important than local contacts. Formulated in another way, the new type of combat has not influenced the time consumption of Danish senior officers, even if the risk for soldiers in combat areas is higher than it was in the Cold War period.

Tensions between multinational military contingents may have influenced the role perception of Danish senior officers, as well. They define themselves as ambassadors and mediators only after defining themselves as professional soldiers. Due to the civil war's tragic consequences for local populations, 53% of senior officers now include "humanitarian worker" as their fourth most important role.

---

[56] The Danish public has now come to accept the possibility that its soldiers may have to participate in war-like operations.

It is problematic that the high-level military authority MND (N) causes tensions for the lower-ranking brigades and battalions. These tensions are caused for a number of reasons, including differences in military values and organizational principles, rules of command and control, and daily work relations. The most tension is probably caused by the latter, where U.S. Army officers demonstrate that they are out of touch with and do not understand (and are not interested in) European perceptions of military leadership and the importance of CIMIC.

"Military to political/humanitarian" relations were rather modest, and no tensions were reported between Danish senior officers and international political organizations such as the UN, OSCE, and EU. NGOs caused some tensions, as did local authorities, the Republika Srpska, and the Federation, which was to be expected. Although relations between Danish senior officers and the local population were problematic, they were nearly without tension, which might have to do with the balanced attitude of Danish senior officers toward the three ethnic groups.

In short, tensions were found neither at the internal military level within DANBN nor at the "military-to-international" political level (toward international political organizations or the local population). Some tensions were identified with NGOs, the national external military unit DLR, the multinational external military unit NORDPOL BDE, and local authorities. Major tensions existed with the U.S. Army, created by the Americans' military values, rules of command and control, and in particular, daily work relations. Here, improvements are called for in the behavior of the U.S. Army for the sake of its IFOR/SFOR partners and their mutual cause.

5. IRISH DEFENSE FORCES IN THE BALKANS

Jean CALLAGHAN

Outline:

1. BACKGROUND

This chapter will examine the history of the participation of the Republic of
Ireland's Permanent Defense Forces (PDF)[1] in peace operations; the motives
for this participation, both in general and in the case of the Former Republic of
Yugoslavia; and the experiences of the Irish soldiers and officers who participated in the UN and NATO operations in this region.[2] This analysis is based
on a review of scholarly literature, as well as newspaper accounts, Internet and
database searches, and extensive interviews with Irish scholars, peacekeepers,
and former peacekeepers who served in the former Yugoslavia.[3]

> *Ireland, its leaders, and its peacekeeping forces have helped to contribute
> to the progress of this peace all around the world. There has not been a
> day in the last four decades when an Irish peacekeeper has not been
> somewhere on duty as a sentinel for peace in a distant part of the world.*[4]

William J. Clinton

1.1. IRELAND'S HISTORY IN PEACEKEEPING

Peacekeeping is a central element in Irish foreign policy and a matter of justified public pride. According to a recent publication by the Ministry of Foreign
Affairs, for the Irish, "Peacekeeping is an integral element of how we see ourselves in the world."[5] The *White Paper on Defense* of February 2000 (and
long-standing tradition and practice) states that the Irish believe that it is in
Ireland's interest to "ensure that the conduct of international relations is undertaken in accordance with international law and democratic principles." This

---

[1] When the term Defense Forces is used, it refers to the Permanent Defense Forces established
under Section 18(a) of the Defense Act of 1954, and includes army, navy, and air corps.

[2] Because of the inward-looking nature of the Irish contingent's mission in Sarajevo, information about and analysis of military relations with governmental and international organizations are quite limited, and therefore will be included in the sections on "Irish Involvement
in the Balkans" and "Military Relations with NGOs, Media, and Local Population."

[3] I would like to express my deep gratitude to and admiration of all of the Irish peacekeepers and scholars who helped me with this study. In particular, I would like to thank Ray
Murphy and Colonel Colm Doyle, both patient and expansive experts on this topic, who so
generously shared their time, insights, and considerable expertise with me. Thanks are also
due to Colonel Oliver A. MacDonald, who directed me to many valuable articles and other
sources of information, and especially to Juergen Kuhlmann, who, as always, has been an
insightful reader and editor, as well as a much-valued mentor and friend. Any errors are, of
course, my own.

[4] Remarks by President William J. Clinton at a Presentation for Irish *Taoiseach* Bertie Ahern,
17 March 1998. http://www.whitehouse.gov/WH/New/html/19980317–5661.html

[5] *Ireland and the Partnership for Peace: An Explanatory Guide* (Dublin: Department of Foreign Affairs, May, 1999), p. 6. Also available at http://www.irlgov.ie/iveagh.

is supported and reinforced in a very direct way by Ireland's willingness to provide peacekeepers to the troubled spots of the world. [6]

For more than 40 years, Ireland has been actively engaged in UN peace-keeping. There have been few UN peace missions in which the Irish Army has not been represented. During this time, the Defense Forces have built up an enormous reservoir of international respect for the Irish ability to keep extremely difficult and protracted UN operations "on the road." [7]

Ireland's involvement in peacekeeping began soon after its admission to the United Nations Organization in 1955. [8] Within three years, the first Irish volunteer observers joined the UN Observer Group in Lebanon (UNOGIL). Lebanon was destined to become the cornerstone of Ireland's UN peacekeeping contributions. During 1958, Ireland contributed observers to the UN Truce Supervision Organization (UNTSO), which assisted and helped coordinate other UN missions throughout the Middle East. [9]

It was UNOC, the Congo operation that ran from 1960 – 1964, however, which was a true watershed in the Republic's peacekeeping activities. Until this time, the PDF was in danger of losing its military identity and becoming a "glorified *Gendarmerie*." [10] The Congo was a costly investment by the Irish in peacekeeping. Irish troops arrived in July 1960. In less than four months, nine Irishmen lost their lives as a result of an ambush by the Congolese. They were the first Irish soldiers to die abroad since the establishment of the Republic. In September 1961, Irish troops in the Congo, also for the first time in the history of the Republic, took offensive action against a military opponent; two more soldiers died and 15 more were wounded. Moreover, a detachment of 150 Irish troops associated with this operation was surrounded by mercenaries and rebels and was forced to surrender after four days of fighting. Between 1960 and 1964, the Irish deployed more than 6,000 soldiers to the Congo. At the height of their contribution, Ireland had more than 1,400 troops on this mission, with average troop strength of more than 700.

---

[6]   *White Paper on Defense*, Section 6.1.2.

[7]   "Ireland: National Overview," in Charles Heyman (Ed.), *Jane's World Armies* (Coulsdon, Surrey: Jane's Information Group, 1998).

[8]   Ireland's attempt to join the UN has an unusual history. The *Dáil* approved membership on 26 July 1946. The government did not hesitate to exercise its mandate; the Soviet Union, however, vetoed the country's initial application in the Security Council, in a "tit-for-tat" move repaying Catholic Ireland for refusing to support the "godless" Soviet Union's application to the League of Nations. See also Ray Murphy, "Ireland, the United Nations, and Peacekeeping Operations," *International Peacekeeping* 5, No. 1 (Spring 1998), p. 25.

[9]   Harold J. Kearsley, "The Blue Helmets of Ireland," *Army Quarterly and Defense Journal* 128, No. 4 (October 1998), p. 391.

[10]   *Ibid*, p. 391, referring to John P. Duggan, *A History of the Irish Army* (Dublin: Gill and Macmillan, 1991).

In total, 57 Irish soldiers were wounded or injured in this deployment, and Ireland lost 26 of her soldier's lives. This sobering set of experiences changed the perception of the Irish peacekeepers both at home and abroad. Internally, the Irish saw the high cost of their participation in this UN peace-keeping mission as "the membership fee paid by the Republic for Ireland's new international role. These Irish soldiers were not to die in vain, but [instead] became symbols of Irish efforts to help bring peace to the international stage." [11] Abroad,

> [t]he difficulties experienced by the Irish [in the Congo] provided the basis of a broader Irish policy at the UN. This emphasized Ireland as a model peacekeeper, both in practice and in their proposals for improvements, and also as a model for how the smaller UN members should endure existing arrangements. In both of these, the willingness to accept costs was a crucial part of the policy. [12]

In the years since this deployment, 80 Irish peacekeepers have lost their lives on UN missions. This sacrifice, however, has not deterred the Irish from seeing their overall contribution toward the UN as positive.

1.2. PRIDE IN SUPPORT OF UN PEACE OPERATIONS

Though the contributions of smaller states to UN operations rarely seem to make headlines, it is largely thanks to their work that UN peacekeeping is possible. The Republic of Ireland is such a state. Generally, international news coverage about the Republic focuses on the "Troubles" across the border in Northern Ireland. Unfortunately, many of Ireland's international activities, including those within the UN, are not normally considered newsworthy, although Ireland's contribution to and involvement in the UN is certainly disproportionate to its size and wealth. It is one of the most active of the nearly 190 members. [13] For example, Ireland is regularly listed as among the top ten contributors to UN peace missions over the last 40 years. [14] Despite the fact that the UN very often owes Ireland (which for most of its history has been one of the poorest countries in Western Europe) large sums of money, the Re-

---

[11]   *Ibid*, p. 392.
[12]   *Ibid*, pp. 391 – 394. See also *The Blue Helmets: A Review of United Nations Peace-Keeping*, 2nd edition (New York: United Nations Department of Public Information, 1990), especially Chapter XI, "UN Operation in the Congo," and Paul Sharp, *Irish Foreign Policy and the European Community* (Aldershot, UK: Dartmouth Press, 1990), pp. 51 – 52.
[13]   Kearsley, "Blue Helmets," p. 390.
[14]   Speech by Mr. Michael Smith, Minister for Defense, on the Occasion of the Visit of the Secretary General of the United Nations, Mr. Kofi Annan, to the UN Training School in the Curragh, 21 January 1999. See also Heyman, "Ireland: National Overview."

public is one of only a handful of member states to consistently pay their dues on time. [15]

Ireland's commitment to the UN is the bedrock of the Republic's foreign policy outside Europe. The importance of Ireland's involvement can be summed up in the words of David Andrews, former Defense Minister:

> I regard Ireland's commitment of military personnel to UN-sponsored peacekeeping missions as one of the most important elements of Irish foreign policy .... [P]eacekeeping has become the mainstay of our involvement in the affairs of that organization. [16]

For many years, prior to Ireland's accession to the European Community, the UN was the only forum where Ireland could express its concerns across a wide range of international issues, including decolonization, disarmament, human rights, and peacekeeping. [17] The Irish are proud of their tradition of involvement in the UN, from Frank Aiken's initial proposal for nuclear nonproliferation in UN Resolution 1665, adopted in 1961 (still referred to as "the Irish Resolution"), which led to the Nuclear Non-Proliferation Treaty, through their June 1998 effort, in collaboration with seven other countries, to launch a new international drive to rekindle efforts at nuclear disarmament. [18]

The building and maintenance of a strong and effective UN, especially in the area of conflict prevention, form a key objective of Irish foreign policy, within which peacekeeping operations occupy center stage. [19] The Defense Forces' decades of active participation in peacekeeping operations demonstrate this longstanding Irish commitment to support of the UN, as does the fact that

---

[15] For a small country that has only recently started to see a turn in its economic tides, the sums owed Ireland by the UN are rather large. "On 1 February 1999 the total amount due my department from the United Nations was 8.1 million Irish pounds, as opposed to the amount due on 1 May 1998 of 9.6 million pounds, which was the greatest amount due for any month in 1998. The total extra costs, excluding pay and allowances, net of reimbursement, in respect of Defense Forces personnel currently in UNIFIL, UNFICYP, and SFOR is estimated at 2.1 million Irish pounds per year." *Testimony of the Minister for Defense*, Mr. Michael Smith, *Dáil* Debates Official Reports, *Tithe An Oireachtais,* 25 February 1999.

[16] Kearsley, "Blue Helmets," pp. 390, 395. Mr. Andrews made this statement during a speech in the *Dáil* in March 1993 and again in Lebanon in June of that year.

[17] For an interesting discussion of these issues and the history of Ireland in the UN, see Murphy, "Ireland, the UN, and Peacekeeping Operations," pp. 22–45.

[18] Speech by Mr. Michael Smith, Minister for Defense, on the Occasion of the Visit of the Secretary General of the United Nations, Mr. Kofi Annan, to the UN Training School in the Curragh, 21 January 1999.

[19] *Challenges and Opportunities Abroad, White Paper on Foreign Policy* (Dublin: Department of Foreign Affairs, 1996).

peacekeeping has been part of the stated mission of the Irish Defense Forces since the 1960s. [20]

The advent of the Cold War made the concept of collective security and enforcement under the UN Charter seem obsolete. It was replaced by the UN policy of "political-military control of local conflict by impartial, essentially non-coercive methods." [21] This changed situation offered Ireland a new and important role as "peacekeeper" and "middle power." [22] It was against this background that peacekeeping became a central feature of Irish foreign policy in the early 1960s. Ireland, in terms of its size and resources, has made a disproportionately significant contribution to peacekeeping operations that continues to the present day. [23]

Currently, the Irish Defense Forces and, to a lesser extent, *An Gardai Siochána* (the Irish police force) participate in a wide range of UN-sponsored activities dedicated to the maintenance of international peace and security. As of this writing, peacekeeping and related activity involves some 900 Irish military personnel deployed in more than a dozen different countries; in the future, this will include the UN Standby Arrangements System (UNSAS), which the government has agreed to support. This initiative involves the commitment of up to 850 military personnel at any one time for rapid deployment to a UN mission area. Participation can be fulfilled by the redesignation to UNSAS of personnel currently serving with the UN. There would be no obligation to participate, and, as in the case of all UN missions, the approval of the lower house of the Irish parliament, the *Dáil*, would be required before any contingent could be dispatched to UNSAS.

Participation in overseas peace support operations is the largest single military activity currently undertaken by the Defense Forces. Since 1958, members of the Irish Defense Forces have completed more than 50,000 tours of duty on 51 different peacekeeping missions. [24] The largest single mission in which the Irish have participated was UNIFIL (UN Interim Force in Lebanon), to

---

[20]   Murphy, "Ireland, the UN, and Peacekeeping Operations," p. 44.

[21]   *Ibid*, p. 26. See also the section on peacekeeping and preventive diplomacy in Larry Fabian, *Soldiers Without Enemies* (Washington, D.C.: The Brookings Institution, 1971), pp. 16, 88.

[22]   *Ibid*, p. 28. The term "middle power" is commonly used in speaking of peacekeeping and the countries best known for their participation in these operations. It has never been clearly defined and can have different connotations depending on the context in which it is used. Dag Hammarskjöld referred to the term frequently when discussing peacekeeping. In some circles, the term has been used to describe the disproportionate influence that can accrue to a state as a result of being a reliable troop-contributor. Fabian discusses this range of definitions in *Soldiers Without Enemies*, p. 88; regarding peacekeeping however, he says, "... a Canada, a Sweden, an Austria, or an Ireland has repeatedly acted out the middle power role."

[23]   *Ibid*, p. 29.

[24]   *White Paper on Defense*, February 2000, Section 6.3.

which Ireland contributed more than 600 personnel at any given time, including an infantry battalion and administrative and support personnel. [25] Although
personnel are drawn from right across the Defense Forces, the vast majority
comes from the army; with up to almost 10% of the army serving abroad at
any one time, this is a very significant manpower commitment. [26] Irish soldiers have recently served with peacekeeping and military observer missions in
Afghanistan/Pakistan, Cyprus, Kuwait, Lebanon, the Middle East, East Timor,
the Western Sahara, and the former Yugoslavia. Some have also been seconded
to the UN High Commission for Refugees. Irish officers, in an effort to facilitate cooperation with non-governmental organizations (NGOs), have also
been seconded to NGOs carrying out humanitarian work in Africa, mostly in
Rwanda. [27] In addition, Irish officers have participated in UN observer missions
since 1958. [28] The combined commitment of the Defense Forces and the *Garda*
to UN peacekeeping operations has become a significant part of Ireland's foreign policy.

Ordinary people in Ireland have a sense of pride about their national contribution to international peace. Within the UN, Ireland is rewarded for its activities in this arena; the country's influence is more significant than its size
and wealth would usually suggest. Though there are many more powerful and
wealthy countries than Ireland, there is most certainly a need for states like Ireland (as well as Austria, Sweden, and the other middle powers) to continue to
contribute to UN operations. Without the aid of Ireland and other such states,
the UN mandate to bring global peace and security may never be achieved. [29]

1.3. RECONCILING NEUTRALITY WITH MILITARY SUPPORT OF UN PEACE OPERATIONS

The idea of military neutrality is very popular with the Irish people and thus
plays a key role in Irish security policy formation and decision-making.

> Irish military neutrality is a policy to which this government is deeply at-
> tached. The Government do [sic] not intend to join mutual defense alliances
> such as NATO. Ireland, however, has never been ideologically neutral, nor
> morally indifferent to the major international and security challenges of the
> day. Ours is not doctrinaire neutrality, frozen in time and isolated from the

---

[25] Department of Defense, *Defense Strategy Statements 1997–1999* (Dublin: Department of
Defense, 1997), p. 8, and *Defense Strategy Statements 1998–2000* (Dublin: Department of
Defense, 1998), pp. 10–12, available at http://www.irlgov.defence.strat.htm.

[26] *White Paper on Defense*, February 2000, Section 6.3.2.

[27] "Ireland: Current Developments and Recent Operations – UN Service," in Charles Heyman
(Ed.), *Jane's World Armies* (Coulsdon, Surrey: Jane's Information Group, 1998).

[28] Murphy, p. 22.

[29] Sean Boyne, "Ireland Edges toward EU Security Identity," *International Defense Review* 28
(Business Section), No. 4 (1 April 1995), p. 56.

evolving international security realities .... . Irish neutrality has not been imposed from outside, nor is it guaranteed by international treaty. It is a policy espoused by successive Irish Governments, and its core, defining characteristic is non-membership of military alliances. Our neutrality has gone hand in hand with a strong commitment to international cooperation for stability and security. [30]

Current Irish policy maintains that there is no conflict between Ireland's military neutrality and full and active support by Ireland of collective security efforts based on international law. [31] Still, as one of Europe's five neutral, non-aligned states (the others being Finland, Austria, Sweden, and Switzerland), [32] the Irish place strict conditions on whether and how their military forces will participate in peace operations. Irish participation in these operations therefore always requires not only a UN mandate but also the approval of the *Dáil*.

It is noteworthy that parties in conflict often accept the Irish as peacekeepers and military observers because of a combination of factors, including Ireland's extensive successful experience in peacekeeping operations; the country's neutrality; its policies at the UN; its history under colonial rule; and its non-membership in any military alliance. [33] The international awareness that the island has survived (and is now flourishing) despite a long history of political and ethnic strife often makes "those whose peace is being kept" [34] even more prone to accept Irish peacekeepers as neutral and fair intermediaries. This decades-long reputation for effectiveness and for acceptance by disputing parties also helped Ireland to achieve and maintain "middle power" status at the UN. [35]

This idea is linked with the belief that neutrality does not have to mean impotence on the world stage. In 1946, while advocating in the *Dáil* that Ireland seek UN membership, Eamon de Valera emphasized this reality, not[ing] that declarations of neutrality are not enough. De Valera said, "Small nations have

---

[30]   *Ireland and the Partnership for Peace*, p. 7.

[31]   *Ibid*, p. 8.

[32]   Much has been written about the question of whether Ireland is a truly neutral state. Though Ireland has a policy of military neutrality and (the recent debate on PfP notwithstanding) has not thus far participated in military alliances, some commentators have raised the question of whether Ireland's western and European oriented voting record in the UN is consistent with claims of neutrality. Despite this dispute on the question of true neutrality in the international community, in the realm of peacekeeping, the Irish are widely accepted as neutral and impartial brokers in peacekeeping operations. For a detailed discussion of this issue, see Brefni Lynch, "Irish Neutrality and UN Peacekeeping," *An Cosantóir Review* 4 (1997), pp. 64–73.

[33]   Murphy, p. 23.

[34]   Larry Seaquist first coined this phrase at the Inter-University Seminar on Armed Forces and Society in Baltimore, MD, in October 1999.

[35]   Murphy, p. 28.

a particular reason for wishing to have security maintained by a combined or collective effort." [36] Following this logic, Ireland, notably through the UN, and now also through regional organizations like the European Union (EU) and the Organization for Security and Cooperation in Europe (OSCE), has consistently sought to play a proactive role in preventing and managing conflicts and keeping peace. [37]

A major evolution in UN peacekeeping has been taking place in light of the UN's reliance on regional security organizations to carry out missions on its behalf, and in light of the increased complexity of situations to which peacekeepers can be sent. Ireland has demonstrated its acceptance of the new UN approach to European regional peacekeeping through its participation, alongside many other non-members of NATO, in the Stabilization Force in Bosnia and Herzegovina (SFOR), established to maintain the peace agreement contained in the Dayton Accords of 1995. SFOR is mandated by the UN Security Council, but is conducted on the UN's behalf by NATO. [38]

2. INTERNAL MILITARY DIMENSION

2.1. IRISH INVOLVEMENT IN THE BALKANS

Early in the conflict in the former Yugoslavia, the Irish government took note of the human tragedy occurring there and volunteered forces and resources to aid in promoting peace in the region. The following statement by the Minister for Foreign Affairs, David Andrews, reflects to a great extent Irish popular opinion on this issue:

> If any warning is needed of what happens when conflict prevention activities are not effective, we need look no further than the Western Balkans. The 1990s will be remembered for the appalling carnage and atrocities which first took place in Croatia and Bosnia, and which are now being replicated in Kosovo. The overriding imperative is a moral one – a Europe which turns a blind eye to gross abuse of human rights is a Europe which allows the seeds of its own self-destruction to take root. [39]

Although this study will focus on the experiences of the MP company in Sarajevo working as part of SFOR, it should be noted that this is not Ireland's only contribution to building peace and working toward a settlement in this region.

---

[36] *Ireland and the Partnership for Peace*, p. 8.

[37] *Ibid*, p. 8. See also Department of Defense, *Defense Strategy Statements 1997–1999*, p. 8, and *Defense Strategy Statements 1998–2000*, pp. 10–12.

[38] *Ibid*, p. 6.

[39] *Statement on Partnership for Peace/Kosovo*, Mr. David Andrews, TD, Minister for Foreign Affairs, *Dáil Eireann*, 20 May 1999, p. 7.

The first UN mission there was established in March 1992 as the United Nations Protection Force in Yugoslavia (UNPROFOR), with Irish PDF officers
acting as observers, as well as *Garda* personnel. Since the demise of UNPRO-
FOR,[40] the Irish have contributed troops and police to the four replacement
missions:

- UN Preventive Deployment Force, Macedonia (UNPREDEP) in March
  1995;
- UN Mission in Bosnia and Herzegovina (UNMIBH) in December 1996;
- UN Transitional Administration for Eastern Slavonia, Baranja, and Western
  Sirmium (UNTAES) in January 1996; and
- UN Observer Group, Prevlaka (UNMOP) in January 1996.[41]

In 1996, Peter Fitzgerald, a member of the *Garda*, was appointed as the
assistant commissioner of the UN International Police Task Force. The UN
Civilian Police Support Group to Croatia was set up in March 1998, using
civilian police advisors, including Irish *Garda*,[42] to help the Croatian police
in the Danube region to monitor displaced persons.[43] Ireland has also contributed personnel and expertise to the United Nations Civil Police, the European Community Monitor Mission, the European Community Task Force
(Humanitarian), and the International Conference on the Former Yugoslavia (a
sanctions monitoring group, based in Serbia).[44] Many other Irish people are to
be found in this region on a secondment, leave of absence, or contract, working in a civilian capacity with all the above organizations and in a plethora of
humanitarian agencies.[45]

Irish military participation in the peacekeeping forces in Bosnia began in
May 1997, after the following motion passed the *Dáil*:

> I move that *Dáil Eireann* approves the dispatch ... of a contingent of the
> Permanent Defense Force for service with the UN-authorized Stabilization
> Force (SFOR) in Bosnia and Herzegovina, in accordance with UN Security
> Council Resolution 1088 of 12 December 1996, and that it further approves
> the terms of the exchange of letters on Ireland's financial responsibilities
> arising from participation in SFOR.[46]

---

[40] For a frank discussion of the performance of UNPROFOR by an Irish officer who served in
this mission as a military observer, see Comdt. Michael Beary, "UNPROFOR: Success or
Failure?" in *An Cosantóir Review* 4 (1997), pp. 4–21.

[41] These operations were followed by the UN Mission in Kosovo (UNMIK) in July 1999.

[42] "Smith Visits Sarajevo Troops," *Irish Times*, 11 August 1999, p. 2.

[43] Kearsley, "Blue Helmets," p. 393.

[44] An Irish officer, Colm Doyle (at the time a commandant), was head of the European Monitoring Mission for Bosnia-Herzegovina.

[45] O'Shea, "UNPROFOR," p. 32.

[46] *Statement by the Tánaiste and Minister for Foreign Affairs, Mr. Dick Spring, TD, on the Motion to Approve the Dispatch of a Contingent of the Permanent Defense Force to Participate*

2.2. COMPOSITION OF IRISH CONTINGENT

Following this motion, the Irish government approved sending an Irish contingent in the middle of May 1997. The first contingent arrived in Bosnia and Herzegovina on July 1st. "We left Ireland in a hurry," according to Cmdt. Jerry Cleary, Commander of the Irish Military Police (MP) Contingent. "On May 18th, our government approved our departure. People were selected and trained in 5 weeks. But we arrived here ready for work." [47]

All Irish peacekeepers are volunteers who have recently become eligible for additional incentive pay (approximately $15 per day) for participation in overseas missions. Units are formed from a pool of volunteers in the weeks prior to departure for a mission. In recent years, Irish military leaders have noted that it has become increasingly difficult to staff a mission, leading to speculation that one day the traditional "all volunteer" peacekeeping units will be filled out with soldiers and officers ordered to deploy on these missions. A number of women served with the Irish contingent in Sarajevo, as well. [48]

2.3. PRE-DEPLOYMENT TRAINING

Prior to their departure for their six-month rotations in Bosnia, all commanders, officers, and selected NCOs reported to the UN Training School Ireland (UNTSI), which is co-located with Ireland's military college. UNTSI has institutionalized a debriefing and "lessons learned" program, in which returning commanding officers (who are supposed to have debriefed their own people prior to arrival at UNTSI) discuss the salient issues of their deployment with UNTSI staff and faculty. The results of these debriefing sessions are incorporated into UNTSI's curriculum and passed on to future commanders, who report to UNTSI for training prior to their departure for their next mission. Topics covered in pre-deployment training include briefings on the area's political-military situation; dealing with the media; stress management; local cultural norms; basic words and phrases in the local language; and administrative and procedural issues germane to the given deployment. Normally, the officers and senior NCOs attending this "train the trainer" course are responsible for passing this information on to their troops.

Peacekeepers interviewed for this chapter reported that MPs selected for the Bosnia deployment were brought to the Irish MP school, co-located with UNTSI, for additional training with returning MPs who had served in the last

---

in SFOR in Bosnia and Herzegovina, Dáil Eireann, 14 May 1997.

[47] 2LT Lionel Hamnoun, "Irish Military Police in Ilizda," *SFOR Informer Online,* accessed August 1999, http://www.nato.int/sfor/nations/various/irish/irish.htm.

[48] An Irish military policewoman, Corporal Lorraine Coss, was the first Irish woman in the history of the army to be injured while on peacekeeping duties overseas. She received shrapnel wounds to the legs when a cache of grenades exploded at the base where she was on duty.

rotation to Bosnia. As is the usual practice, the MPs received instruction on lessons learned; the military situation on the ground; basics of the political landscape; and cultural "do's and don'ts."

2.4. THE IRISH IN A FOREIGN LANGUAGE ENVIRONMENT

The Irish benefit from the fact that almost all UN operations use English as their official language. The NATO-led operations in Bosnia also had English as the primary language, which proved to be quite useful to the Irish in their role as MPs for SFOR headquarters. As one peacekeeper related, tongue-in-cheek, "One good thing the Brits left after 800 years of occupation was the English language!" [49] As has been their practice on peacekeeping missions for decades, the Irish contingent hired professional interpreters for their work in Sarajevo. Irish officers have extensive experience working and negotiating through interpreters and are quite comfortable working with them. Although the Irish do not generally get training in foreign languages for peacekeeping deployments, they have, in critical instances when no other secure means were available, utilized "Connemara [50] boys" to relay messages in Irish over open lines. The Irish initially encountered some communications problems with the other platoons in the MP company but were able to work around them through cooperation with another contingent. [51]

2.5. NATO MEMBERS WORKING DIRECTLY WITH THE IRISH CONTINGENT

The military police company at SFOR headquarters was an international one, made up primarily of Irish (one platoon), Spanish (one platoon), and Italian (one platoon) MPs. The "fourth platoon" – an affectionate nickname of at least one former commander – is made up of civilian interpreters who speak the main languages in Bosnia and Herzegovina. There was a small investigative section, as well. Finally, a small multinational NATO composite platoon was assigned to support the company commander.

This is the first time, as far as the interviewed officers were aware, that a non-NATO country has been placed in command of NATO troops. Within the command group at the International MP company, however, the Irish commanding officer has three NATO positions: the deputy commander, the NCO-in-Charge (NCOIC) of the investigating unit, and the sergeant major. (As of this writing, the deputy commanders were from Germany and Italy, the NCOIC

---

[49]   He went on to make clear that he has had good experiences with the British military, saying, "We work well together. They're extremely helpful and competent whenever we work with them ... *off the island!*"

[50]   An Irish-speaking area on the west coast of Ireland.

[51]   See "Working with Other Contingents," below.

of the investigative unit was from the U.S., and the sergeant major was from the UK.)

Some serving in Sarajevo felt that, although an Irish officer was designated to be commander of the MP unit, NATO "kept an eye on us" with the three key NATO positions in the command group. The Irish had worked with U.S. observers in UNTSO, and the Irish were aware that NATO would be sending in assessment teams (for instance, KFOR sent an assessment team to Ireland before the Irish KFOR deployment); many in the Irish contingent saw these three NATO representatives as a mini-assessment team evaluating Ireland's capabilities for these (and perhaps future) operations.

2.6. MISSION AT SFOR HEADQUARTERS

In many ways, the duties of the MP company at SFOR headquarters were similar to those of any other peacekeeping operation. The Irish contingent was responsible for performing a wide variety of police tasks, including ensuring the security of SFOR headquarters; maintenance of discipline among SFOR troops; conducting speed controls; investigation of accidents involving SFOR vehicles and criminal incidents involving SFOR members; enforcing curfews; and manning checkpoints. These tasks are consistent with the experiences of Irish contingents in classical peacekeeping missions, as well, which have often consisted of self-reliant teams at the lower levels, performing duties such as manning checkpoints and outposts. [52]

2.7. IRISH "COPS ON THE BEAT?" WHY THE IRISH MAKE GOOD PEACEKEEPERS

How or why have Irish soldiers been so successful at conflict resolution and peacekeeping duties in general? A number of factors contribute to this phenomenon. While the Defense Forces are organized and trained to fulfill their stated primary role of defense of the state against aggression, their most important function evolved to that of providing military assistance to the civil power. In the 1970s, internal security tasks expanded, due primarily to the conflict in Northern Ireland; "Aid to the Civil Power" became the major operational task of the Defense Forces. In this way, much of the daily work of the army over the past 30 years has in fact been the performance of duties of a police nature. In this role, the Irish military (among other tasks) mans checkpoints, assists in transportation of large amounts of cash or weapons, and performs cordon and search missions. Experience in this role is one of the reasons why Irish troops have adapted so successfully to a UN peacekeeping role, where the duties per-

---

[52] Oliver A. K. Macdonald, "Peacekeeping Lessons Learned: An Irish Perspective," *International Peacekeeping* 5, No. 1 (Spring 1998), p. 44.

formed up to recently have also, for the most part, been similar to those of a robust police force.

Ray Murphy, a former infantry officer and peacekeeper, suggests that Morris Janowitz's characterization of the "constabulary concept" [53] for the use of conventional military forces in peacekeeping operations was probably an unfortunate choice of words, as it conjures up an image of "an unarmed English bobby keeping the peace along his beat," hardly a description that the "warriors" in many of today's armies would wish to have applied to themselves. At the same time, however, this definition does have several elements that do indeed describe traditional peacekeeping operations, including the constant readiness to act, the commitment to minimum use of force, and the search for successful relations rather than military victory. Janowitz recognized the dilemma, which troubles military attitudes toward peacekeeping operations even today, wherein the military would look upon such "police-type" work as less important and prestigious than traditional military operations. While this may be true in large military forces, this view does not appear to be widely shared within the Irish Defense Forces. [54]

The mission of the Irish contingent in Bosnia was consistent with this characterization of peacekeeping operations as being of a police nature. It is important to note, however, that none of the Irish peacekeepers interviewed and the written sources reviewed for this chapter mentioned discontent with this role; rather, the evidence shows that those who served in the MP company at the headquarters in Sarajevo generally found this mission to be similar in many respects to others on which they had served, albeit a bit more dull, given all of the additional rules, regulations, and restrictions imposed under NATO leadership.

Interviews with current and former peacekeepers consistently make mention of some or even all of the four main characteristics listed by Murphy that render a military force (in this case, the Irish Defense Force) suitable for UN peacekeeping missions:

- An emphasis on a high degree of adaptability in the military sector, including an ability to operate independently of large-scale supporting forces;
- A major emphasis on the differentiation of skills and the development of initiative in professional training;
- A distinctly non-political role;
- A high degree of discipline combined with a democratic professional structure. [55]

---

[53] Morris Janowitz, *The Professional Soldier* (New York: Free Press, 1960).

[54] Ray Murphy, "Ireland, the United Nations, and Peacekeeping Operations," p. 44.

[55] Murphy cites the work of John A. Jackson, "The Irish Army and the Development of the Constabulary Concept," in Jacques Van Doorn (Ed.), *Armed Forces and Society: Sociologi-*

The Irish Defense Forces clearly satisfy all of these requirements. The first two bullets could be said to be characteristics applicable to any viable small military force. The third bullet also is germane to the Irish case, where the army is, constitutionally and by tradition, prohibited from any involvement in politics. (Indeed, since the end of the Irish Civil War and the establishment of the modern Irish state, no suggestion of partiality on the part of the army has ever been made by any Deputy in the course of Defense and other debates. [56]) The internationally acknowledged success of Irish peacekeepers in peacekeeping operations is evidence of a high level of discipline and professionalism. Finally, the Irish army is well integrated into Irish society, living not on isolated military bases or in military enclaves but rather in homes and apartments alongside their civilian counterparts. The Irish soldier is, like his post-war German counterpart, truly a "citizen in uniform:" Irish servicemembers are drawn from all segments of society and remain part of civil society, thus ensuring that their ties with the rest of Ireland are strong and well-rooted. [57]

2.8. RULES OF ENGAGEMENT

When discussing the rules of engagement (ROE) for the MP company, one must bear in mind that this unit looked inward; its mission was to provide internal security and ensure law and order within SFOR. Although there was very little contact with the local population, the ROE were clear; according to one of the officers interviewed, the ROE used in Sarajevo were almost the same as the ROE the Defense Forces use at home. When working in their "Aid to the Civil Power" role, the Irish military must remember two concerns while accomplishing the mission: respect for and protection of the civilian population's civil and human rights, and force protection in a civilian environment. Both peacekeeping operations and anti-IRA work are sometimes risky non-traditional military environments, but the Irish army has extensive experience with both. In Bosnia, for instance, use of deadly force is a last resort, but the MPs are allowed to use sufficient force to accomplish the mission.

2.9. VALUE OF THE MISSION TO MILITARY AND COUNTRY

Although Ireland has grown in international stature, the PDF has been one of the greatest beneficiaries of this international appreciation. To quote Duggan's history of the Irish military, "There was a time when Irish troops might have envied Imperial [British] soldiers their chance of foreign travel; not anymore. Empires have withered away, leaving in their wake a growing peacekeeping

---

cal Essays (The Hague and Paris: Mouton, 1968).
[56] *Ibid,* p. 34.
[57] *Ibid,* pp. 33 – 34.

requirement." [58] Peacekeeping duty is highly valued in the Irish army. It is important for promotion. All applicants are carefully screened prior to assignment to peacekeeping missions, and a clean record is essential for selection. A report for the Irish Minister for Defense states:

> Service on a UN mission is now almost a rite of passage. A soldier is not deemed to have soldiered unless he/she has done so. For this and other reasons, it is perhaps true to say that the culture of the Irish Defense Forces today is a culture of peacekeeping. [59]

In addition to the international goodwill that participation in peacekeeping has generated, and as an added benefit of working to alleviate suffering worldwide, peacekeeping missions have provided an important training and development opportunity for the Defense Forces. [60] A recent analysis of the strengths and weaknesses of the Defense Forces attributes the success of the army in peacekeeping missions to a widespread "can do" attitude of Irish military personnel at all levels, and "the extent to which conventional military skills have been retained within a system, notwithstanding the many barriers preventing implementation of an optimum training program." [61]

Particularly since Ireland joined the Partnership for Peace (PfP) in December 1999, service with NATO forces has become an advantage for promotion, and is seen as advantageous to the army as a whole. Of course, peacekeeping operations anywhere in the world have long been seen as beneficial to the training and readiness of the Irish forces. Whether serving in SFOR in Bosnia or on any other peacekeeping operation, the advantages of participation in such a mission, which accrue to Ireland's army as a whole, include the facts that:

- Peacekeeping experience reinforces training for missions also performed at home.
- Troops are given operational experience with equipment and foreign forces that the PDF would not otherwise encounter.
- Leadership skills and professionalism have been improved.
- Peacekeeping operations have given Irish soldiers battlefield experience. [62]

---

[58] Kearsley, "Blue Helmets," p. 394, citing Duggan, *History of the Irish Army*, p. 272.

[59] *Ibid*, pp. 394–395. See also *The Irish Defense Forces: Peacekeepers and Custodians of Peace*, (Dublin: Irish Defense Forces Headquarters, 1993).

[60] *Defense Strategy Statements 1998–2000*, pp. 12–13.

[61] Ray Murphy, "Ireland, the United Nations, and Peacekeeping Operations," pp. 32–33. Murphy goes on to point out that "... the difficulty with the 'can-do' work ethos is that in the long run it can be counter-productive if it perpetuates the illusion that all is well, when this in fact is not the case." See also *Defense Forces Strategy Statements, 1997–1999* (Dublin: Department of Defense, 1997), p. 8.

[62] Kearsley, "Blue Helmets," p. 394.

The 1998–2000 *Defense Mission Statement* evaluates the strengths and weaknesses of the Defense Forces, as well as the opportunities and threats they face. The first bullet listed under "External Threats" clearly shows the importance of peacekeeping to the Irish defense establishment: "Competition from other better equipped and trained armed forces in the provision of modern peace-support forces." [63] Three of the seven weaknesses listed in this evaluation clearly underline the importance of peacekeeping as a mission to the Irish. They are:

- Personnel – operational units are seriously under-strength;
- Equipment & Infrastructure – inadequate expenditure on equipment and infrastructure; [64] and
- Training – insufficient dedicated collective conventional military training. [65]

The presence of such clearly stated concerns over maintaining the country's capabilities in peacekeeping operations in the *Defense Mission Statement* reflects the importance of the mission to military decision-makers.

3. MILITARY TO MILITARY DIMENSION

3.1. A MILITARILY-NEUTRAL, NON-ALIGNED STATE IN A NATO-LED OPERATION

Virtually since their founding, the Defense Forces have closely followed the development of the military doctrine of the Western allied military forces; thus, the current doctrine of the Defense Forces is very close to those of the military forces of the Euro-Atlantic powers. "Since the inception of NATO, the Defense Forces have sent personnel on training programs and maintained a military doctrine that reflects NATO's." [66] Arms and ammunition purchases for infantry rifles are all interoperable with NATO equipment. [67] Without exception, those interviewed for this chapter were positive about the Irish experience of working with NATO and for the most part believed that the mission was successful.

---

[63] *Department of Defense and the Defense Forces Strategy Statements: 1998–2000*, p. 33.

[64] The need for improved equipment and infrastructure comes up frequently in recent writings. See, for example, in the same document under "The Defense Forces Environment," where it states (p. 31) "The Stabilization Force in the former Yugoslavia (SFOR) is an example of this new approach – the mandate is undertaken on the UN's behalf by NATO, which demands high operational and equipment standards." New initiatives are designed to address these shortfalls.

[65] Interviews with Irish peacekeepers have consistently brought up the need to enhance combat skills within the PDF, should the current trend away from traditional peacekeeping and toward peace enforcement operations continue.

[66] See Jim Cusack, "Irish Forces Facing up to Changed Role," *The Irish Times* (City Edition), p. 11.

[67] *Ibid.*

Although a few officers remarked upon a perception of being observed and evaluated by their NATO colleagues, no one expressed irritation about this (although one officer wryly observed that NATO was new to peacekeeping, not the Irish).

One high-profile exception to this generally positive attitude was published in a recent editorial in the *Irish Times,* in which a prominent retired general complained about the problems that Ireland encountered working with NATO forces in the following manner:

> Operating as we are in Bosnia under NATO command, our non-membership of PfP also places us at a serious and potentially dangerous disadvantage. Detailed intelligence is restricted to NATO members, but a less-classified level of intelligence is available to PfP members adequate to their requirements. This arrangement covers all the nations that make up the force except Ireland. This lack of proper intelligence could prove life-threatening to our soldiers. [68]

This assessment, however, does not find much resonance with those interviewed and with the rest of the literature reviewed. Although it is going too far to say that the general was deliberately overstating the case or perhaps trying to campaign in favor of the controversial question of Irish involvement in PfP, it is true to say that most of the evidence points to Irish versatility and resourcefulness at getting around such problems. Overall, it appears that the Irish contingent worked well with their NATO partners in Sarajevo and those interviewed didn't share this view. For example, several of the Irish peacekeepers interviewed on this topic praised their NATO colleagues for "watching out for" them and their interests whenever there was sensitive NATO-only information that could affect anything within the Irish contingent's AOR.

3.2. DOCTRINE, EQUIPPING, NATO EXPERIENCE

Virtually since their founding, the Defense Forces have closely followed the development of the military doctrine of the Western allied military forces. There has long been keen interest in and awareness of the potential importance of being able to work with NATO, and the Irish military has kept this in mind when making decisions about their own armed forces. Thus, the current doctrine of the Defense Forces is very close to those of the military forces of the Euro-Atlantic powers. Moreover, since the inception of NATO, the Defense Forces have not only sent personnel on training programs and maintained a military doctrine that reflects NATO's, but have also ensured that arms and

---

[68]   Lt. General Gerry McMahon (former Chief of Staff of the Irish Defense Forces), "Campaign Against PfP Full of Misinformation," *Irish Times,* 12 May 1999, "Opinion" section.

ammunition purchases for infantry rifles were all interoperable with NATO equipment. [69]

3.3. WORKING WITH OTHER CONTINGENTS

There were no significant difficulties mentioned when asked about relationships between the Irish contingent and other units within SFOR. At the time of this writing, only one Irish officer was serving on the SFOR international staff: a lieutenant colonel who was serving in a protocol position. When asked whether the Irish encountered any problems or felt any resentment over what the Dutch termed "Star Wars games" [70] at SFOR headquarters, one former Irish peacekeeper who had served in Bosnia commented:

> Certain nationalities make decisions for 30 other countries. I am not complaining, as the military is not a committee and someone must take decisions, but I can see why certain contingents have complaints about this situation. For the most part, it wasn't really a problem for us.

One officer did relay, with a combination of amusement and irritation, that he had once arranged to meet with an American officer at a local restaurant to discuss an upcoming project. He was quite surprised when the American arrived, "armed to the teeth," in the company of three other American soldiers similarly outfitted. At the same time, however, he did say that he realized that U.S. officers were under orders to put force protection first, and that the risks to American forces could be higher than the risks to forces from other countries. Nevertheless, he said he would never again make such a suggestion to an American peacekeeper.

3.4. PERCEPTIONS OF RELATIVE DEPRIVATION

The following statement from an interview with an Irish officer pretty much summarizes the outlook of the Irish in Bosnia toward their experiences working with the other contingents:

> We don't have the resources the U.S. can offer their soldiers and officers. We sometimes envy the Americans' wealth and equipment, but we make do the best we can, and when we get the resources we need, we can do the job even better.

Although there is an awareness of relative deprivation when compared with some other Western contingents (as seen above, interviews have revealed some evidence that there is a perception that the "rich Americans" often have better equipment and living conditions), and there were times, especially at the

---

[69]   Jim Cusack, "Irish Forces Facing up to Changed Role," *The Irish Times* (City Edition), p. 11.
[70]   See chapter on the Netherlands in this volume.

beginning of the deployment, when the Irish contingent was definitely lacking in creature comforts (for instance, they initially lived in the ice stadium!), it appeared in general that there was no real resentment of such differences.

The Irish who served in Bosnia seemed very optimistic, cheerful, and well-inclined toward those they worked with (primarily the Americans with whom they, for instance, shared a mess hall, and the Spanish and Italians within their platoon), and they made the best of even the most inconvenient situations. For instance, when discussing the living conditions at the ice stadium, more than one peacekeeper told me, "We all had same bad conditions for sleeping, washing, etc. But in summertime, it was not so awful." Upon arrival, they were still de-mining the Butmir (former MiG fighter base). There was not always hot water. But the work was done, and a "can do" attitude appears to have prevailed.

Like the peacekeepers from some of the former Warsaw Pact states discussed in other chapters in this volume, the Irish appear to be proud of their ability to overcome adversity and to adapt to difficult circumstances, even when under-resourced or lacking in necessary equipment or provisions. For example, although the officers in the Italian and Spanish platoons of the MP company generally spoke English, most of the enlisted troops did not. The Irish did not, for the most part, speak Spanish or Italian, either. In an effort to avoid communications problems with their Spanish and Italian counterparts in the MP company, the Irish worked out an informal arrangement with the U.S. contingent, in which the Americans provided the assistance of bilingual Italian-Americans and Hispanic-Americans, who worked as unofficial interpreters. Although these young soldiers were of course not professional interpreters, the cooperation between the different contingents improved the ability of the MP company to successfully perform their mission.

4. MILITARY RELATIONS WITH NGOS, THE MEDIA, AND THE LOCAL POPULATION

4.1. NGOS

A former peacekeeper and commandant of the UN Training School Ireland, Colonel Oliver MacDonald, writing about changes in peacekeeping over the last four decades, had this to say about the relationships between the military and NGOs in the 1990s:

> Peacekeeping operations have for many years included a humanitarian dimension. Now, humanitarian operations have assumed a military operation. This has led to confusion between peacekeeping and humanitarian operations, with fairly dire consequences in terms of expectations of results

from missions, and to uncomfortable overlapping of areas of authority and responsibility. [71]

Though there are many reasons that the cultures of these two very different sorts of organizations may clash, the military must learn to deal with increasing numbers of humanitarian missions and the NGOs which are key to the success of any such mission. Ireland has tried to promote synergistic and symbiotic relationships between the Irish military and NGOs, which often are the very agencies who have the money, experience, expertise, and commitment required to help a region move beyond peacekeeping into peace building and post-conflict reconstruction and reconciliation. The Irish military has a policy of permitting its members secondments to work within NGOs in an effort for both sides to aid the other and to familiarize themselves with one another's professional ethos, practices, and environmental culture. The Irish military has successfully seconded representatives to Irish charities as well as international organizations like *Médecins Sans Frontières*/Doctors Without Borders. The Irish military has also reached out to NGOs through UNTSI, which has run training seminars for aid agencies working with the military overseas.

4.2. MEDIA RELATIONS

The Irish military also realizes that relations with the media can be problematic for armed forces. Therefore, prior to departure to Bosnia, the MP company received training on dealing with the media. The Irish military's approach is cautious but not adversarial. Senior staff officers receive at least a full day's training, but every Irish soldier is trained in the basics: nothing is ever "off the record," for example. Even a private who is the senior man at a checkpoint may make a factual comment to the press, but is expressly not permitted to speculate or express opinions.

UNTSI also runs training courses for media representatives destined for service in Bosnia. In this operation, mine awareness training was considered especially important and was thus a focus of training efforts.

4.3. DEALINGS WITH LOCAL GOVERNMENT

The Irish contingent primarily had contact with those inside of and working with SFOR headquarters in Sarajevo. Because of the nature of this mission, the bulk of their concerns and dealings were usually with other peacekeepers, and not with the local government or international organizations. Nevertheless, the MPs did encounter a few instances where their ability to negotiate (through their locally hired interpreters) ensured that large-scale social events that could have ended in disaster came off without a hitch. The Irish were pleased with

---

[71] Macdonald, "Peacekeeping Lessons Learned."

several examples of successful cooperation with the local authorities, which allowed a number of high-profile public events to proceed. In August 1997, for example, Denmark played against Bosnia in the World Cup Tournament in Bosnia. Danish soldiers wanted to go to the match, and their commander gave them permission to attend as long as SFOR police would accompany them. The MP company worked with the local authorities to do all they could to ensure the safety of the (unarmed) Danish soldiers. Though the Danes lost in a surprise upset, from an SFOR security point of view, the event was a successful demonstration of good local civilian–SFOR relations.

A related success story was the U2 rock concert held shortly thereafter, which was attended by 5,000 SFOR troops. The MP company, in cooperation with the local police and the U2 organizers, provided security within Sarajevo for the concert. This was the first large-scale mixing of SFOR troops with Serbs, Croats, and Muslims, as well as the first large-scale cultural event shared by all three ethnic groups since the onset of hostilities. Because of careful advance planning and cooperation with the local authorities, more than 50,000 people from all of the formerly warring factions gathered in a stadium, along with many SFOR peacekeepers, to hear the first major rock group to play in the capital since the war ended in 1995. The concert was considered a success from a security standpoint.

4.4. CONTINGENCY PLANNING PAYS OFF

The Irish MP unit also conducted extensive contingency planning and training. One of the MP officers interviewed gave the following example:

> We had a tense situation outside Butmir camp (which is on the line be-
> tween the Federation and the Republika Srpska). SFOR had closed down
> local radio transmitters in September-October 1997 to stop anti-SFOR pro-
> paganda. In response, the Serbs blocked the road to the Butmir base on
> the same Saturday that the 20-kilometer SFOR "Viking Run" (sponsored
> by the Norwegians) was scheduled. In fact, the Serbs had already begun
> blocking access to the base after the run was already in progress, and sol-
> diers and officers from all over SFOR had already begun the Viking Run.
> The Irish were tasked with providing traffic control for this activity. Unfor-
> tunately, the Serbs blocked the roads and stopped buses and other SFOR
> vehicles after the run had commenced, without any prior warning. Most of
> the headquarters staff were on the run when news came in that the Serbs
> had begun this operation, with about half of the group on each side of
> the line. At one point early in the day, about 20% of the runners were
> not accounted for. Fortunately, the MPs were able to implement Operation
> CLAMPDOWN, which had already been planned and exercised in case
> such a situation would ever arise. The MPs put in checkpoints, rerouted

traffic, and were able to negotiate the release of buses full of troops that the Serbs had detained.

According to those interviewed, extensive peacekeeping experience around the world often helps the Irish to anticipate and train for this sort of (normally unexpected) problem.

4.5. YOUTH OUTREACH

An innovative example of promoting positive relations with local populations can be seen in a popular sports-based initiative of the Irish contingent. In October 1998, Comdt. Johnny Molloy, who used to coach the Irish army rugby team, spotted a number of young men playing rugby in a field outside Zenica, where he was stationed with the European Community Monitoring Mission. Molloy discovered that there were five clubs in the town, composed mainly of Muslims, but also containing Croats and a small number of Serbs. Molloy, who a year later was still coaching the team from his new base in Sarajevo, found that the multi-ethnic teams had virtually no equipment and played on rented soccer pitches. As he believed that this sport would help minimize tensions in the area and promote goodwill between the opposing parties, he began coaching the teams, in cooperation with other Irish monitors and soldiers serving as military police with the multinational UN peacekeeping forces stationed in the area. At the same time, he also applied to Irish Army Headquarters for help, explaining that rugby was one of the few activities in the region that was entirely non-sectarian and brought different ethnic groups together in an – almost – entirely peaceful way. In response to his request for aid, the Irish army provided the team with training equipment, including tackle and rucking bags, balls, cones, and training bibs just before Christmas of 1998. [72]

5. CONCLUSION

The Republic of Ireland, despite its small size, limited military power, and history of neutrality, has played a disproportionately influential role in UN peace missions for more than 40 years. The Irish people are justifiably proud of the sacrifices and contributions made by the men and women who serve in their Defense Forces. Ireland has continued this tradition in the Balkans, from the first days of UN involvement in the region (with the European Community Monitoring Mission) to the deployment of Irish troops to Kosovo. Although the military culture and national security interests of Ireland (and several of the other traditionally neutral European countries) differ from those of many of the

---

[72] Jim Cusack, "Irish Troops Use Rugby as an Improbable Peacekeeping Tool in Bosnia," *Irish Times*, 19 March 1999, p. 8.

other larger countries studied in this volume, the newcomers to peacekeeping (including the U.S. and Russia) may have lessons to learn from Ireland and her fellow traditional peacekeepers.

Ireland, the old hand at peacekeeping, finds itself facing new choices, as well, as we enter a new era in peace operations. The recent somewhat acrimonious debates over Irish membership in PfP and the draft White Paper (finalized in February 2000) reveal an evolution in the understanding of Irish neutrality on the part of both the military and society, as well as a growing awareness among the public about the potentially more robust sort of peace operations that Ireland may face in the future.

Although these recent events have received a fair amount of attention, Ireland had in fact already begun, several years earlier, to take steps to adjust the legal basis of Irish participation in peacekeeping operations. These legal changes were necessary to give the Irish military the ability to adapt to the changing reality of peace operations after the end of the Cold War. The impetus for these changes was the most controversial Irish troop contribution since the Congo: the second UN operation in Somalia, UNOSOM II, which began in 1993. UNOSOM II required the Irish government to rethink parts of the Republic's Constitution, as this was not a traditional peacekeeping mission. Irish legislators, when considering participation in UNOSOM II, were forced to face the question of whether the country would – for the first time – send its soldiers to participate in a peace enforcement operation. Even though in the end no constitutional amendment was necessary, the unusual nature of this mission, and the changing role of UN peacekeeping, heightened debate within Ireland concerning the Republic's future role in peace operations. As a result of this issue, the Defense Act was amended in 1993, eliminating the phrase "for the performance of duties of a police character," thereby making peace enforcement and participation in UNOSOM II possible. [73] An Irish transport platoon of 80 soldiers and 30 vehicles was sent to Somalia to provide logistical support to UN combat troops already stationed there. All 80 soldiers had prior UN service and were volunteers. This deployment broke a long-standing post-Congo tradition that the Irish armed forces did not participate in active peace enforcement operations.

---

[73] Kearsley, "Blue Helmets," pp. 393, 395. See also Ray Murphy, "Ireland: Legal Issues Arising from Participation in United Nations Operations," *International Peacekeeping* (Kluwer) 1, No. 2 (March-May 1994): 61 – 64. The Defense (Amendment) Act of 1993 amended and extended the Defense (Amendment) Act of 1960 in significant respects. Section I defines an "International United Nations Force" as an international force or body established by the Security Council or General Assembly; this goes beyond the definition which limited participation to peacekeeping or police-type forces. See also Ray Murphy, "Ireland, the UN, and Peacekeeping Operations," p. 30.

Nothing is certain about the future of peace operations. If political support remains to continue them, however, there are decisions to be made on both sides. As some in Ireland start to contemplate moving away from the country's traditional neutrality following the signing of the Maastricht Treaty, additional demands may be made on the Defense Forces within a common European defense arrangement. [74] The Irish military, at least, seems interested in playing a more active role in formulating and participating in activities related to the EU's Common Foreign and Security Policy as well as the European Security and Defense Policy, and being able to contribute to the Petersberg Tasks. There is also increasing interest in taking part in the sort of coalition military operations that membership in PfP will allow.

The Irish experience in working with NATO thus far appears to have been good. This cooperative relationship, which has the additional benefits of mutual comprehensibility due to the shared English language and Ireland's training, doctrine, and weapons/equipment interoperability, will most likely grow even better as time passes.

Other countries could take a page or two from the Irish book, as well. The Irish, with their experience in "Aid to the Civil Power" missions as well as decades of peacekeeping experience, are in an ideal position to train others about peacekeeping. Their methods of pre-deployment training and troop selection, their cooperative and synergistic relations with NGOs, and their highly developed "lessons learned" system – which is used to facilitate troop rotations in and out of mission areas and incorporated into training at the UN Training School in the Curragh – should serve as examples to be emulated by newcomers to peace operations. Though the situations that call for peacekeeping forces are never happy ones, the future certainly seems to promise that Ireland will continue to play a leading role as a model troop-donating country in future UN peace operations of all stripes.

---

[74] "Ireland: Armed Forces Overview," in Charles Heyman (Ed.), *Jane's World Armies* (Coulsdon, Surrey: Jane's Information Group, 1998).

6. Dutch Experiences with International Military Operations in Bosnia-Herzegovina

Hans BORN, Tessa OP DEN BUIJS, and Ad VOGELAAR [1]

---

[1] We would like to thank Erik-Hans Kramer and Nancy Peters (both of the Royal Military Academy) for their contribution to the fieldwork for this research project. We also thank Marina Caparini (King's College, London), Jean Callaghan (George C. Marshall European Center for Security Studies), and Pieter van Nispen tot Pannerden (WHA Consulting Firm) for their comments.

1. Introduction

1.1. The Netherlands and Peace Missions: From Korea to SFOR

The Royal Netherlands Army has a long tradition of participating in peace missions. Since the founding of the United Nations, the Netherlands has always supported the UN in its peacekeeping policy. However, until the 1970s, the UN Secretariat usually refused the offers of the Dutch government to provide large-scale military assistance in major UN peace operations. The UN Secretariat never explained this refusal. We can only guess, but it is likely that the role of the Netherlands in the de-colonization process in the former Dutch colonies (the Dutch Indies and New Guinea) played a role. Perhaps the Netherlands was also regarded as too loyal a member of NATO, and therefore it was believed that it could not play a neutral role in peacekeeping operations. [2] Hence, until the end of the 1970s, the Netherlands played only a minor role in smaller UN peace operations. The only exception to this general picture was the Netherlands' contribution to the UN force in Korea at the beginning of the 1950s.

This non-participation changed in 1979 when the UN Secretariat asked the Netherlands to participate in a UN peace mission in Lebanon. From 1979 until 1985, 8,000 peacekeepers from the Netherlands were on duty in Lebanon. This was a troublesome mission, especially in the beginning, because of the Netherlands' lack of experience in dealing with peace missions. Manning the battalion was another problem, predominantly due to the fact that the government filled the battalion with professional officers and NCOs as well as conscripts, who had explicitly volunteered for the UN peace mission in Lebanon. At that time, military personnel could not be sent on peace missions against their will.

The fall of the Berlin Wall changed the role of the Dutch armed forces in international peace missions. Since 1989, the armed forces have been involved in 30 peace operations, disaster relief operations, and humanitarian aid operations. This is twice the total number of peace operations that the Netherlands had been involved in during the years of the Cold War. As of this writing, approximately 3,000–4,000 Dutch military personnel are serving abroad in international operations, mainly in the Balkans. [3] In this article, we focus mainly on 1 Netherlands (NL) Mechanized Battalion (MECHBAT), which is the contribution of the Netherlands, first to IFOR and subsequently to SFOR. 1

---

[2] Chris Klep, "Peacekeepers in a Warlike Situation: the Dutch Experience," in Erwin Schmidl (Ed.), *Peace Operations between Peace and War: Four Studies* (Vienna: Landesverteidigungsakademie/Militärwissenschaftliches Büro, 1998).

[3] *Framework Memorandum for the 2000 Defense White Paper* (Den Haag: Ministry of Defense, 1999), p. 4.

(NL) MECHBAT operates under British command in the Multinational Division Southwest in the Southwest sector. In this multinational division, Turkish, British, German, Bulgarian, and Dutch military units worked together. The Bulgarian military engineering unit fell under the command of 1 (NL) MECH-BAT. The area of operations of the Multinational Division Southwest contains the entire western part of Bosnia-Herzegovina. [4]

1.2. THE NETHERLANDS' CONTRIBUTION TO IFOR AND SFOR

At the end of 1995, the warring parties in Bosnia signed the Dayton Accords. The Dayton Accords established two autonomous regions within Bosnia: the Republika Srpska for the Bosnian Serbs in the northern part and a Muslim-Croatian Federation in the southern part. Furthermore, the agreement called for a phased withdrawal of military forces to their barracks, dissolution of the armed forces, the setting up of elections, as well as the return of refugees to their homes. The agreement also authorized NATO forces to enforce the implementation of this agreement through its Implementation Force (IFOR).

The Netherlands contributed an armored battalion and a logistics battalion, both under English command, to IFOR. The armored battalion was deployed to enforce the agreement between the parties. The operation, with its enforcing mission, was quite risky for this armored battalion, because anything could happen: for example, the former warring parties could comply with the agreement, they could continue fighting each other as they had before, or they could try to prevent IFOR from performing its tasks. Therefore, the battalion had to be prepared for many possible scenarios. The logistics battalion was already deployed in Bosnia, so they had to continue driving their convoys. When peace returned to Bosnia, the logistics battalion was reduced to one company under the command of the armored battalion.

The armored battalion was divided into three teams of equal components (infantry, cavalry, military engineers, medical units, etc.) of about 200 soldiers each. One team was located in the Republika Srpska; the other two teams were in the Muslim-Croatian Federation. The battalion staff and many support units were based at a central location between the team areas.

At the end of 1996, IFOR was replaced by a somewhat smaller Stabilization Force (SFOR). The former warring factions had withdrawn to their barracks, peace had returned to Bosnia, and normal life had resumed to a certain extent, but the refugees had only started to return to their homes. Furthermore, it was felt that if NATO were to leave Bosnia, the fighting would start again within months. Therefore, a military force – SFOR – had to stay in Bosnia.

---

[4]   *Informatiebundel crisisbeheersingsoperaties* (Information on crisis management operations) (Den Haag: Operational Staff of the Commander in Chief of the Army, 1998).

The Dutch contributed an armored battalion to SFOR. The area for which the Dutch battalion is responsible has been divided into two parts, each covered by one team: one in the Muslim-Croatian Federation and one in the Republika Srpska.

The situation for SFOR is different from that of IFOR. Because of the relative peace in the area, the mission of SFOR changed from a purely military mission into a more or less police mission. The teams had to patrol the area, gather information about possible hostilities between the parties, and monitor elections as well as the return of refugees to their homes. Further, they had to inspect sites in which the weapons and ammunition of the former warring factions had been stored and check military movements in the area. Moreover, they had to support all kinds of activities to restore roads, public buildings, and the infrastructure of the area. Although the situation was mainly peaceful, it sometimes changed suddenly and became very tense, for example, when war criminals were arrested by SFOR, when SFOR was involved in an accident, or when SFOR noticed that one of the former warring parties did not adhere to the agreement. The situation also became tense when refugees, thinking they would be supported by SFOR soldiers, tried to provoke the other party. The possibility of such abrupt changes in the situation meant that SFOR soldiers had to "walk on eggshells."

1.3. RESEARCH QUESTIONS AND METHODS

In this section, we will briefly outline the experiences of Dutch soldiers in their encounters with:

- Other Dutch military units within 1 (NL) MECHBAT, i.e., internal military relations;
- Military contingents of other countries, i.e., external military relations;
- Local authorities and the former warring factions;
- The local population, i.e., the Croats, the Muslims, and the Serbs.

We are especially interested in points of tension experienced in these encounters and relations, i.e., the frictions and problems that arose when people from different cultures and backgrounds had to work together. By and large, we limit ourselves to the operational units, i.e., the infantry, cavalry, and military engineer units. Our time scope is from the beginning of IFOR in January 1996 until June 1999.

In addressing our research questions, we used two different sources of information. First, we analyzed the transcripts of 25 interviews we held with military personnel belonging to IFOR and SFOR. Second, we analyzed 13 journals that contained articles on Dutch participation in IFOR and SFOR. These articles were written mainly by military personnel who were stationed on the territory of the successor states to the Yugoslav Federation. In total, we analyzed approximately 150 articles published between 1995 – 1999.

2. INTERNAL MILITARY DIMENSION

In this section, we describe a number of tensions that occurred within the Dutch contingents of IFOR and SFOR. We begin by describing the tension that existed between the mission and reality in Bosnia, as perceived by the Dutch soldiers. We go on to describe tensions in vertical relations, i.e., tensions between the higher and lower command levels within 1 (NL) MECHBAT. Finally, we discuss the tensions that arose in horizontal relations among the different military units, such as the cavalry, infantry, and military engineers.

2.1. DIFFERING PERCEPTIONS OF THE USEFULNESS OF THE MISSION

NATO and its political and military leaders considered IFOR to be a very important mission. After the fiasco of UNPROFOR, NATO was given the responsibility of implementing peace in Bosnia. Where UNPROFOR failed, IFOR succeeded. The parties demilitarized according to schedule. Although it was clear to everyone that IFOR was successful, after some time, however, a number of doubts arose. Soldiers, in particular, were very ambivalent about the mission. On the one hand, they argued that it was very important for SFOR to be there, to ensure safety and security in the area, to allow the refugees to return to their homes, and to facilitate the resumption of normal life. On the other hand, soldiers realized that when they left, people would begin to fight each other again. Following this argumentation, the situation seemed hopeless. Therefore, differences in soldiers' attitudes about IFOR were directly related to which of the two realities the individual soldier stressed.

Another aspect of the perceived usefulness of the mission concerns the usefulness of tasks that had to be performed. On the one hand, soldiers had the feeling that they had to be in the area to guarantee the safety of the local population. For example, SFOR troops were to demonstrate their presence in the area by means of patrols, but only a few patrols a day, because otherwise the population might think that something was wrong. On the other hand, it was often very difficult to determine what to do; therefore many questions arose among the soldiers. Frequently asked questions included:

- Should the unit gather as much information as possible?
- What type of information should be gathered?
- What does it contribute to the progress in the area?
- Is the performance of the missions worth risking the safety of the soldiers?

- What exactly should SFOR do in the area besides keeping themselves busy and maintaining good relationships with the local population and the former warring factions?

2.2. TENSIONS OVER THE AUTONOMY OF SUB-COMMANDERS

In peace support missions, small units operate far from base, many times in remote locations. Therefore, lower-level commanders must be able to solve many problems on their own. Team commanders are responsible for the operations in their relatively large areas. Platoon and group commanders are responsible for the patrols that they lead. These sub-commanders may be confronted with all kinds of problems, which are completely new, not only for them, but also for their commanders.

Problems may arise from at least four sources. First, the behavior and the underlying norms and values of the local population or the local belligerents may be rather different from the soldiers' norms and values, a situation that may lead to many misunderstandings, conflicts, and even mutual dislike. Second, cooperation with soldiers from other countries and with relief organizations may be far from smooth. Third, local belligerents may not comply with the agreements, a situation that in turn may lead to many disagreements about what to do in specific situations, especially when the peace support unit is not fully equipped to fight the belligerents. Fourth, soldiers may be confronted with all kinds of violations of human rights and with human suffering. In peace support operations, it is very likely that small units will be confronted with these problems, especially because of the dispersion of units during operations. Therefore, the on-scene commanders are often lieutenants or sergeants; operations are most effective if they are capable of dealing with these problems and taking the initiative in a professional manner. This is even more important if the problems must be dealt with in a very limited period of time and if no suitable procedures for taking action have been established. This requires decentralization of command and trust of higher commanders that their sub-commanders are able and willing to correctly assess the situation and subsequently take appropriate action.

We found a tension between this tendency toward autonomy and the need to control. In the first rotation of IFOR, commanders enjoyed a high level of autonomy of action. Each team had a broad assignment: each team commander was, within his assigned territory, responsible for the implementation of the Dayton Accords according to the official schedule. The battalion provided extra support only when needed and coordinated only if necessary. Each team was assigned an area and a forward base in that area. Each team commander had to independently decide how to implement his mission. In practice, this resulted in completely different methods of operating.

One of the team commanders developed a style of operating in which he tried to cover the area as much as possible by means of patrolling with mixed platoons (infantry and cavalry soldiers together). Each patrol was performed with a different composition of soldiers. The most experienced soldiers – a platoon commander or a deputy platoon commander – led the patrols. These patrols often took longer than one day.

Another team commander developed another style of operating. He decided that it would not make sense to conduct many patrols in the mountainous area for which he was responsible. He decided to focus his contingent's efforts on the control of the borders of his assigned area. In this way, he would know what persons and material passed into and out of his area. The group commanders performed the controlling tasks with their men. The platoon commanders got separate assignments.

The third team commander's style of conducting operations differed yet again from that of the other two. He decided that one platoon would be permanently located at a post that was located two hours (driving) away from the forward base; the platoon had to perform their patrols from this second post. The other platoons conducted patrols from the forward base.

Therefore, the overall finding is that many commanders experienced significant autonomy in the performance of their tasks, especially at the beginning of the mission. As one platoon commander remarked in an interview conducted by Frusch, "When IFOR started, we had to find out everything for ourselves. During our half-year tour, many regulations had been written about proper clothing, scheduling, how to perform patrols, etc." [5] Frusch also reported similar results on the autonomy of action. In his study, he surveyed commanders and sub-commanders of the IFOR-1 soldiers on the level of autonomy and mutual trust. He found a relatively high level of autonomy, because leaders did not constantly check on how their subordinates performed their tasks. They relied on their subordinates' abilities and judgment. On the other hand, he also found that there was a rather large number of regulations that limited autonomy of action.

In SFOR, the teams – and the platoon commanders and group commanders within these – teams had less autonomy of action. They were bound by even more regulations and standard operating procedures. The team commanders were responsible for the performance of routine tasks within their area, such as gathering information, patrolling, monitoring refugees, and site inspections. However, when problems arose – for example, when local inhabitants and re-

---

5   J.M.H. Frusch, *Kernthema's van de beleidsvisie 'Leidinggeven in de KL: meetbaar'?* (Is it Possible to Measure the Core Themes of the Dutch Army's Leadership Policy?), internal unpublished report (Den Haag: Ministry of Defense, 1996).

turning refugees started to fight each other – the battalion commander would take over command with means the battalion possessed, such as a crowd and riot control platoon or a reconnaissance platoon. The work within the teams was generally routine and also bound by many rules and regulations. Each patrol was planned by the operations room (ops room), which also gave specific instructions on what information should be sought. Patrol commanders received detailed lists of information.

There was also a directive that patrol commanders should keep in touch with the ops room on a regular basis. If something unexpected happened, it should always be directly communicated to the ops room. The ops room then gave instructions about what should be done, because they claimed to have the correct procedures to be used in virtually every situation. One ops manager reported in his interview that nothing had happened during his six-month tour for which the ops room did not have a procedure.

There were also many rules about how to perform site inspections and what should be done in a situation in which shortages or surpluses of weapons and ammunition were found. Furthermore, there were many restrictions regarding the safety of the soldiers. Team commanders felt a huge responsibility for the safe homecoming of their men. Therefore, they tried to restrict the behavior of their men during the patrols and other activities as much as possible. They did not want them to run any unnecessary risks; hence, they tried to prevent the patrols from driving or walking on roads that had not been officially cleared of mines. Additionally, many safety rules about the handling of weapons inside and outside the encampment were issued and enforced. Furthermore, they did not want to have any contacts between potentially dangerous "locals" and SFOR soldiers. This limitation in autonomy of action resulted in friction between higher and lower levels of command.

2.3. TENSIONS AMONG DIFFERENT BRANCHES

We believe that there was significant rivalry among different branches. IFOR consisted of an infantry battalion minus one company, a tank squadron, military engineer units, and medical units. As has been mentioned before, these units were divided into three teams, of which one was led by a cavalry major and two by infantry majors. In 1996, this kind of structure for peace support operations was not very well known, meaning that a team commander had units under his command that he did not know how to use very well. For instance, once the former warring factions were demilitarized, the mayors asked IFOR not to use their tanks anymore. The team commanders then had to think creatively about how to use their cavalry soldiers. This was not hard for the cavalry officer, but the other two officers had greater difficulty in fulfilling this request. On one team, only cavalry soldiers were allowed to perform guard duty. Some conflicts also arose between one of the team commanders and the military engineer platoon commander who was part of his team. The conflicts were about how fast the roads could be cleared of mines. The military engineer was much more cautious than the team commander, who wanted to use as many roads as possible for his patrols.

Tensions among the different branches were much higher during SFOR than during IFOR. At one camp, many different branches were located at one spot: maneuver units, medical units, repair units, etc. These units all had their own tasks and their own accompanying culture. The maneuver units were busy preparing and executing patrols. They also performed patrols at night. Therefore, it was not uncommon for a number of them to be sleeping during the day or early in the evening in order to be able to rise in the middle of the night or early in the morning. The repair unit, on the other hand, worked from nine to five. In the evening, they had free time and they relaxed.

To a certain extent, differing responsibilities and tasks for different units within the contingent helped create clashes among the Dutch peacekeepers. On the one hand, the maneuver units thought they had an operational task with certain risks; on the other hand, the repair units and medical units, which did not leave the encampment, believed they were in a completely safe area. Consequently, the maneuver units felt that the risks of the mission were unfairly distributed among the different army branches. They had to do "the real work," whereas the other units had a safe nine to five job. Furthermore, the differences in working hours led to all kinds of misperceptions about the other branch having nothing to do. There were also many complaints about each other's noise.

3. RELATIONS WITH MILITARY UNITS FROM OTHER COUNTRIES

We shall now discuss the external relations between Dutch soldiers and soldiers from other nations involved in I/SFOR. We make a distinction between units in the field and the multinational military headquarters. The reason for this distinction is that field units and headquarters had very different types of tasks and working styles. Furthermore, the (educational) background and age of those involved were different. In the field, soldiers are generally young and from the lower ranks, whereas in the headquarters, the reverse is usually the case.

3.1. FIELD UNITS

Here we present the data gathered from IFOR-1 (January–July 1996) and IFOR-2 (July–December 1996). The soldiers worked in cavalry, infantry, and military engineering units. We studied how Dutch soldiers perceived soldiers from the other countries taking part in IFOR. At the start and end of the mission, we asked for respondents' opinions of their own performance in relation to the performance of other soldiers. The exact question was: "Do you think that the Dutch units perform worse, as well as, or better than the units of other nations?"

One must bear in mind that the soldiers generally did not operate in units of mixed nationalities. For the most part, soldiers of different nations worked in their own national units, many times even in different areas from one another. Hence, the opinions mentioned below are not always based on daily relations, interactions, and encounters, but are also based on incidental encounters, encounters in the private sphere, stereotypes, and other images. It is also important to bear in mind that the 1 (NL) MECHBAT worked in the British sector, under British command.

The following trends may be observed (Table 1) over the course of Dutch soldiers' deployment. First, Dutch soldiers increasingly believed that their units were as good as the units from other countries. Second, there was a decreasing feeling that Dutch soldiers were worse than other soldiers. Third, Dutch soldiers' perception that they were better than other soldiers (with the exception of the British troops) had to be adjusted downward.

Table 2 presents the experiences of IFOR-2 soldiers. Similar trends are evident here. Again, Dutch soldiers generally felt they were as good as the soldiers of other countries. At the end of the mission, the Dutch found themselves "less bad" in comparison with the units of other countries than at the beginning of the mission. It may be seen that, in the beginning, the Dutch had much respect for the British and American soldiers, who had initially been regarded as highly professional. By the end of the mission, however, this respect had disappeared. Compared to the IFOR-1 tour, Dutch soldiers in IFOR-2 had a more positive self-image.

From these trends, we may conclude that observation of the performance of other countries' soldiers during the six-month period of the mission led to a more positive self-image among Dutch soldiers. In general, at the end of the mission, only a few soldiers thought that they were not as good as soldiers in other contingents. The difference between IFOR-1 and IFOR-2 was that IFOR-2 soldiers tended to see themselves as better than the other units.

3.2. Working with Bulgarian Military Engineers

During IFOR and SFOR, Dutch soldiers were involved in one bi-national (Dutch/Bulgarian) military unit. Hence, we will take a closer look at the cooperation between Dutch and Bulgarian troops. These troops worked together in a single military engineer unit of 1 (NL) MECHBAT under the command of

Table 1: Opinions of Dutch military personnel (IFOR-1, 1 NL MECHBAT, MND-SW) on their own functioning compared with military units from other countries, at the start (January 1996) and end (June 1996) of their mission (percentages).

IFOR-1	French units		British units		Canadian units		U.S. units		Russian units	
N =	170	104	178	115	162	96	167	104	155	95
Time frame in mission	Start	End	Start	End	Start	End	Start	End	Start	End
Dutch units are better than others	31	16	29	38	28	17	24	14	56	43
Dutch units are as good as others	48	75	44	49	61	80	47	67	31	50
Dutch units are worse than others	21	9	27	13	11	3	29	18	13	7
Total	100	100	100	100	100	100	100	100	100	100

a Dutch officer. There were several cultural differences between the Bulgarian and Dutch soldiers.

The biggest disparity was the difference in wealth. The Dutch soldiers received higher salaries, while the Bulgarians were sometimes not paid for months. The Dutch military engineers also enjoyed better and more sophisticated equipment than the Bulgarians did. According to one Dutch officer, the Bulgarians regarded the Dutch equipment storehouse as a big toyshop because of the "high-tech" equipment. Another difference was that the Bulgarians did not have any women in their army, so they had to get used to working with female soldiers.

Despite these differences, Dutch officers were quite satisfied with this co-

Table 2: Opinions of Dutch military personnel (IFOR-2; 1 NL MECHBAT, MND-SW) of their own functioning compared with military units from other countries, at the start (July 1996) and end (December 1996) of their mission (percentages).

IFOR -2	French		British		Canadian		U.S.		Russian		Scandinav.	
N =	147	138	150	155	145	134	148	148	142	135	144	132
Time frame in mission	S	E	S	E	S	E	S	E	S	E	S	E
Dutch units are better than others	29	39	24	38	20	36	22	29	44	49	31	36
Dutch units are as good as others	53	57	45	52	68	59	42	56	45	45	62	59
Dutch units are worse than others	18	4	31	10	12	5	36	15	11	6	7	5
Total	100	100	100	100	100	100	100	100	100	100	100	100

S = Start, E = End

operation. There are several possible explanations for their satisfaction. For instance, the Dutch and the Bulgarian soldiers lived and worked in separate areas. Each nationality had its own living quarters, its own workplaces, and its own distinct tasks. This segregation decreased the chance of tensions. Second, the Dutch soldiers undertook several actions to give the Bulgarians the feeling that they were very welcome within the unit. For example, the Netherlands introduced a new badge for the bi-national military unit and the Dutch commander gave a welcome speech, which was partly in phonetic Bulgarian. Finally, and probably most important, the Dutch soldiers acknowledged that the Bulgarians were professional traditional craftsmen. The Bulgarians were able to improvise and solve technical problems with only little and simple equipment. In this way, the Bulgarians made an indispensable contribution to the tasks of the military engineer unit, such as the rebuilding of damaged schools and hospitals.

4. RELATIONS WITHIN THE INTERNATIONAL HEAD-QUARTERS

How did the Dutch military officers view their work experience in the international headquarters? In this section, we describe their experiences by focusing on the headquarters of the multinational brigade, part of the Reaction Force, and SFOR Headquarters. For these descriptions, we use two articles written by Dutch officers who were stationed at these headquarters. [6] We selected these two articles because they contain insights and detailed information on the internal functioning of multinational military headquarters. The description of the headquarters of the multinational brigade covers the period September 1995–June 1996, and the description of the headquarters of SFOR covers the period October 1997–April 1998. In the headquarters of the multinational brigade, a Dutch officer filled the position of Assistant Chief of Staff. Within SFOR headquarters, a Dutch officer was the deputy CJ3.

4.1. HEADQUARTERS OF THE MULTINATIONAL BRIGADE, 1995 – 1996

The multinational brigade fought successfully against the Bosnian Serbs in Operation DELIBERATE FORCE. During this operation, the multinational brigade used mortars and cannons against targets of the Bosnian Serbian army, which had besieged Sarajevo during the previous two years (1993 – 1995). The multinational brigade consisted of two French units, four British units, and two units from the Netherlands. The headquarters staff of the multinational brigade was, of course, international. However, the dominant nationality in the headquarters was French; moreover, the commander was of French nationality. Three observations can be made about this international cooperation.

First of all, it appeared that the multinational brigade operated more slowly than a national unit, due to differences in language, culture, and doctrine. Because of the large differences in language and doctrine between the French and British troops, it was decided to separate the French and British geographically, into separate units with separate lines of command. In addition, even those French officers who could speak English spoke only French and used translators during meetings. All orders and reports were bilingual, which caused many delays. However, during times of crisis, for example when shooting incidents occurred, only the French line of communication was used. All

---

[6] J.R. Mulder, "Een paar ervaringen als ACOS bij de MNB van de RRF in Bosnië-Hercegovina" (Some experiences as ACOS within the MNB of the RRF in Bosnia-Herzegovina), *Militaire Spectator* (1996): 555–559. See also Sjaak Duine, "Werken en leven in HQ SFOR" (Working and Living in HQ SFOR), *Militaire Spectator* 167, no. 9 (1998): 451–455.

orders and situation reports were given in the French language. These delays in the pace of operations were the price of international cooperation. From the Netherlands' perspective, this price was easily accepted, because it was the wish of the political leaders of the countries involved. Nevertheless, it was very difficult to accept when, during crises, French domination resulted in an all-French approach, i.e., orders and communications only in French. Hence, the Dutch officers felt excluded and redundant.

Second, the nations involved had different management and communication styles. The Dutch and French soldiers approached management problems and tasks in a different manner. In the Dutch and British view, it was preferable first to work out several distinct solutions and to present these solutions to the commander. Based on these proposed solutions, the commander could then, along with his staff, make a choice between his options. When a management problem arose in the headquarters, however, the French commander deliberated briefly, put forward his own solution, and ordered the staff to implement this solution. The French commander also became upset when he heard that (British) subordinates had tried to solve a problem without informing him. The British officers had only done what they always did: they tried to support their commander by working out solutions to problems in advance.

Moreover, the French commanding officer had a more theatrical management style. He used various strategies, such as shouting, displaying anger, and banging his fists on the table. Consequently, many (French) officers were afraid of the general and did not dare to criticize his decisions. In addition, military orders were communicated in a different way. The British and Dutch issued orders in a rather collegial way: "Would you please issue that order?" The French commanders, however, issued military orders in a much more peremptory manner: "Issue that order, now!"

A final point of observation is related to rank and hierarchy. The international headquarters of the multinational brigade was top heavy. The French and British sent high-ranking officers to the international staff, in order to guarantee influence on the senior level decision-making process. However, from the Netherlands' perspective, this practice resulted in an inflation of ranks: lieutenant colonels were doing the work that a captain in Holland normally does. One Dutch officer noticed with amazement how sensitive the British and French were to differences in rank. For example, it was very difficult for a French lieutenant colonel to work on the same team with a British captain who was doing the same work. Within the Dutch context, hierarchical differences play a less dominant role.

4.2. SFOR HEADQUARTERS, 1997 – 1998

The organizational structure of the headquarters was not based on efficiency or span of control, but on power and access to information. Every participating country wanted to have a strong position in the headquarters. The Dutch called the struggle that arose among these countries for the best positions "Star Wars." This game involved lobbying, persuasion as well as give-and-take – in order to collect as many high positions as possible. This resulted in a great number of generals and colonels, not all of whom had meaningful functions. This did not mean that the headquarters was ineffective. On the contrary, if necessary, the organization was able to react quickly and decisively, due to the high quality of personnel and the networks of relationships that existed among officers of the same nationality.

Very interestingly, these national networks formed shadow organizations within the formal organization of SFOR headquarters. The different countries formed their own lines of communications between their officers on various levels. The highest-ranking officer from each country headed the national networks. This senior officer was responsible for representing, defending, and carrying out the national interests of his country. These national networks did not stop at the gate of SFOR headquarters but continued throughout the lower echelons and units of SFOR.

Many countries involved had their own national networks, such as France, the United Kingdom, and the United States. The U.S. had an especially powerful national network, as the U.S. occupied many powerful positions within and outside SFOR headquarters, including the positions of military commander of NATO, commander of SFOR, and, within SFOR, commanding positions in intelligence, operations, civil–military relations, public information, special operations, and support command. Consequently, the Americans dominated the process of policy development and implementation within the headquarters. On many occasions, the Americans had already decided upon future actions before the headquarters reached a decision. The officers of other nations, especially those from Europe, could understand the supremacy of the U.S. in SFOR, because Europe in the past had been rather indecisive concerning the conflict in the Balkans. However, it was difficult to accept the supremacy of the U.S. In the opinion of the Dutch officer who worked in SFOR headquarters, the Netherlands did not play the "Star Wars" game very well. The Netherlands sent only a very small number of highly qualified senior officers and they did not form a national network.

Language was an advantage for the Anglo-Saxon countries and a big disadvantage for the other countries. Especially for the countries of Southern Europe, it was difficult to comprehend what was said and meant during the formal and informal meetings. The use of English abbreviations, acronyms, and dialects contributed to the language barrier and to the dominant position of the Anglo-Saxon countries. Consequently, the non-Anglo-Saxon countries, including the Netherlands, sometimes felt excluded. Officers from these countries felt that they were not able to communicate their experiences and knowledge effectively within the headquarters. Therefore, we make a distinction between the Anglo-Saxon countries, calling them the "Haves," and the non-Anglo-Saxon countries, which we shall call the "Have Nots." The "Haves" possess information on policies and operations; they use the (English or French) language as their mother tongue; and they have the most powerful positions. The "Have Nots" must operate without these assets.

Policymaking within headquarters could be characterized as micro-management; details and the generation of detailed information were very important. On some occasions, for instance in the case of shooting incidents, micro-management resulted in overreaction and escalation because higher echelons took measures that were not proportional to reality. This was a big shock for Dutch officers. In the Netherlands, officers are taught to deal with modern governance models and to treat brigades as business units with decentralized management. The Americans, in particular, managed SFOR in a very detail-oriented way. While many new American management theories are very popular in the Netherlands, it seemed that the Americans did not implement these management theories themselves.

5. RELATIONS WITH LOCAL AUTHORITIES AND FORMER WARRING FACTIONS

The previous two sections described the relations within IFOR and SFOR. In this section, we describe civil–military relations among Dutch military units, local authorities, and the former warring factions.

5.1. LOCAL AUTHORITIES

Within the 1 (NL) MECHBAT of IFOR, a special team of four officers was tasked with managing contacts with the local authorities. One officer dealt with the military commanders of the former warring factions. A second officer dealt with all representatives of local governments, non-governmental organizations, as well as minorities in the Muslim-Croat Federation. A third officer dealt with representatives in the Serbian region. Finally, a team commander coordinated all of these contacts. The consequence of this organization was that local authorities always had to deal with the same officer.

The Netherlands' approach to dealing with local authorities was aimed at establishing cooperation and commitment. The town mayors were promised substantial aid – e.g., for (re-)building schools, and building and maintaining field hospitals – if they cooperated. The policy was also designed to raise expectations that more aid would follow if the authorities continued their cooperation. Another way to foster the commitment of the local authorities was to give them seats on SFOR task forces.

The relationship between local authorities and the Dutch military could be characterized as "tit-for-tat," with a mutual perception of interdependence. The mayors needed the support of the Dutch troops because such support was crucial for obtaining financial support for rebuilding their villages. The Dutch government financed the reconstruction of bridges, schools, roads, and the electricity network in Bosnia. The Dutch troops played an important role in acquiring these funds. The Dutch troops also needed the help of local authorities, because cooperative authorities contributed to stability in the regions, which was essential for implementation of the Dayton Accords. Cooperative, friendly mayors made the lives of Dutch soldiers in Bosnia much easier. For instance, with the help of local authorities, the heating system of the Dutch base in Knezevo was restored and showers were repaired. In addition, Dutch soldiers were able to influence local radio stations with the help of local authorities, for example, when local stations broadcast programs with anti-I/SFOR sentiments.

Maintaining good relationships with local authorities also proved to be a valuable asset when I/SFOR personnel arrested alleged war criminals. Many times during and after these detentions, Dutch contact officers visited local authorities in order to clarify I/SFOR actions. These meetings had a de-escalating effect that was very important in containing a hostile atmosphere in the villages, which became very tense during and after the detention of alleged war criminals.

Dutch military units also maintained good relations with the informal representatives of local communities, such as the directors of factories, farms, and schools. By setting up a social network with these authorities, it was possible to acquire information about possible sources of tensions and problems. This sort of information about the local situation was vital, as it allowed the peacekeepers to take a proactive rather than a reactive approach to dealing with potential problems and stumbling blocks.

Not surprisingly, a great deal of animosity existed among local authorities from the different population groups. For instance, when Dutch soldiers used tanks in times of local unrest, Serbian local authorities immediately spread rumors that these tanks were specifically aimed at the "evil Muslims." Because of the undesirable effects of local authorities' misinformation, Dutch soldiers made a great effort to continuously inform all the different local authorities and their populations about the actions of Dutch troops.

Dutch military perceptions of the local authorities varied greatly from person to person. Some authorities were seen as unqualified politicians (sometimes even as criminals), who were elected only due to patronage and promises of "golden mountains" to their electorate. According to the military, however, other authorities were very qualified politicians who tried to create a better world for their people. One might say that these different perceptions are typical not only with regard to Bosnian politicians, but to politicians in general.

5.2. FORMER WARRING FACTIONS

Relations with the former warring factions can be illustrated by one of the elements of the Dayton Accords: the de-mining of Bosnia. In carrying out these de-mining activities, it was important that Dutch military engineers maintained good relations with the former warring factions. Most of all, the Dayton Accords stipulated that the former warring factions should clear their own mines in the zones of separation. The former warring factions could only fulfill this condition, however, with the help of I/SFOR. In an attempt to reach an understanding and to promote good working relations with the former warring factions, the Dutch army gave the former warring factions necessary de-mining equipment without asking anything in return.

Dutch military engineers were also careful not to present themselves as liberators or to humiliate the former warring factions when they were powerless. In their relations with the different ethnic groups, Dutch soldiers tried to be neutral and to avoid favoring any of the former warring factions. This was an important concern, which was reinforced by the fact that Dutch soldiers noticed a hostile attitude on the part of the Croatian HVO towards the British. This hostile attitude was a legacy of the UNPROFOR period, when the HVO fought the British (in the Vitez area).

6. RELATIONS WITH THE LOCAL POPULATION

We begin this section by describing the nature of the IFOR/SFOR mission and its impact on relations with the local population. Second, we focus on the different types of relationships that arose between soldiers and the local population. Finally, we discuss the soldiers' views of the local population.

6.1. INTRODUCTION

During both the IFOR and SFOR missions, Dutch soldiers had contact with the local population. The extent of these contacts was dependent, however, on the contingent's (as well as the individual soldier's or officer's) assigned tasks under the auspices of I/SFOR.

The main task of IFOR was to implement the peace; it was a purely military operation. IFOR was concerned with the warring parties' abandonment of the declared zone of separation; the withdrawal of heavy weapons to the barracks; the organization of elections; and the return of refugees to their homes. During this operation, the situation was very uncertain; therefore, contacts with the local population were restricted. Because of these restrictions, there was generally very little contact with the local population. On the other hand, contacts with the warring parties occurred, but the frequency and extent of contact was dependent upon the individual tasks of IFOR.

The goal of SFOR was to control and stabilize the situation in Bosnia. The situation was much more peaceful than during the IFOR period. Peace had returned, so the rebuilding of public buildings, schools, hospitals, and roads could start. In addition, a first effort was made to return refugees to their homes.

During SFOR, there were also rules concerning relations with the local population. Contacts between IFOR and the local population had been kept limited. With SFOR, however, rules governing contact with the locals changed along with the tasks. SFOR was designed to stabilize the situation in this region; therefore, SFOR began to behave more like a police force. In addition, SFOR also had a more humanitarian task; during this period, peacekeepers (mainly those from the engineer units) began to cooperate with the local population and help them rebuild public buildings and restore roads. Because of these tasks, SFOR had more contacts with the local population than did IFOR. Of course, situations remained in which SFOR had to demonstrate military functions, as well. This was especially the case when SFOR had to monitor the return of refugees, inspect weapon depots, or escort weapon transports.

The perceptions of the local population changed with this change in mission. Not many years before, they viewed the Dutch troops as occupiers. SFOR made a better impression. During the SFOR period, the local population began to see these troops more as a solution to their problems. Nonetheless, The Hague in the Netherlands has a bad name among the locals because the International Criminal Tribunal, which takes war criminals into custody, is located there.

6.2. DIFFERENT TYPES OF RELATIONS WITH THE LOCAL POPULA-TION

During their work, soldiers had contact with the different population groups. Muslims, Croats, and Serbs lived in the I/SFOR area of operations. Ten years before, these groups had been living together in peace. Now, the different groups hated each other. Consequently, soldiers had to operate as if they were on good terms with all these population groups; it was also important that they were neutral in their dealings with these different groups.

During I/SFOR, there were three types of relationships with the local population. The first type developed because of tasks such as patrolling, information gathering, etc. Second, there were special projects such as the inspection of weapon depots, escort duty for weapon transfers, and the monitoring of the return of refugees to their homes. In such situations, mainly commanders had contact with the local population; they had to be very careful to stay on good terms with the local parties. Third, there were incidental contacts with the local population, for example, when I/SFOR vehicles were involved in accidents with "locals" because of the often poor driving habits of the local population. Furthermore, there were contacts with local women who worked on the base. They helped SFOR in the kitchen and in the bar, and also did the cleaning and the laundry. The soldiers were not allowed to have steady relationships with the local women. If a soldier started a relationship with one of these "locals," s/he was repatriated.

A study of SFOR soldiers in Bosnia from November 1997 – November 1998 (SFOR-3 and SFOR-4) [7] revealed that not all soldiers had contacts with the local population. Indeed, only one third of the soldiers had such contacts (see Table 3). SFOR soldiers mentioned that most contacts were made with Bosnian Serbs (43%). Relatively more commanders were represented in this category.

Table 3: Frequency of Contacts with the Local Population during Work (percentages).

SFOR	N	Often	Sometimes	Few
Bosnian Serbs	219	43	33	23
Muslims	250	37	38	26
Bosnian Croats	227	30	35	35

6.3. OPINIONS ABOUT RELATIONS WITH THE LOCAL POPULATION

In addition to the kinds of relations and the frequency of the contacts, we saw that soldiers had differing opinions about their contacts with the local population. Opinions varied with the tasks the soldiers had to perform, but in general most soldiers were positive about cooperation with the "locals."

---

[7]   Tessa op den Buijs, *Assessment of the Factors that Influence the Functioning of Dutch Soldiers Deployed in Bosnia,* internal unpublished report (Breda: Royal Netherlands Military Academy, 1999).

They were very positive about "social patrols." During these patrols, soldiers distributed newspapers with information about SFOR, as well as *Mirko,* a publication for young people. In exchange, soldiers received information about the area and different local populations. This was very useful for SFOR; for example, the local population often knew the exact position of mines. In these situations, the "locals" were always very friendly, especially the very poor elderly people living in the mountains. When soldiers gave food or potato peels for the pigs, these people thanked the soldiers with a kiss or hug. Sometimes the soldiers were invited for coffee or even a nip to drink. The soldiers had to restrict gifts of food because there was a chance that the entire population of the village could come to the base the next day, hoping to get more food. Soldiers viewed wealthier people living in the villages as more arrogant, because they did not greet the soldiers at all. In addition, soldiers viewed their informal contacts with the women on the base as friendly, despite the language barrier. This may have been a consequence of the fact that the greatest problem in Bosnia was unemployment; these women may have been grateful that they had a job with SFOR and earned a lot of money in comparison to other "locals." A soldier said, "When you are friendly to these women, they are also friendly to you."

It was not always easy for the soldiers to cooperate with the local population, however. When soldiers had to inspect and check weapon depots or escort a weapons transport (mostly Muslim moves), they often had to negotiate with the local population. For the most part, the "locals" wanted to deal with the soldiers; however, when "locals" offered vital information to the soldiers, they generally expected money in return. The "locals" were very crafty negotiators; the reasons for certain requests and stumbling blocks during negotiations were not always clear to SFOR. Soldiers sometimes had the idea that the "locals" were playing games. Studies on the work and life of IFOR and SFOR soldiers confirmed these findings. [8] For instance, soldiers were asked to rate on a scale how often they experienced negotiations at checkpoints. During IFOR, almost 30% of the soldiers reported that they had to negotiate at checkpoints on an almost daily basis. (For 25% of the SFOR soldiers, however, this rarely occurred.) After the mission, many IFOR soldiers rated the population in Bosnia as unreliable and cruel.

The local population sometimes threatened soldiers. For example, when SFOR arrested two Croatian war criminals in December 1997, the Croatian population reacted by throwing a hand-grenade and putting up roadblocks.

---

[8]   Ad Vogelaar, Joseph Soeters, and Hans Born, "Working and Living in Bosnia: Experiences of Dutch Soldiers," *NLARMS: Netherlands Annual Review of Military Studies* 1, No. 1 (1997): 113–140. See also op den Buijs, *Ibid.*

The soldiers perceived this situation as very threatening. In addition, refugee monitoring was sometimes very stressful for the soldiers because of the aggressiveness of the local population, who did not want the refugees to return to their homes. Relations were strained and stiff in the Serbian area, in particular; therefore, there was always tension in this area concerning the monitoring of the refugees returning to their homes. Earlier studies reveal that more than 30% of the I/SFOR soldiers reported witnessing aggressive acts between civilian population groups. [9] A good example of how seriously the leadership perceived the general state of aggressiveness and its potential threat to I/SFOR can be seen in cases of accidents and injuries. Soldiers were not allowed to leave base alone or to give medical help to the "locals." For instance, when an accident occurred and "locals" were injured, soldiers had to request a local medical doctor or ambulance. When the situation was critical, soldiers had to decide whether to give first aid. This situation could be very dangerous for the position of I/SFOR, however, because if the injured local died, the local population could blame I/SFOR for the death.

After the mission, the soldiers mainly rated contacts with the local population as neutral (see Table 4). This confirms that soldiers had to cooperate in an unbiased and neutral way in order to be on good terms with all the population groups. Between roughly 20–25% viewed their contacts with the locals as pleasant. This number may represent the soldiers who experienced only positive welcomes by the local population and did not negotiate with "locals" or experience difficulties at roadblocks.

Table 4: Opinions about Contacts with the Local Population (percentages).

SFOR	N	Pleasant	Neutral	Unpleasant
Bosnian Serbs	202	24	73	4
Muslims	236	28	67	6
Bosnian Croats	205	20	72	7

7. CONCLUSIONS

Peace missions in Bosnia may be characterized as very complex situations for many reasons. Among others, they are complex because of the encounters that soldiers have with individuals from distinctly different national and cultural backgrounds. On the one hand, this makes the peace missions challenging and interesting. On the other hand, however, it also makes peace missions difficult

---

[9]   Vogelaar, Soeters, and Born, *Ibid,* and op den Buijs, *Ibid.*

and sometimes disappointing. In this study, we explored the points of tension in the complex encounters between people with different backgrounds. We described four different types of relationships in which points of tension could arise:

- Internal relations within the Dutch military units;
- External relations among Dutch military units and soldiers of other nations;
- Civil–military relations between the Dutch army and the local authorities and former warring factions;
- Civil–military relations between the Dutch army and local population groups.

Within the military, we found two points of tension, one in the vertical relationship between hierarchical levels and one in the horizontal relations between units and colleagues. Regarding the vertical relations, there was a point of tension between the need and desire to control (from above) and the need and wish for autonomy (from below). There was a constant tension between the hierarchical levels. The balance of power between the higher and lower levels of command was not stable and shifted during the subsequent mission in favor of higher-level commanders. Because of standardization and an increased knowledge of the area and its typical problems, the battalion commanders of later tours (IFOR-2, SFOR) were more able to control their sub-commanders than the commander of IFOR-1 (the first tour). A second point of tension is located in the horizontal cooperation among soldiers of different army branches, such as the infantry, cavalry, and military engineers. During IFOR, soldiers and officers from these various branches had to work together in teams, an unfamiliar situation that resulted in friction. In addition, differences in areas of expertise and competencies resulted in tensions.

The external relationship between the Dutch army and the militaries of different nations was our second dimension. In our opinion, it is important to distinguish between working in the field and working in international headquarters. In order to better manage complex international military operations in the field, military units from different countries were usually geographically separated from each other in the field. Consequently, we could not find explicit points of tension. However, Dutch soldiers had some contacts and relationships with soldiers from other nations, and they formed clear opinions of one another. During the mission, it appears that Dutch soldiers' self-image and self-esteem improved when they compared themselves with soldiers from other nations. Soldiers from the United States and United Kingdom did not turn out to be as outstanding as Dutch soldiers had expected, and Russian soldiers turned out to be not bad at all. Franz Kernic draws a similar conclusion concerning Austrian soldiers. [10] Another implication of our observations of international cooperation in the field is that soldiers from other countries are not evaluated by their nationality, but rather by their concrete actions. For example, a soldier is evaluated as good or bad not because s/he is an American, but because s/he performs well. Hence, international cooperation may result in fewer stereotypes and a better understanding of one another.

A different picture applies to the situation at the international headquarters. I/SFOR headquarters were internationally staffed. Access to information, language, and power seem to be the crucial variables of working with other nationalities in headquarters. Each country tries to realize and to institutionalize its position and interests within the headquarters. We distinguish between the "Haves" and the "Have Nots" based on the possession of information on policies and operations, use of one's own (English or French) language as a native tongue, and possession of the most powerful positions. The "Haves," mainly those from Anglo-Saxon countries, formed powerful national networks, through which they controlled the policy process at headquarters. The "Have Nots," including the Dutch military officers, sometimes felt redundant. Here we see that culture and power are interrelated. Cultural aspects, such as language, can strongly influence the ability to attain positions of power in international relations; without such powerful assets, a culture can become marginalized.

The third scope of our research is the relationship between Dutch troops and local governments. This interaction can be characterized as an interdependent and "tit-for-tat" relationship. Both parties needed each other in order to achieve their goals. The Dutch troops tried to maintain good relations with the civil authorities in a democratic way; they held many meetings and discussions and invited the civil authorities to become members of various task forces. The strategy for dealing with the former warring factions was to be as neutral as possible and not to favor any faction over the others.

The fourth dimension is the relationship between Dutch soldiers and the local population. This relationship was influenced by the tasks of I/SFOR. Relations were more tense within the strict military aspects of the Dayton Accords: inspecting weapons depots, escorting weapon transports, and checking traffic at roadblocks. Relations with the local population were more relaxed when it came to the humanitarian side of the soldiers' work in Bosnia. In this case, Dutch soldiers experienced the local population as friendly. In general, back home after the mission in Bosnia, Dutch soldiers rated their contacts with the local population as neither good nor bad.

---

[10]   See Kernic, this volume.

7.1. THE DYNAMICS OF INTERCULTURAL RELATIONS AND THE NEED FOR INTERCULTURAL MANAGEMENT

We may derive some more general and theoretical implications from our conclusions. In reference to our conclusions on the relationships between Dutch soldiers and soldiers of other nations, we see that the opinions of Dutch soldiers about soldiers from other countries were not stable, but changed over time. These changes over time can be attributed to two main factors. First of all, the experiences of working together caused each side to form an opinion about the other, which is based on real life experiences instead of stereotypes about "foreign" soldiers. Second, each international cooperation mission passes through several transitional phases. [11]

The first phase is the euphoric period or the so-called "honeymoon" period, when everything is new and exciting. The second phase is that of cultural shock, when one notices that the other nationality has different values, belief systems, and customs. The third phase is the acculturation phase, in which one learns to deal with the new foreign circumstances and individuals. The final phase is the equilibrium phase, which can be a positive, neutral, or negative mental equilibrium. A negative equilibrium means rejection, irritation, and feelings that the others are foreign and different. The neutral equilibrium implies a more indifferent attitude. A positive equilibrium means that both parties partially adjust to each other and realize that they have mutual interests, understanding, and trust.

These dynamics show us that a positive attitude toward international cooperation and toward soldiers of other nationalities cannot be taken for granted for the whole mission. Responsible authorities and managers should therefore deliberately and systematically try to influence the culture of international relations, or, to put it in other words, use intercultural management. This implies recognition of the national and organizational differences between the nations involved. Intercultural management does not mean that cultural differences should be diminished at all costs. On the contrary, intercultural management means mutual respect, and recognizing and reinforcing what the nations have in common. Intercultural management also implies that senior management promotes the equality of each member of the international organization. [12] We

---

[11]   Geert Hofstede, *Cultures and Organizations: Software of the Mind* (London: McGraw-Hill, 1991). See also A. Furnham and S. Bochner, *Culture Shock: Psychological Reactions to Unfamiliar Environments* (London: Methuen, 1986). Furnham and Bochner developed this transitional phase model in reference to individuals who work abroad. It is therefore a social-psychological model, which is, in our opinion, also applicable to international cooperation projects.

[12]   Axel Rosendahl Huber, Paul Klein, and Joseph Soeters, "Het Duits-Nederlands legercorps: meningen en ervaringen van Duitse en Nederlandse militairen" (The German-Netherlands

think it is especially important that the powerful countries (the Haves) and less powerful non-Anglo-Saxon countries (the Have Nots) find a balanced way of working together.

A second aspect of intercultural management is the "management of meaning" of the mission goals and strategy. It is important that these goals and subsequent strategy are perceived as a win-win game. Management has a special responsibility to avoid situations, in which participants from different nations view the mission as a zero-sum game, with losers and winners. The result of a zero-sum game perception will be distrust and the employment of strategies, such as "Star Wars" and information games that can be useful from a national perspective, but not from the perspective of the international mission. In our study, we saw a good example of the management of meaning by the Dutch commander of the Dutch-Bulgarian military engineer unit. By making new symbols and badges of the bi-national unit, and by speaking in the Bulgarian language, he tried to give the Bulgarians the feeling that they were welcome and at home.

The third aspect of intercultural management is the organization of international military units. Are the soldiers of the different countries working together in mixed units or are they separated into different areas and units? The advantage of separate units is that the mission can be better controlled. Confusing situations and "Tower of Babel" complications will be avoided. On the other hand, many opportunities for mutual understanding, decreasing stereotypes, and learning from each other will be lost. One can also learn from points of tension and from encounters in complex cultural environments.

Army Corps: Opinions and Experiences of German and Dutch Military Personnel), *Militaire Spectator* 168, No. 3 (1999): 134 – 144.

7. FROM A BLUE BERET TO A GREEN HELMET: THE BACKPACK OF SWEDISH PEACEKEEPERS SERVING WITH THE UN AND NATO IN BOSNIA-HERZEGOVINA

Eva JOHANSSON

Outline:

1. INTRODUCTION

In recent years, the number of peace support operations launched by the UN or NATO has increased dramatically. During this period, several media and other reports concerning peacekeeper misbehavior, both as individuals and in groups, have surfaced. [1] Has the peacekeeper changed character, have peacekeeping missions changed, or is the concept of peacekeeping not up to date with the patterns of conflict now experienced in different parts of the world? The answers to these questions may be complex, reflecting interaction between mission factors and peacekeeper characteristics. This article will discuss some aspects of this interrelationship from a Swedish perspective.

1.1. SWEDEN'S EXPERIENCES IN PEACEKEEPING OPERATIONS

Sweden has a long tradition of peacekeeping operations and has, for many years, provided personnel especially for United Nations (UN) peacekeeping efforts. However, as early as 1935, Sweden took part in the Saar operation, at that time under the auspices of the League of Nations. Sweden also took part in another League operation, namely the one in Spain during the Civil War of 1936–1939, though only with military observers. During this operation, World War II broke out and the League of Nations collapsed. After the Second World War and the formation of the UN, the first Swedish contribution to a UN operation took place, with the selection of Count Folke Bernadotte as a mediator in the conflict between the Israelis and the Arabs in 1948. That assignment ended tragically, when Count Bernadotte was killed in Jerusalem in September that same year. Since 1948, Sweden has taken part in nearly every operation launched by the UN; by 1998, over 80,000 Swedes (including 2,000 women) have served within the framework of these peacekeeping forces. Sixty-six persons (five in Bosnia) have lost their lives during their service; most died in accidents or similar circumstances while only a few were killed in combat. [2]

From the viewpoint of most Swedes, certain individuals could be said to have had a significant impact on the views of international work aiming to prevent war or to defend human rights. Two people in particular can be said to have given the UN "a human face" in the minds of the Swedish population, namely Dag Hammarskjöld, who was appointed UN Secretary-General in 1953 and, as mentioned above, Count Folke Bernadotte. Another person who worked for the UN was Alva Myrdal. In 1949, she received an offer to

---

[1]   See, e.g., Donna Winslow, "Misplaced Loyalties: The Role of Military Culture in the Breakdown of Discipline in Peace Operations," *Canadian Review of Sociology and Anthropology* 35, No. 3 (1998), pp. 345–367. See also Franz Kernic and Harald Haas, *Warriors for Peace* (Frankfurt am Main: Peter Lang, 1999).

[2]   Swedish Armed Forces, *Facts and Figures 98* (Stockholm: Swedish Armed Forces, May-June 1998), pp. 20–23.

become head of the UN Department of Social Affairs; this was a great honor, since no woman had ever occupied any top positions in major international organizations at that time.[3] Over a period of 12 years (1962 – 73), she worked as a disarmament negotiator at the UN Conference on Disarmament in Geneva. She was also awarded the Albert Einstein Peace Prize in 1980, and two years later she shared the Nobel Peace Prize with Alfonso García Robles. A further person worthy of mention is Olof Palme, who first became Prime Minister in 1969. Olof Palme became well known outside Sweden during the Vietnam War, when he became a persistent critic of U.S. policy. He also stressed the importance of introducing democracy and human rights in Namibia and South Africa. In 1980, he was appointed the special representative of the Secretary-General on the conflict between Iran and Iraq. After the Cold War, persons like Rolf Ekéus, Jan Eliasson, and Carl Bildt all had prominent appointments in different branches within the UN. For a small country like Sweden, these persons, together with others, awakened an interest in international matters among the population, not always because of what they did, but also because of the domestic debate they stimulated through their different statements. In the political establishment, this was not always without friction. Persons like those described above could be seen as social or mental models for Swedes. Thus, in the absence of recent war heroes, Swedes can be said to have been brought up with "peace heroes."

1.2. THE BACKPACK OF THE SWEDISH PEACEKEEPER

Today's peacekeepers are very much a product of their heritage. They have been brought up in a small country with a rather peaceful history, at least in recent centuries. Sweden has managed to stand outside the two world wars, a fact sometimes criticized, but the wars have had an impact on the society in different ways. Principles and values of importance to or cherished by Sweden, including respect for international law, the rights of smaller or weaker states, non-aggression, tolerance, and human rights, developed during these decades. These principles have also permeated the educational system and the development of curriculum. Significant efforts have been made to foster a respect for peace and understanding in students and to introduce co-determination between students and their schools. How powerful this was in reality is hard to say, but it did reflect the spirit of the society.

Swedish peacekeepers have also been brought up with the idea of a conscription army. Compulsory military service for males, nowadays also possible on a voluntary basis for females, might influence how Swedes participate in or view peacekeeping operations. As Sweden does not have professional soldiers,

---

3   Lars G. Lindskog, "Alva Myrdal and the Disarmament Struggle," in Peter Wallensteen (Ed.), *Sweden at the UN – Eight Profiles* (Borås: Centraltryckeriet, 1996), pp. 35 – 43.

there is nothing ordinary about the business of being a soldier; it is very rarely thought of as a profession for the man in the street. The only time it is seen as a job, except for those who are regular officers, is when Swedish soldiers participate in international missions. The importance of participation in these operations has become more prominent since the 1996 Defense Bill stated that international operations are one of the Swedish Armed Forces' four main tasks.

Sweden has also taken part in different organizations that have worked for peace, democracy, and human rights during the 20th century. Besides participating in the League of Nations and the UN, many individuals have also made contributions by working for the Red Cross, Save the Children, Amnesty International, and so forth. Some of these persons gained respect for their international work, serving as models for society due to their efforts to prevent acts of war and protect human rights.

Peacekeepers are also products of the educational system, which has been strongly influenced by a political vision of a society based upon the principles of peace, cooperation, and equal opportunity for all individuals. Sweden is also a society built on the idea of "people's defense," a notion that took root in society through compulsory military service. As Stig Hadenius writes in the book, *Swedish Politics during the 20th Century*,[4] Sweden's 20th-century history differs from that of most other countries because of its relative calm and slowness to change. One underlying reason, of course, is that Sweden has been spared from war and is relatively homogeneous in both ethnic and religious terms. Extremism in politics, religion, and other spheres has never managed to make much headway.

Can one speak of a national character? An attempt has been made in this section to present a part of this character, but this is, of course, incomplete since there are other important aspects aside from democratic development, the educational system, conscription, and a tradition of peacekeeping. Nevertheless, the cultural heritage transferred from generation to generation through education and early life experience in family and schools and through socialization in organizations and institutions has left its mark on Swedish citizens.

Hofstede and others have looked at cultural differences, especially in the business world.[5] Scandinavian managers are, for example, characterized by the following cultural traits:[6]

- Support for equality and democratic values;
- Regard for order and honesty;

---

4   Stig Hadenius, *Swedish Politics during the 20th Century: Conflict and Consensus* (Trelleborg: Skogs Boktryckeri AB, 1997).
5   Geert Hofstede, *Culture's Consequences: International Differences in Work-related Values*, abridged edition (Newbury Park: Sage Publications, 1984).
6   Björn Bjerke, *Affärsledarskap i fem olika kulturer* (Lund: Studentlitteratur, 1998).

- Concern for private life;
- Do not want to play a conspicuous role;
- Scrupulousness and deliberation;
- Rationality and practicality;
- Disdain for aggressiveness;
- Tendency to avoid confrontations.

Furthermore, Bjerke writes that there is a strong commitment to democratic values and fair play in Scandinavian countries. He also states that the character of Scandinavian societies can be described as collective individualism.

Since the mid-1970s, however, Sweden has often been described as a country in crisis. Tighter government budgets and higher unemployment rates have made it difficult, to some extent, to live up to many of the goals of the "People's Home" and the welfare state. It is difficult to say how these changes will affect the peacekeeper's backpack.

1.3. WHY GO TO BOSNIA?

In 1993, the Swedish cabinet and Parliament decided to contribute a major combat unit to operations in Bosnia. A number of factors appear to have contributed to this decision. Robert Dalsjö,[7] a Senior Analyst with the European Security Group of the National Defense Research Establishment, sees at least three motives for the decision to send troops to Bosnia. First, a certain sense of embarrassment was evident, both internally and externally, that Sweden did not provide a major and more visible unit in the area of operations, despite its long peacekeeping tradition. Second, the conflict in the former Yugoslavia had a stronger direct and indirect connection to Swedish national security interests than did, for example, Somalia. If aggression and violent nationalism were allowed to run unchecked in the Balkans, it might set a pattern for other parts of a continent still in turmoil after the fall of the Berlin Wall and might eventually have direct repercussions on Swedish national security. Thus, it could be said that by helping the UN to uphold international order and principles of justice, Sweden would also be defending herself. Third, during recent decades, Sweden had shifted its foreign policy focus from the Third World to Europe. During this time, Sweden had also applied for EU membership. Since Sweden's policy of neutrality was sometimes criticized abroad for being egotistic and opportunistic, particularly during World War II, it was important for Sweden to demonstrate its determination to participate actively in building a common European security order, even if this involved risks or costs.

---

[7]   Robert Dalsjö, "Sweden and Balkan Blue Helmet Operations," in Lars Ericson (Ed.), *Solidarity and Defence* (Västervik: Ekblads, 1995), pp. 103–105.

1.4. PUBLIC OPINION

How does the public regard Swedish involvement in international missions and the new types of missions that are emerging? The National Board of Psychological Defense (SPF) conducts an annual poll of public attitudes about Swedish society, security policy, international affairs, and defense. In their report, *Opinion 98,*[8] 75% of those surveyed considered it appropriate for the UN to resort to direct acts of war to restore peace and security. Furthermore, an equal percentage (75%) approved of Sweden's decision to contribute troops to the operations in Bosnia. Sweden's non-alignment policy was supported by 59% of the population, but 25% wanted Sweden to apply for full membership in NATO. Almost half of the population (46%) approved of Sweden's participation in EU efforts to build a common foreign and security policy and a joint military defense, while 39% were opposed to such a development.

In a 1993 study of conscripts' attitudes towards military service,[9] respondents were asked their opinions of Sweden's decision to provide troops for UN missions like those in the former Yugoslavia. In all, 58% approved of Swedish participation in UN missions. Among conscript NCOs, the figure was even higher: 72%. Respondents were also asked whether they themselves would consider applying for such missions after completing military service. Over a third (37%) answered yes, while an equal percentage answered no. Conscript NCOs were again more positive: 54% stated that they would consider applying for UN duty. Apparently, the base for recruitment to peacekeeping operations seems to be rather broad, even despite the change in the type of mission represented by Bosnia. One problem, though, is the decreasing number of persons who actually complete compulsory military service and are therefore qualified to apply for peace support operations. It is already difficult today to find and recruit certain mission-essential personnel; this situation may become even worse over the next few years if the recruitment base decreases.

1.5. PEACEKEEPING IN THE FORMER YUGOSLAVIA

The conflict in the former Yugoslavia began in 1991 with the wars in Slovenia and Croatia. In the wake of the euphoria that accompanied the fall of the Berlin Wall in 1989, the entire world seemed paralyzed by the fact that a war raged in Europe. When the international community finally understood the magnitude of military aggression in the Balkans, and when the EU and UN became seriously involved in efforts to end the conflict, the peace process got caught up in many problematic situations.

---

[8]   Styrelsen för Psykologiskt Försvar, *Opinion 98, Svenskarnas syn på samhället, säkerhetspolitiken och försvaret*, Göran Stutz (Stockholm: SPF, 1999).

[9]   Eva Johansson, *Inskrivningsskyldigas attityder till försvar och värnplikt* (Karlstad: FOA, PM 55:183, 1994).

The United Nations Protection Force (UNPROFOR) in the former Yugoslavia started in 1992. The UN's initial mandate called for contributing states to send troops to Croatia and to establish headquarters in Bosnia-Herzegovina for the operation in Sarajevo. The reason for locating UN operations headquarters in Sarajevo was the assessment that this would have a dampening effect on developments in Bosnia-Herzegovina, then considered likely to be the next Balkan powder keg. [10] Despite these efforts, however, war spread to Bosnia-Herzegovina. The headquarters were thus caught up in the outbreak of fighting in Sarajevo in spring 1992, necessitating the relocation of headquarters from Sarajevo to Zagreb (after a brief interlude in Belgrade).

At the beginning of March 1992, Swedish participation in UNPROFOR consisted of military observers, civilian police, and a headquarters company. As UNPROFOR's task and mandate grew, the first Nordic battalion (Nordbat 1) was deployed to Macedonia in January 1993. The Nordic commitment, and therefore the Swedish commitment, was subsequently increased to include the deployment of a mechanized infantry battalion (Nordbat 2) to Bosnia-Herzegovina in October 1993. This Nordic battalion was situated in the Tuzla area, in northern Bosnia. Since December 1995, Sweden has also provided personnel within the framework of NATO, since UNPROFOR changed hands to become a NATO-led operation. Participation in the Implementation Force (IFOR) and later the Stabilization Force (SFOR) was something new from a Swedish point of view. As mentioned above, Sweden had extensive experience in working under UN missions; however, it had considerably less experience with NATO, since Sweden is not a member. The culture, traditions, terminology – and to some extent participants – were all quite new to the Swedes.

As of this writing, Sweden has personnel serving in the former Yugoslavia under the auspices of the EU, OSCE, WEU, UN, and NATO.

1.6. METHODOLOGY

Although Sweden has extensive experience in peacekeeping operations, very few systematic attempts have been made to document the lessons learned; such lessons learned could benefit the Swedish Total Defense organization as well as other entities intending to serve in international operations. Swedish international missions could, to a certain degree, be compared to a "black box." When commanders and soldiers begin a mission, it is as if they disappear into a black box, to reappear again six months later. What remains after the mission is a final report that provides a technical description of the period in the mission area. After demobilization, the erstwhile peacekeepers take their personal experiences with them. Stories about events and people are spread in different

---

[10] Eva Johansson, *In a Blue Beret: Four Swedish UN Battalions in Bosnia* (Karlstad: Klaria AB, 1997).

ways, rather like wanderers' tales. [11] Professional evaluations of Swedish units on international duty were rare before Bosnia. [12]

This article focuses on Swedish peacekeeping experiences in Bosnia from 1993 to 1998. Swedish battalions were deployed in an area dominated by Muslims. Empirical data were collected through the distribution of questionnaires to 10 mechanized infantry battalions that served during both the UN and NATO periods. Most of the questionnaires were distributed to personnel during their demobilization procedure. The survey group consisted of 3,505 individuals from the UNPROFOR period and 2,351 individuals from the IFOR/SFOR period, for a total of 5,856 persons. The fifth battalion that served with both UNPROFOR and IFOR is not included. At its peak, the battalion consisted of 1,020 individuals (UNPROFOR), but that number was gradually reduced to 405 individuals, which was the battalion size in 1999.

The questionnaire contained 45 items during the UNPROFOR period and 53 items during the IFOR/SFOR period, most of them with fixed response alternatives. The purpose of the survey questionnaire was to gather information from a broad spectrum of experiences in order to get a better understanding of how Swedish personnel react, adapt, and cope during international operations.

Since the IFOR/SFOR period, however, questionnaires were distributed both before departure to and after return from the mission area. The pre-deployment questionnaire emphasized issues concerning expectations, recruitment principles, mental preparedness, and hesitations about going on duty. Both the pre-deployment and post-deployment questionnaires were answered anonymously.

In addition, several field studies were conducted during the Swedish deployment in Bosnia. In this article, data from these studies are used mainly to provide a broader understanding of the results of the questionnaire study. The results are presented with the aim of comparing Swedish peacekeepers' experiences during tours of duty, depending on whether they served during the UN or NATO period.

---

[11] Lars Andersson and Eva Johansson, *Developing Military Leadership by Making Leadership Problems Visible* (Karlstad: National Defense College, 1999), p. 13.

[12] Results of behavioral science research on the functioning of Swedish commanders and soldiers in peacekeeping missions are described in several articles and reports, including Lars Andersson et al., *Utbildning av FN-bataljoner för Libanon. Utvärdering och diskussion* (Karlstad: FOA 55, PM 55:124, 1987); Lars Andersson et al., *Kvinnor i FN-tjänst* (Karlstad: FOA 55, PM 55:134, 1988); Anders Carlström et al., "Mental Adjustment of Swedish UN Soldiers in South Lebanon in 1988," *Stress Medicine* 6 (1990), pp. 305–310; Tom Lundin et al., "Swedish UN Soldiers in Cyprus, UNIFICYP: Their Psychological and Social Situation," *Psychotherapy and Psychomatics* 57 (1992), pp. 187–193; and Bertil Kettner, "Combat Strain and Subsequent Mental Health," *Acta Psychtriatrica Scandinavica, Supplement 230* (Copenhagen: Munksgaard, 1972).

2. INTERNAL MILITARY DIMENSION

2.1. CURRENT CONDITIONS FOR SWEDISH PERSONNEL SERVING IN BOSNIA

Swedish personnel participate in UN service on a voluntary basis. This is true for officers as well as all other ranks. It is possible to apply for UN service twice a year. For the battalions in Bosnia, however, recruitment principles were slightly different with regard to regular officers. During this period, selected brigades in Sweden were responsible for supplying the battalions with suitable personnel. This meant that many regular officers were recruited from those or nearby brigades.

Male applicants who are not regular or reserve officers must have completed their compulsory military service with a good record. Military service is usually completed by the age of 20. The situation for female personnel is somewhat different, as Sweden does not have compulsory military service for women. Female candidates must apply for service and go through a multi-stage application process. First, they are screened and tested, then they complete a very short basic military training course; finally, if they are successful, they may apply for UN service.

Different types of skills are emphasized depending on the position for which an individual applies. For instance, civilian skills are important for certain expert positions in the battalion, such as medical personnel, computer experts, hygienists, carpenters, etc., while soldiering skills are emphasized for purely military positions. All personnel, however, must have some basic military competence and knowledge.

Before departure to the mission area, all personnel receive special training, which is normally conducted by the Swedish Armed Forces International Center (SWEDINT). The length of this training period is dependent on one's position in the unit and the mission's degree of difficulty, and whether or not the mission is new. For service in Bosnia, the training period varies from four to eight weeks.

The normal tour of service is six months, but some individuals are contracted for a shorter period of time while others sign up for additional service in a subsequent battalion. The battalions rotate as a body, stretched over a period of three to four weeks.

2.2. THE BATTALIONS AND THEIR PERSONNEL

The personnel in the battalions serving in Bosnia are young; about half of the personnel were between 20–25 years of age; 76% stated that they were single. Even though such a large proportion was relatively young, 35% during the UN period and 39% during the NATO period had previous UN or NATO experience. The proportion of female participants was 3% during the UN period and 5% during the NATO period. Although in general the women were older than their male colleagues, about the same proportion was single. The employment situation of recruits upon their return to Sweden varied; among personnel from the UN period, 34% stated that they were unemployed while the figure from the NATO period was 27%. Of those who stated they were unemployed when they returned home, about 70% had also given unemployment as an important reason for applying for UN service. The questionnaire also included a question on the attitude of the recruit's family toward his or her participation in the Bosnian mission. During the UN period, families for the most part accepted or supported the person's participation in UN service. Only 4% were definitely against participation. During the NATO period, even fewer (1%) reported that their families were against participation, while participation was supported by 56% and accepted by 43%.

The following five tables present figures on the age distribution, marital status, previous UN or NATO mission experience, employment situation, and level of family support level during both the UN and NATO periods.

Table 1: Age distribution (UN and NATO periods, in percent)

Age	UN period N = 3,487	NATO period N = 2,340
20 – 25	52	50
26 – 30	32	28
31 – 35	8	12
36 – 40	4	4
41 – 45	2	2
45 and over	2	4

Table 2: Marital status (UN and NATO periods, in percent)

Marital status	UN period N = 3,484	NATO period N = 2,330
Married/cohabiting	23	25
Single	77	75

The tables show that data on battalion personnel do not differ greatly between the UN and NATO periods concerning these background variables. The level of experience in peacekeeping missions was somewhat higher among personnel serving during the NATO period. The decrease in reported unemployment among NATO-period respondents may reflect the fact that the em-

Table 3: Participation in Earlier UN/NATO Missions (UN and NATO periods, in percent)

Earlier service	UN period N = 3,492	NATO period N = 2,337
None	65	61
One tour	20	24
Two or more tours	15	15

Table 4: Employment Situation of Personnel Returning Home (UN and NATO periods, in percent)

Employment situation	UN period N = 3,428	NATO period N = 2,257
Full employment	46	49
Casual employment	11	12
Intend to study	9	12
Unemployed	34	27

Table 5: Families' Views Regarding Participation in Service. (UN and NATO periods, in percent)

Family Attitudes toward Service in Bosnia	UN period N = 3,448	NATO period N = 2,298
Full support	39	56
Acceptance	57	43
Firm opposition	4	1

ployment situation in Sweden has improved during recent years. The increase in family support could be explained by a reduced uncertainty factor, since the mission became well known among the population, and many people have served in the area without much trouble.

In Sweden, cautionary voices have urged that peacekeeping should not be turned into an ordinary profession. Principles regarding selection have therefore been revised; now, the recommendation is that persons who have served on a peacekeeping mission should stay at home, in Sweden, for at least 12 months before applying for a new tour. Furthermore, no one should be deployed more than three times to the same mission area. Efforts to prevent personnel from spending too much time away from family and friends serve to reduce the risk of adjustment problems after a tour of duty, thereby making it easier for former peacekeepers to fit into society again.

2.3. VIEW OF HOW WELL THE TASK WAS ACCOMPLISHED

The greatest differences among battalions in their attitudes toward how well they had fulfilled their task occurred during the UNPROFOR period. The first battalion was decidedly more convinced than the following ones that they had fulfilled their tasks. In the first battalion, a clear majority thought that they had succeeded in alleviating the suffering of the civilian population, that they had protected the civilian population against attacks and assault, and that they had acted to calm the conflicting parties. In the other battalions, however, substantially fewer believed they had succeeded in achieving these goals. Comments included the following:

- "There was no suffering among the civilians; anyway, if there were villages that needed help, we were prevented from getting there."
- "We were not allowed to protect the civilian population and there wasn't any peace to keep, so we didn't have a calming effect on the conflicting parties."

The statements may well reflect the frustration that arises when one is given a job to do in a very complex situation and does not have or cannot use the right tools to perform the job. The tasks and, more importantly, the conditions for conducting the mission changed substantially when NATO was responsible for operations in the area. Apart from the tasks of protecting the civilian population against attack or assault and acting to calm the conflicting parties, the battalion had to maintain and supervise the zone of separation and secure freedom of movement in the area. For the first time since the beginning of the conflict, the troops felt they had the ability to perform their tasks successfully. Therefore, during the IFOR/SFOR period, the troops felt more positive about their chances of succeeding with their tasks. Over 80% thought that they had succeeded fairly well or to a great degree in performing their tasks.

Table 6 describes the different tasks, with figures for both the UN and NATO periods. Respondents were asked to indicate how well they considered that these tasks had been fulfilled. The table shows the percentage of respondents who believed the battalion had succeeded *fairly well* or *to a great degree* in solving the tasks given as examples.

The NATO period, to a great extent, was characterized by the view that the battalion had succeeded in accomplishing its various tasks. The same feeling, to a certain degree, also applied to the first battalion in UNPROFOR, but to a significantly lesser degree among the rest of the UN battalions. Many (80%) also stated that they generally felt their efforts were appreciated.

Several comments indicated that the Swedish personnel felt the success or failure of the mission depended on circumstances in the area or overall situation, and not on the individual soldier or unit.

Table 6: Respondents who believed the battalion had succeeded to a great degree or fairly well in performing given tasks (UN and NATO periods, in percent)

Tasks	UN period	NATO period
Contribute to relief of suffering among civilian population (UNPROFOR only)	69	–
Contribute to protecting civilian population against attack/assault	47	86
Act to mollify the conflicting parties	43	94
Maintain and supervise zone of separation (only IFOR/SFOR)	-	94
Secure freedom of movement in the area (only IFOR/SFOR)	-	83

Segal and Waldman have studied the background and effectiveness of UN peacekeeping operations. [13] They found that a central element to mission success involves (i) whether the conflicting parties have experienced the costs of violence and (ii) whether they have at least a potential stake in pursuing non-violent options. Furthermore, peacekeeping interventions have been most likely to succeed in controlling the conflict when both conflicting parties have something to gain from the success of the peacekeeping operation.

2.4. FACTORS HINDERING THE PERFORMANCE OF TASKS

As can be seen from the results so far, the situation for the peacekeepers looked quite different during the UN period compared to the NATO period. While the UN period was characterized by increasing complexity regarding the performance of tasks or even the fulfillment of the mandate with its ever-changing resolutions, the conditions of the NATO period provided greater leverage for implementing the Dayton Accords and starting a peace process.

From the questionnaire data, it is possible to identify certain factors that personnel in the various battalions felt hindered, or did not hinder, the performance of their tasks. These factors can be divided into three groups: (i) factors involving the conflicting parties or the local situation, (ii) factors involving material or human resources, and (iii) factors involving higher levels of command or other authorities.

The personnel responded on a 4-grade scale from *not at all* to *a high degree*. Table 7 provides figures on hindering factors, divided according to factor

---

[13]   David R. Segal and Robert J. Waldman, "Multinational Peacekeeping Operations: Background and Effectiveness," in James Burk (Ed.), *The Adaptive Military: Armed Forces in a Turbulent World*, 2nd ed. (New Brunswick: Transaction Publishers, 1998), pp. 183 – 199.

group and mission period. The figures reflect the percentage of respondents who answered "quite a lot" or "to a high degree," which are reported together in the table.

Table 7: Factors Representing Obstacles to the Performance of Tasks (percentage of respondents answering "quite a lot" or "to a high degree," UN and NATO periods)

Factor Group	Hindering Factors	UN period	NATO period
Conflicting parties/ local situation	Lack of freedom of movement	73	4
	Action of local authorities	57	10
	The difficult situation itself	23	5
Resources: materiel/personnel	Poor maintenance	30	10
	Lack of suitable materiel	33	19
	Lack of suitable personnel	12	13
Higher levels of command or other authorities	Restrictions from BHC/UN or NordPolBrig/IFOR/SFOR	42	23
	Lack of support from OP command, SWEDINT	34	14
	Political actions in Sweden	21	22
	Circumstances within UNHCR	15	3

During the UNPROFOR period, one factor in particular, "lack of freedom of movement," was the greatest obstacle to the performance of tasks. This also appears to have been a growing problem from the first battalion up to the time when NATO took over. The conflicting parties, in particular the Bosnian army, did not consent unconditionally to the UN operation, but rather gave sporadic consent. Thus, they often acted in their own interests, which were seldom in accordance with those of the UN.

The hindering factors listed in Table 7 were much weaker during the NATO period. However, the number of respondents who stated that political actions in Sweden were a hindering factor remained constant. This could have several explanations depending on the period of deployment. During the first battalion's tour, the Swedish government refused to send units to Srebrenica, a Muslim village outside the Swedish battalion area, after a request by the UN. This decision was based on concerns over the UN's capacity for successful command and control over national contingents. Another criticism directed toward internal Swedish politics focused on the issue of remuneration, i.e., a considerable number of Swedish UN soldiers felt that Sweden did too little to raise salaries to a decent level, comparable with, e.g., other Nordic countries. Lastly, the debate in Sweden over whether UN soldiers might participate in combat may have been of significance for personnel serving in 1995 – 1996.

Aside from internal Swedish politics, restrictions from higher levels of command (e.g., NORDPOLBDE) were viewed as a hindering factor by 23% of respondents serving during the NATO period. Swedish (UN) soldiers are used to taking responsibility for their tasks in a highly autonomous manner; under NATO, some felt that the organization was ruled too much from the top, especially as the chain of command became much more evident, a somewhat new experience for the Swedes. (At the same time, however, one must acknowledge that during the UNPROFOR period, most critics felt that the UN, as a bureaucratic organization, did not have enough resources and accordingly very often had to retreat from the conflicting parties.) Overall, hindrances to performance almost vanished during the NATO period, at least with regard to factors listed in the questionnaire.

2.5. PREPARATION AND TRAINING REQUIREMENTS

Since the operation in Bosnia, there has been a change in the way Sweden organizes its participation in peacekeeping missions. This involves a greater responsibility for selected brigades in Sweden to recruit, equip, and train units before deployment to the mission area. Some have claimed that this "brigade" principle has caused each brigade to invent the wheel over and over again. The lack of continuity has had a negative effect on the transfer of lessons learned. Others argue that this principle increases good fellowship among officers before deployment to the mission area; this argument seems only partly true since, according to the pre-deployment questionnaire, 75% of the officers were positively inclined toward the "brigade" principle before departure to the mission area, compared to 51% after the end of their tour (according to the post-deployment questionnaire).

In connection with the operation in Bosnia, pre-deployment training has been increased and varies from four to eight weeks, depending on one's position within the unit. Besides traditional pre-deployment training exercises, much more emphasis has been placed on military training such as live firing exercises, patrol duty, and worst-case scenarios. The training seeks to increase the brigade's ability to handle the heavier and more modern armaments now included in the equipment for international units, as well as to give the units experience in working within a hostile environment. However, questionnaire responses indicated that the training did not match the local situation in Bosnia; some respondents pointed out that training in worst-case scenarios could affect individuals by fostering aggressive and provocative attitudes. This issue is also mentioned by Hårleman, who states that "Overly offensive training may contribute to aggressive behaviour, which may create unpredictable and dangerous situations, not only for the soldiers, but also for others who may be involved." [14]

A number of items in the questionnaire asked respondents to identify areas in which they had needed more preparation and training before traveling to the mission area. The answers may have been influenced by the fact that the questionnaire was completed after the tour. Respondents had by then served in the area for at least six months, which strongly affected their perspective on how pre-deployment training corresponded to the actual mission. If, for example, the respondent felt during the tour that he/she mastered the equipment or weapons well, this probably meant he/she did not feel a need for more preparation or training in this respect. This applies regardless of whether the skill had been developed in the mission area or during pre-tour training.

The questions regarding training needs can be grouped into four different blocks or themes. The first block involves training related to "tools" for understanding the "new" service situation. The second block involves "tools" for better handling the new situation. The third block involves more traditional military knowledge, and the fourth involves training related to leadership. Table 8 shows the proportion of Swedish peacekeepers who believed they would have benefited from additional preparation or training.

About half the respondents believed they could have benefited from additional training to better understand the situation they had worked in. Many respondents stated they required better pre-deployment training in local languages and the local population's traditions and values. Many also emphasized the need for more practice in NATO terminology.

It is not wrong to say that cultural understanding is of significant importance to peacekeepers and, since language is closely associated with culture, knowledge of local languages becomes an advantage in understanding that culture. Many respondents made corresponding comments in the questionnaire's open-ended section, such as "try to learn about the culture and the people be-

---

[14] Christian Hårleman, "Psychological Aspects of Peacekeeping on the Ground," in Harvey J. Langholtz (Ed.), *The Psychology of Peacekeeping* (Westport: Praeger, 1998), pp. 101–110.

Table 8: Respondents who Believed They Required Additional Preparation/Training (According to training area and mission period, in percent)

Area of training	Subject	UN period	NATO period
Understanding the new situation	Different population groups' traditions and values	65	65
	Political situation in the area	54	53
	The UN/NATO role in the area	54	40
Handling the new situation	Language skills (local language)	66	62
	Negotiation techniques	42	26
	Ability to assess consequences and risks	36	24
	Ability to counter threats and provocations	45	29
	NATO terminology	–	52
Military/technical	Physical training	31	25
	Ability to fix own unit's material	36	24
	Ability to use materiel/equipment	35	30
	Living under primitive conditions	14	8
	Use of weapons	22	19
"Leadership"	Recognizing stress in others	40	30
	Mastering one's own stress	18	14
	Ability to take initiative and lead others	21	17
	Cooperating with others	15	14

fore you go there," or "to know just a few words in the local language can serve as an icebreaker and facilitate daily life in the mission area, for both parties."

2.6. Assessment of Morale, Cohesion, and Leadership

During the UN period, many individuals wrote comments in the questionnaire regarding unit morale, cohesion, and leadership. For that reason, a couple of new questions were added to the questionnaire at the start of the IFOR period.

The questions were constructed to elucidate the internal climate at both the company/section and battalion levels. The question consisted of nine different statements, and answers were given on a 4-point scale from *not at all* to *to a great extent*. Table 9 presents the nine different statements and the extent to which personnel found these significant for their company or battalion.

Table 9: Factors that Affected Morale, Cohesion, and Leadership (At Company and Battalion Levels, in percent)

Factors	Level	Not at all	To some degree	Fairly much	To a great extent
Offenses against rules	Company	51	38	8	3
	Battalion	*35*	*40*	*16*	*9*
Strict boundaries	Company	44	35	15	6
	Battalion	*29*	*37*	*24*	*10*
Tendencies toward racist behavior	Company	80	16	3	1
	Battalion	*70*	*26*	*3*	*1*
"Rambo" behavior	Company	76	19	4	1
	Battalion	*56*	*32*	*10*	*2*
Struggle for a good service record	Company	50	29	14	7
	Battalion	*38*	*35*	*18*	*9*
The opportunity of taking personal responsibility for deciding how to implement tasks	Company	9	25	38	28
	Battalion	*13*	*40*	*35*	*12*
Cohesion	Company	6	14	40	40
	Battalion	*9*	*32*	*43*	*16*
Good leadership	Company	12	22	38	28
	Battalion	*15*	*35*	*37*	*13*
Good comradeship	Company	2	7	31	60
	Battalion	*4*	*18*	*46*	*32*

The overall climate was perceived to be rather good, especially with regard to comradeship and unit cohesion. All companies in the different battalions rated their own unit's (company) climate more highly than the climate of their battalion. Concerning the "offenses against rules" factor, the major comment was that most offenses were against the unit's alcohol policy. Each battalion wrote a policy document before departure to the mission area that contained rules of conduct. This document was supposed to be agreed upon by all personnel and was a battalion document alongside official standard regulations such as the Standard Operating Procedure (SOP). Normally, writing the policy document is part of the team-building process before departure to the mission area. For example, racist behavior is forbidden; in most documents there is special emphasis on dealing appropriately with other nationalities. Respondents stated that tendencies toward racist behavior were low among the different battalions, especially within their own units, but 20% believed such tendencies existed to some extent within their own unit and 30% within the battalion as a whole. During the UN period, many respondents stated that Sweden should not send "Rambo soldiers" to the mission area, as these "warriors" do more harm than good. Few stated that "Rambo behavior" had occurred frequently during the mission, but 24% stated that it occurred to some degree at the company level and 44% at the battalion level.

To a certain degree, different battalions and companies show different profiles. To a large extent, these profiles have their origin in the unit culture or climate. To varying degrees, internal conflicts have affected behavior within units as well as the overall evaluation of the service period. Participants in all battalions studied declared that the overall result was good and that the battalions performed their tasks in the best way possible, a fact that is reflected in final reports. There is no need to disagree with this, but, in looking closely at each battalion, an "organizational iceberg" appears. [15] What can be seen above the surface level is the result of the operation, which for the battalions in Bosnia is considered well done. However, beneath the surface and hence barely detectable, power struggles, policy violations, crises of confidence, leadership problems, unresolved moral dilemmas, and symptoms of "group-think" are to be found. This is not unique to battalions deployed in Bosnia, but it is surprising to observe the level of amazement and sometimes paralysis displayed by many commanders when confronted with these covert problems. Since battalions operate on a 24-hour basis for six months, it is impossible to "hide" problems, and – in contrast to the ordinary workday in Sweden – there are no escape routes in terms of family support or free weekends.

In light of different studies now being conducted among Swedish soldiers deployed in peace missions, together with the somewhat changed image in the media (due to accusations of alcohol abuse and prostitution among Swedish soldiers in peacekeeping operations), these signs should be taken seriously by those responsible for selecting and deploying units, especially since other

---

[15] Eva Johansson and Lars Andersson, "Assessment of Factors Affecting Morale, Cohesion, and Leadership in Swedish Peacekeeping Forces," paper presented at the 14th World Congress of Sociology, Montreal (1998).

countries taking part in peacekeeping operations have experienced similar phe-
nomena, and sometimes worse, in their units.

3. MILITARY TO MILITARY DIMENSION

3.1. SOLDIERS' MOTIVES FOR VOLUNTEERING FOR THE PEACE-KEEPING MISSION IN BOSNIA

The most common reasons motivating Swedes to serve in the UN peacekeeping operation in Bosnia were to make a personal contribution, to experience
something exciting, to belong to a closely knit group, to improve one's qualifications for the future, and to leave routine, day-to-day life at home. Some
respondents also stressed the importance of personal development. Since the
NATO period, the questionnaire has been changed slightly with regard to motives. The same alternatives remain in the question, but instead of responding
to each alternative and answering on a 4-point scale from *of no significance*
to *very important,* respondents were asked to select a maximum of three most
important motives, or to provide their own written alternative. Another change
was that the issue of motives was also addressed in the pre-deployment questionnaire.

The most significant change in the results was that the motive "to have
the opportunity to save money" was emphasized as one of the most important motives, especially in the post-deployment questionnaire. Another change
was that the motive "to belong to a closely knit group" was not among the
five most common motives in both the pre- and post-deployment questionnaires. The greatest change between pre- and post-deployment assessments
involved the motive "to make a personal contribution," which 45% marked as
important in the pre-deployment questionnaire, compared to 36% in the post-
deployment questionnaire. Otherwise, the motive structure was very much the
same before and after the tour of duty. Regular officers had a somewhat different motive structure since they stressed the importance of the opportunity
to make "proper" use of their military training and to improve one's qualifications for the future. For officers nowadays, a successful period of international
duty is essentially a prerequisite for the positive development of one's military
career. Furthermore, some officers stressed that they were more or less obli-
gated to participate because their regiment was responsible for sending a unit.
A trend is seen in recent battalions towards an increased interest in adventure
and moneymaking. However, it is possible that responses concerning motives
reflect socially acceptable answers.

As mentioned above, a pre-deployment questionnaire was used in recent
studies, beginning with the IFOR battalion in 1996. One question dealt with
the issue of expectations regarding tour of duty. This was an open-ended ques-

tion in which respondents could write down the expectations they had for the upcoming tour. Altruistic expectations were often expressed, but some differences among personnel also appeared. Stated briefly, young soldiers who were being deployed for the first time had very strong beliefs that they would learn more about themselves, develop as persons, have a stimulating time, experience excitement, and have a chance to help others. Soldiers with previous UN experience, on the other hand, had a more pragmatic view of their period of service. Answers like earning money, meeting old friends, and having fun dominated. Officers generally had expectations concerning their professional development. Those without any previous period of service abroad often emphasized the actual task and the importance of doing a good job in a realistic environment. Officers with previous experience in peacekeeping operations stressed the importance of taking care of their personnel and having the chance to do humanitarian work.

All these different expectations (and motives) might influence the way in which the service period is looked upon and how people valued their tour. On the one hand, personnel seemed to be highly motivated, wanted to achieve a great deal, and had high expectations. On the other hand, the demobilization questionnaire indicates that many would advise persons going to Bosnia against having high expectations. Below is a random selection of comments on this theme:

- "Don't set your expectations too high."
- "Be patient and don't expect to accomplish too much."
- "Don't expect to be able to help – the UN's role in [the] former Yugoslavia is deplorable and unfortunate."
- "Don't imagine you'll be able to do any good, save lives, stop the war, or anything like that."
- "It is better to keep expectations low; furthermore, don't think that the humanitarian efforts are that great."

The motivation structure, and the trend towards more excitement and pragmatic motives, at the expense of altruistic motives, might reflect greater awareness among applicants regarding the nature of the conflict as highly complex encounters that will not be solved during one 6-month period of service. The common image of the peacekeeping soldier could also be said to have changed since the deployment in Bosnia. Very often, the media have portrayed the peacekeeping soldier as a "combat soldier," heavily armed and well equipped. This depiction differs significantly from that of peacekeeping soldiers carrying light armaments and wearing blue helmets, which was portrayed in photos and booklets from Cyprus and Lebanon. Today's "peacekeeping" might thus attract a different kind of person. Moreover, it is clear that a mechanized infantry battalion will attract a different type of person than, for example, a logistics battalion, which was one of Sweden's major contributions to previous UN peacekeeping operations. It might also reflect the fact that the previous mental image of peacekeeping soldiers is slowly but steadily changing from that of "peace angels" to "warriors for peace" in the minds of Swedes. [16]

4. MILITARY RELATIONS WITH NATIONAL AND INTERNATIONAL ORGANIZATIONS

4.1. POINTS OF CONTACT DURING THE PERIOD OF SERVICE

Peace support operations imply that the range of contacts during a tour of service involve more than the national or purely military domain. To gather information on the groups and individuals with which personnel had contact during their periods in service, the questionnaire elicited responses regarding 14 different groups/units and the extent to which Swedish peacekeepers had contact with them. The group "own commanders" comprises platoon, company, and battalion commanders. Answers were on a 4-point scale from *never* to *daily*.

Table 10 presents figures on the extent to which various battalions came into contact with (a selection of) different groups. The alternatives *fairly often* and *daily* are presented together in the table.

Table 10: Units/Groups with which Battalions Came into Contact during their Tours
(Respondents answering "fairly often" or "daily," in percent)

Unit/groups	UN period	NATO period
Own commanders	61	63
Other UN/NATO units	56	62
EU monitors	10	4
IPTF	–	19
UNHCR	21	4
Red Cross	7	2
Civilian population	74	70

Contacts within the battalion and with the civilian population remained high during both the UN and NATO periods. So did contacts with other UN/NATO units, while contacts with the UN High Commission for Refugees

---

[16] Cf. Franz Kernic and Harald Haas, *Warriors for Peace* (Frankfurt am Main: Peter Lang, 1999).

(UNHCR), in particular, decreased. This decrease can be explained by a change in the local situation, in which military escorts were no longer needed for humanitarian transports conducted by the UNHCR or other NGOs. Contacts with the International Police Task Force (IPTF) were especially frequent during the NATO period in connection with riots that occurred when people tried to return to areas where they had lived before the conflict. The most common point of contact with the civilian population involved work relations, i.e., when local people were employed as interpreters or support personnel; contacts were also established between soldiers and the local population during so-called "social patrols."

The data presented in Table 10 allow the speculation that the presence of other UN/NATO units or organizations in a particular area does not automatically mean frequent contact with these other entities. Rather, each unit mainly acts only within its own organization to achieve its own goals and accomplish its own tasks. There seems to be a limited number of individuals responsible for collaboration and cooperation with other organizations and entities; moreover, this cooperation appears to take place at higher command levels or within units that have support functions.

Regarding cooperation in civil–military operations, Major General and Deputy Chief of Joint Operations Staff Johan Hederstedt [17] points to Swedish experiences in operations like the one in Bosnia. These experiences reveal the central problem: that commanding personnel, in both civilian and military organizations, have insufficient competence or knowledge to solve problems beyond the direct task of commanding their own units. This inability leads to passiveness and sometimes negative attitudes, for example, on the part of military leaders who do not want to cooperate with civilians, or civilians who regard the military as the major threat. These attitudes hinder the rational use of joint resources in an operation area. Of course, if civilian or military commanders have negative views of cooperation efforts, this can affect the views of the rest of the personnel. The same applies if commanders have different understandings of the mission mandate.

---

[17]   Johan Hederstedt, "Cooperation in Peace-Keeping/Peace-Enforcing Civilian/Military Operations," in Bo Huldt, Annika Hilding, and Arita Eriksson (Eds.), *Challenges of Peace Support into the 21st Century* (Stockholm: Norstedts, 1998), p. 111.

5. RELATIONS WITH THE (NATIONAL) MEDIA AND THE LOCAL POPULATION

5.1. DIFFERENT ANGLES OF NATIONAL MEDIA COVERAGE FROM THE FORMER YUGOSLAVIA

The events in the former Yugoslavia have been quite extensively covered by the Swedish national media, which have also provided extensive coverage of Swedish battalions' work in the area. At the beginning, the tone was quite positive, but as time passed, more and more criticisms surfaced, first towards the impotent management of the UNPROFOR operation but later also towards Swedish achievements in the former Yugoslavia. In several reports, the media have pointed out conditions that might indicate gaps in the leadership of the international Swedish units. Tabloids featured headlines on alcohol abuse and the exploitation of prostitutes among Swedish officers and soldiers. [18] In addition, during the changeover from a UN- to a NATO-led operation, a discussion took place in the media that was caused by a statement from the Minister of Defense at that time, who indicated that Swedish units did not have the ability to "attack." The media discussion was rooted in the ongoing debate about how and whether Sweden would or could participate in a NATO-led operation. The basic theme of this debate was "Swedish soldiers cannot attack," implying that they would be given special treatment and could not cope with the same problems that battalions of other nations did. Irritation among military personnel in general, and in the Swedish battalion in particular, was high.

The 1990s have brought changes to Swedish defense and security policy. Sweden's neutrality and non-alignment policy, once highly cherished, has to some degree been given new meaning. One step in the direction of change occurred when Sweden joined the Partnership for Peace (PfP) program in 1994. The goals of Swedish participation in PfP are to enhance Swedish capacity and interoperability, to facilitate operations with NATO, and to support other countries (i.e., the Baltic States) in their efforts to participate in PfP exercises and peace support operations. Furthermore, Sweden became a member of the European Union (EU) in 1994, and has been an active observer in the Western European Union (WEU) since 1995. In 1995, Sweden participated with troops in a NATO-led operation for the first time.

A study by Peter Berglez [19] analyzes how the Swedish media, in this case the leading daily *Dagens Nyheter*, reported on the integration of Swedish UN troops into the NATO-led operation in Bosnia. Special attention was paid

---

[18] See, e.g., Viveka Hansson and Thomas Mattsson, "Officer sköts på bordellen," *Expressen*, 8 January 1997, pp. 6–7, and Ulrika Häggroth, "Den hemliga rapporten om FN-befälen," *Expressen*, 10 July 1997, pp. 6–7.

[19] Peter Berglez, *Bilder av FN och NATO* (Örebro: Stadstryck AB, 1999).

to media treatment of this issue from the perspective of neutrality and non-alignment. The analysis demonstrated that journalists at *Dagens Nyheter* took no substantial initiative in discussing the transition from a UN- to a NATO-led operation from the perspective of neutrality and non-alignment. On the contrary, the media could be said to have contributed to a social consensus on the redefinition of Swedish security policy. This redefinition includes, above all, the concept that it is possible to combine Swedish participation in a NATO-led operation with the traditional Swedish principle of neutrality and non-alignment.

In the questionnaires, many comments addressed the media coverage from Bosnia; most comments criticized the media's tendency to exaggerate and to some extent give a false picture of the everyday reality in Bosnia. One explanation of the criticism of the media may be that the image respondents had before leaving Sweden, painted mostly by the media, created entirely incorrect expectations about what the tour might entail. In addition, while deployed, respondents might have developed perceptions of the situation that were different from those presented in the media. If one lives with a "reality" 24 hours a day, a 30-second news item may appear to be superficial or just plain misleading.

It is obvious however, that the media, through their coverage, have managed to move the theater of conflict into the living room. One result has been an increased pressure on regional, national, and international authorities to act. Furthermore, it is also obvious that peacekeepers in different situations will be subject to media attention and must deal with that reality in a constructive way.

5.2. VIEW OF THE CIVILIAN POPULATION AND THE CONFLICTING PARTIES IN THE FORMER YUGOSLAVIA

During their periods of service, battalion members had varying opportunities to come into contact with the civilian population and the conflicting parties. The personnel of the first battalion (UNPROFOR) came into contact with practically all the parties in the area, while those of subsequent battalions had extremely little or no contact with the Serbian civilian population, the Bosnian-Serbian population, the Bosnian Serb Army (BSA, later VRS), or the Croatian Army (HVO). During IFOR/SFOR, however, contacts with different Serbian factions reappeared. In the questionnaire, three questions were asked. First, peacekeepers were asked to describe their various experiences with the civilian populations and conflicting parties. Second, they were asked to describe their opinions of how the civilian populations and conflicting parties viewed them. Third, they were asked whether their attitudes toward the local population groups had changed during the tour.

Generally speaking, there was a trend towards more negative views regarding the different groups with whom the personnel came into contact during the

UN period. The same could be said about respondents' opinions of how the local population and the various conflicting parties viewed them; in this case, an even more negative trend appeared for most of the groups. Quite a few also stated that they had no experiences of contact with the various groups in the area. During the NATO period, however, attitudes became more positive; this applies especially to the Bosnian Serb and Serbian civilian populations. Contacts with the Bosnian civilian population were mostly positive throughout the periods studied.

The reasons for experiencing the contacts as positive or negative were not elicited in the questionnaire. However, one reasonable explanation could involve the changed situation in the area. The first battalion serving for UNPRO-FOR was greatly needed in the area, particularly by the civilian population. In addition, it was the first unit in the area and thus had extensive contact with civilians and the conflicting parties. This battalion also enjoyed strong from both the Bosnian population and the Bosnian Republican Army. Later, when the local situation became more stable, the UN, including the Swedes, became a source of increasing irritation for the conflicting parties. They had no use for the UN; UN personnel were not taking sides but rather acted as neutrals and hence stood in the way of the conflicting parties' advances. This irritation, with the UN seen by the conflicting parties as its source, found expression in the obstruction and humiliation of the UN and its operations. Sometimes it was even a kind of game in which the conflicting parties tried by all available means to cause the other party to appear as the sinner in the UN's eyes. One example was to start bombardments and then persistently blame one's opponent for doing so. When IFOR was deployed in the area, the war in Bosnia had been going on for several years. A certain war-weariness, certainly among the civilian population, could be seen after years of hardship. From the point of view of the conflicting parties, they had agreed upon a cease-fire and they now also faced a large number of heavily equipped troops in the area, a perceivable change compared to the UN period. In a way, all parties in the conflict, including the peacekeeping troops, could believe in a more peaceful future, or at least a reliable status quo. One could imagine that the contacts and experiences between the local population and the different armies became less burdened by friction and more positive, as long as everyone followed the rules of the game.

The personnel in the fifth battalion, who served with both UNPROFOR and IFOR, were asked an additional question, namely whether they believed the conflicting parties' attitudes toward peacekeeping troops have changed since IFOR took over. Among those who answered the question and thus had experienced a change (65%), nearly half (46%) stated that the different groups in the area viewed IFOR more positively than UNPROFOR. The civilian populations on all sides and the VRS especially contributed to that change. On the other hand, 9% stated that a negative change in attitude had occurred, especially within the Army of Bosnia-Herzegovina. Some comments shed light on these changes:

- "Greater freedom of movement increases possibilities for contacts, which is positive."
- "People are starting to believe in peace."
- "They saw that there were opportunities and a chance to receive support and assistance."
- "They felt safer."
- "Both in a positive and a negative way for all. Some hated us and some liked us; opinions were very localized."
- "Some saw us as an occupying power."

Table 11 illustrates Swedish peacekeepers' opinions of how attitudes among the different local population groups (Serbs, Bosnian Serbs, Croats, and Bosnians) toward peacekeepers changed during the tour.

Table 11: How Attitudes among the Local Population Groups toward Peacekeepers Changed during the Tour (in percent)

Group	Change	UN period	NATO period
Serbs	Positive	10	18
	Negative	31	12
	No change	59	70
Bosnian Serbs	Positive	10	26
	Negative	36	12
	No change	54	61
Croats	Positive	11	9
	Negative	41	13
	No change	48	78
Bosnians	Positive	17	21
	Negative	46	15
	No change	37	64

Most respondents stated that no change had occurred in the attitudes of local population groups toward peacekeepers. However, respondents clearly stated that negative attitudes were much more common during the UN period compared to the NATO period. Thus, if there was a change between the UN and NATO periods, it is in a positive direction for most of the groups. These figures are in line with earlier discussions that showed more positive views during the NATO period compared to the UN period.

The environment in which peacekeeping soldiers must operate is complex in many ways. In the case of the former Yugoslavia, the presence of the UN aroused great hopes, chiefly among the civilian population, for an early peace and a chance to live in safety. In Bosnia, these hopes were not fulfilled, at least not within the time frame the people had anticipated. Dissatisfaction with this spread among the people and was directed to a large degree against the UN. Disappointment, frustration, and powerlessness naturally grew as time passed and "nothing happened." The UN soldiers came under criticism not only from the conflicting parties but also from the civilian population. This was not an easy situation for the individual soldier to handle and it generated frustration among many. Brought up with a mental model in which peacekeepers were the "good guys" and then confronted by a reality in which this view was not always shared, peacekeepers understandably found the situation "unfair."

Changes in the attitudes of peacekeepers became evident when IFOR was deployed in the area; many also expressed concern about the backward construction of the mission. With enough power and personnel, and with a strong enough mandate, IFOR should have been in-theater first, and only afterwards should UNPROFOR have begun. Among the first Swedes to join IFOR were many who had also been serving in UNPROFOR. The frustration that some Swedish peacekeepers felt during the UNPROFOR period found expression in, for example, printing new T-shirts for IFOR service with the text, "Back on track; time to show the colors."

Attitudes towards other people, to a certain extent, seem to depend on how specific individuals felt they were treated. In complex cultural encounters, as was in the case in Bosnia, tensions surfaced. Many of these tensions, though, had their origin in ignorance and misunderstandings. When the situation was ambiguous and difficult to understand, some Swedes found it hard to live up to the democratic values and the positive outlook on mankind, which are so strongly emphasized by Swedish society.

6. FINAL REMARKS

The peacekeeping operation in the former Yugoslavia, and especially in Bosnia, has implied a new phase in Swedish peacekeeping. First, international operations have become one of the main tasks of the Swedish armed forces. Partly because of this, the pendulum regarding the value of international service for officers has swung from one extreme to the other. Today, international service is more or less explicitly a condition for positive career development among officers. Second, it is the first UN operation on the European mainland. To some extent, this has meant that the conflict scenario has come much "closer" to the Swedes; it is not only in remote places that conflicts occur. Third, in connection with the operation in Bosnia, many "new peacekeepers" joined an operation that, among other things, meant working with new collaborators, some of whom probably had different motives [20] for participating than those of the "old peacekeepers." Fourth, it was the first time that Sweden joined a NATO-led operation; it is significant that this occurred without any major debate within Sweden regarding the principle of neutrality and non-alignment. In connection with the changeover from a UN- to a NATO-led operation, Sweden also had ambitions to be elected to a position on the Security Council for the years 1996–1998, a situation that, to some extent, could have affected various (political) decisions made at this time. Fifth, the quite extensive media coverage of the conflict in Bosnia was something new for Swedish peacekeepers. All of a sudden, peacekeeping was nothing anonymous; on the contrary, news about what the battalion had accomplished in different respects traveled quickly back to Sweden. There was also a need to have at least one person always ready to answer questions from the media.

One might assume that Swedish soldiers, with their background and traditions, would be better suited for a UN mission than for a NATO mission. The empirical data presented in this article show no indication of this. Somewhat paradoxically, many experienced a change for the better starting with IFOR. The change in situation and improved resources possibly accounts for much of this positive evaluation. One could also say that the IFOR/SFOR mission, to a large extent, resembled a traditional peacekeeping mission and, because of that, suited the Swedish peacekeepers well. Nevertheless, Swedes have now "shown their colors" in a NATO-led mission; in some respect, this shows that the "mental model" for the Swedish peacekeeper has also changed, both with respect to serving with NATO, but also by deploying a more combat-like unit. This has probably had an effect on potential applicants for such operations, as well as on the selection process, preparation, training, and the views of peacekeeping among the general public.

As far as data are analyzed today, it appears that at least two types of peacekeeper have emerged within Swedish units. The first type is comprised of individuals who have a more traditional view of peacekeeping and who are very much influenced by the backpack presented at the beginning of this chapter. In this group, there is a tendency to view heavy armaments as a factor that may provoke the conflicting parties and the local population. Another type of peace-

---

[20]   See, e.g., Trevor Findlay, "The New Peacekeepers and the New Peacekeeping," in Trevor Findlay (Ed.), *Challenges for the New Peacekeepers* (New York: Oxford University Press, 1996), pp. 1–31.

keeper seems to have adopted a more "warrior-like" strategy of peacekeeping. This means, among other things, that one can also be a diplomat in combat gear. These persons have created their own image of "peacekeeping heroes." Many examples of this type of peacekeeping hero came from the stories of those deployed in Bosnia during the more "combat-like" conditions encountered by the first battalion. Nevertheless, both types of peacekeepers emphasized that more training is needed regarding the cultural aspects of operations, such as knowledge of the different population groups' traditions and values. The need for understanding the conflict seems to be of importance to Swedish soldiers, regardless of type, not least to reduce tensions between different actors in the area. Some of the negative feelings that have been found in the data could certainly have been dispelled if the personnel had had this understanding. This is very much in line with Canadian research findings from Somalia and the former Yugoslavia, which concluded that "an understanding of the cultural factors affecting the behavior of military forces in these increasingly complex and irregular interventions will contribute to the stability of these operations in the future." [21]

Overall, members of all battalions thought the service period was a positive experience and many would consider applying again, despite the frustration, crises of confidence, and moral dilemmas that can, be part of the daily life of peacekeepers.

Our analysis of the data reveals the advantages of this study's longitudinal approach, since there are noticeable differences between the battalions. These differences can be attributed to many causes, such as the changing course of events, leadership, and unrealistic expectations. The important point is that the evaluation of Swedish peacekeeping efforts is not based on the experience of just one battalion.

Swedish peacekeepers will almost certainly be involved in future peacekeeping missions, and there is no evidence that these missions will be less complex and demanding than the ones we have seen during the 1990s. The backpack of future peacekeepers might look different but, in a sense, peacekeepers are what we make them, through such factors as selection, training, guidance in the field, and aftercare.

---

[21] Donna Winslow, "Misplaced Loyalties: The Role of Military Culture in the Breakdown of Discipline in Peace Operations."

8. FRANCE AS PEACEKEEPER IN BOSNIA-HERZEGOVINA

Bernard BOËNE

Outline:

1. Background
2. Points of Tension Internal to the Military
3. Military to Military Dimension
4. Relations with Official Organizations and their Representatives
5. Relations with Non-Governmental Organizations and Local Population
6. Military-Media Relations
7. Conclusions

1. BACKGROUND

France can fairly be said to have extensive experience with peace support missions. It is probably one of very few countries with a peacekeeping and humanitarian assistance record dating back to the 19th century. In 1860, Napoleon III, having persuaded other European powers to follow suit, sent some 7,000 French troops to Syria as part of a 12,000-strong multinational intervention force to protect the Christian Maronite minority, then suffering massacres at the hands of the Muslim majority. French forces later played a major role in the enforcement of post-World War I treaties, interposing troops (with only, at best, mixed success) between ethnic groups or nascent states: Hungarians, Serbs, and Romanians in the Timisoara province (1918–1919); Greeks and Turks across the Dardanelles (1920–1922); and Poles and Germans in Upper Silesia (1920–1922). In cooperation with the Red Cross, the new League of Nations' Relief Fund Committee, and several religious charities, French troops helped and rescued 200,000 defeated Russian soldiers and refugees who crossed the Black Sea in 1920–1921, after their defeat at the hands of the Bolsheviks.[1]

During the Cold War, as was then the case with most major players in the international arena, France did not take part in many UN peace support

---

[1]   Olivier Forcade, "Les missions humanitaires et d'interposition devant l'histoire," *Revue Tocqueville* XVII, No. 1 (1996): 39–52.

operations; notable exceptions were the "Police Actions" in Korea in the 1950s and Lebanon in the late 1970s and early 1980s. Nevertheless, from the 1960s to the 1990s, France played an active role in stabilizing the regimes it had left behind after de-colonization in French-speaking sub-Saharan Africa, on the strength of bilateral agreements with most of those newly independent states.

The post-Cold War era has seen France active in almost all major peace enforcement, peacekeeping, and humanitarian assistance operations: the Gulf War, Cambodia, Bosnia, Somalia, Haiti, Rwanda, and Kosovo, as well as a few others. In fact, French participation in such missions has been uninterrupted since 1990, and French force levels in these operations have usually been among the highest mobilized by the international community. Over half of the army's battalions now have post-Cold War peace support experience. With the shift to an all volunteer force (AVF), which should be completed in 2002, and its attendant decrease in active-duty force levels, planning now proceeds on the assumption that, in the future, *all* battalions will be rotated in succession and, over time, see service overseas in the cause of peace as part of multinational contingents.

The political motivations behind such an active stance are but thinly veiled. If it is to maintain an international status worthy of its past as a major player in world politics (notably expressed through its permanent seat on the UN Security Council), France must assume responsibilities commensurate with such pretensions. Activism also serves to influence the future European Union defense identity in accordance with French views on how it should be configured, and for what political purposes. Finally, when dealing with its former colonies, France has realized that it may no longer have the military resources (or even, now that strategic interests have been redefined, the political will) to intervene as it did for so long, and that UN-sponsored multinational emergency missions there may help spread the burden of averting the worst in nations precariously poised on the brink of economic, social, or political disaster.

France has been in Bosnia since the collapse of Yugoslavia unleashed ethnic-nationalist strife and led to atrocities the international community could not condone. With up to 10,000 troops in the region as a whole, France has been a major participant in peace support efforts there. French forces in Bosnia have been central components of UNPROFOR, IFOR, and SFOR, with a large sector of responsibility and share of multinational command. Adding to the list of motives offered above, specific political reasons for participating in successive multinational peace support arrangements there included moral imperatives and the determination, shared by other European powers, not to allow such atrocities (reminiscent of the darker days of 20th century European history) to take place on the fringes of EU territory. Another concern is the avoidance of huge, uncontrolled flows of refugees into neighboring states (and eventually into countries to the north and west). Later, a further reason, reinforcing the initial option to intervene early as part of a collective security effort, may have been the realization that prolonged conflict in the Balkans would generate increased military cooperation among Europeans and accelerate the forging of a European defense identity.

This chapter draws mainly on a series of (questionnaire and interview) surveys, conducted by the army on a regular basis, of troops rotated out of the theater. [2] Other data sources include participant observation reports from the field, documentary evidence, and general social science literature on the topics of interest here.

2. POINTS OF TENSION INTERNAL TO THE MILITARY

Participation in the peace operations in Bosnia reinforced a point previously driven home by the Gulf War: that the mixed armed force of Cold War days (comprising a majority of conscripts, a minority of regulars, and a professional cadre) was poorly adapted to the "new times" of the post-Cold War era. The policy pursued early on, which consisted of inviting conscripts to extend their period of compulsory service under arms and volunteer for peacekeeping duty overseas, actually worked rather well. Sufficient numbers volunteered, and (to the surprise of many) conscripts proved up to the difficult tasks that awaited them. It was felt, however, that the favorable image of the new peacekeeping duty thrust upon French armed forces – an image that went far to explain why so many signed on – might one day sour if casualties occurred or the media turned against them, and could eventually lead to a dearth of military personnel in emergencies. Sound manpower planning could not proceed on such a brittle basis. Moreover, while public opinion held that peacekeeping was a legitimate mission, leaders had cause to fear that conventional war waged for purposes other than defense of the national sanctuary, with possibly much higher casualty levels, would *not* be. For that reason, as early as 1990, a presidential decision prudently excluded the deployment of conscripts who did not specifically volunteer for duty in the Gulf. It can be safely said that this early post-Cold War experience led to the realization that the country would have to relinquish the draft system that had served it well throughout the 20th century but was no longer adapted to current and future needs.

Another consequence of post-Cold War peace support efforts, not least in Bosnia, has been the army's return to a central role, which it had lost after the final retreat from empire in 1962 to the air force and navy, then the main

---

[2]   This chapter relies heavily on the work of the Army's *Centre des Relations Humaines*. It also draws on studies conducted as part of the Military Academy's research center.

vehicles of deterrent power. This has restored the army's sense of self-esteem as well as its *raison d'être,* and changed its organizational climate for the better.

French troops have proved easily adaptable to a kind of peacekeeping operation that was different from the Cold War type. Officers' ethos took the change in stride, and other ranks followed rather effortlessly. This is probably related to France's imperial past, in which troops earmarked for colonial duty – Marines and Foreign Legion (i.e., today's elite formations) – performed many of the same tasks that are now needed in contemporary peacekeeping missions: interposing and mediating between rival ethnic groups or factions; policing whole areas; constructing roads, railways, and bridges; operating schools and infirmaries, etc. Thus, in French military culture, particularly that of the army, such duties are not felt to be beneath the dignity of even elite professionals and regulars – those who set the tone. The only surprising factor was that such skills, which had not been taught in military schools since the early 1960s, could be spontaneously reactivated almost immediately (a testimony to the resilience of institutional memory, probably passed on through military families).

One of the first difficulties encountered had to do with unit rotation frequency. The initial tour length in Bosnia-Herzegovina was six months, which was soon found to be less than optimal. It included a three-week leave at home, which should ideally have taken place at the mid-point of the deployment but was very often erratically placed because of operational requirements or constraints related to the use of airports in the area. Moreover, as entire battalions could not be allowed to take home leave as a unit, they were chronically under strength and often lacked crucial skills when they were needed. A study conducted in 1994 by the army's social science division concluded that a four-month tour without leave would be better [3] and recommended it for future deployments; this has been the case ever since and has proved a satisfactory solution for field units. [4]

Selection for service in Bosnia and other such theaters was voluntary, though it was difficult for career-minded regulars and professionals to refuse deployment with their unit. To begin with, a mix-and-match configuration was the basis on which selection proceeded, with one battalion providing the core

---

[3]   Interestingly, four months was the period needed in World War II, as reported in Samuel Adam Stouffer's *The American Soldier,* for rank and file U.S. infantry soldiers to reach optimal effectiveness, after which time a law of diminishing returns seemed to set in. See Samuel Adam Stouffer et al., *The American Soldier: Combat and its Aftermath,* Studies in Social Psychology in World War II, Volume 2 (Princeton, NJ: Princeton University Press, 1949), p. 285.

[4]   Survey results suggest, however, that four months may be too short for staff officers. Six-month tours are now generally the rule for staff positions.

human and materiel resources to which volunteers with required additional skills were added. The army's new modular structure, then being phased in, made the process smoother. In those days, conscripts who agreed to serve overseas and to extend their service beyond the legally mandated 10-month period made up a sizeable part of the force. Now that the shift to an AVF is nearing completion, the proportion of such conscripts has decreased dramatically. Reservists were mostly used as individual specialists, not least in areas of civil–military cooperation (CIMIC) [5] where experts were often not otherwise available from the peacetime active-duty table of organization and equipment.

Training for peacekeeping deployments includes short courses in international law, history, and politics relevant to the theater of future deployment; UN and NATO procedures; and English. [6] This ideally takes into account the latest lessons learned from troops rotated out of the theater. Attendance at a three-week "cohesion camp" allows members of different modules to get to know those with whom they will functionally serve in the field or on staff, and to practice specific tactical missions such as convoy protection, crowd control, hostile checkpoint searches, etc. [7] All battalions deployed, except perhaps the more specialized ones (signals, engineers), are expected to master simple infantry tactics and operate as infantry personnel if the need should arise. As experience has accumulated over time, French contingents can be said to be among those best adapted to "second-generation" peace support operations of the post-Cold War type. In particular, restrictions imposed by the rules of engagement (ROE), which early on were a frequent source of frustration, are no longer regarded as a major problem.

Perceptions of relative deprivation in the Bosnia operations were hardly apparent, at least compared to other national contingents. Pay used to be very high (it multiplied basic compensation by a factor of three or more), however for budgetary reasons, pay rates for overseas operational service were recently set at only 50% above the basic rates in continental France. Food was envied by other contingents: at one point, French rations could be exchanged for three U.S. Army MREs (meals ready to eat) among international soldiers on the informal market. Accommodation was seldom comfortable, but no one ex-

---

[5]   According to the agreed NATO definition, CIMIC encompasses the array of "resources and arrangements, which support the relationship between NATO commanders and the national authorities, civil and military, and civil populations in an area where NATO military forces are or plan to be employed. Such arrangements include cooperation with non-governmental or international agencies, organizations, and authorities."

[6]   Survey respondents in the early years thought not enough stress was placed on UN, OSCE, or NATO organizational structures, as well as on those of foreign armed forces.

[7]   The three-week cohesion camp is often thought to be too short and formal. Its benefits are viewed as sub-optimal in terms of cohesion, as troops are not shipped directly to their theaters of destination but rather return to their garrisons prior to departure.

pects to enjoy first-class hotel conditions while serving on overseas operations. Rest and recreation opportunities, initially a problem, were judged to have become more satisfactory as additional facilities were built. Freedom of individual movement was greater than in most other contingents whenever tactical circumstances allowed (though it seems to have decreased under IFOR/SFOR, as some of the troops scattered under UNPROFOR were regrouped in large camps, to the chagrin of many). In Bosnia, as well as on other peacekeeping missions, French forces made a point of establishing friendly relations, indeed as frequent contact as possible, with local populations – so far with little to regret.

One important source of deprivation in the early years of the Bosnian mission resided in the scarce opportunities to communicate with families back home.[8] There were instances of frustrated (and somewhat humiliated) French soldiers having to use U.S. facilities in order to talk with spouses or children. Since then, cell phones have become nearly universal, and, thanks to satellite coverage, this problem has vanished (though another has arisen: the use of mobile phones within units in the field, even while on operations, a situation that naturally raised security concerns within the leadership). The main reason for discomfort has been the increasingly sorry appearance of heavy equipment, which stayed on the spot and was passed from one to battalion to another at each successive rotation. This policy was certainly justified in economic terms, as it saved the cost and time of moving heavy items to and from France every four months; however, it did not guarantee optimal maintenance because units felt they were operating materiel that did not belong to them (or to anyone in particular) or was not in optimal condition. Comparison with the heavy equipment of other, comparable national contingents often embarrassed soldiers.

Relative deprivation was stronger as regards different terms of service among French personnel. Tensions existed early on between those who were deployed and those volunteers who were not.[9] The decline in force levels has been taking care of that problem, however, since at the present pace of overseas intervention, almost everyone will be deployed at one time or another. In the theater itself, some areas were more tense than others, and conditions in the field were apt to vary considerably. Headquarters (HQ) and staffs were reported to enjoy very enviable living and working conditions, as well as privileges unheard of in field units. While hard feelings were barely in evidence, such discrepancies cannot be expected to improve in-theater cohesion or or-

---

[8] At the start of IFOR, soldiers were entitled to only one phone call home every nine days.

[9] Personnel left behind on regimental bases back home were often frustrated because they felt overburdened and deprived of the high pay and recognition enjoyed by those deployed. To some extent, the same applied to spouses, who often said they were entitled to their share of recognition.

ganizational climate. Yet this was tempered by levels of satisfaction that were unrelated to material conditions. Staff personnel, whose services are often underused, were reported to have been disappointed by realities that did not live up to their pre-deployment expectations, leading to classic dysfunctions such as bureaucratic formalism and infighting. Overstaffed HQs appear to have been the root of such dysfunctions: numbers were set according to wartime norms that were apparently out of touch with peace support realities under the conditions prevailing in Bosnia. In particular, it was often the case that mid-level staffs were short-circuited due to the time pressures generated by real-time communications systems and media coverage. On the other hand, those units that performed the roles for which they were trained (infantry, engineers, signals, traffic regulation) reported much higher levels of satisfaction and morale even though their service conditions were more exacting. A similar divide separated junior cadre personnel, who enjoyed the increased level of responsibility and autonomy typical of peacekeeping operations, from their more frequently frustrated mid-level superiors. This has led on a number of occasions to frictions between staff and field unit personnel.

Since 1992, the casualty count has risen to over 80 dead and 400 wounded, mostly due to accidents rather than skirmishes with belligerents. [10] This has not given rise to outcries in domestic public opinion, probably because deaths and injuries were spread over time and came in very small numbers (often one or two) on each occasion. Risk was not considered excessive by military personnel. However, a fundamental issue, common to most national contingents on peace support operations, has emerged. This was pithily expressed by *Time Magazine*'s cover story when U.S. troops first arrived on the spot some five years ago: *"Is Bosnia Worth Dying For?"* From the viewpoint of peacekeepers and the nations that stand behind them, the stakes involved in terms of national interest were low and thus could not possibly justify high casualty rates, even in cases where domestic public opinion, as in France, proved tolerant in that regard. Therefore, force protection loomed large in the conduct of operations (although among French troops it did not take on the – as they see it – extreme forms prevalent in U.S. contingents). For soldiers steeped in the notion that the mission is sacred and takes precedence over the security of military person-

---

[10] The fact that objective danger is low does not lessen subjective perceptions of risk. That was the case in Bosnia at the height of the UNPROFOR mandate, when Blue Helmets were routinely targeted by snipers and at one point taken hostage. The frustration born of not being able to respond in kind when attacked, or of perceptions of a lack of heavy weapons when faced with hostile factions, was an important factor under UNPROFOR. The guarantee that wounded personnel would be quickly evacuated and taken care of by a highly professional medical service effectively served to lessen anxiety in the face of such perceptions.

nel, this amounted to a reversal of classical military norms and generated some disorder in even a fairly pragmatic military ethos.

In this regard, the events of 1995 were a defining moment. When, in late spring that year, Bosnian Serb soldiers took hostage a rather large number of UN Blue Helmets, little could be done immediately to rescue them. Given the norms then governing the use of force and the risks involved for the hostages themselves, UNPROFOR was shown to be weak, a fact that was confirmed (among other things) by the tragedy of Srebrenica. This was to lead, at President Chirac's instigation, to the deployment of "Green Helmets" prepared to use force in a more muscular way. Eventually, after the Dayton agreements were signed, the UN subcontracted peacekeeping operations to NATO, and UNPROFOR gave way to IFOR. Within that framework, the battle between French and Bosnian Serb soldiers for the Verbanja Bridge dramatized the dilemma faced when pitting mission effectiveness against the avoidance of casualties, and the problem of shifting gears and priorities when the need arises to revert to classical military norms. After the Serbs had taken the bridge by surprise and captured those French soldiers guarding it, a general decided (apparently on his own initiative, though he was immediately backed by President Chirac) that the French contingent had taken enough humiliation, and that further weakness in the face of Serbian daring would prove entirely counterproductive with respect to peacekeeping objectives. He ordered offensive action to secure the bridge again and to free the hostages. This succeeded at the cost of a few casualties (including the deaths of one French soldier and several Serbs). Such action drew an almost universally positive response, as nobody deemed it unjustified. But for the military, after the fact, it raised the issue of the criteria to be applied if similar circumstances should arise in the future. When does the mission become sacred again, to the point of risking casualties? Should the decision be left to the intuitions of junior field commanders? Is it possible to set rational criteria in advance to assist leaders in coming to sound decisions on the spur of the moment? Such an issue remains to be doctrinally settled; meanwhile, it is a burning one, and not just for the French contingent.

Interestingly, while the military ethos in that instance dramatically resurfaced to everyone's satisfaction, interviews suggest that ordinary soldiers were nonetheless grateful to their superiors for sparing them unnecessary risk to life and limb. The key here seems to have been the principle that superiors did not issue orders they themselves would have hated to obey. This brings to light the need for a high level of confidence in vertical command relationships, which was present in the case under consideration as it is in many others. Horizontal relations in the field were less of a problem, as they were powerfully strengthened by shared pressure and hardships – in no short supply in Bosnia (or for that matter in any post-Cold War peace support operation). The only shadow in this picture, as regards successive French contingents, was the relative lack of confidence in politicians, whether at home or in international organizations. It must be added, however, that such lack of trust was not in any way related to peace support missions, since it is to be found throughout the services under ordinary circumstances in garrison life.

French soldiers were under no delusions about what peace support can achieve. Like others, they were apt to be demoralized by what they sometimes perceived as the lack of effectiveness inherent in peacekeeping (especially when atrocities occurred that they were unable to inhibit or restrict). But national culture does not accustom them to thinking in black and white terms or believing that the decisive use of force can solve problems once and for all, and thus spare one the trouble of living with them. They felt they were there to avert the worst and to help local populations as much as they could. They saw their mission as difficult and stressful, [11] though not dangerous. As one captain once put it, if the choice is between peace support action and remaining in the barracks throughout their careers as their predecessors did in the closing decades of the Cold War, officers will gladly take the former alternative any day. Similar sentiments were to be found among young non-commissioned officers. Likewise, short-term volunteers, whether regulars or conscripts, did not see peacekeeping as devoid of meaning. Indeed, they saw peace support as a noble mission, and its high legitimacy, both at home and in the international community, was a major factor in the level of morale they exhibited. [12]

Personal motives, as sampled by surveys, were idealistic. The leading motives included preserving the peace; fostering international justice and stability; upholding universal values; and giving a good account of France on foreign

---

[11] One clear sign of the increased salience of stress is the new use of professional help from chaplains and doctors, who now routinely engage in counseling in the field. Junior officers report that they spend more time listening to their subordinates and advising them on how to cope with ambiguities and keep cynicism at bay. Psychology used to be a dirty word in army circles, as only weak personalities were reputed to be in need of support. But this is no longer the case. Psychological support programs now play an important role for soldiers who do not regard themselves as weaklings (all the more so because senior officers, including generals, are reported to be more susceptible to fatigue and stress due to the burden of responsibility and the complexity they must face). Such programs now extend to military families in garrisons, as morale has been found to be sensitive to developments affecting spouses and children, with whom direct communication is now much more frequent.

[12] Another factor is the degree of cohesion that characterizes units. As could be expected, organic outfits fared better in that regard than mix-and-match formations. Also, the fact that groups lived in close confines meant that junior leaders shared all aspects of their subordinates' lives, which greatly enhanced their role and the group's morale. Conversely, isolation can be a very negative factor when small groups are scattered in order to cover as much territory as possible (which was often the case under UNPROFOR).

soil. Among conscripts, the acquisition of skills and experience that are useful in civilian life and look good on résumés (because of the favorable public image of peacekeeping back home) usually came next; the equivalent was found among regulars in the form of career interests that are enhanced by overseas tours. While financial motives generally come last, satisfaction in that regard was high (and engendered the envy of neighboring contingents), since monetary incentives were strong and felt to be justified. There was no hypocrisy about the importance of pay, as the topic was freely discussed with interviewers. At the beginning, in 1992 – 1994, some senior officers, mostly to be found in heavy armor or artillery units, expressed skepticism and discomfort at the thought of serving as "UN mercenaries." They explained that they had entered the military to serve the motherland, not some weak and confused international organization upholding abstract humanitarian values. But that was a minority phenomenon; the fact that such sentiments are no longer publicly expressed suggests that norms have turned against them.

There were women in-theater, but their numbers did not make them highly visible: most performed their duties in service support units and HQs. They did not seem to raise particular problems. One interesting phenomenon was that peacekeeping duty has modified the way in which various branches of service view one another. Disdain for logistics or auxiliary branches has disappeared, as scattered small units, typical of peacekeeping operations, tend to perform the same (basic infantry) way in such theaters irrespective of branch; specialized roles tend to be more visibly useful at grass-roots levels in the vertical integration of forces than they would be in conventional warfare.

All in all, despite inherent difficulties, Bosnia and other such missions were widely seen as a positive experience, and a plurality of professional, long-serving career soldiers appeared to have been fully reconciled with the prospect of serving several tours in the region.

3. MILITARY-TO-MILITARY DIMENSION

Relations with other national contingents have been more problematic. For one thing, the fact that France had withdrawn from the integrated military structure of NATO in 1966 made its military (the army to a greater degree than either the navy or air force) more isolated from its Alliance partners during the late Cold War than was the case with most other countries, with the possible exception of Spain. English, while widely taught in secondary and military schools, was not a requirement for successful careers in the armed services: only a few years ago, some army generals who had made it to the very top could hardly speak a word of it. Likewise, NATO procedures had become unfamiliar to most soldiers. UN norms and ways were *terra incognita*. This being the case, things proved fairly difficult to begin with; after it became clear that such multinational operations were here to stay, it took a few years for the situation to improve gradually.

Yet the situation has not improved sufficiently for French officers to be fully at ease in multinational staff conferences. These officers tend to resent the fact that French, though it is one of two or several official languages in NATO or UN circles, nearly always takes a back seat to English, the *de facto* working language of multinational missions. It is not rare for French officers in staff proceedings to insist on translations by professional interpreters. This demand obviously slows the pace of work and often irritates colleagues of other contingents who possess greater language skills or are native speakers of English.

This tension has combined with considerations of power politics to produce relationships that have been rather tense at times, especially with the Americans. Under UNPROFOR, when the U.S. was absent from Bosnia, relations with other major players (Britain and Italy) were good. UNPROFOR was undoubtedly less effective, or more disorganized, due to weak UN command structures (and political will), but there was much more freedom of action at all levels, and major contributors of manpower and political capital were on an equal footing. At that time, meetings between British and French generals serving together in Bosnia were friendly and easygoing. IFOR was apparently an entirely different matter. [13] Belligerents were now more subdued, and NATO procedures and norms were strictly applied. American generals provided a stronger lead than French officers were used to, and a more bureaucratic style set in that French officers would have preferred to do without. Action by the book, which contradicts traditional French resourcefulness and devolution of initiative to junior levels, was pronounced "boring" by many interviewees. It took some time before they adjusted to a situation in which the French style was cramped.

One distinctly French response to the problematic cultural adjustment and interoperability of units and staffs was to regroup and concentrate in areas where the French were in charge (notably in and around Sarajevo). However, it was soon realized that this could only result in further isolation and loss of influence, so the practice was discontinued whenever possible. [14]

---

[13] Under IFOR, survey findings registered a rise in the number of soldiers who said they suffered from boredom. This led to situations in which junior leaders performed tasks normally assigned to subordinates; under these circumstances, organizational climate took a distinct dip. Intemperance was reported to have risen to levels higher than normal.

[14] Concentration in some areas or offices resulted in an under-representation of French officers elsewhere. Interestingly, however, this also applied to French civilian UN representatives under UNPROFOR.

Political rivalry compounded matters. Paris had expressed doubts about the prospects of success for the U.S.-brokered peace settlement signed at Dayton in 1995, and one French army general voiced this sentiment out loud in-theater. The realist stance that had earlier led the U.S. to supply weapons to Bosnian Muslims in defiance of a UN embargo – with a view to making the local balance of forces less unequal – had generated misunderstandings and was viewed by many members of the French contingent as a sign of American duplicity. Later, French soldiers were more or less openly suspected of being unduly sympathetic to the Serbian side and were thus at times left out of the intelligence or information loop, a fact that infuriated numerous French soldiers. The feeling of being dominated by an arrogant newcomer also contributed to tensions. At the same time, French participants could not help but perceive both the extent of U.S. military might as reflected by the assets deployed by the U.S. to Bosnia, as well as the increased effectiveness of peace support efforts under IFOR/SFOR compared with UNPROFOR.

These misunderstandings and rivalries stemmed in part from a clash of cultural styles, which by far predated joint action in Bosnia. [15] They also, in part, reflected structural opposition within West between two exceptionalist, messianic nations with claims to being beacons of liberty and democracy to the world. France, being by far the less powerful of the two and consequently reduced to the status of junior partner (albeit of the first rank), has, since de Gaulle's day, developed contrarian attitudes in foreign policy (backed by an independent nuclear strike force). These attitudes are deemed by more subtle analysts or commentators to be generally beneficial to the Alliance as a whole, but they do not always go down well with the Americans, especially since other European countries are known to support French positions whenever it suits their specific interests. The pressures and different approaches generated by a problematic return to peace in Bosnia have undoubtedly added fuel to old fires. French participants, in particular, have been known to complain that their share of influence on the theater was not commensurate with the extent of their experience and their contribution to the multinational effort in Bosnia.

Relations with national contingents other than the U.S. varied according to contingent and the extent to which such contingents were long-established or

---

[15]   In the closing months of World War II, surveys conducted among U.S. Army soldiers saw the esteem in which they held the French general population plummet in just four months, while their opinions of Germans improved over the same period. See Stouffer et al., *Ibid,* p. 577. The French, for their part, although they rejoiced in being liberated from German occupation and welcomed American soldiers, could not entirely obliterate mixed feelings about the latter's apparent lack of schooling in the art of precision bombing (which had reduced parts of many towns to heaps of rubble) and less-than-strict discipline, which obliged them to keep their daughters off the streets. While ambivalence toward U.S. power and its uses is not restricted to the French people, it often seems to be especially acute among them.

inexperienced peacekeepers. French soldiers were by this time accustomed to serving alongside Italian, German, Dutch, Spanish, and British soldiers, most of whom they regularly encountered in overseas theaters or as part of Euro-corps and other European formations. European sentiment, contrary to conventional wisdom (and indeed to what could reasonably be expected since military institutions are among the last bastions of nationalism), ran rather strong among French service members and was shared by other European soldiers. In point of fact, such sentiment was stronger on average among service members (apparently even in the British case) than in the domestic public opinion of their respective countries. This was because they understood that, in a period of declining military budgets and force levels, there was not much that national military establishments in Europe could hope to achieve on their own. Also, their realization of the full extent of U.S. military superiority has served to unite them. But it probably goes beyond that, as well, to include truly shared attitudes in a number of dimensions.

Things may have been different with contingents coming from further afield, although no openly hostile feelings have been reported in surveys or any other data source. However, it is always a burden to serve alongside a "sloppy" contingent whose discipline leaves something to be desired, because then someone must take up the slack. This happened, for instance, when neighboring contingents decided that their duty in Bosnia was a 9-to-5 job and deserted the positions they were supposed to hold at all times (as was reported time and again in post-deployment interviews). Worse still was the spectacle of foreign soldiers engaging unchecked in various types of trafficking, including the most objectionable (weapons, women, aid, etc.). This sort of behavior is liable to ruin morale by lowering expectations and standards, if not by fostering cynicism – a highly dangerous ingredient, apt to deprive strenuous peace support efforts of any real moral meaning.

One interesting aspect of military-to-military relations in peace support operations, including Bosnia, is what happens in HQs and higher staff levels. There, political rivalries translate into rank inflation, as players soon learn that if influential positions are to be secured, it is best to assign a colonel to do a captain's job. Much lobbying took place in Bosnia. Although they have been learning, French officers did not – especially at the outset of the mission – prove very adept at this game and tended to resent it. The same applied to garnering future reconstruction contracts on behalf of French firms when it came to CIMIC work. Further, the formal organization of the multinational force was paralleled by purely national shadow networks, among which the covert struggle for influence could be fierce.

French soldiers' perceptions of how other contingents judged them were positive. Indeed, French peacekeepers believed that the attitudes of neighboring contingents toward the French, e.g., in the areas of discipline and dedication, were rather flattering. Discipline and dedication, for instance, were reputed to be high. But, as always, there was reason to believe that such mirror images, while probably not unjustified, were overly optimistic. In particular, there was little evidence in survey findings or interviews that French peacekeepers were aware of complaints that – where and when the French military dominated the scene (e.g., in the sector for which it was responsible) – French officers and other ranks often acted in ways very similar to the behavior they resented on the part of the Americans.

4. RELATIONS WITH OFFICIAL ORGANIZATIONS AND THEIR REPRESENTATIVES

This is an area about which knowledge is in short supply, because questionnaires or interviewers have not identified it as crucial. This is probably true as far as troops in the field were concerned, but it leaves wide open the issue of how senior military leaders related to civilian authorities at both the international and local levels.

French officers and service members were rather uneasy in their relations with all but the highest-ranking civilian officials. However, this also applies at home as well as in peace support theaters. French peacekeepers welcomed top-ranking policymakers with strong personalities and leadership qualities. A French general, reminiscing about his UNPROFOR days, recently declared to a military audience that he saw the advantages in serving with a man like his former boss, Mr. Akashi, whom the general described as a man who took responsibility and stood by his word, although the general acknowledged that Akashi's directives could only be as clear as the usual instructions from the UN Security Council or UN bureaucracy (i.e., often tortuously unclear or liable to change overnight). Such positive qualities make an army general's task easier as he tries to translate political goals into attainable military objectives. At lower levels, however, civilian officials were less welcome. Their lack of rank insignia sometimes made them difficult to place in a hierarchy, and the roles they were assigned were often seen, rightly or wrongly, as interfering with the responsibilities of proper military professionalism. Another factor was that the arrival of civilian officials generated protocol problems and disturbed the work at hand. But a lot depended, in such circumstances, on the civilian official's style and his or her ability to calm undue fears or avoid any inconvenience caused by his or her presence.

Local authorities, whether at "national," district, or municipal levels, were an entirely different matter. It is always politic for a military force trying to restore peace and bring democratic order to a war-ravaged area to maintain good relations with the functional equivalent of ministers, prefects, governors, or mayors, and their administrations. Therefore, goodwill can be presumed, at least initially, on the part of military leaders. The question is the extent to which such goodwill will engender cooperation from the other side – and this is variable. When local authorities are truly concerned about the welfare of those in their charge, cooperation is usually straightforward. If, on the other hand, such authorities act in a strategic manner so as to compromise the peacekeepers' impartiality, the situation is apt to become difficult, especially where local authorities effectively control their population. In such cases, peacekeeping forces cannot hope to bypass such authorities, e.g., when it comes to distributing aid. This has been the case a number of times with the Republika Srpska, although the Muslim and Croatian sides were not above using the French contingent's supposed pro-Serbian leanings to suit their purposes indirectly by embarrassing or implicating both the peacekeeping force and their foes.

It is undeniable that, due to historical and cultural factors, [16] some French service members (like many members of the French general public or the intellectual elite in France) sympathized with the Serbs. However, official policy has steadfastly maintained, in word as well as in deed, the impartiality that is central to peace support efforts. More will be said on this topic below.

5. RELATIONS WITH NON-GOVERNMENTAL ORGANIZATIONS AND LOCAL POPULATIONS

Humanitarian non-governmental organizations (NGOs) have multiplied spectacularly in the last decade or so and now come in all shapes and sizes. Sadly, some are fronts for mafia-like criminal organizations (though this seems to have affected Kosovo much more than Bosnia), so military intelligence must discriminate between those who do important work in an effective manner, those for whom charity is just a business, and those apt to prove a nuisance.

Given the wide differences in attitudes, motivations, and procedures among military and NGO personnel, tensions could initially be expected. Those who work for NGOs tend to dislike force and to be much more informal than soldiers are ever likely to be. Yet, and the French case is probably no exception, after a while the two sides have come to know each other and to learn that they play complementary roles in peace support efforts. NGOs now realize that without the security provided by military forces, there is often little they

---

[16] Interviews suggest that French soldiers are sometimes impressed with the pride and tenacity of the Serbs in the face of ill-fortune and severe hardships. This easily resonates with the heroic dimension of French Army culture. The historical factor involved is a throwback to the French-Serbian alliance in World War I.

can do in a violent climate to help the local population. Without that security, aid ends up benefiting belligerent factions rather than refugees, and volunteer activists can be targeted or become casualties. In turn, the military soon learned that, without NGOs around, they would have to distribute bags of food, provide shelter, or care for infants, orphans, the old, and the sick, which detracts from what they perceive as their real role and somewhat disturbs their collective self-image. Far from breeding contempt, familiarity has generated grudging respect and appreciation on both sides in many instances.

However, these sentiments seem to apply mostly to emergency situations. Things may be somewhat different where and when pressure is low, since the military is less busy in such circumstances and may appear to compete with NGOs where their activities converge. In such cases, differences in styles and attitudes are apt to separate the two communities, and mutual suspicions (notably of partiality) are likely to resurface. Competition among private voluntary organizations can at times be a problem for mission effectiveness, as it complicates relations with them. On the other hand, such relations are made easier by the strong French or French-speaking tradition among voluntary organizations with established reputations (e.g., *Médecins Sans Frontières*/Doctors Without Borders); here, language and cultural barriers are apt to be less of an issue with NGOs than with other national military contingents.

Relations with local populations were seen as mostly unproblematic where and when local authorities did not interfere for political purposes. Ever since colonial days, French troops on overseas duty have honored the habit of mingling with locals rather than building fortresses that they would leave only for patrols or other military missions. Such a time-honored habit applies from time immemorial to the mother country in relations between the *Gendarmerie* and rural populations. This generates affectual ties, reduces the fears that armed force can create among civilians, enhances support, and provides a major source of intelligence. Supplies of fresh food and other basic products are procured locally rather than imported from home, whenever practical, secure, and in accordance with multinational doctrine. This boosts the local economy and creates ties of mutual dependence, which in turn enhances trust. Such behavior is in sharp contrast to the usual practice of some other national contingents, notably U.S. forces. [17]

The amount of help, both formal and informal, accruing to local civilians from French contingents is far from inconsiderable and is generally valued by local populations (though there are complaints of ingratitude among soldiers).

---

[17] It is true that French soldiers are less likely to be targeted than U.S. service members are, and thus do not have to take the same onerous type of precautions when relating to locals. Belligerents know that the potential political impact of a terrorist attack against U.S. military personnel resulting in deaths is much stronger than in the case of French soldiers.

CIMIC roles and G5 staff branches are now fully integrated into operational structures and processes.

As a result, relations with local populations were usually good.[18] As French troops were assigned to areas of different ethnic make-up, local ties did not put impartiality at risk. This was underscored by staff conferences internal to the French military, in which disagreements have been reported on a number of occasions between French army officers serving in predominantly Serbian or Muslim areas, who tended to support, respectively, the interests of *their* locals. These examples contradict the external suspicion of pro-Serbian sympathy on the part of French soldiers and can only be interpreted as social ties getting the better of supposed cultural leanings.

6. MILITARY-MEDIA RELATIONS

French military personnel, as a rule, harbor a deep mistrust of journalists. The usual complaints are that journalists tend to be superficial, intrusive, abrasive, lacking in proper appreciation of what the military is all about, afflicted with a short attention span, obsessed by the search for "scoops" or sensational pictures, and occasionally disloyal. French military personnel also presume that media representatives distrust communitarian and hierarchical institutions like the armed forces. During the Cold War, military suspicions fed on the indifference or vague hostility of the press and electronic media with respect to defense issues (as well as on the institutional memory of negative images of the military portrayed by the press during the de-colonization conflicts of the 1950s). In turn, during the Gulf War, journalists were infuriated by the restrictions placed on their freedom of movement.

Surprisingly, given such a hostile track record, relations during the decade following the Gulf War have been good. This has to do with the (very) favorable image of peacekeeping held by journalists, which both reflects and amplifies the attitudes of the French public at large. Peace support operations are highly legitimate, and they have, to a considerable degree, restored the military's prestige after decades spent in comparative limbo during the late Cold War. Media coverage is positive to an astonishing degree, to the point of bordering on tribute. This writer has yet to see a negative portrayal of French peacekeepers in a television program or press article.

While media people have made significant progress toward bridging the wide gulf that used to separate the two communities, those serving in the military have done their part, as well. Media-savvy public relations officers are now part of the table of organization and equipment at battalion level and above.

---

[18] This obtains despite important differences between Croatia and Bosnia, registered by surveys.

These officers often oblige journalists with up-to-the-minute pictures, sound bites, or video footage that illustrate the latest hot stories in a timely manner, and they have learned not to provide such information in a manipulative or high-handed way that would instantly backfire.

However friendly, though, a permanent media presence creates tremendous pressure on military organizations: the rise of the soldier-communicator can, in part, be traced back to a race against the clock triggered by media-worthy events. One revealing example of this was provided several years ago by an officer just back from Bosnia. A landmine close to the Croatian border had damaged a French armored personnel carrier, and casualties had occurred. A Croatian military observer had seen the event through his binoculars and mentioned it to an acquaintance of his, a French journalist who happened to come his way. The news was aired on French national radio about an hour later. It took a few hours for the battalion commander to gather the relevant information (notably the identity of casualties, the exact circumstances, and the significance of the event) and send his report up the chain of command all the way to the Operational Situation Room in Paris. Care was taken that the families of the deceased and wounded soldiers would not first hear of the event through the press, but rather from the regimental home base.

Such developments are novel and account for unprecedented short-circuits along the chain of command that now characterize military organizations. This entails a de-layering process, which, as in private firms operating in international markets, probably affects the military more than it cares to recognize. However, pressure and in-depth organizational transformation, while they stem from the presence of journalists in the field, do not result in a deterioration of media–military relations, since there is no way the media can be barred from access to military theaters short of war conditions. Moreover, most of the difficulties encountered arise from emerging technology rather than media ill-will. An important countervailing factor is that, however uncomfortable such situations may be, media attention – in sharp contrast to what was the case in the 1960s, 1970s, and 1980s – puts the military at the center of things and makes it feel appreciated.

This being the case, the last few remaining tensions are to be found at the grass-roots level between field reporters and junior leaders or rank-and-file soldiers. The latter sometimes complained that they were not getting the recognition they deserved; that reporting was technically incorrect in various aspects so that families back home got the wrong idea of local conditions; that journalists are interested in unimportant details, etc. More serious are complaints that reporters tended to concentrate on the areas most likely to yield tragic events (e.g., "Sniper Alley" in Sarajevo) and neglect quieter zones where peacekeeping was more successful; that they were biased against Serbs to the point of "satanizing" them in a nearly systematic manner; or that they tried to turn young soldiers into paid informants in order to beat competitors whenever a hot story was to be had. But all in all, a mutually satisfactory working relationship was established, which certainly broke new ground in the military's institutional history.

7. CONCLUSIONS

In France, as elsewhere, the past decade has witnessed tremendous changes. Bosnia has represented a central experience, because intervention there as part of the successive and continuing multinational efforts to keep an elusive peace started as early as 1992. The navy and air force, which during the Cold War's final three decades had been at the center of the country's military power, have become comparatively marginalized, while the army has recovered its former primacy under these new circumstances. The post-Cold War era has brought major changes to the French armed forces' organizational format, thereby raising fundamental issues, including the search for new civil–military equilibria and a new *raison d'être* for the military establishment.

Peace support operations have proved beneficial in bringing rather satisfactory answers to these questions. They have provided a positive test of the services' operational status and capabilities and put an end to the disuse of force, which had somewhat depressed morale and motivation to serve in the military before 1990, thereby changing the military's self-image for the better. Likewise, they have restored the military's prestige, not in any unconditional way, but in the form of popular support and legitimacy that conventional war could not possibly enjoy. Media relations have improved beyond recognition and public opinion has shown itself to be tolerant enough with regard to casualties, although questions remain as to the limits (so far untested) of such attitudes.

Peacekeeping has brought the country closer to NATO than it had been for over a quarter century. Bosnia was the theater most instrumental in this shift until Kosovo came on the scene. Yet, at the same time, the Bosnian operation has enabled France to maintain a fairly autonomous foreign policy, balancing U.S. influence within the West (thereby providing other European nations with breathing space in the face of unrivaled power), and to play a leading role in the shaping of the future European defense identity – the second pillar that had been so often talked about in the late stages of the Cold War but had failed to materialize.

Despite the rise in prestige that usually makes for the return of radical professionalism, peace missions have confirmed and reinforced the pragmatic military ethos, which had gradually (and painfully) emerged from the 1960s onwards. This is because peace support is *not* war, but rather obliges the military to take into account a wide range of roles and to blend military with political considerations at *all* levels. Popular support and positive media coverage have not been lacking. The French military ethos has proved well adapted to the tasks of peace support, even though these tasks raised the important issue of meaning. While participants were proud of serving in Bosnia and elsewhere in the cause of peace, justice, and humanitarian aid (motives that by far exceeded self-interest, whether related to pay or subsequent career chances), uncertainty as to the primacy of mission vs. personnel security in perilous circumstances has engendered a mute questioning of classical military norms and traditions. These issues hang heavy on leaders' minds and have not yet received clear-cut answers, probably because such issues are difficult to conceptualize and articulate, and they involve a redefinition of military identity that all concerned are as yet unready to address. The characteristics of peace support, the practical consequences of emergent technology (notably in the information and communications field), as well as the pressures of real-time media coverage are transforming military organizations in ways that parallel similar developments on the outside and lead the services (especially the army) away from familiar, well-trodden ground. All of this adds to the stress of operations that are objectively not dangerous but tax soldiers' and their families' endurance in new ways. This may be the reason why psychological support, previously almost unheard-of, has become part of the military scene. However, eagerness for action easily overcomes these difficulties, and there has been no reluctance to volunteer for such missions.

In Bosnia, cultural complexity has been one of the most serious obstacles to effectiveness. What is at issue here is not so much the complexity deriving from relations with local populations and authorities, because France's imperial past has accustomed the French military to dealing with people of diverse origins and traditions. Nor is it the complexity that stems from relations with NGOs, despite the comparative novelty of the diversity and omnipresence of NGOs in the field). Rather, the primary problem involves cultural interoperability with other national contingents. Part of the difficulty lies in the fact that culture is not a separate phenomenon, but rather a dimension that pervades all aspects of inter-group relations. Some of the more tangible factors, such as harmonization of procedures and norms, have given rise to formal and informal adjustments over time and no longer seem to create problems, at least among habitual partners. Other factors, such as the lack of sufficient command of foreign languages (particularly English), cannot be remedied quickly and call for long-term educational investment. French troops are now earnestly grappling with this problem, as they have correctly identified it as one of the weaknesses that prevent them from reaping the full benefits of what is more often than not a highly valuable contribution. But there are still other difficulties, of a political nature, that can hardly be helped. These are part and parcel of any coalition venture that inextricably blends functional with diplomatic considerations. Hence, those in-theater must grapple with lines of authority that are less clear than would be optimal because multinational chains of command are often troubled by shadow national networks; rank inflation through "strategic" postings of officers; lobbying on behalf of special political or economic interests; the resistance of smaller contributors to the domination of larger ones, etc.

While accumulated experience has brought practical solutions to the first set of problems, there is little that social or cultural engineering can do to alleviate the interference of political interests in the functioning of command relations (if only because social engineers have careers that are controlled by national authorities in their respective countries). The UN, reflecting the politics of the Security Council and General Assembly, has so far lacked the strong leadership that only it could provide. NATO, though more effective in managing the operational side of military intervention, no longer boasts the kind of alliance discipline that came with the common threat of the Cold War period. Yet players in Bosnia have learned over time that politics can be taken too far and become a losing game that benefits no one. As a result of that learning curve, restraint in the pursuit of national interests seems more in evidence on the part of all concerned (including France) than in the early years. This is no doubt the legacy of collective action in the oldest second-generation peace support theater, a legacy that makes the Bosnian experience unique.

9. THE UNITED STATES IN BOSNIA-HERZEGOVINA: POINTS OF TENSION AND LEARNING FOR THE U.S. MILITARY

John GAROFANO

Outline:

PREFACE

Two thousand, six hundred U.S. troops began deploying to Bosnia and Croatia on December 29, 1995. Approximately 30,000 U.S. troops would eventually participate in the Implementation Force (IFOR) resulting from the Dayton Accords. The duty fell primarily to the 1st Armored Division and to numerous combat support and combat service units from throughout Europe, who

223

deployed for one year. Authority was transferred to the Stabilization Force (SFOR) on December 20, 1996, to which the U.S. contributed an expanded brigade. This task went to the 1st Infantry Division, which deployed for a year before being replaced by elements of the 1st Armored Division and then transferred to the 1st Cavalry Division in 1998. The U.S. task force operated in the northeastern third of the Republic of Bosnia and Herzegovina, around Tuzla and Brcko.

The prospects for "tension" were tremendous. A region with an already struggling economy was devastated by political decisions and by war that destroyed much of the remaining social, political, economic, educational, and communal infrastructure. The process of rebuilding these institutions could begin only after warring entities, driven by deep and lasting hatreds, were first separated and relations among them normalized to some minimum degree.

To accomplish all of these tasks, NATO had no institutionalized strategic planning process for out-of-area crises, and no combined or joint doctrine on Rules of Engagement (ROE), command and control, or indeed most of the social and political tasks on which they were about to embark in December of 1995. New NATO members had limited resources or not fully compatible systems and organizations. This was even more true for Partnership for Peace (PfP) nations and of course for the Russian peacekeepers. In addition, other international organizations, from the Organization for Security and Cooperation in Europe (OSCE) to the United Nations (UN) and several hundred non-governmental organizations (NGOs), attempted to carry out their tasks with similar deficits in organization, doctrine, and relationships. The U.S. contributed its share to this potential cacophony, since it embarked on this ambitious mission without an integrated political–military plan, with minimal training, and little help from international and non-governmental organizations.

In this context, the accomplishments of IFOR and SFOR were remarkable – successful national and local elections, some refugee resettling, and the groundwork for economic growth and a civil society. The group project that has resulted in this book represents an attempt to understand the points of tension encountered along this path to essential mission success, based on the assumption that similar missions will arise in the future.

This paper is an overview of the U.S. peacekeeping experience in Bosnia with observations arranged more or less in accordance with the project's outline. The primary foci are the impact of peacekeeping on readiness and troop morale, relations with other NATO and non-NATO countries, and lessons learned. I have used secondary sources, many of which are based upon first-hand experience; I have supplemented this research with interviews as well as insights derived from two after-action conferences held in 1996 and 1997 at the U.S. Army War College (USAWC) in Carlisle, Pennsylvania. [1]

1. BACKGROUND

1.1. U.S. POLICY BEFORE BOSNIA

The Bush administration (1988 – 1992) took a wary approach to peacekeeping; its policy was shaped largely by Chairman of the Joint Chiefs of Staff (CJCS) Colin Powell and Secretary of Defense Dick Cheney. In one of the administation's final significant documents, *Presidential Decision Directive* (PDD) 74 of January 1993 rejected language that might have supported either a standing UN force or active participation by the U.S. milityry in the entire spectrum of peace and humanitarian operations. This apporach revealed itself in the administration's opposition to deeper involvement in Bosnia and in its choice of a peace operation in Somalia instead.

Presidential candidate Bill Clinton took issue with this tack, emphasizing the moral obligation to use American power to intervene more forcefully in Bosnia. It appeared the new president would make good on his campaign rhetoric when he appointed Secretary of State Warren Christopher, Ambassador to the United Nations Madeleine Albright, and National Security Advisor Anthony Lake. Their speeches seemed to signal that this administration would dare to tread where the previous one had not. dare to tread where the previous one had not. However, General Powell and the military at large continued to resist such changes. Powell cited the need to retain a warrior culture as well as the primary mission given to the military by official U.S. National Security Strategy – to fight and win major wars that threaten vital national interests. [2] Other relevant factors were the military's limited experience with peacekeeping and the perceived lessons of Vietnam. Although a small number of officers had served in the Sinai and the disastrous Beirut deployment, these experiences and those of northers Iraq and Somalia had yet to "filter up" or significantly alter overall perspectives. [3] Finally, the primary lessons learned by the military from their experience in Vietnam did not suit the limited de-

---

[1]   These after-action conferences were held on a non-attribution basis. They were held in May 1996 and April 1997 and will be referred to as *Bosnia-Herzegovina After-Action Review I* (BHAAR I) and *Bosnia-Herzegovina After-Action Review II* (BHAAR II). BHAAR I can be found at http://cbnet/orgs/usacsl/org/pki/military/aars/bosniaframe/bosfram.htm. The findings of both are also summarized in Max Manwaring, "Peace and Stability Lessons from Bosnia," *Parameters* 28, No. 4 (Winter 1998 – 1999), pp. 28 – 38.

[2]   Colin Powell, "U.S. Forces: Challenges Ahead," *Foreign Affairs* (Winter 1992/1993).

[3]   Ivo Daalder, "Knowing When to Say No: The Development of U.S. Policy for Peacekeeping," in William J. Durch (Ed.), *UN Peacekeeping, American Policy, and the Uncivil Wars of the 1990s* (New York: St. Martin's Press, 1996), pp. 35 – 67 (37 – 8).

ployment of force for non-vital interests. Secretary Weinberger had posited as early as 1984 that force should only be used as a last resort, in defense of vital natianal interests, and only if public support was clearly forthcoming. The so-called "Powell Doctrine" modified this approach to include the notion that if U.S. forces were committed to battle, politicians should authorize the use of "overwhelming force."

Such a panoply of strictures made peace operations unlikely, since they frequently do not protect vital national interests, are not suited to doctrines of overwhelming force, and are likely to expose leaders to political attacks when casualties occur. A further constraint was the apparent continuing opposition of the senior military leadership to humanitarian operations. The President's lack of military service in the 1960s and his decision, later partially reversed, to allow gays in the military, got the administration off to a rocky start with the institution that consistently ranks at the top of those respected by the American people. Together with the high regard in which General Powell was held, these factors weighed heavily on peacekeeping policy.

Such was the setting for a major review of U.S. policy that began with the new Clinton administration and that asked four questions: When should the international community engage in peace operations? Who should conduct them? How can UN operations be improved? How can the U.S. contribute? [4]

The National Security Council (NSC) proposed the creation of a standing rapid reaction unit modeled on the 82nd Airborne Division. This time, both Chairman Powell and Secretary of Defense William Perry opposed the idea, and it was rejected. Powell stated that, as long as he was Chairman, U.S. units would under no circumstances be committed "to an unknown war, in an unknown land, for an unknown cause, under an unknown commander, for an unknown duration." His opposition killed the idea. [5]

Apart from this issua, general agreement was secured on the other elements of the policy. The most significant departure from the Bush administration was the statement that peace operations were a key element in national security strategy and sometimes the best way to secure importatn national interests. Other aspects of the emerging Clinton policy were not new or unique. U.S. forces could be placed under the operational command (OPCON) of UN or foreign commanders in certain circumstances, as had been done in Somalia, but there would be no open-ended commitments and U.S. unit commanders would always maintain separate channels of communication to U.S. authorities. A UN army would not be created but a database of available forces and equipment

---

[4]   *Ibid*, p. 42.
[5]   *Ibid*, p. 43. See Colin L. Powell, *My American Journey* (Random House, 1995), 260 – 61, 490 – 91, 558 – 567, 574 – 589, and 605 for his views on the use of force in Somalia, Bosnia, and similar conflicts.

would help get them to the field when necessary. These issues were written into the early drafts of the policy document that were completed in the spring of 1993.

Events in Somalia, compounded by attacks at home on the administration's multilateral policy, derailed the policy process and almost changed the policy dramatically. Four Americans were killed in Mogadishu in August 1993. Congressional and other eminent critics argued against the commitment to multilateralism and especially the UN. During this period, the Pentagon's views once again moved to the fore; these views stated that UN peace operations could not be a substitute for the necessity of fighting and winning wars. They argued that U.S. forces should not be committed to peacekeeping operations without a cease-fire first in place. An end point and specific objectives to UN participation should be identified, open-ended commitments avoided, and a firm budget figure estimated. Most importantly, the Pentagon restated a more extensive version of the Weinberger-Powell doctrines: U.S. troops should become involved only when:

- The operation is in the U.S. national interest;
- There is a clear intention to achieve objectives decisively;
- Sufficient forces are committed and reassessments and adjustments to the force are made when necessary;
- U.S. forces are used as a last resort, after other policy options have failed;
- There is domestic support for U.S. involvement. [6]

In October, 18 U.S. soldiers were killed in a battle in Mogadishu. This was a searing moment for most policymakers and members of the armed forces. The sight of the bodies of U.S. soldiers dragged through the streets of a country in which most Americans perceived no vital interest highlighted what many viewed as a misguided policy. A storm of criticism buffeted the Clinton foreign policy team and its multilateralist approach. All of this influenced the final product of the interagency review, *PDD-25*, which, because of Somalia, was not signed until May 1994. *PDD-25* noted that peacekeeping should be "more selective and more effective" in the future, and it excluded support for a UN standing force or U.S. forces earmarked for use by the UN. The document also laid out an extensive series of criteria that had to be met before U.S. forces were committed to a peace operation.

The administration would therefore ask, on a case by case basis, whether the operation:

- Advances U.S. interests;
- Addresses a case of security, humanitarian disaster, or violation of human rights;

---

[6]   Daalder, p. 51.

- Has clear objectives and fits within UN Charter Chapter VI or VII operations;
- Includes a cease-fire (if Chapter VI) or a significant threat to national security (if Chapter VII);
- Provides the means to accomplish the tasks;
- Has an unacceptable consequence if no action is taken;
- Is tied to clear criteria and a timeline for ending the operation. [7]

Yet the document continued to step away from the Bush administration's approach by stating that the U.S. was prepared to make available the full spectrum of its military capabilities for UN-sanctioned peace operations. A new formula, created to share financing between the State and Defense Departments, might make increased funding available for the operations. Plans would also be proposed to strengthen the UN's capability for action. [8]

Thus, before IFOR and SFOR, U.S. policy was characterized by a duality. The Clinton administration was more willing to become involved in humanitarian operations than was the Buch administration, but it was constrained by the lessons of Vietnam and Somalia as well as by the bureaucratic and wider political opposition created by the latter experience.

1.2. POLITICAL MOTIVATIONS FOR SENDING A CONTINGENT TO BOSNIA

The U.S. may be said to have become officially involved in Bosnia beginning with UN Security Council Resolution 743 of 21 February 1992, which called for a UN Protective Force (UNPROFOR) to act as a peacekeeping force between Croat and Serbial forces in Krajina and Slavonia. Shortly thereafter, the Moslem and Croat population voted for independence. Large-scale fighting broke out in April when the international community recognized Bosnia-Herzegovina.

A series of European Union (EU) and UN efforts in 1992 and early 1993 failed to end the fighting in Bosnia-Herzegovina. By 1994, Serb forces controlled 70% of the territory of this former Yugoslav republic and were condemned for pursuing a policy of ethnis cleansing. During this period, the U.S. was involved through the five power contact group consisting of the U.S., Russia, Germany, France, and Great Britain.

UNPROFOR's mission gradually expanded to include conflict limitation; the halting of arms deliveries; the enforcement of a no-fly zone over Bosnia; the prevention of ethnic cleansing; the imposition of economic embargoes against

---

[7]   *The Clinton Administration's Policy on Reforming Multilateral Peace Operations* (Washington, D.C.: Office of the President, May 1994).

[8]   *Ibid.*

Yugoslavia; the provision of safe havens; the policing of artillery around Sarajevo; and the improvement of living conditions for refugees and civilian populations.[9] In the spring and summer of 1995, its position, and that of the international community in general, was on the verge of collapse. NATO undertook air strikes after Serbian troops allegedly fired mortars at the Sarajevo market, causing many deaths and injuries that were immediately broadcast by the media. Serb forces responded to the air strikes by taking UNPROFOR prisoners. The UN negotiated their release, which probably only emboldened the Serbs to take Srebrenica. The massacre of Muslims at Srebrenica, while under UN protection as a "safe haven," was not met by a renewal of international will. This failure led to redoubled American efforts, which initiated the process that led to the General Framework Agreement for Peace (GFAP), or Dayton Accords, in December 1995.

There are at least four reasons, then, why the U.S. became more deeply involved in Bosnia. First, the Clinton administration was forced to confront the failure of the Europeans and the UN to stop ethnic cleansing and massacres, which steadily grew in import to the American and global public. Second, a change in personnel in the White House meant that the Clinton administration's views were in stark contrast to those of the Bush administration on both the nature of the *security threat* and on the import of *humanitarian aid* to the suffering. Bush's Secretary of State Baker had stated that the U.S. "didn't have a dog in this fight" while his successor, Lawrence Eagleburger, believed the matter had to be settled by internal participants or by the Europeans.[10] In contrast, Clinton's Secretary of State, National Security Advisor, and other close advisors believed there *were* serious national security implications to Bosnia. They feared a spillover of the fighting into Macedonia, perhaps bringing Turkey and Greece into conflict, as well as the danger of a war for or against a Greater Albania.

Third, NATO'S involvement and possible failure had serious implications for the U.S. due in no small part to U.S. influence on the UN Security Council, NATO was tasked by the Security Council with the following: enforcing a weapons embargo and no-fly zone in 1992 and 1993; protecting UN personnel and providing air cover for safe havens in 1994; bombing targets in August 1994; planning for withdrawal and escalation simultaneously in 1995;

---

[9] "Lessons and Conclusions on the Execution of IFOR Operations and Prospects for a Future Combined Security System: The Peace and Stability of Europe after IFOR," A Joint U.S./Russian Research Project of the Foreign Military Studies Office, Center for Army Lessons Learned, U.S. Army Combined Arms Center, Ft. Leavenworth, Kansas, p. 5. Also at http://call.army.mil/call/fmso/fmsopubs/issues.ifor/toc.htm (8 July 1999).

[10] See Richard Holbrooke, *To End a War* (New York: Random House, 1998), pp. 26–33 for a discussion of Bush administration views.

developing a rapid reaction force in 1995; and again with launching air strikes against the Serb army in August and September of that year. Ultimate failure by NATO would have been a grave setback to U.S. interests in promoting an increasingly robust and independent security organization whose expansion it had recently ensured.

Finally, after running on a platform of doing more about Bosnia, withdrawal and defeat would have opened the way for major attack from political opponents within both the Democratic and Republican parties.

1.3. U.S. DOMESTIC SUPPORT FOR PEACE OPERATIONS

As a RAND study asserted in 1996,

> It is now an article of faith in political and media circles that the American public will no longer accept casualties in U.S. military operations, and that casualties inexorably lead to irresistible calls for the immediate withdrawal of U.S. forces. If true, this would not only call into question the credibility of the U.S. Armed Forces in deterring potential adversaries, but would be profoundly important in decisions concerning force structure, doctrine, and military campaign planning, as well as the nature of the country's broader foreign policy, including its alliances and other commitments. [11]

However, a study of U.S. public attitudes toward conflicts since the World War II showed that "the public's aversion to losses of U.S. life in some recent military interventions has had less to do with a recent decline in tolerance for casualties than with the debatable merits of the operations themselves." The underlying problem, in this view, is the fact that in Somalia, Haiti, and Bosnia, "U.S. interests and principles are typically much less compelling or clear and success is often elusive at best." Additional findings included, first, the fact that attitudes reveal an awareness of the *costs and benefits* of the new operations. Second, at the outset, the public was willing to accept significant casualties in virtually all limited interventions from Korea to Panama, due to the perception that there were significant stakes. [12]

These findings are complemented by other studies. Between 1992 and 1995 there was general support for airdrops of humanitarian aid, U.S. assistance in protecting UN peacekeepers, and the use of U.S. airpower to protect UN troops or Bosnian Muslims in safe havens. Support slowly grew during this period for active U.S. involvement on the ground, although it stayed in

---

[11]   RAND Research Brief, "Public Support for U.S. Military Operations" (Santa Monica: March 1996), p. 1. This brief is based on a book by Eric V. Larson, *Casualties and Consensus: The Historical Role of Casualties in Domestic Support for U.S. Military Operations* (Santa Monica: RAND, 1996).

[12]   *Ibid.*

the minority until just before the signing of the Dayton Accords. A large majority thought Bosnia was largely a European problem. While the proportion that viewed Bosnia as an American problem grew somewhat between 1992 and 1995, after Dayton it dropped again. If there were no other way to get aid to civilians, or if atrocities occurred, 58% of Americans agreed that the U.S. had an "obligation to use force;" 27% agreed strongly with this statement. A plurality of 37% thought the main reason the U.S. should take military action was that it had "a moral responsibility to stop ethnic cleansing." [13]

From 1992 to 1995, the public generally supported presidents when they acted decisively or took strong positions, while the public did not offer such support when the president appeared to be indecisive. A majority supported President Clinton's decision at the end of 1995 to send troops to Bosnia. 63% thought U.S. troops should be deployed to Bosnia if a wider war could be prevented, and 64% thought that the humanitarian desire to stop more killing justified sending U.S. forces. These majorities turned to minorities just after deployment. Furthermore, public support dropped significantly when confronted with the possibility that U.S. soldiers might die for Bosnia. Two-thirds supported a deployment if no Americans were killed; however, only a third, 29–31%, approved if 25 to 200 soldiers were to die. On the other hand, perceived success seems to be important, since 60% believed that if the operation were successful, the U.S. would have done "the right thing in contributing troops" even if 50 Americans were killed. [14]

In early 1995, 67% of Americans surveyed supported UN peacekeeping in principle, including the contribution of U.S. troops to UN peacekeeping, the payment of UN peacekeeping dues in full, and support for most UN peacekeeping operations. There were no significant differences based upon party affiliation. Fully 89% embraced the argument that "When there is a problem in the world that requires the use of military force, it is generally best for the U.S. to address the problem together with other nations, working through the UN, rather than going it alone." These figures were, in fact, a decline from a February 1994 poll, which found that 84% favored UN peacekeeping. 88%, however, still believed the U.S. should generally be willing to contribute some troops to an operation for which the U.S. endorsed a Security Council vote. [15]

---

[13]   Steven Kull, "Americans on UN Peacekeeping: A Study of Public Attitudes," Program on International Policy Attitudes, University of Maryland, 27 April 1995, "Summary Findings."

[14]   Richard Sobel, "The Polls – Trends: United States Intervention in Bosnia," *Public Opinion Quarterly* 62, No. 2 (Summer 1998), pp. 250–278.

[15]   Kull, *Ibid*. The following discussion is based upon this study (n. 13) and on Steven Kull and Clay Ramsay, "Americans Support U.N. Peacekeeping, with Conditions," *Foreign Service Journal* (December 1998), pp. 34–40.

A majority felt that the U.S. was paying more than its fair share of UN peacekeeping costs, but these were based on gross errors in estimates of how much the U.S. was actually contributing. The median estimate was that 40% of UN peacekeepers were American; the actual percentage at the time was 4%. When asked what the appropriate amount would be, the median response was about 20%! Similarly, the median estimate of how much of the U.S. defense budget was spent on peacekeeping was 22%, more than 22 times the actual amount. Asked what an appropriate amount would be, the median response was 15%, a large amount of money. Other mistaken impressions of the American public include those concerning casualties: one poll found that 63% of respondents believed Americans had died as a result of the Bosnia operations. [16]

Strikingly, at this time 73% of Americans would have accepted placing U.S. troops under the operational control of a foreign officer in situations where other countries contributed more troops than did the U.S. One might therefore postulate that the sentiment favoring U.S.-only OPCON is based on the belief that the U.S. is contributing 40% of all UN peacekeeping troops.

Finally, there was much frustration with the lack of assertiveness or muscularity in UN peacekeeping, with 79% agreeing that the UN did "just enough to keep the situation from getting totally out of hand but not enough to really solve the problem." About the same percentage of respondents agreed that UN peacekeeping operations were dangerous "because they send troops into civil wars without the means to defend themselves or the ability to deter attacks by being able to retaliate effectively. UN troops end up being sitting ducks." Again, the same number, 79%, wanted to see the UN take a more muscular approach. In February 1995, on a scale of 1 to 10 measuring frustration with UN actions in Bosnia, the median answer was 3, with 32% giving a 1. Two out of three favored intervening with a large military force of 150,000 – 300,000 troops, if necessary, to stop ethnic cleansing. Even more thought the UN should have intervened to stop ethnic cleansing in Rwanda, and, if limited means proved ineffective, 62% thought the UN should have "gone in with a large military force to occupy the country and stop the killings" in Rwanda. 86% of these individuals favored sending U.S. troops to participate in such an operation. Similarly, in a June-July 1994 poll taken while genocide was occurring, 60% favored setting up safe havens in Rwanda. Similar numbers in an April 1995 poll, a strong 62%, thought that the U.S. should send peacekeepers and contribute troops to Burundi. [17]

---

[16] *Ibid.*
[17] *Ibid.*

Support for prior operations also demonstrated significant staying power. Of those surveyed in this April 1995 poll, 52% thought U.S. troops should remain a while longer in Haiti and more than 60% thought the U.S. did the right thing when it first threatened to use force and then landed troops to reinstate President Aristide.

There is a great deal of misperception and cynical misuse of the facts when it comes to the American public's support for military and peace operations in the face of casualties. The flagship event is Somalia, where cries for withdrawal quickly followed the deaths of 18 servicemen. But polls by CNN/USA Today, ABC, and NBC, taken just after the event, showed that between 55% and 61% supported sending in *more* U.S. troops in response. [18]

Other polls support this. When asked how they would feel if they "saw the bodies of Americans on television," only 16% said they would want to withdraw all American troops, with 73% favoring a more active and engaged response and 30% favoring "striking back hard at the attackers." In a June-July 1994 poll, fewer than 25% said they would want to withdraw troops from UN peace operations in Rwanda or Haiti if American lives were lost. On the other hand, while in 1995, 82% supported the delivery of humanitarian aid to Somalia by UN peacekeepers, 46% thought it was a mistake to try to end the civil war. [19]

In the U.S., despite conventional wisdom to the contrary, it appears that public support is sufficient to sustain peace operations, provided the administration takes an activist approach to maintaining that support. This means clarifying the nature of the mission and its relationship to American interests and engagement abroad, explaining why the mission may evolve (if that is the case), and making an argument for why the U.S. military must be used.

2. INTERNAL MILITARY DIMENSION

2.1. GENERAL

A major source of internal tension in the U.S. case arises from the fact that the end of the Cold War brought a tremendous increase in the number, forms, and pace of military operations. At the same time, however, resources were substantially cut. The U.S. government and public appeared at times to be divided on the purpose of these operations. Despite continued political disagreement over the extent to which the U.S. ought to be involved in humanitarian or peace operations, the military has nevertheless been repeatedly asked to carry out such tasks. Operational tempo (OPTEMPO) – a rough measure of such factors

---

[18] Kull and Ramsay, "Americans Support," p. 40.
[19] Kull, "Americans on Peacekeeping."

as the number of troops and units deployed; miles driven, flown, or sailed; rate of rotation within units; and stress caused to logistical, combat, and combat support systems – has increased dramatically since 1991. During the time period discussed in this volume, the U.S. military averaged daily deployments of 55,000 personnel in approximately 70 countries, in addition to having 100,000 forward-deployed troops in Europe and Asia. Yet the army was reduced from a force of 781,000 in 1987 to one of 495,000 in 1997, and defense outlays were reduced from 6% of GDP in 1985 to 3.2% in 1997. [20]

The U.S. military is in the process of overcoming a natural and rational opposition to peace operations. For some 50 years, the U.S. government asked the military to prepare to perform the critical task of defending the country against threats to vital and important national interests. These threats were almost always conceived as those requiring large-scale conventional military operations, such as those conducted in Korea, Vietnam, and the Gulf War. Resources were provided for planning and training for these missions. These primary missions of deterring and, if necessary, defeating threats to vital u.s. interests remain the bedrock of the official national military strategy.

Within this context, the military has done a tremendous job of making a difficult transition to a new world. Some aspects of this adaptation are discussed below.

2.2. Readiness

The tension caused by increased OPTEMPO is magnified by widespread concern that the military is no longer ready to execute its prescribed mission of responding to two nearly simultaneous major theater wars. News reports; testimony to Congress by respected military officers; General Accounting Office studies; think tank reports and strong anecdotal evidence support this argument. The September 1998 hearings of the Joint Chiefs before the Senate Armed Services Committee, in which the Chiefs were subjected to near-humiliation, drove the point home. [21]

---

[20]   United States General Accounting Office, *Military Readiness: A Clear Policy Is Needed to Guide Management of Frequently Deployed Units*, Report NSIAD-96–105 (Washington, D.C.: April 1996).

[21]   Center for Army Lessons Learned (CALL), *The Effects of Peace Operations on Unit Readiness* (Fort Leavenworth: U.S. Army Training and Doctrine Command, February 1996); U.S. General Accounting Office, *Military Readiness: A Clear Policy is Needed to Guide Management of Frequently Deployed Units,* Report NSIAD-96–105 (Washington, DC: April 1996); U.S. General Accounting Office, *Heavy Use of Key Capabilities May Affect Response to Regional Conflicts,* Report NSIAD-95–51 (Washington, D.C.: March 1995); U.S. General Accounting Office, *Military Readiness: Observations on Personnel Readiness in Later Deploying Army Divisions* (Washington, D.C.: March 1998). A major RAND Corporation study concluded in 1997 that this ability persisted, although there are shortages in support units, such as water purification, petroleum supply, and maintenance teams. See Ronald

The mechanism by which peace operations affect conventional combat readiness is fairly clear. Deployed units are unable to practice the skills normally deemed essential for combat missions. They may not have the time, terrain, support units, manpower, or resources for conducting such training. But the impact of peace deployments goes far beyond the units deployed; such deployments affect supporting units, the unit just returned from the mission, and the unit preparing to deploy as well. Other costs include those incurred when, for example, a brigade cannot train for combined arms combat because a subordinate armor or infantry battalion deploys. Peace operations also divert equipment necessary for effective combat training. [22]

How these effects are interpreted is a different matter. Three factors influence one's argument on the readiness issue: institutional perspective, risk acceptance, and risk assessment. If one is considering the overall readiness of the U.S. military to respond to any one or two of the plethora of scenarios that might challenge the national interest, it is more difficult to argue that peace operations critically undermine overall or "general" readiness. From the perspective of a brigade or other commander in a first- or second-to-fight division, however, peace operations can seriously weaken readiness. Although the issue is seldom discussed due to the politically charged atmosphere, one's judgment about readiness is also deeply influenced by one's attitude toward risk. A risk-acceptant leader might look back on U.S. history and argue that the nation as a whole always rose to the occasion when it was necessary, and that during peacetime it is prudent to expend resources on domestic needs. Such a leader might reasonably be willing to risk that neither Iraq nor North Korea is likely to explode without offering the U.S. and its allies the opportunity to prepare. All foreign policies involve risk; in some instances, however, it is prudent to accept a minimal risk. Finally, risk assessment is central to views of readiness. If one assesses favorably the international community's efforts to contain Iraq and to contain and engage North Korea, readiness can rationally be allowed to "slip" while resources are directed to peace operations or to military priorities such as research, development, and procurement.

Hard evidence bearing on the actual effects of peace operations on potential combat operations is still another matter. It is mixed, but it appears that

---

E. Sortor, *Army Forces for Operations Other than War* (Washington, D.C.: RAND Arroyo Center, 1997).

[22] COL William J. Blankmeyer, "Sustaining Combat Readiness during Peace Operations" (Carlisle, PA: USAWC Strategy Research Project, 1998), pp. 5 – 7. For a study of the impact of one battalion's participation in a peace operation on brigade and division, see LTC James L. Huggins, Jr., "The Impact of Peace Operations on Rapid Deployment Force Readiness" (Carlisle, PA: USAWC Strategy Research Project, 1999), pp. 16 – 25.

peace operations in and of themselves do not make most units any less ready for future combat. A sample of opinion follows.

The next generation of senior military leaders appears to share the view that readiness to fight conventional wars suffers from peace operations. According to surveys of the USAWC classes of 1997, 1998, and 1999, future military leaders perceive a mismatch between the skills in which they have been trained and the skills necessary to execute peace operations. Only 9% of the Class of 1999 felt that their Mission Essential Task Lists (METLs) – the basic tasks that a unit must be able to perform in order to fight successfully – included the tasks executed during the peace operations in which they participated. This was down from 30% of the Class of 1998, and far below the 60% of the Class of 1997. [23]

Fully 50% of combat units felt they had significant training shortfalls, and most felt even less ready to perform peace operations. Once in-country, "overall 60% of the senior leaders participating in these operations saw little opportunity to reinforce or validate the level of proficiency" with which they embarked. [24] This finding was reinforced by a survey of the Class of 1997, in which 65% reported that peace operations had a negative impact on combat training readiness, and 72% reported a decrease in training opportunities during peace operations. [25]

There are, however, contrary views of the perceived impact of peace operations. Laura Miller's work reveals that nearly equal numbers believe that a peace operation makes them better – or less well – prepared for combat. Small-unit and leadership skills, as well as the general skills of many supply and support units, were perceived to improve. [26] Other research finds even stronger support for the notion that peace operations contribute to readiness in some aspects; for instance, 65% of officers in one survey agreed with the statement that "the skills/tactics learned/employed during MOOTW [military operations other than war] missions are useful to warfighting," while 83% agreed with the statement that such missions made no difference in their own willingness to employ lethal force. [27]

---

[23] 69% of the Class of 1998 participated in at least one peacekeeping operation. The figures are 63% for the Class of 1997 and 51% for the Class of 1999. Response ran at about 30% (97 of 320). LTC Joseph P. Nizolak, "Peace Operations and their Impact on Combat Readiness," (Carlisle, PA: USAWC Strategy Research Paper, 1999) pp. 4 – 11.

[24] *Ibid*, pp. 11 – 12, 18.

[25] LTC Alan D. Landry, "Informing the Debate: The Impact of Operations Other than War on Combat Training Readiness" (Carlisle, PA: USAWC Strategy Research Paper, 1997).

[26] Laura L. Miller, "Do Soldiers Hate Peacekeeping? The Case of Preventive Diplomacy Operations in Macedonia" *Armed Forces & Society* 23, No. 3 (Spring 1997), pp. 415 – 450.

[27] MAJ Robert G. Young, "The Impact of Operations Other than War on the Midgrade (O-3/4) Army Officer" (Fort Leavenworth, KS: MA thesis, June 1997).

The views of recent students at the Army's Command and General Staff College (CGSC) at Fort Leavenworth, Kansas, support this benign interpretation of the impact of peace operations on readiness. Students who had served in one or more peace operations were asked whether their deployment helped or hindered their combat readiness and effectiveness. As a result of their experiences in peace operations, 70% felt that participation had increased their ability to carry out a future combat mission; another 20% felt it stayed about the same; 7.8% felt it decreased a little; and none felt it decreased a lot. [28]

These students were also queried on five characteristics assumed useful to unit effectiveness in combat: self-discipline, initiative, decision-making ability, leadership skills, and ability to function for a sustained period in an austere environment. The majority opinion on most factors was that it had "stayed about the same" as a result of the peace operation. Still, 33% felt their self-discipline had increased; 47% felt their initiative had increased; 59% felt their decision-making ability had improved; 54% felt their leadership skills had improved, 57% felt they had increased their ability to function in a difficult environment; and 75% felt that unit cohesion had improved. [29]

More research is needed to discern the effect of peace operations on combat readiness according to unit type, organizational level, and mode of deployment. [30] For example, despite the above-cited results based on Army War College students, among the Class of 1999 the majority of combat support and special forces units believed that combat readiness increased, as did 100% of respondents in health service units. [31] This fits with the intuitive thesis that branches that use their combat skills will have enhanced readiness. [32]

By organizational level, skills improved at the individual, crew, squad, and to some extent the platoon level but decreased at the company and battalion level. [33] By type, skills that improved included those relating to command and control, intelligence gathering, deployment training, staff experience, and logistics/supply. On the other hand, basic combat skills are not exercised in most

---

[28] MAJ Mark S. Martins, "The 'Small Change' of Soldiering? Peace Operations as Preparation for Future Wars" (MA Thesis: Fort Leavenworth, June 1998), pp. 123–124. N=90 of a possible 126.

[29] *Ibid*, p. 126.

[30] There is a major limitation to existing research. In the absence of a war or combat training center evaluation immediately following redeployment from a peace operation, virtually all such studies rely on self-assessment.

[31] Nizolak, p. 19.

[32] The Army divides its service into the following branches, with some exceptions: Combat Arms (armor, artillery, aviation, infantry, and special forces), Combat Support (chemical, engineering, military police, military intelligence, and signals), and Combat Service Support (adjutant, finance, medical, ordnance, transportation, and quartermaster).

[33] Nizolak, pp. 19–21.

peace operation environments. Thus, mechanized infantry, armored units, and units dependent on heavy equipment are likely to suffer the most. A final factor concerns whether or not a unit deploys in its normal configuration or is extensively adapted to fit the environment of a peace operation. This will be determined by the zone of operation to which a unit deploys and existing military commitments at the time the unit is called. [34]

These more optimistic or benign interpretations of peace operations and readiness may be due to that literature's focus on individual assessments of specific traits and skills. While these may improve, the wider effects on unit readiness may nevertheless suffer from the lack of training and group skills. Observers/controllers at the Combat Maneuver Training Center (CMTC) report a tendency for soldiers returning from peace operations to respond overly methodically to typical warfighting challenges. They inordinately request and require detailed plans and clearances by senior commanders – a tendency not appropriate to high-intensity conflict. A U.S. officer who served in Tuzla discovered this when he saw the difference in reactions by a new, elite unit trained for combat that had just rotated into his base. After a tour in Bosnia, his own soldiers responded as policemen to harassment around the perimeter of his base camp. The new troops (i.e., soldiers who had never been on a peacekeeping mission) were much less tolerant and more rapid in their reactions than those who had served on a peacekeeping mission, leading the officer to realize how the tone of his unit had been affected by the deployment. [35]

2.3. STRESS AND THE "PSYCHOLOGICAL CONTRACT"

Apart from their effects on combat readiness, peace operations such as the IFOR and SFOR missions present difficult social-psychological challenges and operational stressors. In order to track these effects, the U.S. Army Medical Research Unit-Europe (U.S.AMRU-E) regularly conducts studies on the psychological health of U.S. soldiers stationed and deployed in Europe. Since senior U.S. military leaders increasingly recognize that stress can increase the likelihood of injury or death due to accidents, errors of judgment, or inattentiveness, new "Combat Stress Control" units now deploy along with combat troops.

A survey of 3,000 troops prior to deployment to IFOR revealed as primary sources of stress, in descending order: the need to complete personal

---

[34] U.S. General Accounting Office, *Peace Operations: Effect of Training, Equipment, and Other Factors on Unit Capability*, Report NSIAD-96–14 (Washington, D.C.: October 1995); MAJ Robert J. Botters, "The Proliferation of Peace Operations and U.S. Army Tactical Proficiency: Will the Army Remain a Combat-Ready Force?" (Fort Leavenworth, KS: School of Advanced Military Studies (SAMS) monograph, December 1995).

[35] MAJ George Krivo, interview with author, 8 September 1999, Arlington, VA.

business before deploying; the loss of educational opportunities; preparation of family for deployment; imminent separation from family and friends in the U.S.; concern about how the rear detachment will care for their families; and lack of job advancement opportunities, among other factors. [36] During the first month of deployment, the principal stressors included having to leave one's family just before the Christmas holidays; isolation once deployed; high "OPTEMPO" and long hours; fatigue and sleep deprivation; crowded and spartan living conditions; and one of the harshest winters the region witnessed in years. During the second month, weather and living conditions improved and working conditions became more predictable and reasonable. In order of decreasing saliency, stress factors were ranked as follows: isolation; uncertainty and confusion about the mission; lack of recognition; workload; boredom; lack of recreation/entertainment; lack of privacy; and doubts about mission importance. [37]

During the third month (February–March 1996), morale continued to improve as living and working conditions improved. The main stressors remained uncertainty, lack of recognition, isolation, and OPTEMPO. The major stressor was the absence of knowledge about the larger mission of the unit, its next move, and command policies. Most soldiers expressed doubts about the importance of the mission during this phase. Compounding the feeling of being in a bleak environment far from home was dissatisfaction with the telephone and mail systems. And although working hours had improved somewhat from the first month, many units continued to work seven long days per week. Other stressors included limited recreation opportunities, lack of privacy, boredom, and monotony. [38]

Other, less easily identifiable stressors were noted by the authors of this study. One hidden stressor may be described as an

> intra-psychic conflict or dissonance, a mis-match between the personal sacrifices and discomforts that being deployed on such missions entails, and the limited perceived pay-off or benefit. Many soldiers perceive the benefit of the mission as minimal; a common belief is that the peace established by IFOR under the Dayton Accords will not be a lasting one. Soldiers also typically see little of value coming to them personally from this deployment. Their jobs are often boring and lacking in meaning, the extra pay they re-

---

[36] "American IFOR Experience: Psychological Stressors in the Early Deployment Period," Army Medical Research Unit-Europe, May 1996.

[37] *Ibid*, p. 2.

[38] *ibid*, pp. 2–4. On dire living conditions, cold weather, high OPTEMPO, but generally good morale, see COL Peter G. Dausen, "Signal Preparations for Operation JOINT ENDEAVOR in the Former Republic of Yugoslavia," Personal Experience Memoir, in Douglas V. Johnson, II (ed.), *Warriors in Peace Operations* (Carlisle: Strategic Studies Institute, January 1999), pp. 3–30.

ceive is modest, and recognition is often lacking. This situation leads to an
intra-psychic conflict that may be psychologically very damaging.[39]

At a minimum, the authors note, soldiers must suffer painful separations from
loved ones (they do not state the percentage that are happily married). When
these sacrifices cannot be offset by meaningful work activities, frustration and
anger can result. Indeed, anger and depression were the most common problems among soldiers arriving at the Combat Stress Control service in Croatia. "In a majority of cases, there were profound worries about the welfare
of spouse and family members at home, coupled with a sense in the soldier
that his/her presence on this mission was insignificant." Additionally, soldiers
frequently experienced feelings of guilt over leaving their families.[40]

Such studies are suggestive but do not prove a causal relationship between
peace operation-induced stress and mental health. One attempt to do so postu-
lates that the causal relationship is between soldiers' perceptions that their job
was important, relevant to their training, and possessed clear rules of engagement (ROE), on the one hand, and low levels of depression and higher levels
of morale on the other.[41] These emphases on mission importance and relevance point to what some have called the "psychological contract" between
nation and soldiers. This contract consists of an unwritten set of expectations
and reciprocal relations that give value to members who voluntarily subscribe.
Soldiers enlist and officers persist in part because they feel their service has
value. Many feel that their sacrifice in Bosnia will be of a fleeting nature. The
fact that their fellow citizens appear not to understand this only exacerbates
this tension.[42]

Differences in findings on stress did not appear to be based upon unit type.
Gender differences did not show up in the primary screening rates, but gender
did account for a statistically significant difference in referral rates (4.6% of
men vs. 8.5% of women). Two additional findings related to length of time
deployed and rank. Longer-deployed soldiers tended to score positive on the
stress screenings, and the data suggest that the trend would continue for longer

---

[39] "American IFOR Experience," p. 5.
[40] *Ibid.*
[41] "Soldier Beliefs about Peacekeeping Operations as Predictors of Depression, Morale, and
      Responsibility," Walter Reed Army Institute of Research, 22 February 1996.
[42] For an excellent study on the Canadian forces, see COL Glenn W. Nordick, "Exploring the
      Psychological Contract of the Canadian Forces" (Carlisle, PA: USAWC Strategy Research
      Project, 1999). See also Denise M. Rousseau, *Psychological Contracts in Organizations:
      Understanding Written and Unwritten Agreements* (Thousand Oaks, CA: Sage Publications,
      2000).

periods of deployment. Also, lower-ranking soldiers scored positive more frequently than did higher-ranking soldiers. [43]

These findings are more interesting when compared with those for a non-deployed group. From April–July 1998, 790 non-deployed personnel participated in the screening. The roughly 19% of deployed troops who exceeded criteria on at least one of the primary scales was lower than the 25.6% of non-deployed active duty Army personnel. Similarly, 4.8% of deployed personnel exceeded criteria on the Post-Traumatic Stress Disorder (PTSD) checklist, while 7.5% of non-deployed personnel exceeded criteria. For alcohol abuse, there were no significant differences. Overall, significantly fewer deployed soldiers received a referral (2.8%) than non-deployed soldiers (11.3%). [44] The same differences between deployed and non-deployed personnel in both primary and secondary testing were found in sub-samples of male and female junior enlisted soldiers and in female enlisted soldiers. Differences were not found for male officers, while there were too few non-deployed female officers to compare with the deployed group. [45]

In general, then, deployed troops exhibited greater general psychological well-being as measured by such surveys. There are several possible explanations for this, apart from the fact of deployment. These include the timing of the testing, which for the deployed group coincided with the pleasure of re-deployment, the stress of extra garrison duties, and self-selection in deploying troops. In any case, the findings are strong enough to indicate that the Army has dealt with many of the concerns noted by observers of deployed troops. A sense of mission was instilled through news broadcasts and official praise noting the good that the deployment is doing. Isolation was overcome to a certain extent by mail, Internet, and telephone services. Recognition for superior performance was granted through meritorious awards and ceremonies. Rear detachment functions, as well, have improved significantly in recent years. For example, the overwhelming majority of spouses felt that the Army was doing everything it could to train (66%) and protect (67%) its soldiers. The Family Assistance Center system appeared helpful to a much larger portion of spouses (roughly 90%) than in Somalia (45–75%) or the Gulf War (70%). 85% claimed to have had an active Family Support Group, as opposed to 80% in Somalia and 50% in the Gulf War. [46]

---

[43] "Soldier Beliefs."

[44] It should be noted that General Order Number 1 prohibited alcohol consumption.

[45] "Psychological Screening with Deployed and Non-deployed Soldiers," Army Medical Research Unit-Europe, 19 March 1999.

[46] *Ibid.*

2.4. TRAINING

A key decision by the U.S. Army European Command (USAREUR) to com-
mence training *before* political decisions were made to deploy forces "probably saved lives" and meant that U.S. forces were better prepared for many tasks
than they would have been otherwise. Mine awareness and cold-weather training proved highly effective, as was borne out by the extremely low number of
casualties from these hazards. [47] More generally, "[by] the time the force was
deployed, virtually every soldier, civilian, and family member in USAREUR
had been exposed to special training or orientations related to Operation JOINT
ENDEAVOR." [48] Initially, training was geared towards a possible major extraction effort on behalf of UNPROFOR. For this task, basic warfighting skills
were deemed most appropriate. During the summer of 1995, training centered
on the possible swift extraction of smaller groups. Major exercises were held
for such tasks. In late summer, planning shifted to peace implementation; after September, they focused on a possible extended stabilization mission. The
most significant exercises during this September–December time frame covered: crew gunnery; tactics, techniques, and procedures to separate warring
factions and to develop IFOR doctrine on this issue; a political–military exercise designed to sensitize deploying officers to history, geography, and current conditions; three combat maneuver training exercises; reconnaissance;
and family support and other rear detachment issues. USAREUR conducted
frequent "lessons learned" and after-action studies. [49]

  Thus, training for the most dangerous missions was adequate. As an example, one brigade, the 3 – 325 Airborne Battalion Combat Team, focused on
Bosnia on and off for at least two years prior to deployment. They maintained
a contingency plan, participated in several rotations to the Combat Maneuver
Training Center in Hohenfels, Germany, and conducted several complete re-
hearsals for various missions under a variety of weather and time conditions. [50]

  Training for such missions requires a paradigm shift from the warfighting
goals of "attack, defend, and delay" to the peacekeeping goals of "secure, protect, and supply [populations]" and to the peace enforcement goals of establishing zones of separation and joint military commissions, working with political
and religious leaders, and other tasks. [51] The U.S. military has made important
steps down this long path. Training evolved as the mission progressed. Con-

---

[47]   U.S. Army Europe (USAREUR), *After Action Report, Operation JOINT ENDEAVOR,* Vol-
     ume I, p. xvii.
[48]   *Ibid,* p. 137.
[49]   "Lessons and Conclusions," pp. 1 – 2.
[50]   COL Curtis M. Scaparotti, "The Blue Falcons in Bosnia," in Johnson, *Warriors in Peace
     Operations,* pp. 31 – 82 (31 – 36).
[51]   *Ibid,* pp. 138 – 139.

tinuous after-action reviews took place based on information provided by almost 600 observer/controllers and the supervision of two retired generals, who
served as informal advisors to the commanding general. Exercises were also
expanded and revised until a series of major, simultaneous, multi-echelon exercises were developed to train the force for most of its anticipated missions. [52]

Other non-warfighting skills were honed, as well, during the train-up period. While training in Germany, one U.S. officer ordered his troops to block
a public road running through a large military training area. Many soldiers did
not speak German but had to learn to communicate while dealing with justifiably ill-tempered German citizens. In general, units in Germany were able to
prepare for "patrolling, convoy escort missions, tank crew gunnery skills tests,
tank crew proficiency courses, and other training, all while commanding and
controlling the events from the Tactical Operations Center and sustaining ourselves in the field. What we were doing turned out to be more realistic than I
could ever have dreamed." [53]

The U.S. Army Peacekeeping Institute (PKI), located at the Army War
College, was a central source of training for non-warfighting skills. *PDD-56*
directs the National Security Council to work with the Peacekeeping Institute and other agencies to provide training for the Political–Military Plan and
other aspects of complex contingency operations. [54] Established in 1993, PKI
conducts research and studies, plans, and exercises to refine leaders' skills for
peace operations. It also teaches courses at the Army War College and exports
these and other courses to the field. In addition, PKI specializes in negotiation and mediation training for Army civil affairs personnel; runs International
Conflict Resolution Education and Skills Training (ICREST) seminars with
the United States Institute of Peace; supports regional training exercises for
CINCs to prepare for complex contingency operations; and provides training
assistance to the UN Department of Peacekeeping Operations. PKI's support
to Task Force Eagle-bound units is found in Appendix A.

While virtually all units had specialized training relevant to their tasks,
there was also a minimal amount of cultural training. The sorts of messages
taught in political–military training to one engineering unit's leaders in the
pre-deployment phase included:

- "Nationalism replaces logic and it is always viewed as the proper response."
- "Ethnic problems do not have solutions; thus, conflict must be managed."

---

[52] *Ibid*, pp. 141 – 143.

[53] LTC Michael D. Jones, "The 'Iron Dukes' [2nd BN, 67th Armor] Supporting Operation
Joint Endeavor," in Johnson, *Warriors in Peace Operations*, pp. 83 – 118 (85).

[54] PKI is a central clearinghouse for material on strategic and high operational employment of military forces in peace operations; its web page can be found at http://carlisle-
www.army.mil/usacs/pki.

- "Ethnic cleansing is final and non-reversible."
- "In managing conflict, remember there is no clear mission; no clear plan to execute; no clear distinction between military and civilian; and no clear lines of command."
- "The official aim (separate states) will not be the true aim (manage conflict)."
- "If the operation fails, there is serious potential for NATO security failure."
- "Attitudes and perceptions are critical, so watch who [sic] you help and be fair."
- "It is not a people's war but a war of politicians."
- "They only respect strength and force."
- "Keep to the moral high ground in our actions and dealings." [55]

The depth of such training was not extensive. In medical units, 41% of nurses received less than one hour of cultural training prior to a mission, 48% received between one and three hours, and 11% received more than three. Topics included local values, politics, economics, education, health care, religion, technology, and family relations. [56]

After-action reviews, studies, and "lessons learned" pamphlets continued to refine notions of the skills required by unit type and level of organization. [57] On the other hand, training never strongly emphasized intercultural relations. Rather, mine awareness, patrolling, squad-level forward observer activities, cold weather survival, and rules of engagement were stressed during training. [58] This is somewhat understandable in view of the mission required of U.S. forces, which is discussed next.

The U.S. military must make further progress in training for peace operations, however. [59] Rotations through the Joint Readiness Training Center (JRTC) involving civilian organizations were minimal before 1994 and nonexistent for at least two years after. Peace operations are not included in unit METLs. *Field Manual 100–23, Peace Operations*, states: "Peace Operations

[55] COL Randall J. Butler, "94th Engineer Combat Battalion (Heavy) – Operation Joint Endeavor," Personal Experience Monograph, USAWC, p. 19, table 2.
[56] Julie M. Stola, "Medical Readiness in Humanitarian and Civic Assistance Missions: Significance of Cultural Training for Nurses" (University of Colorado, Boulder, MA Thesis, 1997), pp. 41–46.
[57] See, e.g., Kenneth P. LaMon, "Training and Education Requirements for Humanitarian Assistance Operations" (Center for Naval Analysis, April 1996); "Lessons Learned Report: Bosnia Contingency Planning and Training" (Fort Leavenworth, KS: CALL, September 1994).
[58] LTC Jeffrey Hammond, "Commanding a Field Artillery Battalion in a Peace Enforcement Environment – Operation JOINT ENDEAVOR," in Johnson, *Warriors in Peace Operations*, pp. 119–168 (124).
[59] BHAAR I, pp. 10–11.

are not a new mission and should not be treated as a separate task to be added to a unit's METL … For planning purposes, units require from 4 to 6 weeks of specialized training" to be prepared to conduct peace operations. The military will have to move beyond a "just in time" training philosophy once it recognizes that peace operations will remain part of its brief.

2.5. FORCE PROTECTION

The issue of force protection has become both a source and a symbol of intra-IFOR/SFOR tension. Operation JOINT ENDEAVOR strictly enforced a four-vehicle convoy rule to deter ambush and kidnapping. [60] There was no vehicle movement unless the plan was briefed, rehearsed, and certified by the battery commander. Vehicles were either off the road or moving in groups of four. The two-minute rule meant that if a vehicle was stopped for more than two minutes, drivers disembarked to clean windows, block the wheels, and assume a force protection stance. [61]

U.S. force protection policies generated tension both within the U.S. military structure and between the U.S. and other militaries. A Force Protection Program and Force Protection Working Group were set up by USAREUR (Forward) and permeated the working environment. This was done outside of the established NATO command and control structure. This, together with the perception that force protection prevented closer relations with local civic groups, annoyed many in the European contingent, who had a much more relaxed approach to the issue. Many Americans, in turn, did not feel their allies appreciated the different regard with which U.S. soldiers were held by certain of the Former Warring Factions (FWFs).

Force protection also generated tensions within the U.S. military. Although a unit's METL is not prioritized, it was assumed by the vast majority of officers in IFOR and SFOR that (1) force protection was an imperative with roots at the political level, and (2) one's assessment as a successful or failed leader in Bosnia would be critically influenced by the number of casualties in one's unit.

At the tactical level during IFOR, force protection was the highest priority. It was even part of the Operational Plan (OPLAN) mission statement: for US-AREUR, it was listed second on the METL after "provide and sustain trained and ready forces" and ahead of promoting regional stability; information dominance; power projection operations; operating a strategic support base; and providing for the well-being of soldiers and families. [62]

---

[60] Task Force Eagle, "Operation JOINT ENDEAVOR Lesson Learned," No. 68, 12 August 1996.

[61] Hammond, p. 158.

[62] United States Army Europe, "Mission Essential Task List," found at http://www.ullos.army.mil/public/plsql/ullos).USAREUR (accessed 22 July 1999).

Many officers felt that the policy seemed to be politically motivated rather than being based on actual, daily threat assessments. [63] In this respect, they agreed with some of their European counterparts. Virtually all of the officers interviewed by the author believed the concern with force protection was official policy. Virtually all interpreted this as meaning that a fatality would be a tactical "failure" for which they would be held accountable. But beyond this, none of the officers felt that force protection policies caused deep damage to the mission. They generally regarded it as a wise approach given the nature of the fighting that had recently taken place and the mission that the U.S. had to fulfill.

Several stated that the goal of the U.S. going in was to be "the meanest dog in the neighborhood" and to accomplish the primary goals of: separating FWFs; establishing a Zone of Separation and enforcing the cease-fire; providing for the handover of detainees and the withdrawal of personnel to proper zones; and providing for the disarmament of civilian formations and the withdrawal of heavy weapons. These missions required a clear demonstration that someone "meant business," thus necessitating the rules about convoys, flak jackets, ready weapons, and the highest standards of appearance and discipline.

The experiences of most officers bore out the wisdom of this policy. Most cited either harassment or direct attacks on NATO and PfP forces, but none on U.S. troops. A typical story involves the stopping and harassment of British troops in a clearly IFOR-marked military vehicle. When a U.S. convoy arrived on the scene, a British officer complained loudly about the behavior of the Serbs and said another route might have to be found. An American noncommissioned officer approached the group of Serbs, asked for their leader, demanded his weapon and identification papers, emptied the weapon, feigned a radio report on the individual's papers, recited current law on free passage, and demanded and received immediate dispersal and right of passage.

Other stories involve sniping at non-U.S. troops, minor disturbances (in non-U.S. sectors) that became more dangerous than necessary, and the failure by non-U.S. troops to deal with serious disturbances. In short, U.S. officers generally felt they had a difficult task and that force protection was usually justified, always helpful as a deterrent, occasionally excessive, but not excessively unwise or counterproductive. The section on "Military-to-Military Relations" below argues that the show of potentially overwhelming force was a necessary building block for political and social progress in Bosnia and the Republika Srpska.

---

[63]   BHAAR I, pp. 23 – 24; BHAAR II.

2.6. FORCE REQUIREMENTS AND THE RESERVES

Forty-five thousand Reserve Component (RC) soldiers participated in Operation JOINT ENDEAVOR and Operation JOINT GUARD, primarily in civil affairs positions. In fact, 95% of the Army's civil affairs specialists and 85% of its psychological operations units are found in the RC of the Army. [64] Deployment requires a Presidential Selected Reserve Call-up (PSRC), allowing the involuntary mobilization of up to 200,000 Reserve Component soldiers and officers for up to 270 days. The Joint Chiefs did not request such a call-up during RESTORE HOPE and CONTINUE HOPE in Somalia, perhaps out of sensitivity to the political pressure such a move places on the President. This decision limited the ability of the Civil Affairs forces to execute their tasks, since the Active Component (AC) Civil Affairs force consists of only 212 personnel with worldwide requirements, whereas the RC have 5,000 serving in the USAR. [65] A PSRC was used in both UPHOLD DEMOCRACY and JOINT ENDEAVOR; however, the latter used almost 50% of the total Reserve Component Civil Affairs force. [66]

Effective use of civil affairs personnel requires that they be in-theater 30 days prior to the start of an operation. In JOINT ENDEAVOR, the PSRC order was not signed until after the deployment had begun; the first mobilized RC soldiers began arriving only 30 days after deployment. The gap was filled by active components and by some Reserve personnel who arrived early. Effective use of Civil Affairs personnel is further limited by the law's restriction on the activation of doctors for only 140 days and of civil affairs personnel for only 179 days. The utility of many RC personnel is significantly less than their legally allotted service because of the time necessary for mobilization, processing, minimal training, movement, and leave. A 270-day tour works out to an effective tour of only seven months and a 140-day tour to less than three months. [67]

Reserve Component members also volunteer on a regular basis for peace operations. At least 18,000 volunteer reservists participated in peace operations between 1992 and the end of 1996. More than 7,500 supported Operations DENY FLIGHT and PROVIDE PROMISE to Bosnia. [68] Service head-

---

[64]   U.S. Army Europe (USAREUR), *After Action Report, Operation JOINT ENDEAVOR*, Volume I, p. xvii.

[65]   John T. Fischel, *Civil Military Operations in the New World* (Westport, CT: Praeger, 1997), p. 247.

[66]   Chadwick, pp. 19 – 20.

[67]   U.S. Army Europe (USAREUR), *After Action Report, Operation JOINT ENDEAVOR*, Volume I, p. xviii.

[68]   United States General Accounting Office, "Peace Operations: Reservists Have Volunteered When Needed," April 26, 1996, pp. 3 – 4.

quarters state that they are satisfied with the general level of volunteer support, a conclusion supported by several studies of specific units. The Air Force is by far the most active user of volunteers. Volunteer forces generate extra costs to the service, which are paid for by funds taken out of the active component. Other restraints on their use include differing philosophies across services about the purpose and use of the reserves and the adequacy of planning for their use. [69]

2.7. PROMOTION

The majority of officers felt that deployments to peacekeeping operations affect their careers, as would any other responsibility – success helps in promotion while failure hurts. For certain officers who have focused on a particular kind of career track, peace operations can be irritating and incline them to chafe against established procedures and policy. This could lead to unnecessary conflict and poor performance. For others, such as Specialist Michael New, who in the mid-1990s tried to make a legal case against donning a blue helmet, religion and narrow patriotism are the motivations. New had made the claim that he had sworn to defend the U.S. Constitution with the words, "so help me God," but this did not oblige him to take orders from the United Nations, which he found "ungodly." [70]

For the majority, however, it is simply another career milestone requiring the development of existing or new skills. Pentagon spokesman Kenneth Bacon stated that a peace operation is "a pass for promotion, just as if someone had commanded in war. The importance and complexity of major peacekeeping operations today makes the officers who command them prime candidates for promotion." [71] The first commander of Task Force Eagle similarly stated that sustained peace operations

> should be, for our junior leaders, a career-defining experience that internalizes into their professional souls the lessons of doing things right. We must take advantage of this unique opportunity to create a cadre of professional soldiers that are able to sustain operations to standard and have the moral courage to do what is right all the time. [72]

---

[69] *Ibid*, pp. 8 – 10.
[70] MAJ Robert G. Young, "The Impact of Operations Other than War on the Midgrade (O-3/4) Army Officer" (Fort Leavenworth KS: MA Thesis, 1997), pp. 20 – 21.
[71] Elizabeth Becker, "War Colleges Now Training Soldiers in Art of Peace," *New York Times*, 6 August 1999.
[72] Cited in CPT Robert Murphy, CPT Fred Johnson, *et al.*, "Maintaining Warfighting Skills While Keeping the Peace in Bosnia," 139.161.168.16/lessons/reports/news4/sec1.htm, accessed 21 July 1999.

3. MILITARY-TO-MILITARY RELATIONS

Several papers in this volume have noted antipathy between U.S. and other NATO forces. These should be placed in context. First, it should be noted that U.S.–Russian cooperation was one of the great success stories of IFOR. Despite serious problems in the early stages, the deployment of Russian soldiers laid the foundation for the signing of the NATO–Russian Founding Act of 27 May 1997. There was great potential for political conflict, given the history of Russian–Serbian relations, Russian–U.S. relations, and the fact that the supreme commander was a U.S. General. Russian forces were placed under General Joulwan, but operational control was exercised through General Joulwan's Deputy for Russian Forces, Colonel-General Shevtsov. Thus the Russian brigade assigned to Multi-National Division (North) [henceforth, MND (N)] was under the tactical command of the MND (N) commanding officer, under the operational control of the Deputy for Russian Forces, and under the strategic control of the IFOR commander.

Much of the groundwork for the successful coordination between U.S. and Russian forces was laid during peacekeeping exercises at Totskoe and Fort Riley. As described by a joint review of the MND (N) experience, the importance of these exercises

> cannot be over-emphasized. Despite whatever goodwill may exist between nations, there can be no vibrant military cooperation until the mechanics of interoperability are developed and tested. The meetings, discussions, and exercises between the U.S. and Russian militaries prior to IFOR being deployed were absolutely critical to its success. Without the prior development of this language and understanding, such cooperation would have been impossible.[73]

Together the units accomplished their mission goals, each provided fire or other support for the other at various critical junctures, and trust generally increased between the two national contingents at high levels.

U.S. troops also worked closely in MND (N) with the Nordic–Polish Brigade and, for Combat Support branches, at one time or another with most other contingents. A series of not-for-attribution interviews conducted by the author revealed several views within an overall picture of sufficiently smooth relations. First, these U.S. officers generally considered their allies to have less discipline, as revealed in appearance, promptness, adherence to chain of command, and after-hours behavior. Second, there was a perception that non-U.S. units "improved" in each of these categories within a short span of time and as

---

[73] "Lessons and Conclusions," p. 4.

a result of the example and expectations set by U.S. troops. Third, none of the interviewees reported any serious tensions.

Tensions were more frequently cited by individuals with experience at higher levels of command, where the divergent national visions of mission and execution are more likely to come into relief. One officer working in Sarajevo suggested that "we caused a lot of the problems" by bringing an attitude of knowing best how to deal with problems with which other allies had longer experience. Frequent rotations did not ease the problem. This situation would be improved should NATO take the major steps of trying to agree on a political–military vision at the start of such a major operation and subsequently developing the concepts, doctrine, and resources to execute that vision.

4. MILITARY RELATIONS WITH GOVERNMENTAL AND INTERNATIONAL ORGANIZATIONS (IOS): EVOLVING "GRUNT DIPLOMACY"

U.S. officers were largely effective in dealing with local political leaders. There is a growing recognition at the middle levels of the U.S. officer corps that many of the conflicts to which the military will be sent are "political–military" operations and that many political skills must be honed for these jobs. One soldier-author has referred to this as "grunt diplomacy." In Brcko, for example, the U.S. military was the key player in issues of resettlement and reconstruction, successfully using its strong force presence to bring together opposing political and social leaders. The existence of hostility and the absence of any NGOs or international military presence meant that the reinforced battalion of U.S. soldiers that arrived shortly after the signing of the Dayton peace agreement faced a number of immediate difficulties. With opposing armed entities poised for new conflict, the task force occupied key terrain and coaxed military units from their trenches to their allotted zones of separation. Warned by both Serb and Bosniak commanders of imminent attacks, this IFOR task force was able to deter all such challenges. It then began the process of building sufficient confidence among farmers, police chiefs, and opposing military leaders to begin the process of reconciliation. During this period, the U.S. battalion commander acted as a third-party quasi-mediator. [74]

Confidence-building was apparently sufficient to carry the reconciliation process through some difficult times. When Serb and Bosniak groups began massive reconstruction and resettlement projects that violated the peace agreement, the civil entity that was supposed to deal with such problems was not yet

---

[74] LTC Tony Cucolo, "Grunt Diplomacy: In the Beginning There Were Only Soldiers," *Parameters* 29, No. 1 (Spring 1999), pp. 110–126 (116–117).

capable of functioning. Thus, the U.S. task force commander had to reveal the details of the violations while continuing to hold weekly meetings; the confidence in both the battalion commander and regular meetings carried all parties through the crisis with the process intact. As one officer described the process:

> [D]uring the first four months of the implementation, there was simply no one else in the international community available to do it. By the fifth month, personnel from the International Police Task Force (IPTF) had taken over the increasingly important joint police meetings, and by the eighth month, the chair of the task force's civil–military seminars was passed to UN Civil Affairs. In the beginning, however, there were only soldiers. [75]

5. MILITARY RELATIONS WITH NGOS, PRIVATE VOLUNTARY ORGANIZATIONS (VOS), AND INTERNATIONAL ORGANIZATIONS (IOS)

5.1. GENERAL

U.S. Joint Doctrine does recognize that the military will be working with a wide variety of organizations in humanitarian and peace operations. *Joint Publication 3 – 08* defines the different types of organizations as follows.

- *International Organizations* (IOs) are those with "global influence, such as the United Nations, and the International Committee of the Red Cross."
- *Non-governmental organizations* (NGOs) are "transnational organizations of private citizens that maintain a consultative status with the Economic and Social Council of the United Nations. NGOs may be professional associations, foundations ... or simply groups with a common interest in humanitarian assistance activities. NGO is a term normally used by non-U.S. organizations."
- *Private voluntary organizations* (PVOs) are "private, nonprofit humanitarian assistance organizations involved in development and relief activities. PVOs are normally United States-based."

This paper will use the blanket term "NGOs" to cover the three groups unless otherwise noted.

The problem with the U.S. approach to civil–military operations in Bosnia may be summed up in the following list from a "lessons learned" web page of the U.S. Army's Center for Lessons Learned. One has to go to the bottom of a long list in a chapter on "Tactics, Techniques, and Procedures (TTP) for

---

[75] *Ibid*, p. 119.

Supporting the Peace in Bosnia-Herzegovina" [76] to find civil–military lessons
learned.

- Pre-deployment Training
- Situational Training Considerations
- Mine and Booby Trap Awareness
- Force Protection
- Security of the Force
- Personal Awareness
- Sniper Threat
- Information Gathering
- Intelligence Preparation of the Battlefield
- Photo Support
- Use of Standardized Priority Intelligence Requirements Checklists
- Area Assessment Checklist
- Patrols
- Fire Support Considerations
- Suppression of Artillery
- Mine Warfare Operations
- Checkpoints
- Convoy Vulnerability
- Convoy Debrief Checklist
- Direct Fire during MOUT Operations
- Use of Underground Sewer Systems
- Clearing Multi-story Buildings
- Urban Communications
- Use of Weapons in an Urban Environment
- Converting an Urban Structure into a Strongpoint
- Correct and Timely SALUTE Reporting is Crucial
- Civil Affairs Plays an Integral Part in any U.S. Peacekeeping Operation

The military–NGO relationship is a daunting one. At the start of the United
Task Force (UNITAF) in Somalia, for example, there were 38,000 soldiers
from 21 nations as well as 49 UN organizations and NGOs, increasing to 90
by the time the U.S. pulled out. During UPHOLD DEMOCRACY, there were
400 NGOs and PVOs, many already in the country when the military arrived.

Until recently, the Combined Joint Task Force Commander (CJTF) did
not adequately utilize the expertise of NGOs. One reason was the leadership
style of most CJTF commanders. Utilizing NGOs requires "consensus-style
decision-making; the realization that the military may not have all the an-

---

[76] "Supporting the Peace: Bosnia-Herzegovina." Newsletter 95 – 13, Center for Army Lessons
Learned, http://call.army.mil/call/newsltrs/95 – 13/bhc4toc.htm.

swers; some humility towards the local population; and flexibility towards non-military ways of doing business," according to one NGO official. Another claimed that military communities need greater cultural awareness and sensitivity. [77] NGO workers saw the military in Somalia as "inflexible, conservative, and bureaucratic." [78] The military – and NGO members themselves – frequently identify the latter as "children of 60s" – liberal, anti-military, and wasteful in their efforts. [79] For their part, NGOs are frequently unfamiliar with military logistics and transportation systems. [80]

There is an inherently ambivalent relationship between NGOs and the military, in that NGOs note the sometimes dire need for security yet chafe at both the restrictions that this entails and the loss of security that will come when the military leaves while NGOs inevitably remain to fulfill civic functions. [81] NGOs have frequently been overlooked by the military as a source of information. Many in the U.S. military view NGOs as obstructionist by definition, and military leaders frequently assume they already possess sufficient knowledge of a complex situation. An example is the quick deployment of mobile surgical tents and military rations ("Meals Ready to Eat" [MREs]) after Hurricane Andrew, while the local Red Cross was aware that tents were not needed and the population in question was unlikely to eat MREs. Elsewhere, in Mogadishu, the military brought such a huge supply of food that, when it arrived, it disrupted NGO plans for economic recovery and displaced merchants. [82]

Another perception is that NGOs do not provide intelligence but only general information. There is a lack of appreciation for information that comes in forms not usually seen by the military. Additionally, the desired nature of coordination is not always understood by the military. A CJTFC will prefer a clear delineation of duties. In Rwanda, this worked out well from the military's perspective, with the military handling bulk water purification processes while the NGOs handled individual distribution. In other cases, the military may be most

---

[77] Mark Dearfield, "The CJTF and NGOs – One Team, One Mission?" (Newport, RI: Naval War College, 15 May 1998), p. 4.

[78] MAJ K.E. Bruno, "The Regional Civil–Military Operations Center: A Force Multiplier in Military Operations Other Than War" (Newport, RI: Naval War College, February 1999), p. 10.

[79] J.T. Dworken, "Military Relations with Humanitarian Relief Organizations: Observations from RESTORE HOPE" (Alexandria, VA: Center for Naval Analysis, 1993), p. 38.

[80] COL Guy C. Swan III, CDR Richard R. Beardsworth, *et al.*, "Uneasy Partners: NGOs and the U.S. Military in Complex Humanitarian Emergencies" (Cambridge, MA: John F. Kennedy School of Government, May 1996), p. 28.

[81] *Ibid*, p. 5., p. 17, n. 13 citing InterAction's petition to President Clinton to maintain a U.S. troop commitment in Bosnia past the June 1998 deadline.

[82] *Ibid*, p. 7.

effective as a "gap-filler," not a role military leaders have been very interested in assuming. [83]

Finally, humanitarian mission advisors have a mixed role on the staffs of the military branch most likely to take the lead in humanitarian operations. They have had a formal place on the staffs of the Pacific Command, for example, a lesser role in Southern Command, but they had no role in European Command in 1995. [84]

5.2. EVOLVING CIVIL-MILITARY COORDINATION

The U.S. military is learning, however. [85] It knows that Operation PROVIDE COMFORT in Northern Iraq benefited greatly from having a Civil–Military Operations Center (CMOC) staffed by the right people. [86] A CMOC may be defined as "a coordination center established and tailored to assist the unit CMO officer in anticipating, facilitating, coordinating, and orchestrating those CM [civil–military] functions and activities pertaining to the civil population, government, and economy in areas where armed forces, GOs, IOs, NGOs, and PVOs are employed." [87]

The U.S. experience in Somalia, Haiti, and Bosnia demonstrated that civil–military tasks are essential to a successful mission, yet the U.S. was ill-equipped to manage them. In Haiti, a lack of coordination led to insufficient planning for a viable police force, the failure of aid shipments once the economic embargo was lifted, and the inability to complete plans for a Haitian Justice Department. Knowledge that important NGOs were wary of working with the military led to the establishment of a Humanitarian Coordination Center, physically separate from the CMOC but subordinate to it. This led to some confusion on the part of the NGOs, although overall the arrangement worked effectively. [88]

In Bosnia, the U.S. did not initially integrate plans with NATO or international partners and concentrated on enforcement issues, failed to plan for the hard political tasks, and in general did not integrate military support with

---

[83]   *Ibid*, p. 10.

[84]   BHAAR I, pp. 10–11; BHAAR II.

[85]   Some thinking along these lines is contained in Kurt E. Muller, "Toward a Concept of Strategic Civil Affairs," *Parameters* 28, No. 4 (Winter 1998–99), pp. 80–98; Capt. Chris Seiple, "The U.S. Military and NGOs: A Window into an Age of Windows," unpublished manuscript; Chris Seiple, *The U.S. Military/NGO Relationship in Humanitarian Interventions* (Carlisle, PA: PKI, 1996). See also Swan, Beardsworth, *et al.*

[86]   See LTC George F. Oliver III, "Who are These Guys? Non-Governmental Organizations in Humanitarian Relief Operations" (Naval War College: May 1996) for discussions of useful meetings in Kigali.

[87]   US Army John F. Kennedy Special Warfare Center and School, *White Paper*, Civil–Military Operations Staff Support to Army Corps Division G5 Sections.

[88]   *Ibid*, pp. 47–48.

civil implementation. [89] Early coordination with humanitarian organizations was particularly inconsistent, so that NGOs did not know who was in charge of CIMIC (the NATO acronym for Civil–Military Cooperation) activities. In Sarajevo, there were actually three layers of CIMICs, including IFOR, the Allied Command Europe Rapid Reaction Corps (ARRC), and the French division. This was one reason why civil actors did not coordinate early with the military, thus later requiring the military to step into civil actions that it had wished to avoid. Except where necessary, the military clearly focused on the peace enforcement mission, and low priority was given to the development and execution of a civil–military campaign plan. [90]

There are several general reasons for such shortcomings. First, planners worked under a force cap of 20,000, as stipulated by political authorities. Second, political authorities announced a 364-day end date for the operation, thus providing a disincentive to plan for the longer tasks of civil–military rebuilding. Third, NATO invented a new concept known as the Combined/Joint Civil–Military Cooperation staff at the IFOR level. This was inadequately staffed and less well regarded than the usual (neutral) CMOC. [91] Fourth, there was a gap between civilian and military understandings of the strategic goals. Military leaders did not believe they had a mandate for nation-building (and may have wanted to avoid the burden of one), while political leaders assumed such a mandate but did not make it explicit. [92] A further problem is the unclear status of the political–military officer within the military establishment. A clear track of professional advancement is not in evidence, due mainly to the military's perceived central task of fighting and winning wars. [93]

The Clinton Administration's response to such problems was *PDD-56* (May 1997), which had the objective of creating an Executive Committee (ExCom) to coordinate and implement a political–military plan for a complex contingency. According to *PDD-56*, the political–military plan should include a comprehensive situation assessment, a mission statement, agency objectives, and the desired end state. The ExCom should consist of members accountable to the President for coordination and responsibility.

As LTC Bob Chadwick has pointed out, two critical levels are left out of this formulation. First, the CINC, in effect the theater commander, is respon-

---

[89]   LTC Bob Chadwick, "Civil Affairs Campaign Planning for Complex Contingency Operations: Getting it Right" (USAWC Strategy Research Project, 12 April 1999).

[90]   BHAAR, II.

[91]   *Ibid.*

[92]   Chadwick, pp. 7–12.

[93]   Norvell B. De Atkine, "Soldier Scholar or Cocktail Commando?" *American Diplomacy* IV, No. 1 (Winter 1999), http://www.unc.edu/depts/diplomat/archives/arcframe.html (accessed 14 January 1999).

sible for developing a "campaign plan" that includes all elements of national power – diplomatic, economic, political, and military. Yet *PDD-56* does not give him the authority to do this, since he follows the strategic plan of the Ex-Com. Second, the IOs, NGOs, and PVOs are usually a crucial component in executing the political side of the equation and are always a force to be reckoned with in the theater commander's plan. Yet they are not included *ipso facto* in the plans at either the theater or strategic level. [94]

Suggestions for improving the integration of these organizations include expanding the role and authority of the Political Advisor's office within the Combatant Commander's headquarters in order to facilitate communication and planning. Another is to deploy a Multi-Agency Support Team consisting of interagency experts to assist the Joint Force Commander or Combatant Commander. A third is to expand the Civil Affairs staff (and develop concomitant doctrine) to provide a wider basis for a knowledgeable CMOC. [95]

Despite these problems, the achievements of the CIMIC in Bosnia-Herzegovina were many, including successfully facilitating cooperation between IFOR and the state electrical supply company; facilitating the installation of safe power lines and gas distribution systems to much of Sarajevo; coordinating the work of the World Bank, IMF, IFOR/AARC engineers, and local agencies on the construction of bridges and roads; assisting the European Bank for Reconstruction and Development in planning and legislating for a cellular telecommunications system; inspecting the main water supply for Sarajevo; developing and employing plans for the IPTF's reorganization of regional Bosnia-Herzegovina and Republika Srpska police forces; contributing to the revision and rewriting of property laws and assisting in processing the claims of displaced persons; and assisting the OSCE in elections support. [96]

6. CONCLUSION: LEARNING FROM TENSIONS

Operations JOINT ENDEAVOR and JOINT GUARD ensured that the territorial integrity and sovereignty of Bosnia-Herzegovina as a unitary state have been guaranteed and ultimately accepted by all parties. Thirty-four nations, including many non-NATO states, together accomplished a series of complicated missions. The roughly 12,000 troops that Partnership for Peace nations contributed comprised approximately one-third of the overall SFOR contingent. The transition from IFOR to SFOR took place as planned and tasks were handed over to civil organizations. The economy has started to recover.

---

[94] Chadwick, pp. 15 – 17.

[95] *Ibid*, pp. 17 – 18.

[96] James J. Landon, "CIMIC: Civil Military Cooperation," in Larry Wentz (Ed.), *Lessons from Bosnia: The IFOR Experience* (Washington DC: NDU Press), pp. 119 – 138 (122 – 124).

More importantly, unified governmental institutions have begun to function, and democratic elections have taken place.

The extent of adaptation by the U.S. military has been remarkable, particularly if one keeps in mind the potential hindrances to this adaptation. First, as stated above, the U.S. government and public remain uncertain of the desired U.S. role in peace operations. This does not make it any easier for the military to know the contingencies for which it ought to prepare. Second, the political and moral basis for peace operations continues to increase in complexity. The killing of Kosovar Albanians, for example, presented a difficult ethical dilemma for European and American polities. East Timor presented another difficult situation for the international community.

A third potential hindrance to adaptation is a basic incompatibility between what one historian has called "the American way of war" and the requirements of peace operations:

> Once American military power became great enough to make the destruction of the country's enemies an object worth contemplating, a central theme of the history of American strategy came to be the problem of how to secure victory in its desired fullness without paying a cost so high that the cost would mock the very enterprise of waging war. [97]

This "strategy of annihilation" is difficult to square with long-term peace enforcement, peacekeeping, or civil-society-building missions. To the extent that it is a part of the American psyche, the American military has absorbed it as well.

Now, the U.S. military must recognize that humanitarian missions are not likely to go away in the near future. International and domestic norms have changed, and public opinion and foreign policy have changed with them. Skills, missions, and standards unique to peace operations must be better integrated into U.S. and NATO doctrine and training. The military must also adjust its conception of its mission to include close relations with civilian organizations, both governmental and private.

Together, these challenges may be said to require a revolution in thinking. If, as Clausewitz and most military men believe, war is an extension of politics, peace operations deal with the politics flowing from war. Max Manwaring has pointed this out and added that such operations therefore entail a political-psychological struggle for limited goals and the "hearts and minds" of peoples. [98]

---

[97]   Russell F. Weigley, *The American Way of War: A History of the United States' Military Strategy and Policy* (New York: Macmillan, 1973), p. xxii.

[98]   Max Manwaring, "Peace and Stability Lessons from Bosnia," *Parameters* 28, No. 4 (Winter 1998 – 1999), pp. 28 – 39 (30).

The military will likely continue to adapt successfully to the challenges of the new millennium but needs assistance from two general sources. One is the alliance of nations with whom it is likely to intervene. NATO and PfP states must dramatically increase their ability to deploy, operate, and supply a versatile force on a more equal footing with their American ally. The UN, too, must move ahead more rapidly with the development of doctrine and standing agreements that will allow the U.S. to use its capacities where they are needed most, and for limited periods of time. Unity of effort is required at the strategic level of peace operations. Representatives from NATO countries must begin now to define shared ends, ways, and means of carrying out peace operations. Each national contingency, not to mention international and non-governmental organization, pursues its own doctrinal and organizational imperatives in planning and implementing peace operations. This cannot stand; strategies must be harmonized. NATO has taken a major step forward with the drafting of its Joint Publication 3.4.1, *Peace Support Operations*. This document tackles the difficult issues of the definition of success; the timing of involvement; mission planning; force structure; public information; degrees of force; rules of engagement; unity of effort; civil–military cooperation; and – significantly – how many of these issues are to be decided. [99]

The U.S. military also needs assistance at home. Political authorities must clearly define the kinds of missions the military is likely to encounter, the scope of those missions in terms of time and assumed costs, and the nature of public, Congressional and fiscal support that the administration will do its best to secure. At the very least, an administration must seek to avoid the kinds of problems created by delaying the call-up of RC forces after Dayton, or by failing to build a sufficient domestic consensus behind the Somalia operation. This is a task for both political parties and for the legislative as well as executive branches of government.

---

[99]   NATO AJP-3.4.1, *Peace Support Operations* (3rd Study Draft, October 1999).

U.S. Army Peacekeeping Institute
Support to Task Force Eagle-bound Units and JRTC Peace Operations Rotations

Topic of training	Duration	Target audience	Summary
Civil–Military Operations	3 hours	Down to Senior NCOs	Overview of civil–military operations. Trains officers and NCOs who may deal with civilians. Instructor takes cultural approach with real world examples.
Negotiations	3 hours	Commanding General (CG), Division (DIV) Staff, Brigade Commander (BDE CDR), BDE Staff, Battalion (BN) CDRs	Provides basic framework on strategy and process of conducting successful negotiations with civilians, host nation officials, belligerents, military leaders, and NGOs. Provides conceptual framework and thought process. Contents are practical and have proven successful. Same class taught to 2ACR and European units deploying to Bosnia and 25th Infantry Division. Class is very interactive; a read-ahead packet is provided.
Joint Military Commissions (JMCs)	2 hours	CG, BDE CDR, DIV/BDE Staff, BN CDRs	Provides training in the conduct of JMCs and the mechanisms enabling relevant military and civilian authorities, at all levels, to implement a peace plan within the theater. JMCs enable military leaders to explore options across the difficult political, military, and social issues that face them.
Political –Military Plan	2 hours	CG, DIV Staff	Focus is *Presidential Decision Directive 56*, "Managing Complex Contingency Operations," signed May 1997. Lays out format for U.S. Government interagency coordination. Designed to synchronize operations at the strategic level and provide political guidance to the operational level for the formulation of the CINC's theater campaign plan and tactical actions.
Civilian Humanitarian Assistance Architecture	2 hours	CG, BDE CDR, DIV/BDE Staff, BN CDRs, Company (CO) CDRs	Explains which civilian organizations, both international (IO) and non-governmental (NGO), provide humanitarian assistance for complex emergency and peace operations and what roles they play. Explains the hierarchy of organizations and functions (food, water, refugees, medical, etc). Helps the military understand what these organizations provide and how to interact with them to accomplish the mission. Will enable units to avoid failure in integrating these agencies into the mission in the crisis country, preventing excess costs and mission creep.
Role Player Training	4 hours	DIV/BDE/BN Staff	Demonstrates attitudes and perspectives of how actual participants in a peace operation can react to certain stimuli. Helps leaders to understand what motivates people to take action in a complex contingency operation. Helps leaders understand hidden/overt agendas, and will provide the unit being trained a realistic picture of what could actually happen in a peace operation.

Other PKI support available:

- *Role players for a brigade level or higher (DIV, JTF, ARFOR, CINC-level) command post exercise or field training exercise – Special Representative to the Secretary General (SRSG), U.S. Ambassador, Humanitarian Assistance Coordinator, UN Official, NGO Field Representative, etc;*
- *Limited copies of doctrinal manuals, after-action reports, publications, papers, articles, etc;*
- *Scenario development;*
- *Recruiting of role players from other agencies and institutions;*
- *Access to PKI network;*
- *Instruction on civil affairs capabilities, multinational logistics, rules of engagement, and legal issues of peace operations.*

10. CZECH SOLDIERS IN PEACEKEEPING OPERATIONS IN THE FORMER YUGOSLAVIA

Štefan SARVAŠ and Marie VLACHOVÁ

Outline:

1. BACKGROUND

1.1. OBJECTIVES AND METHODOLOGY OF THE STUDY

The objective of this national study is to summarize and analyze the experiences resulting from Czech military participation in the Implementation Force

(IFOR) and Stabilization Force (SFOR) missions and to present a structured overview of Czech participation in these peacekeeping operations. This study was based on:

- An analysis of documents (official materials, specialized publications, articles in specialized periodicals and daily press, etc.);
- Results of a survey of ideas and opinions conducted among participants in IFOR/SFOR operations by the Research Department of the Ministry of Defense during 1996 – 1998. This study consisted of three stages and was designed to examine peacekeepers' opinions before departing for the IFOR operations (194 respondents), during the mission (211 respondents), and after return from the mission (518 respondents). The third stage, which was focused on mission veterans, included an examination of the reactions of soldiers' spouses to their partners' deployment abroad (312 female respondents); [1]
- Interviews with journalists and employees of non-governmental humanitarian organizations.

1.2. A BRIEF HISTORY OF THE CZECH REPUBLIC'S PARTICIPATION IN PEACEKEEPING OPERATIONS

Up to the year 1989, participation of Czech, or more precisely Czechoslovak, armed forces in peacekeeping operations was very sporadic. The only operation worth mentioning is Czechoslovakia's representation in the Monitoring Commission of Neutral Countries in Korea from 1954 – 1993. It is not certain, however, whether this diplomatic mission, which included a small group of soldiers, can be considered a peacekeeping mission as this term is understood today. In the beginning of 1989, Czechoslovakia was asked to take part in the United Nations Angola Verification Mission (UNAVEM) and, later that year, in the United Nations Transition Assistance Group (UNTAG) mission in Namibia. From 1989 – 1993, 62 officers took part in these two missions as observers. Although the beginnings were rather humble, the past decade has shown that the Czech Republic is very serious about its participation in United Nations and other international organizations' peacekeeping activities. This stance is supported by the fact that, between 1989 and the end of 1998, the Czech Republic sent almost 7,000 persons on 19 peacekeeping missions in the territories of 13 countries. The majority of them were soldiers from army units

---

[1]   Jiří Hendrych and Marie Vlachová, *IFOR – A Week before Departure* (Prague: Research Department of the Ministry of Defense, 1996). See also Jiří Hendrych and Marie Vlachová, *SFOR – A Month before Return* (Prague: Research Department of the Ministry of Defense, 1997), and Jiří Hendrych, *Former Participants in Foreign Missions: Opinions of Mission Veterans and Their Spouses about Missions and Problems Faced after Return from Abroad* (Prague: Research Department of the Ministry of Defense, 1998).

UN/OSCE, NATO, and WEU Missions and Operations in which the Czech Republic (or the former Czech and Slovak Federative Republic) has taken part since 1989:

Observers (military and civilian)
- UNAVEM I and UNAVEM II (United Nations Angola Verification Mission)
- UNTAG (United Nations Transition Assistance Group) in Namibia
- UNGCI (UN Guard Contingent in Iraq)
- UNOSOM (UN Operation in Somalia)
- EC/MM (European Commission Monitoring Missions) in the former Yugoslavia
- UNPROFOR (UN Protection Force) in Croatia
- UNOMOZ (UN Operation in Mozambique)
- UNOMIL (UN Observer Mission in Liberia)
- UNOMIG (UN Observer Mission in Georgia)
- UNCRO (UN Confidence Restoration Operation) in Croatia
- UNPREDEP (UN Preventive Deployment Force) in Macedonia
- UNMOP (UN Mission of Observers in Prevlaka) in Croatia
- UNTAES (UN Transitional Administration for Eastern Slavonia) in Croatia
- OSCE (Organization for Security and Cooperation in Europe) in Georgia
- OSCE in Bosnia and Herzegovina
- OSCE in Moldova
- OSCE in Nagorno-Karabakh
- OSCE in Croatia
- OSCE in Chechnya
- MAPE-WEU (Multi-National Advisory Police Element – Western European Union) in Albania

Support Units
- Counter-chemical unit in Saudi Arabia

Field surgery hospitals in:
- UNPROFOR/UNCRO
- UNTAES
- 6th Field Hospital in Operation AFOR (Albanian Force)

Battalions independently operating in countries affected by conflicts
- UNPROFOR/UNCRO
- IFOR/SFOR
- KFOR

deployed in four different local conflicts, mostly in the Balkans. The first mission took place in 1990, when Czechoslovakia sent a special counter-chemical unit, comprised of 200 men, to the Persian Gulf. The unit stayed in the Persian Gulf until mid-1991 and actively participated in operations DESERT SHIELD and DESERT STORM.

1.3. PARTICIPATION IN PEACEKEEPING MISSIONS IN THE BALKANS

The Czech Republic's most important contribution to peacekeeping has been participation in observer and military missions in the former Yugoslavia. The first Czech observation mission began in the fall of 1991, when five permanent military observers and three vehicles took part in the European Community Monitoring Mission (EC/MM) in Yugoslavia. Thirty-three soldiers participated in the mission up to January 1993, when the duty was taken over by the Slovak army.

Another group of observers was deployed to this region in March 1992. They took part in the UNCRO mission in Croatia, the UNPREDEP mission in Macedonia, and the UNMOP mission on the Prevlaka peninsula. The UNTAES mission in Croatia in the eastern Slavonian city of Klise included a military field hospital with a staff of 40 Czech physicians and medical attendants. Five Czech officers participated in the OSCE Bosnia and Herzegovina mission, whose tasks included the monitoring of local elections, fulfillment of the Dayton Peace Agreement, and stabilization of conditions in Bosnia and Herzegovina. More than 100 Czech observers have taken part in peacekeeping missions on the territory of the former Yugoslavia since 1991.

Since mid-1998, 12 Czech representatives have been working in the civil-military (CIMIC) Centers in Prijedor and Sanski Most; their aim is to promote cooperation between SFOR units and the local population. The Center workers are active mainly in the sector monitored by the Czech peacekeeping battalion. They take part in the implementation of the so-called Department for International Development (DFID) projects that are financed by the British government and designed to promote the renewal of local infrastructure, the development of small and medium sized businesses, and the creation of new employment opportunities. During the execution of these projects, CIMIC Center workers cooperate with a number of non-governmental humanitarian organizations from the Czech Republic, Great Britain, Norway, Austria, Germany, and other countries. The CIMIC Centers take part in a number of projects that promote the renewal of normal life in peacetime. Examples of these activities include the construction of infrastructure; the repair of schools, cultural centers and factories; the provision of food and teaching supplies; and the establishment of a dental ambulance as well as the procurement of the necessary equipment for it.

The Czech Republic reacted promptly to the serious situation in Yugoslavia. As early as 16 January 1992, the government of the Czech and Slovak Federative Republic approved participation in UN peacekeeping operations on the territory of the former Yugoslavia. The applicable Czech government resolution corresponded to the UN Security Council resolution of 27 December 1991 (Resolution No. 721), in which the UN undertook the adoption of adequate measures to resolve the situation in the Balkans and asked member nations to form peacekeeping forces that could be deployed in the region. The first Czech contingency unit in the UNPROFOR/UNCRO mission consisted of 500 persons. Later, Czech participation was expanded to 1,000 soldiers in a mechanized battalion. In addition to this unit, the regiment included a group of military police officers, a signals unit, and an independent surgery team. The battalion was deployed in Croatia in the operational sector South, where Czech soldiers worked with Canadian, Jordanian, Kenyan, and – up to 1993 – French peacekeepers. This battalion ended its activities in the UNPROFOR/UNCRO mission in December 1995. In the beginning of the following year, the unit was transferred to Bosnia and Herzegovina, where it assumed duties under the NATO/IFOR mission. A year later, the unit was transferred to SFOR.

The Czech army contingency unit deployed in the IFOR, SFOR I, and SFOR II operations consisted of a mechanized battalion of 500 soldiers with an additional 30 persons in headquarters and a cooperation section. The unit was supported by two Mi-17 helicopters (with 22 persons) and an L410 aircraft (with 12 persons). The battalion was equipped with the most modern technology possessed by the ground forces of the Czech army (including infantry combat vehicles, armored personnel carriers, a tank recovery vehicle, grenade launchers, bazookas, heavy machine guns, submachine guns, sniper rifles, pistols, cross-country passenger vehicles and trucks, cranes, tractors, and buses). Responsible for a sector with an area of 3,200 square kilometers, the battalion was deployed in the northwestern part of Bosnia and Herzegovina under the international division SOUTHWEST. The Czech unit was stationed in the British sector; its neighbors were peacekeeping units from Canada and Great Britain. The terrain of the area is highly varied and has large differences in altitude, from 150 meters near the city of Prijedor up to 1,000 meters in the Kozara Mountains. Czech soldiers were deployed on four bases (Bosanka Krupa, Donja Ljubija, Velika Kladusa, and Split) on the territory of both the Republika Srpska and the Muslim-Croat Federation.

Participation of the Czech unit in IFOR and SFOR operations was considered to be the most important and, thus far, the most extensive tangible expression of cooperation with NATO member nations. It is generally acknowledged that the success of the Czech unit in these missions significantly helped to advance the Czech Republic's accession to NATO in the first phase of enlargement.

Even though difficulties persist in Bosnia and Herzegovina, a certain improvement has taken place since the deployment of international peacekeepers under SFOR. The adversaries have retreated to the territories specified in the Dayton Peace Agreement, and heavy weapons have been removed from the zone of separation. Thanks to the presence of peacekeeping forces, municipal elections have taken place in Bosnia and Herzegovina, and parliamentary elections have been held in the Republika Srpska. Moreover, local self-government has begun; relations with neighboring countries have been stabilized; some refugees have returned to their homes; and projects aimed at the renewal of the destroyed national economy have been initiated.

On 14 April 1998, a Czech government resolution (No. 270) and subsequently the Czech Parliament approved continued participation in international peacekeeping operations under NATO command in order to monitor compliance with peace agreements and to stabilize the situation in Bosnia and Herzegovina (SFOR). The original mission was initially extended through the fall of 1999 and was extended several times thereafter up to the time of this writing.

1.4. COMPATIBILITY OF PEACEKEEPING MISSIONS WITH THE NATIONAL SECURITY STRATEGY AND THE MILITARY DOCTRINE

The participation of the Czech armed forces in peacekeeping operations is legislatively supported by both the *Security Strategy of the Czech Republic* and by the Czech *Military Doctrine*. These fundamental documents clearly define duties arising from NATO membership on the basis of the principle of collective defense. The reinforcement of transatlantic bonds is one of the country's main strategic objectives. Additional duties of the Czech armed forces include defending the interests of the international community; strengthening stability, trust and security in Europe; and the deployment of army units in peacekeeping missions outside the Czech Republic. The *Security Strategy of the Czech Republic*, adopted in the spring of 1999, takes into consideration the risks arising from the Czech Republic's membership in NATO. The strategy foresees the participation of Czech army units in various humanitarian and peacekeeping missions as well as in operations that may, in extreme cases, involve "the small-scale, preventive use of armed forces in order to avoid the escalation of an existing conflict." [2]

---

[2]   *The Security Strategy of the Czech Republic* (Prague: Ministry of Defense, 1999).

The deployment of armed forces abroad is decided by the Czech government and must be approved by both chambers of the Czech Parliament. A mission's mandate is based on Section VI or VII of the UN Charter. Due to the fact that the Czech Republic is not represented on the UN Security Council, great emphasis is put on informal consultations with countries that want to take part in a mission with the Czech Republic. These consultations take place before the mandate is approved and allow the Czech army command to participate in preparations for the mission, including the determination of subordination levels with regard to the command of international forces and top UN and NATO bodies.

The Czech Republic respects the applicable chains of command in peacekeeping missions. There have been no fundamental conflicts between UN orders and binding national directives. The UNPROFOR mission showed that the quality of training and equipment in Czech units did not meet the mandate's requirements, a fact that resulted in casualties. This knowledge was used in the preparation of the IFOR mission. The Czech Republic took advantage of the flexibility of the operation's concept, which allowed the transfer of Czech units under NATO operational command, leaving decisions about the format of troops deployed and their weapons and equipment up to the national command.

1.5. MOTIVATION FOR CZECH MILITARY PARTICIPATION IN PEACEKEEPING MISSIONS

1.5.1 POLITICAL MOTIVATION

Czech politicians have decided to accept part of the responsibility for UN peacekeeping missions for a number of reasons. Political reasons – particularly an awareness of the continuing instability of today's world and an effort to incorporate the Czech Republic into Euro-Atlantic structures – have played a decisive role. From the very beginning, Czech political leaders saw participation in peacekeeping operations as an opportunity to demonstrate, through concrete actions, the Czech Republic's often-stated desire to join NATO. Moreover, from both a geographic and cultural perspective, Czechs regard the former Yugoslavia as a nearby region with which the Czech Republic shares a long tradition of friendly relations and similar historical development. These aspects were fittingly expressed in 1995 by the Minister of Foreign Affairs, Jozef Zeleniec:

> We want to build an integrated Europe together with members of the European Union. We want to join NATO. Moreover, we live in the neurotic Central European region. These are several very specific reasons that support our participation in this mission. The NATO Founding Agreement is a

complicated document; however, it clearly expresses a simple principle: all for one and one for all. We have already declared our will to join an alliance based on this principle. But concrete actions speak much more eloquently than all the words in the world. Operation JOINT ENDEAVOR, whose aim is to bring peace to Bosnia – that is, our region – has provided us with an opportunity for such action. [3]

Military reasons were also quite important. In particular, the government wished to prove that the Czech army could be deployed in non-standard operations, while the military wanted to gain experience from participation in the resolution of a regional conflict. Furthermore, economic renewal, to which peacekeeping units contribute, could result in the reopening of traditional commercial contacts between the Czech Republic and the nations on the territory of the former Yugoslavia.

1.5.2 Pᴇʀsᴏɴᴀʟ Mᴏᴛɪᴠᴀᴛɪᴏɴ ᴏғ Pᴇᴀᴄᴇᴋᴇᴇᴘᴇʀs

Czech soldiers join peacekeeping missions on a voluntary basis. [4] The minimum requirement for inclusion in a mission is the completion of basic military service. Most candidates are, however, active professional soldiers or reservists. The view that soldiers are drawn to participation in peacekeeping missions primarily for monetary reasons is quite widespread throughout the Czech populace, however, our survey of members of SFOR/IFOR units showed that it would be simplistic to state that Czech peacekeepers were motivated solely by monetary gain. A survey conducted in an army recruiting and training center among soldiers preparing to leave for Bosnia showed that about a third of the respondents identified monetary gain as their sole motivation. The motivation of the majority of soldiers, however, could be summarized as the desire "to make money and to do something important for our country and the army at the same time." This shows that both financial and unselfish, idealistic motives were somewhat balanced. In this regard, it must be mentioned that the earnings of participants in peacekeeping missions were relatively high, at least in comparison with salaries received by their colleagues at home. This allowed substantial improvements in living standards for soldiers' families, including the possibility to open a business or purchase an apartment. In a situation where it is very difficult to buy an apartment, as has been the case in the Czech Republic since 1990, the latter is a strong reason for participation. Volunteering for a peacekeeping mission is often the only way to achieve the standard of living routinely enjoyed by soldiers in Western armed forces.

---

[3]   Jozef Zeleniec, "The SFOR Operation Has Begun," *Lidové noviny*, 15 December 1995, p. 2.

[4]   The new Act on Professional Soldiers, which came into effect in December 1999, does not include the principle of voluntary participation in peacekeeping operations. Professional soldiers will have to join missions on the basis of an order of the Minister of Defense.

Many soldiers also had career-related or professional motivations, such as the desire to prove one's abilities; to gain experience for future service in the army; to improve foreign language proficiency; or to experience something adventurous and unusual. The example set by peers from the same unit who volunteered for a mission also played a role. It seems that a certain number of soldiers tried to solve their personal, family, or work-related problems by going on a peacekeeping mission. Some soldiers volunteered repeatedly due to their positive experiences from previous missions. Their decisions were not solely based on monetary gain; they enjoyed life on peacekeeping missions so much that they were willing to return to Bosnia repeatedly.

2. INTERNAL MILITARY DIMENSION

2.1. PEACEKEEPERS' PERCEPTIONS OF THE MISSION'S AIMS

The duties of the Czech contingency forces are outlined in the Dayton Peace Agreement. The principal objectives were to fulfill the military aspects of the agreement and to create conditions for the gradual achievement of the agreement's civilian aspects. The Czech battalion monitored the overall military and political situation within the sector for which it was responsible and secured working conditions for international humanitarian and non-governmental organizations (NGOs).[5] In 1996 and 1997, Czech peacekeepers performed duties related to the preparing and holding of general, parliamentary, and municipal elections in the Republika Srpska and the Muslim-Croat Federation. Some tasks were performed in cooperation with the British division, which has taken advantage of the communication skills of Czech soldiers in dealing with local officials. The tasks of the initial military stage of the fulfillment of the Dayton Peace Agreement (separation of the warring parties; transfer of some weapons to international forces; monitoring and gradual liquidation of minefields; and the creation of local institutions, including the formation of common political authorities) were executed relatively successfully. The fulfillment of the second stage, which involves normalization of life in the region (in particular, the return of refugees to their homes), has proved very difficult. This is demonstrated, for example, by the fact that, as of this writing, international forces have not yet succeeded in arresting key war criminals who face international criminal charges in The Hague. These were the main reasons why, in 1998, NATO decided to keep international forces in Bosnia and Herzegovina.

---

[5] This includes supervision of transfers of weapons and armed forces; the removal of heavy weapons from the zone of separation; monitoring the size of local armed forces allowed under the Dayton Peace Agreement; presence at inter-ethnic border crossings; and the removal of mines.

Soldiers who take part in these operations perceive the purpose of peace-keeping missions very much as it is depicted in UN declarations. They consider their main duty to be the protection of and assistance to people in regions affected by crisis. From the viewpoint of the Czech Republic, one specific aspect of participation in peacekeeping missions involves the country's accession to NATO. Soldiers, who from the very beginning have supported the country's accession to NATO (unlike the Czech general public), are well aware of this dimension of peacekeeping. In addition, a great number of Czech soldiers see these missions as an opportunity to showcase their professional abilities. Soldiers who return to military service after completing their peacekeeping duties stress the political aspects of such missions, including the improved prestige of the Czech army and the positive effect peacekeeping has had in facilitating the Czech Republic's accession to NATO. Conversely, those for whom completion of a peacekeeping mission means the conclusion of their military career stress the humanitarian dimension more strongly.

2.2. SELECTION AND TRAINING OF SOLDIERS FOR PEACEKEEPING MISSIONS

Soldiers who volunteer for peacekeeping missions must undergo a selection process that involves physical, psychological, and medical examinations as well as an English proficiency test. Candidates who successfully complete all these tests are included in "cohesion training," which lasts four to six weeks and takes place at the UN Peacekeeping Forces Training Base in the southern Czech city of Český Krumlov. Training consists of four stages: commander training; acquisition of basic knowledge about the mission (tasks, military preparation, information about developments in the conflict region); specialized military training (specialized training for the particular duties with which individual soldiers will be charged); and field skills training. Furthermore, commanders who take part in peacekeeping missions in the former Yugoslavia are trained on foreign training bases and take part in NATO maneuvers (for example, in Sweden, Finland, Denmark, Austria, Canada, and Switzerland). The training base in Český Krumlov was opened in 1990. Since then, the facility's equipment and training concept have undergone several changes. The original two-stage training system has been preserved, but the center currently puts a greater emphasis on the training of commanders who, besides cohesion training, undergo a week-long specialized course intended to provide them the necessary skills to fulfill command duties on peacekeeping missions.

2.3. ASSESSMENT OF BENEFITS OF PEACEKEEPING MISSIONS; DIFFERENCES BETWEEN EXPECTATIONS AND REALITY; AND DIFFICULTIES ENCOUNTERED DURING MISSIONS

A vast majority (73%) of soldiers who have participated in a mission view their peacekeeping duty positively and are satisfied with their service abroad. They are content and proud because they gained new experiences, forged new friendships, fulfilled their duties, and feel that they earned the money they received. Czech soldiers were largely content with free time activities and food. The extent of satisfaction with peacekeeping duties is closely related to the family support received by individual soldiers. Those who went to Bosnia with the approval of their families (60% of respondents) and who had the feeling that all was well at home, that their wives would manage without them, and that would be someone to turn to if necessary viewed their peacekeeping duties much more positively than those who tried to resolve their personal or family problems by volunteering for a mission or those who went to Bosnia despite the disapproval of their relatives.

Difficulties faced by soldiers on the mission included an increased feeling of being personally endangered, homesickness, and some problems of an organizational, materiel, and interpersonal nature. Veterans of the Bosnian peacekeeping mission admitted that their greatest difficulties were ordinary, everyday problems. For example, some felt that their superiors' orders were not always given with the necessary insight; others described insufficient material and equipment provided to the unit as well as problems in interpersonal relations, particularly in detached units with a limited number of soldiers ("submarine disease"). Difficulties faced by soldiers included worries about their families, especially due to the fact that Czech peacekeepers' opportunities to communicate with their families were quite limited in comparison with soldiers from Western contingency forces. The most difficult period for the majority of peacekeepers was the beginning of the mission when they had to adapt to new and unusual conditions. These difficulties were less easily tolerated by older soldiers and those taking part in a peacekeeping mission for the first time.

One-third of peacekeepers experienced a crisis during the mission, regardless of age and previous experience serving abroad. The most frequent cause of crisis was the repetition and intensification of ordinary, everyday difficulties that related more to peacekeeping duties than to family problems. Although an unfavorable family situation may have accelerated and aggravated a crisis, it did not usually cause it. According to soldiers, the most common causes of crises included adaptation difficulties ("I couldn't get used to the work on the mission," and "it was harder than I had expected"), conflicts with superiors, disagreements with comrades in the unit, and organizational problems.

Responses to questions asked of the wives and partners of soldiers who served as peacekeepers in Bosnia showed that the perception of problems related to serving abroad differed substantially as far as men and women were concerned. Soldiers' spouses had much stronger feelings; their greatest fear was that their husbands might be killed, wounded, or captured. In addition, soldiers' spouses were less able to tolerate irregular mail and the absence of up-to-date information about the mission. Hence, it can be concluded that men's problems were related mostly to professional difficulties with peacekeeping duties and homesickness, while spouses were anxious about their husbands' fidelity and lives. Men were better able to withstand separation from their families because they had someone to whom they could turn (including friends in the unit, psychologists, chaplains, or their commanding officers). Soldiers' wives suffered from loneliness, which was deepened by mail problems and difficulties concerning telephone communications with the bases in Bosnia.

2.4. RETURN FROM THE MISSION

Toward the end of the mission, even though most peacekeepers were looking forward to returning home, about one-third expressed a certain apprehension about returning. They voiced concerns about whether they would be able to adapt to "life in peace" and find a good job or an adequate post within the army. Finding work after returning from peacekeeping duty is a significant problem, especially for those soldiers who return to their civilian occupations. Unemployment among those who do not return to active duty reached as high as 40% in the first six months after return, 27% during the first year, and 10% thereafter. The latter figure, in particular, shows that even with the relatively low average unemployment rate in 1997 (4%), peacekeeping veterans had difficulties finding adequate civilian employment.

There were even 4% of soldiers on active duty who (because of the reorganization within the army, which took place while they were serving in Bosnia) lost their original posts in the armed forces and decided to leave. Nonetheless, most professional soldiers returned to their original positions or tried to be promoted to a post where they could utilize their experience from Bosnia. About half of the active-duty servicemen succeeded in doing so. The knowledge and experience gained on peacekeeping duty strengthened their self-confidence, especially as far as their professional, command, and organizational skills were concerned, and they wanted their position in the army to correspond to their ambitions and career expectations. Although most former peacekeepers were optimistic, a number of veterans criticized their superiors' lack of interest in utilizing the experience they had gained during peacekeeping missions.

Adaptation problems may appear in veterans' private life, as well. Coming home meant a return to a lifestyle to which the soldiers became unaccustomed during their foreign service, as well as the necessity to renew relationships with wives and children and to get used to the ordinary problems of family life. The study showed that about 4 – 6% of the marriages of soldiers who have taken part in a peacekeeping mission fall into a long-term family crisis or end in divorce as a result of the separation. In most cases, these marriages already faced problems before departure for the mission and the soldiers opted to serve abroad in an attempt to resolve the situation. [6]

On the other hand, the mission helped strengthen marriages where a strong bond between the partners already existed. The partners began to value one another more and recognized anew each other's respective good qualities. Wives appreciated the fact that their husbands earned money for the family, dealt with the difficulties of the mission, and returned more mature, experienced, and mentally resilient. On the other hand, soldiers valued the fact that their wives managed to take care of their households and children.

The vast majority of soldiers were interested in returning to peacekeeping duty. Their motivation was based not only on potential earnings and fear of unemployment, but also on an awareness of the importance of the mission for the Czech Republic and the Czech army, as well as a desire to take part in an important and beneficial activity and to work once again with a good team of people who shared the same interests. Mission experience also substantially increased the attractiveness of becoming a professional soldier for those who participated in a peacekeeping mission. Almost 60% of peacekeepers who came from civilian life wanted to stay in the service after returning home. Hence, peacekeeping veterans represent an important recruitment source, which can be readily used for the needs of the army.

2.5. WOMEN ON PEACEKEEPING MISSIONS

The army of the Czech Republic, 7% of whose professional soldiers are female, has a relatively high representation of women. The position of female soldiers is comparable with smaller Western European armies, such as the Belgian or Dutch armed forces, with regard to historical traditions, the number of women serving, and the posts that they occupy. Czech female soldiers have actively participated in the Czech army's peacekeeping missions abroad.

Czech women began to take part in foreign missions in 1992, when two female soldiers went to the UNPROFOR mission as military observers. During the following three years, at least one woman was always present on this mission. Since 1994, at least one female soldier has been regularly sent to the UNGCI mission in Iraq. Detailed statistics concerning women in peace-

---

[6]   Before the beginning of the mission, 14% of the respondents stated that the main reason for their departure abroad was an attempt to resolve personal problems through separation from their families or relatives.

keeping missions are not available at this time, as until recently, females were not listed as a special group in statistics. Nevertheless, based on the available information, it can be concluded that Czech female soldiers were present on most military missions in which the armed forces have taken part. For example, eight women participated in the IFOR mission during 1993–1996, and 15 female soldiers served in SFOR during 1997–1999. Altogether, about 30 Czech female soldiers, including those who have served and continue to serve as observers, have personal experience serving abroad.

Similar to their counterparts from many other armed forces, most Czech women are medical attendants, administrative and communications workers, and observers. In 1998, the first two women who performed duties formerly reserved for men – a press agent and a platoon commander – returned from Bosnia. At least one woman is regularly included in the CIMIC mission. Considering the relatively high representation of women among professional soldiers of the Czech army, the 30 females who have served on peacekeeping duty abroad may seem to represent a low number. However, more important than the number is the fact that Czech women soldiers have been provided with an opportunity to test their combat skills in an environment traditionally reserved for men. Despite the initial doubts and problems that the deployment of women abroad caused for the army and for the women themselves, Czech female soldiers have proven that the best ones among them are able to fulfill their duties successfully even under extreme conditions.

2.6. ATTITUDES OF CZECH CITIZENS TOWARD PARTICIPATION IN PEACEKEEPING MISSIONS

Since the fall of the Iron Curtain, the Czech political elite has clearly stated that the Czech Republic is prepared to assume its share of responsibility for international development. This stance has been confirmed by the deployment of a counter-chemical unit in the Persian Gulf War, active participation in the UNPROFOR and IFOR/SFOR missions in Bosnia and Herzegovina, and involvement in other peacekeeping activities.

The Czech public has viewed the country's foreign activities much more cautiously than politicians. Deployment of the Czechoslovak counter-chemical unit in operations DESERT SHIELD and DESERT STORM, the first and only combat operation in which Czechoslovak armed forces have taken part since the end of the World War II, was approved of by 51% of the Czech population in 1992, one year after completion of the operation. The public's stand concerning peacekeeping missions in the former Yugoslavia was ambiguous, as well. In 1992, 51% of respondents agreed that the Czech Republic should take part in resolving this region's crisis. This opinion was maintained by about half of the population until 1998. At the end of that year, support for the participation of Czech forces in peacekeeping missions grew to 58%, while the number of opponents declined to about one-third (see Table 1).

Table 1: Do you agree with the participation of Czech soldiers in peacekeeping missions, such as the deployment of Czech forces in the former Yugoslavia? (%)

	1996	*1997*	*1998*
Yes	50	50	58
No	41	38	32
Don't know	9	12	10

In general, the Czech public favors specific humanitarian activities rather than direct or indirect participation in military operations in countries involved in conflicts. This is clearly shown in the results of public opinion surveys held as the situation in Kosovo increasingly deteriorated:

- Two-thirds of the Czech population agreed with the deployment of a military hospital in Kosovo;
- Should the Kosovo conflict escalate, participation of the Czech Republic in humanitarian activities would be supported by almost 80% of Czech citizens;
- Only one-third of the population approved of Czech participation in military operations in Kosovo, and only 23% agreed with the deployment of Czech soldiers in Kosovo;
- More than one-third of the respondents (43%) thought that the Czech Republic should not get involved should the Kosovo problems worsen, and more than half (56%) were afraid that taking part in the crisis would cause problems for the Czech Republic;
- Even after the Czech Republic became a NATO member, fewer than half of the respondents (42%) approved of participation in resolving the Kosovo crisis and only 27% agreed with deployment of Czech soldiers in Kosovo;
- Forty-four percent of those interviewed maintained that Czech soldiers risk their lives in missions whose objectives are unclear;
- At the end of 1998, more than two-thirds of the Czech population thought that soldiers who take part in peacekeeping missions were mercenaries, motivated solely by monetary gain.

The population's positive attitudes toward humanitarian missions on the one hand, and doubts about the Czech Republic's participation in military operations, on the other, may be due to people's concerns that human lives could be lost, a risk which always accompanies participation in peacekeeping missions. These attitudes are known as the so-called "body bag syndrome," [7] which reflects the belief that modern industrial societies with low birth rates are willing to tolerate neither their own losses nor civilian casualties among their adversaries in military conflicts. [8] The public is highly sensitive to such risks. [9] Another explanation of the hesitant stance of the Czech public with regard to foreign peacekeeping missions is the "free rider syndrome." NATO membership involves advantages as well as disadvantages. The latter become apparent when soldiers must be deployed abroad. Every NATO member tries to minimize its expenditures and the risk of casualties.

Owing in large part to the success of Czech soldiers in peacekeeping missions in the former Yugoslavia, the hesitant stance of the Czech public toward service abroad is gradually changing. This shift is reflected in the opinion that peacekeeping missions have tested the qualities of the Czech army and helped the country's integration into NATO and the EU. More and more people think that participation in peacekeeping activities is the duty of every democratic country. These positive trends are confirmed by the declining number of respondents who think that it is useless to spend taxpayers' money on the deployment of Czech armed forces to peacekeeping missions and that the objectives of peacekeeping missions are not clearly defined.

3. MILITARY-TO-MILITARY DIMENSION

3.1. COOPERATION OF CZECH SOLDIERS WITH OTHER ARMED FORCES

The IFOR/SFOR missions presented Czech soldiers with their first opportunity to participate in an operation alongside NATO forces. At the outset of the mission, there were some glitches in communication between the battalion and the brigade commands. Insufficient familiarity with operating procedures and work at the headquarters level, and problems with the compatibility of communications systems [10] caused tension between the Czech command and higher

---

[7]   Body bags are plastic bags used for transport of the bodies of soldiers killed in military operations.

[8]   It is worth mentioning that, for example, the U.S. had to end the Somalia peacekeeping mission because of casualties. This position was illustrated in a survey conducted by CNN and *USA Today* in October 1995. Its outcome showed that two-thirds of the respondents approved of American participation in peacekeeping operations in Bosnia, on the condition that no U.S. soldiers would be killed; only one-third of the population were in agreement with U.S. involvement in Bosnia if 25 casualties were to occur.

[9]   Edward Luttwak, "A Post-Heroic Military Policy," *Foreign Affairs* 75, No. 4, 1996, pp. 33–44.

[10] Similar problems were experienced by Polish soldiers. See Krysztof Paszkowski, "Partnership for Peace Activities and the Preparation for IFOR: The Polish Experience," in Peter

Table 2: Attitudes toward Statements about Peacekeeping Missions (% of Respondents Answering Yes)

Opinions	1996	1997	1998
Foreign missions test the quality of our army.	62	71	78
Participation in peacekeeping and humanitarian missions improves the image of the Czech Republic.	X	73	77
Participation in peacekeeping missions improves the Czech Republic's chances for integration in the EU and NATO.	X	66	73
The only reason soldiers volunteer for missions is money.	76	72	70
Every democratic country has a duty to take part in resolving problems in regions affected by conflicts.	X	52	59
Missions present an opportunity to create a new type of soldier that will be needed more often in the future.	44	52	56
Our soldiers risk their lives on missions whose objectives are unclear.	55	47	44
It is useless to spend taxpayers' money on sending Czech units on peacekeeping missions.	X	39	35
The Czech Republic should not participate in peacekeeping missions at all.	X	X	25
The Czech Republic should participate in peacekeeping missions to a greater extent than in the past.	X	X	18

Note: X = the question was not asked that year.

command levels, especially at the beginning of the mission. These problems were gradually resolved. Lessons learned by Czech peacekeepers exposed the necessity to respect command structures; to coordinate activities of individual national forces (particularly neighboring units); to ensure cooperation with the command of individual contingency forces already in the preparatory stage; and to share certain classified information. [11]

The Czech unit has worked mainly with English-speaking forces; Czech

---

Talas and Sebestyen Gorka (Eds.), *Lessons Learned from the IFOR/SFOR Experience* (Budapest: Institute for Strategic and Defense Studies, 1997), pp. 29–34.

[11] Dušan Dubový, "The Czech Experience with the IFOR/SFOR Missions," *Ibid*, pp. 41–44.

soldiers' inadequate knowledge of the English language has caused some problems. One Czech officer described the situation as follows:

> We did have some problems in the beginning. During the first two weeks of the mission, we worked with an English brigade that regularly received soldiers from one specific region. It was as if there were a unit in the Czech Republic put together just with soldiers from the Ostrava or Haná regions. [12] To put it briefly, they had quite a strong accent and were using abbreviations we couldn't understand. It took us some time; we had to adjust our ears to their dialect. In the end, we managed... [13]

Participation in peacekeeping operations has exerted pressure on the army to ensure adequate training and preparation of Czech peacekeepers at home. Based on experience from individual missions, the Czech government has concluded that Czech army units must be trained in a way that allows deployment according to NATO requirements. In addition, the government has charged the Ministry of Defense with using the IFOR mission to verify the functionality of existing military structures with respect to their deployment in peacekeeping operations. [14]

3.2. HOW CZECH SOLDIERS PERCEIVE THEMSELVES IN COMPARISON WITH SOLDIERS FROM OTHER ARMED FORCES

Peacekeeping missions have presented Czech soldiers with a unique opportunity to compare their professional qualities and equipment with those of their counterparts from other armed forces serving in the former Yugoslavia. Czech peacekeepers have come into contact mainly with soldiers from Great Britain, Canada, and the U.S., but they have also worked alongside non-European forces (from Jordan, Kenya, Indonesia, and Malaysia) and armies from other post-communist countries (Hungary, Poland, and Slovakia). In light of such exposure, Czech soldiers consider the Czech army to be better than non-European and other post-communist armed forces and, in certain regards, show no lack of confidence as far as Western armed forces are concerned, although they generally view Western soldiers as their models. Czech soldiers see their professional qualities as fully comparable with their counterparts from the U.S., Great Britain, Canada, and France. In their opinion, the Czech contingency forces have better vehicles than the British and German armies, and Czech soldiers are more disciplined than their German counterparts. A clear advantage Czech peacekeepers enjoy in the Balkans is their ability to communicate with local people and representatives of local authorities and the fact that they

---

[12]   Regions in the Czech Republic where a characteristic dialect is spoken.
[13]   "240 Days," *Czech Army Today* 1, 1998, p. 39.
[14]   Resolution of the Government of the Czech Republic No. 677 of 29 November 1995.

are respected by both sides of the conflict, presumably thanks to cultural and linguistic similarities. The respondents who took part in our study agreed that in this regard Czech soldiers are second to none among the above-mentioned armed forces.

In general, Czech soldiers appreciate the combat-related and organizational qualities of Western soldiers, especially their commanders. They greatly esteem interpersonal relations among Western soldiers and their high-quality equipment. Czech soldiers envy the amenities that peacekeepers from Western countries enjoy on their bases, which ensure them the opportunity to spend their free time with relative pleasure: high-quality equipment; good food; and state-of-the-art communication systems that guarantee reliable communications within individual units as well as unlimited contact with families and relatives at home. Peacekeeping missions have taught Czech soldiers that, although their equipment and armaments are inferior to those of their Western counterparts, Czech peacekeepers have similar professional qualities, and that they are even better in some situations requiring specific skills important for peacekeeping missions. All Czech soldiers who have returned from peacekeeping duty exhibit confidence that has been gained thanks to the affirmation of their professional qualities. This aspect is one of the greatest benefits of Czech participation in peacekeeping missions.

4. Military Relations with NGOs and the Local Population

4.1. Czech NGOs' Cooperation with Armed Forces

In conflict areas, army units cooperate with numerous civilian organizations. Some of these institutions are NGOs. Specific features of NGOs include a non-military and often international character, a strategy of presenting their activities in the media in order to raise funds from various sources, and a strong adaptability to local conditions based on good knowledge of local cultures, customs, standards, and politics. Some authors maintain that, in this regard, NGOs possess greater knowledge than military units deployed in conflict regions. On the other hand, Michael Williams, who sees substantial differences between NGO representatives and soldiers, maintains that the successful fulfillment of peacekeeping tasks in conflict-ridden areas can be achieved only through cooperation between these two different types of institutions. [15]

While serving in IFOR/SFOR, Czech peacekeepers dealt with a number of Czech and foreign NGOs. The following Czech NGOs were active in Bosnia

---

[15]   Michael C. Williams, *Civil–Military Relations and Peacekeeping* (London: International Institute for Strategic Studies, *Adelphi Papers*, No. 321, 1998).

and Herzegovina: ADRA, People in Need (*Člověk v tísni*), the Czech Red
Cross, and the Czech Catholic Charity.

These NGOs began their activities in 1991 – 92. The scope of work done by
Czech NGOs is demonstrated, for example, by the fact that the foundation People in Need has, since the signing of the Dayton Peace Agreement in December
1995, participated not only in the provision of humanitarian aid, but also in the
execution of various development projects, including the construction of infrastructure. In addition, the organization has helped establish conditions for
the return of Bosnian refugees to the Sanski Most region by taking part in the
construction and repair of housing in order to create the necessary conditions
for the return of refugees who were given asylum in the Czech Republic.

Further, Czech NGOs have acquired 15 used ambulance vehicles for
Bosnian hospitals; procured incubators for hospitals in the Tuzla region; sent
volunteer doctors to Bosnia and Herzegovina; and supplied seed potatoes.
Most of these activities were carried out with the help of the Czech contingency unit. [16]

In general, cooperation between Czech peacekeepers and humanitarian organizations was perceived as very good on both sides. Soldiers were involved
in the distribution of relief, thanks to their familiarity with local conditions.
A former spokesperson for the Czech battalion commented on the situation as
follows:

> Thanks to the fact that we knew local conditions, we were able to identify
> people who needed aid the most and we helped relief workers with distribution. By doing this, we prevented, to some extent, a situation where most
> of the relief supplies would appear on the black market.

These practical examples of cooperation were specific; soldiers notified relief
workers of localities that needed assistance and helped with humanitarian aid
transportation and distribution. The director of the Czech branch of the Red
Cross has confirmed that with regard to distribution of humanitarian aid,

---

[16] For example, People in Need used the help of a Czech unit during the transport of 80 tons
of sugar, salt, flour, candles, matches, and children's clothing to the surrounded enclave
Gorazde. People in Need was the very first humanitarian organization to come to this area.
Czech soldiers also assisted ADRA in transporting eight tons of potatoes, food, and clothing
to the area where the Czech battalion was stationed in the spring of 1998. Czech peacekeepers were responsible for local distribution of the aid. In addition, ADRA operated a motorized dental ambulance in the Czech sector for three years. The unit provided dental care to
40 – 50 patients a day; its doctors and attendants shared accommodations with the Czech
peacekeeping unit. An ADRA official assessed relations between soldiers and humanitarian
workers as responsive and friendly.

> Czech soldiers worked in a very professional manner. It was apparent that
> they were very familiar with the territory. They knew people and their needs
> and had contacts with the local administration, school principals, etc.

Cooperation between soldiers and humanitarian workers was necessary in
some more complicated cases, such as assistance provided during the road
accident of an ADRA truck. Another instance involved a different Czech truck
that was inadvertently caught in the midst of a conflict between Karadzic and
Plavsic supporters in September 1999; Czech peacekeepers helped resolve the
dangerous situation.

There were some communication problems between the Ministry of Defense and the Ministry of Interior, which was responsible for the official part
of Czech humanitarian aid. A Ministry of Interior employee responsible for
the organization of relief noted:

> The Ministry of Interior was working on its own thing, as was the Ministry
> of Defense. Communications was so bad that the Czech SFOR battalion
> was fixing houses with funds from the British government, not at all aware
> that the Czech Ministry of Interior was cooperating in the same region with
> the foundation People in Need. Direct communication with the battalion
> was good; the problems primarily involved communications between the
> Ministry of Defense and the Ministry of Interior.

Thankfully, insufficient coordination and gaps in communication between the
ministries that took part in the organization of humanitarian aid in Bosnia and
Herzegovina were overcome thanks to good interpersonal relations between
members of the Czech battalion and NGO workers, the accommodating attitudes of Czech peacekeepers, and their willingness to do more than what was
their duty.

4.2. THE LOCAL POPULATION'S PERCEPTION OF CZECH SOL-
DIERS

When discussing the perception of contingency forces from individual countries, it must be noted that the local population was very sensitive to relations
between armed forces and power politics. The attitudes of the local people
are a key aspect of the success or failure of every peacekeeping mission, a
fact shown in lessons learned by Czech soldiers during the IFOR/SFOR mission. IFOR/SFOR units deployed under NATO command with a mandate from
the UN had to communicate with the English-speaking command as well as
with the local population. In this regard, Czech peacekeepers were respected,
thanks to the similarity between the Czech, Serbian, and Croatian languages.
According to one humanitarian relief worker, many Serbian and Croatian soldiers expressed such sentiments about Czech peacekeepers as: "You are Slavs

and we understand and believe you. We have nothing to talk about with Blacks [i.e., Western countries' Black soldiers] who are armed to the teeth." [17]

National interests are a frequently discussed problem of peacekeeping missions. Among others, this problem has been pointed out by representatives of Czech NGOs, especially in relation to cooperation with British and French soldiers deployed in Bosnia and Herzegovina. Igor Blazevic, one of the founders of People in Need, has noted that "it seems as if every country were advancing its own petty politics in the war."

Impartiality was an important factor that helped build trust among the local population and significantly contributed to creation of considerate relations among all sides involved in the conflict region. The Czech contingent was perceived favorably by the local population, thanks to the fact that Czech forces were not seen as representing a superpower like their American, British, or French counterparts. Impartiality was an essential prerequisite in a situation where the Czech battalion was the only unit deployed on both sides of the multiethnic border. This emphasis on neutrality proved to be very important, especially with regard to the municipal elections held in Bosnia and Herzegovina in September 1997. In the Bosnian context, Czech soldiers faced problems related to the defense of "national interests" several times, especially with respect to the British command, a fact that, at the beginning of the mission, caused some tension that was deepened by Czech peacekeepers' insufficient English language skills. Another problem was the fact that the territory, for which the Czech battalion was responsible, had the greatest concentration of persons who were identified as war criminals by the Hague Tribunal.

When discussing the issue of impartiality, it must be mentioned that Czech peacekeepers were sometimes accused of favoring Serbs. There are several interpretations of this issue. First, Serbian soldiers acted in a more professional manner than Bosnian units that, especially in the beginning of the conflict, had behaved like paramilitary forces, a fact that complicated communications. Second, as was mentioned by Jan Urban, a well-known Czech journalist who was active in Bosnia,

> The Czechs did exhibit a certain pro-Serbian orientation; however, this was mostly due to the fact that they did not have enough information about the war. The ministry did not say very much to them and the Muslims were quite upset about the UNPROFOR mission. They thought that it was preventing them from regaining territory that they had lost at the beginning of the war.

---

[17] "In the Service of Peace," *Army of the Czech Republic* 1, 1994, p. 22.

On the other hand, it must be admitted that, particularly at the beginning of the conflict, Serbs harbored a certain aversion to Czech soldiers who were viewed as an obstacle to a "final solution" as regards the Muslim population in Bosnia and Herzegovina.

The Czech field surgery team that was stationed in the headquarters complex of the sector South in Knin, Croatia, played an important role as far as relations with the local population were concerned. Czech military doctors provided health care to the local population, despite that fact that their duty was to serve only the military forces and they did not have sufficient material to provide medical care to such an extent.

Furthermore, the local population appreciated the help provided by Czech demolitions and explosive ordnance disposal experts in the liquidation of mines. Especially important for the establishment of friendly relations with the local population was the consistent fulfillment of the peacekeeping mandate, assistance provided by IFOR units in securing supplies of humanitarian aid, and help in the renewal of local infrastructure. While these activities have proved beneficial to Czech peacekeeping units, they presented an increased demand on the nation's capacities, especially logistics.

The local population's positive perception of Czech peacekeepers was also helped by the fact that, especially in the first half of the 1990s, a large number of soldiers who served in Bosnia came from civilian life, where they had worked as carpenters, metalworkers, locksmiths, etc. These soldiers won the hearts of local people who appreciated that "one gives advice about how to shoe a horse, another helps with house repair, and yet another knows about keeping pigs." [18]

The experiences gained by Czech peacekeepers show that impartiality and maintaining friendly relations with the local population are vital to the success of a national contingency force. This requires an accommodating approach, familiarity with the culture and mentality of the local population, and the ability to communicate in the local language.

5. SUMMARY

Thus far, the participation of Czech soldiers in IFOR and SFOR has been the most important and most extensive example of specific cooperation with NATO member countries. It is generally acknowledged that the success of Czech forces in these missions was very important for the Czech Republic's admission to NATO in the first enlargement phase. Czech military participation in peacekeeping operations in the former Yugoslavia has had an incontestable effect on the transformation of the Czech army. In addition, it has

---

[18]   *Ibid*, p. 21.

brought about a slow but increasingly noticeable shift among the Czech public toward a more positive perception of the army and its members. Peacekeeping missions have provided soldiers with an opportunity to test their military and political skills, abilities, and knowledge. The professional, soldierly qualities that most Czech soldiers gained during the former totalitarian regime, have proven themselves to be apolitical and therefore transferable to the current social and political conditions. In the culturally and historically analogous environment of the former Yugoslavia, Czech soldiers have exhibited a sizable degree of adaptability. Nonetheless, the greatest benefit of Czech participation in the IFOR/SFOR missions is the increased self-confidence that peacekeepers gained while fulfilling combat duties and unusual humanitarian and policing tasks.

Czech soldiers have had to learn to communicate with civilian organizations involved in the conflict, as well as journalists, representatives of non-governmental humanitarian organizations, the local population, domestic political structures, and international organizations active in the former Yugoslavia. The necessity to work alongside contingency forces from other countries has shown Czech soldiers both the strong and weak aspects of their professional skills. These peacekeeping missions have prepared the Czech army for what will likely be a main duty of armed forces in the next millennium: coordinated international operations in regions affected by crises and conflicts.

Influenced by reports about the successful actions of Czech soldiers in Bosnia and Herzegovina, the Czech public has gradually realized the importance of foreign missions for the Czech Republic and its armed forces. There is no doubt that participation in the UNPROFOR, IFOR, and SFOR missions has substantially facilitated the Czech Republic's accession to NATO in the first enlargement phase. Duties arising from NATO membership have been and will be fulfilled through Czech participation in peacekeeping missions. Consequently, the Czech public now perceives itself to be an active player in and co-creator of the new international security environment.

11. BUILDING A NEW FACE: HUNGARY'S ROLE IN PEACE MISSIONS

Laszlo SZABO

Outline:

1. INTRODUCTION

The post-Cold War period has witnessed a substantial increase in both the number and range of peacekeeping activities under the auspices of the United Nations, the Organization for Security and Cooperation in Europe, and NATO. Those countries professing democratic values are making great efforts to support these activities and satisfy these needs and justifiably expect other countries sharing their values to also contribute to peace missions, each in proportion to their capabilities.

Active participation in peacekeeping is a multinational affair, undertaken in the interests of the international community. Since 1988, Hungary has played a very active role in peacekeeping, promoting the noble ideas enshrined in the UN Charter and contributing to peace and international stability all over the world. More and more Hungarian officers and NCOs have had the opportunity to be measured against the challenge of participating in multinational peace missions. Their experience constitutes a particularly important basis for the processes of defense reform and Hungary's integration into Euro-Atlantic structures.

Hungary has accepted the obligations stipulated in Articles 42 and 43 of the UN Charter, namely that, at the request of the UN Security Council, Hungary will supply armed forces for the maintenance of international peace and security. The Constitution of the Republic of Hungary, under section 7, paragraph (1), harmonizes the UN Charter requirements with domestic law in accordance with Hungarian Law No. I of 1956.

High-level legal documents require the Hungarian Defense Forces (HDF) to satisfy their military obligations as detailed in international treaties. These state that the Hungarian armed forces must have at their disposal units that are able to accomplish peacekeeping tasks. The relevant documents are the National Defense Law, the parliamentary resolution on the Basic Principles of the Republic of Hungary's Security Policy and on the Principles of National Defense, as well as the governmental program dealing with national defense matters.

The various political decisions and subsequent decision implementations and structural changes resulted in a situation where, by the autumn of 1994, Hungary had at its disposal a unit suitable for peacekeeping duties. It was deemed ready for deployment in the autumn of 1995; since then, this force has proven itself in Cyprus and the Sinai, as well as within the Implementation Force (IFOR) and the Stabilization Force (SFOR) in Bosnia-Herzegovina.

Although Hungary does not have a long history of peacekeeping deployments, the efforts of Hungarian observer forces have been honored by the UN on no less than three occasions, when Hungarian officers were asked to act as sector commanders. Additionally, on one occasion, a Hungarian officer was made deputy commander of a mission and later (as of this writing) commander of the mission. Almost 300 officers have now served as observers and have done so with distinction. No complaints have been made against Hungarian soldiers while they have been on UN duty. After a short period of service, the majority of those deployed were rapidly promoted to leading positions or staff postings. In the interests of modernizing the HDF and raising as well as harmonizing the domestic level of peacekeeping training, the task of the former Hungarian Peacekeeping Forces Training Center was taken over by another HDF body. This center was designed to facilitate the transfer of knowledge and experience we have gained on recent peacekeeping missions to representatives of other nations.

The European peace, which lasted for over 35 years, was finally broken by the inter-ethnic explosions in the Balkans. The UN Protection Force (UN-PROFOR) was dispatched to address this threat to European peace following the relevant UN decisions. Although Hungary, due to its geographical proximity, was also very interested in securing peace, the country did not participate in this armed peace mission out of concern for the welfare and interests of the large numbers of ethnic Hungarians living in the endangered areas. At the same time, however, there were opportunities for us to support the implementation of the mandate, for example by allowing AWACS monitoring aircraft to be directed from within Hungary. These planes were allowed to fly in Hungarian airspace; in addition, we allowed the option of withdrawing and securing the aircraft in Hungary in emergencies. We also had the opportunity to assist in the deployment and functioning of the mission sent to supervise the UN-mandated embargo. The Hungarian government and parliament subsequently decided to deploy a combat engineer contingent to aid in the successful implementation of the Dayton Accords via the NATO-led IFOR.

Three factors resulting from the experiences of IFOR represented such dramatically new requirements for the HDF that, in interests of satisfying these fully, it was necessary to specifically create an "Operations Group." Since the establishment of the Operations Group, we have acquired experiences with which, in the future, we will be able to create a permanent Peacekeeping, Humanitarian Aid, and Crisis Management Group.

2. HUNGARIAN PARTICIPATION IN PEACEKEEPING

Hungarian peacekeeping dates back to the early 1970s. Following the signing of the Paris Peace Treaty, which put an end to the Vietnam War, more than 100 officers and NCOs participated in the observation of the cease-fire. Although this mission was launched at the request of the signatory powers, its nature was very similar to that of UN peacekeeping missions. Détente in international relations allowed for an increase in the number of peacekeeping missions. In 1988, the UN invited the Republic of Hungary to participate in the observation of the cease-fire agreement concluded between Iraq and Iran. This was a breakthrough, after which more and more professional soldiers, mainly officers, became involved in the work of international peacekeeping missions, although not on a large scale. During the subsequent "study period," which lasted until 1995, approximately 200 officers gained expertise in activities within international missions. These people formed the core of later peacekeeping missions in Cyprus, the Sinai, and in IFOR/SFOR.

At first, in the early 1990s, Hungary faced a serious problem: only a few of those serving in the military had adequate proficiency in English to allow them to participate in such missions. Therefore, the first officers to participate in observation missions were those who were already experienced in working in the international field. Those responsible for training were continuously replaced; unfortunately, a permanent organization that could have carried out peacekeeper training in an organized form did not evolve. Nevertheless, the courses organized from time to time were of good quality, thanks to the participation of experts from the Ministry of Foreign Affairs, researchers specializing in this particular field, and experts representing the Ministry of Defense and the General Staff. These courses had to familiarize students with the professional, legal, and practical tasks of peacekeeping because Hungarian military education lacked an institutional framework to pass on such knowledge systematically at that time.

Although the professional permanent staff was reduced almost by half due to restructuring and staff reductions between 1990–1995, a stable core of 20–30 people was at the government's disposal. These people were almost universally envied, since UN wages were 4–8 times as high as Hungarian ones. [1]

The new experiences and knowledge gained on peacekeeping operations led to continuous change in the training syllabus; by the middle of the 1990s, a new syllabus was developed that formed the backbone of peace operations training. Only occasional special modifications were needed to update it from time to time. Usually, the equipment supplied by the military provided all the necessary means to implement the mission, but it often proved inflexible and did not allow complementary needs to be satisfied. Once they were sent on an observer mission, most Hungarian peacekeepers had only occasional contact with Hungarian military authorities and could not hope for any real help in case of problems. After returning to Hungary, the expertise thus gained during the mission was not put to good use in an organized form. For example, it was only after 1994 that health screening of soldiers returning from missions became a standard practice.

By 1995, a group of officers with considerable international experience had emerged who were capable of commanding a larger contingent as well. First, in partnership with Austria, a military contingent was dispatched to Cyprus. The Sinai mission followed, and finally IFOR began. This latter deployment, in particular, meant a real breakthrough in Hungarian peacekeeping since it was the first time that a considerable contingent had been dispatched. Moreover, in this mission, NATO procedures prevailed. This mission, to a great extent, provided Hungary with the necessary knowledge to participate effectively in NATO's military cooperation system as a member state.

I shall not analyze the whole spectrum of Hungarian participation in this chapter. Not only is it too early for such an undertaking, but such an analysis

---

[1] Later, this fact even prevented Hungarian soldiers from participating in UN missions, because decisive efforts were made at certain decision and planning levels to turn down UN invitations.

also exceeds the scope of this study. Therefore, I will concentrate primarily on the salient political and professional positions that emerged during preparation for deployment, since this was the very first peacekeeping mission in which Hungarian soldiers had participated in large numbers and in cooperation with NATO forces.

3. PARTICIPATION IN IFOR: A POLITICAL DECISION

Hungary's geographic position made it impossible for the country to become involved in the settlement of the conflict on the territory of the former Yugoslavia. In spite of this, we directly took part in the activities of UNPRO-FOR. Since the conflict took place in two neighboring countries, where historic grievances were still alive, our political leaders believed that Hungary should keep as much distance from the conflict as possible. The sensitivity of our situation became even more evident in 1992, when it was revealed that, prior to the introduction of the arms embargo, Hungarian firms had supplied weapons to the Croatian police forces. The Serbs protested, so Hungarian policymakers decided to adopt a neutral attitude towards the countries involved in the conflict. Another factor contributing to this approach was the fact that ethnic Hungarians live in all the Yugoslav successor states. This became a very sensitive issue, especially in Serbia, where approximately 400,000 ethnic Hungarians live. [2]

Of course, the war affected economic, political, and military relations between Hungary and her southern neighbors. In a few cases, ground troops made attempts to use Hungarian territory to launch attacks against opponents. Especially in the early phase of the war, aircraft from the Serbian Air Force violated Hungarian airspace on a number of occasions. As a result of the war, approximately 50,000 displaced persons requested refugee status; tens of thousands left the region through Hungary. At the same time, Hungary served as an economic "background area," because people living near the border came to Hungary to purchase goods that were in short supply at home due to the economic embargo.

There were two fields in which Hungary provided a staging ground for the implementation of UN resolutions. First, Hungarian cooperation made it possible for the EU/WEU mission monitoring the arms embargo to carry out operations on the Danube. Second, NATO's AWACS aircraft were allowed to use Hungarian airspace to control the air traffic inside the peacekeeping mission's area of responsibility (AOR).

When the outlines of the peace agreement ending the war began to take shape and the corresponding NATO authorities made preliminary proposals to

---

[2]   The region lost its autonomy within the Republic of Serbia in 1989.

the Hungarian government on possible Hungarian participation in peacekeeping activities, the Hungarian political leadership faced a difficult decision. The
Hungarian parliament took decisions on two occasions concerning IFOR activities. These decisions permitted the transit of IFOR forces through and their
provisional stationing in Hungary, and also allowed the direct participation of
a Hungarian contingent of limited strength. Afterwards, Hungary became involved in the activities of IFOR/SFOR in three fields:

- Hungary permitted the passage of forces through the country's territory and
  the use of its airspace;
- Hungary took part in activities in a direct form by sending an engineer bat-
  talion;
- Finally, Hungary provided a support base for U.S. forces and the Nordic
  Brigade.

Both resolutions were made after heated internal policy debates. The main
reason for this dispute was that, after the first democratic elections in Hungary, strict regulations were adopted regarding the movement and stationing of
foreign military forces in the country. The regulations were some of the most
stringent in Europe and were formulated with the agreement of the political
opposition. This was required at that time because of the presence of Soviet
troops. In 1995, the parliament faced a situation in which it became necessary
to change this practice.

In the course of the debate in parliament, political, economic, military, and
ethnic questions were discussed. Almost all political parties agreed that Hungary should support any measure suitable for contributing to the achievement
of peace in the region. The arguments put forward in the political debate can
be divided into four groups. First, one set of arguments pointed out that Hungary would greatly benefit from an end to the war in the Balkans and from
the elimination of a serious security threat in the region. Though not perfect,
the Dayton Agreement was certainly better than war, and it would be beneficial for Hungary to become an active participant in this process. Second, it
was recognized that Hungary should support the endeavors of NATO, as this
support would bring about a closer relationship with the alliance.

In addition to a "quasi" security guarantee, policymakers believed that
supporting NATO would increase Hungary's chances of membership in the
alliance. Allowing the stationing of NATO troops in the country would contribute to enhanced interoperability, one of the prerequisites for membership. It
offered the possibility for Hungarian troops to cooperate with NATO forces not
only in exercises but also under real conditions, over a relatively long period
of time, and to adapt our command model to NATO norms. Third, the presence of foreign military forces would also offer economic advantages, as they

would rent installations and purchase goods and services; even more important, their presence would enhance the flow of foreign capital into the country. The fourth set of arguments claimed that, as part of the peace agreement, the status of refugees and ethnic minorities would be settled, a system of democratic institutions could be developed, and human rights and the rights of ethnic groups would be guaranteed. When the war ended, economic reconstruction could start, bringing significant reductions in armed forces personnel in the region. Hungary had a vital interest in all of these developments; it was stressed that Hungarians should not wait passively for all this to happen but should instead take an active role.

Needless to say, the risks involved in Hungary's direct participation were also emphasized. At the time, the majority of members of parliament agreed that the presence of NATO forces would ensure democratic development in the region. Unfortunately, as it turned out later, this expectation was not fulfilled. The question of more direct participation in the IFOR mission was also raised at that point. Though a request in this regard was made informally, parliament did not deal with this question in the absence of a formal invitation.

4. POLITICAL DEBATE

There was a lively political debate in parliament when the government presented its proposal to send a Hungarian contingent to participate in the IFOR mission.[3] The debate was not about substance; rather, it was based upon a difference of opinions about the political environment and anticipated consequences of participation. A week earlier, on 28 October 1995, the question of Hungarian participation had come up when parliament discussed the issue of logistical support for IFOR forces, but at that time the government had received only a verbal request from NATO.

A few days later, an official letter was received by the Hungarian government from General George Joulwan, NATO's Supreme Allied Commander in Europe. In addition to "the use of the territory of the Hungarian Republic and of facilities necessary for the logistic support of peacekeeping forces," General Joulwan invited Hungary to take part in the mission directly by sending a military contingent (engineering and medical troops). On receipt of the letter, direct talks began, during which the form of participation was somewhat modified. The idea of a medical unit was dropped; instead, NATO requested that we send an engineer contingent.

---

[3] Hungarian Parliament, "Draft Resolution on the Participation of a Hungarian Technical Contingent Consisting of a Limited Number of Persons in the IFOR Mission Tasked with Ensuring the Implementation of the Peaceful Settlement of the Southern Slav Conflict," No. H/1775, 5 December 1995.

After having clarified the alliance's needs, we began the political and military preparations necessary for sending the contingent. As a result of a political agreement reached after the first democratic elections in Hungary, much stricter conditions were laid down for the deployment of troops abroad; each proposed deployment now required parliamentary approval. Consequently, participation in IFOR also had to be approved by parliament. The proposal presented to parliament included the following main elements:

- Parliament should limit the strength of the independent Hungarian engineer subunit to a maximum of 500 persons.
- Authorization for the participation of the Hungarian contingent in the IFOR mission should be given by parliament for a limited duration, lasting until 31 December 1996.
- A possible extension of the duration of their participation would require a further resolution by parliament.
- In addition to the necessary technical instruments and equipment, Hungarian soldiers were to be allowed to take only personal weapons. Thus, in the course the Hungarian contingent's discharge of its duties, ground and air protection would be secured by the IFOR contingent of the nationality responsible for the area in which the Hungarian soldiers were to operate. During the talks, Hungary obtained the necessary guarantees in this regard.
- In accordance with the law on national defense, the Hungarian contingent must consist exclusively of volunteers (professional and contract soldiers).
- In view of the fact that at least 35 – 40 days (estimated from the date of the respective decision by parliament) would be required to organize the independent battalion, to prepare its members, to provide the necessary equipment, and to set up accommodation in Croatia, the earliest date when the contingent could start working would be the middle of January.

Parliamentary approval depended chiefly on discussion of the above conditions. The Minister of Defense responsible for the motion stated that:

> In my view, the decision also requires every MP to take a sort of political stand. All parliamentary parties agree with our country's commitments under the United Nations Charter; they support our endeavors toward integration in Western European institutions; they agree with the respective intentions of the government including, among others, the aspiration of Hungary to become a member of NATO and, as pointed out repeatedly, consider it a vital interest for Hungary that peace be secured in the southern Slav region. [4]

It remained to be decided how – through what deeds and sacrifices– the country should support these often-stated interests regarding the conflict in Bosnia

---

[4]   Official Minutes of Parliament, No. 135, p. 15240.

and the establishment of closer relations with NATO. It was the first time after the change in the political and economic system that the Hungarian parliament had the chance to make a sovereign decision, free of any external influence, on an issue that significantly affected our relations with our neighbors and with minorities, since our accession to NATO also meant that we would be taking on a military obligation. It was also important to bear in mind that this decision would substantially affect the modernization of Hungarian armed forces, greatly influence the country's political image, and represent an important step toward preparing for NATO membership. On the other hand, a refusal could delay Hungary's integration within Western European institutions for several years, even though parliament fully supported efforts to achieve this integration.

The protection of the engineer subunit to be deployed (and its weaponry) was also a subject of debate. Although legislators did not deny the advantages of direct Hungarian protection, they concluded that it was acceptable to rely on the protection of IFOR forces after appropriate coordination in close cooperation with the multinational forces. The grave responsibility of the Hungarian military leadership in this respect was also recognized.

Due to the mixed composition of the Hungarian defense forces (HDF), personnel selection for the engineer contingent was also discussed by members of parliament. In addition to the principle of voluntary participation, the basic requirements for selecting participants included experience, professional and practical skills, and the ability to reliably operate the necessary equipment. It was difficult to meet all these requirements, because the number of personnel in the armed forces, including engineer units, was gradually reduced during the period prior to the IFOR operation. Over the course of military restructuring, a number of engineer units were disbanded, while others were merged and redeployed. Because of this process, many officers and NCOs in the engineer units retired. Although the commanders well knew that they could not keep soldiers from volunteering for the task, they were nevertheless none too keen on losing newly appointed career soldiers.

A sufficient quantity of engineering equipment was available, because the equipment of formerly abolished engineer units was no longer needed by those units. In the opinion of NATO experts, who had made a prior survey of the technical assets of the Hungarian engineer battalion to be deployed, the quality of this equipment met and in some cases even exceeded Western European standards.

MPs from the opposition also accepted the fact that it was in Hungary's fundamental interest as well as an obligation for Hungary to become involved in the peaceful resolution of the crisis in the former Yugoslavia, including active participation in the peacekeeping process. However, there was a lively debate on the form of participation. Due to historical factors and the fact that Hungarian minorities live in various parts of the Carpathian basin, the opposition did not consider it desirable to send Hungarian soldiers to the territory of neighboring countries.

The opposition accused the Socialist-Liberal government of promoting an irresponsible policy and pushing for overly hasty action because the Horn government chose not to involve parliamentary parties in the preparation of the resolution. Objections were voiced that the lack of coordination among the six parties involved in the decision-making process could have a fundamental impact on the security and future of the country. Some members of the government, namely the Ministers of Foreign Affairs and Defense, were suspected of having made some "clandestine offers." This accusation was based on the fact that, while at NATO headquarters in Brussels on 21 November, Foreign Minister László Kovács was given a concrete offer. On that same day, and without consulting the opposition, the government made a decision about the participation of Hungarian troops "with exemplary speed and, I believe, with unprecedented irresponsibility." [5] When the question of logistical support for NATO forces was presented before the parliament, the government withdrew its earlier decision and listened to the opinion of the opposition.

Another question debated in parliament was Hungary's failure to assert the position that, as a neighboring country, its contribution should take the form of sending only medical troops. Concerns were expressed about accepting the proposal that Hungarian troops should be equipped with weapons, even though they would be weapons for self-defense only. The controversy divided the government coalition, too, as some of the Social Democrats also opposed the participation of armed Hungarian troops in the IFOR mission.

The argument put forward by the government was that the National Assembly had to make up its mind whether it wished to meet the country's international obligation arising from its acceptance of the UN Charter, as laid down in the Hungarian constitution and in the Basic Principles of National Defense. Article 17 of this document, adopted almost unanimously by the National Assembly in 1993, provides that "the Hungarian national defense should have the necessary forces enabling it to take part in the peacekeeping and peacemaking activities of the United Nations and other international organizations concerned with crisis management."

It was pointed out that if responsible political forces in Hungary really wished to contribute to ending the senseless and brutal massacre in the "neighborhood" and make it possible for refugees to return to their homes, it was

---

[5]   *Ibid*, p. 15245.

their duty to back their intentions with the necessary decisions and actions. The issue of Hungary's political orientation was also discussed with regard to these questions. According to Article 16 of the Basic Principles of National Defense, "it is the aim of the Hungarian Republic to accede as full member to the existing international security organizations such as NATO, and to the European Union." It was clear that the above endeavor, incorporated in a legal regulation, should be supported with actions.

This also raised the necessity of modifying certain legal regulations. As a full member of NATO, Hungary will offer one or two units to participate in the NATO forces. As of this writing, as the law now stands, it will be necessary to ask soldiers whether they wish to serve abroad or not; Hungary's National Defense Act provides that only volunteers can leave Hungarian territory.

The position of the smaller party in the government coalition was put forward by Iván Pető, who supported the idea of Hungarian participation. He pointed out that, as the goal of Euro-Atlantic integration was stated in the program of every political party represented in parliament and also in the program of the Hungarian government, it constituted one of the most important basic principles of Hungarian foreign policy. It was therefore no surprise, based upon previously stated Hungarian intentions, that

> Hungary should take part in the diverse tasks and obligations arising from Euro-Atlantic integration. For security policy reasons, too, Hungary aspires to become a member of NATO, and this aspiration is an integral part of Euro-Atlantic integration. If we expect NATO and the Western European countries to guarantee Hungary's security, we cannot refuse to participate in such an action, and I am speaking on behalf of the majority of the faction of the Alliance of Free Democrats. [6]

In the view of the Alliance of Free Democrats, Hungary's participation was also desirable because this would enable Hungarian foreign policy experts and policymakers to take a more effective stand in support of the ethnic Hungarian minority living on the territory of the former Yugoslavia.

In addition, a relatively large number of refugees fled to Hungary from territories where Hungarians would be required to take part in peacemaking efforts. Hungary had asked for and obtained the support of international organizations to ensure the conditions necessary for refugees to seek and receive shelter in our country. According to Pető, "It would be improper for Hungary to expect such support and yet refuse to take part in the proposed mission due to motives of self-interest." [7]

---

[6] *Ibid*, p. 15262.
[7] *Ibid,* p. 15262.

The proposal tabled by FIDESZ (Alliance of Young Democrats – Hungarian Civic Party)[8] generated a heated debate. It was proposed that the Hungarian engineer subunit should be accompanied by armed troops for protection. To support the motion, six elements were mentioned. First, Hungary had a direct interest in creating and consolidating peace in Bosnia, as it had a national interest in achieving stability in the region. One of the main reasons why exports declined in 1993 was that Hungarian foreign trade with the successor states to the former Yugoslavia came to a halt, resulting in a deficit of approximately two billion dollars. This caused Hungary's balance of payments and foreign trade to deteriorate during the war. During the debate it was pointed out that, once the conflict came to an end, economic and trade relations would be normalized, the security of the Hungarian Republic would improve, and one of the major sources of external threat would diminish and, we hoped, be eliminated. It followed from this that Hungary had direct economic interests in the Balkans.

The second reason mentioned was of a historical character. The region's peoples and nations had been interdependent upon each other for many centuries. Living side by side often meant having a common ruler, but just as often it also meant antagonism and even hostility. During World War II, the Serb and Hungarian people fought on different sides, and both committed serious atrocities against each other. This grievance is deep-seated in the memories of both nations and requires caution in attitudes towards the other side.

Caution was especially justified in the case of Serbia, which at this time seemed to be in an initial phase of its development as a nation state. Its fundamental endeavor was to establish its own identity and to distinguish itself from other peoples with whom it co-existed, either within its territory or in the region. Due to increasing nationalism and disintegration in the early 1990s, it was state policy for Serb leaders to profess the goal of extending state borders to ethnicfrontiers. This centrist, Greater Serb endeavor, which has manifested itself cyclically throughout Yugoslav history, convinced non-Serb nationalities that they should seek separation, because it was impossible to find a mutually advantageous form of common statehood with the Serbs.

The end of the Cold War also meant that the geopolitical significance of Yugoslavia diminished. This in itself had a disintegrating effect. Moreover, there was no longer a great power that had an interest in keeping Yugoslavia a united federation.[9] Slobodan Milosevic, a nationalist himself, deliberately

---

[8]   Before the 1998 election, FIDESZ adopted a new name (Hungarian Civic Party), showing that the interests of the party were those of the new middle class, and in common with civil society.

[9]   For more details, see József Juhász, *A Short History of the Southern Slav Wars: 1991 – 1995* (Budapest: SVKI, 1996).

opposed any compromise. Citing the need for state unity of the Serb nation, he insisted first on the recentralization of Yugoslavia and then, in the period of disintegration, on the revision of the borders of the republic. This inevitably led to the outbreak of war.

Great power interests also played a part in the civil wars on the territories of the former Yugoslavia, but militancy also contributed to the ultimate outbreak of war. The role of the Yugoslav army, in particular, should be mentioned; its political indoctrination, its survival reflexes arising from its unduly large size, and the predominance of Serbs in its officer corps explain why the military was especially receptive to ideas of a Greater Serbia. Nobody denies the Serb people the right to self-determination, but it was unacceptable that the Serbs used a double standard with regard to the rights of ethnic minorities: while defending the rights of Serb minorities, they effectively refused to respect other nationalities' right to self-determination.

FIDESZ put forward several arguments with regard to the issue of historical sensitivities. First, they stated that it is neither possible nor practical to refuse to take part in peacekeeping activities after the end of a conflict. One should recall that Hungary, having permitted AWACS aircraft to use its airspace, was already affected by the conflict. Critics in the former Yugoslavia protested when AWACS aircraft began operations in Hungary. Nevertheless, the warring parties had signed a peace accord and were interested in adhering to it. Consequently, Hungary's intended participation in peacekeeping activities could not be considered as an act against their will but rather as an act in accordance with it. Second, those who put forward historical arguments, whether intentionally or unintentionally, nurture historical prejudices about a guilty nation and the "last satellite state." One FIDESZ representative stressed that it was time that we shed our own stubborn historical preconceptions. One cannot ignore or deny the past, but it is possible to eliminate bad historical reflexes. The representative asked how, if we were not prepared to do this, we could expect our neighbors, with whom we have had conflicts in earlier times, to get over their own historical reflexes against us? In his opinion, the third argument in favor of our participation was that all other countries that also aspired to NATO membership and that intended to take part in the IFOR mission had larger forces than Hungary. This fact should induce us to reconsider our position.

The lessons of the Gulf War were mentioned as the fourth argument. When Hungary sent a medical group to the Gulf, it undertook internal political risks, the risk of terrorist actions, and the risk that there could be Hungarian casualties as a result of the action. Nevertheless, participating in the Gulf War brought only marginal direct political gains for our country. For example, after the war,

Kuwait published words of gratitude in all the major daily newspapers of the world, enumerating the countries to which it owed thanks because of their assistance in overcoming the difficulties that Kuwait had faced. They forgot to mention Hungary. No harm was meant; it was an omission by mistake, since Hungary's participation did not attract great attention. When we consider taking a risk, however, it is worth taking into consideration whether our actions could bring about political gains for the country. It was assumed that this could be achieved if we sent troops who could guarantee the safety of the Hungarian engineer subunit.

Fifth, it was pointed out that our participation could offer great opportunities for cooperation with NATO forces. If Hungary chose to engage in peacekeeping activities more extensive than the one discussed by parliament, Hungarian troops might have to be armed with NATO weapons, since (according to information we had received) Polish forces were supposed to use NATO weapons in this mission. This could be a significant chance for us, the FIDESZ representative pointed out – one that should not be missed. A vote for participation could make it possible for the Hungarian unit to participate with NATO weapons, under a NATO contingent, in more or less peaceful circumstances, but still in a combat situation.

Finally, the sixth argument mentioned by FIDESZ contained a psychological element: the protection of the engineer unit by Hungarian soldiers would give a greater sense of security to the public at home as well as to the members of the Hungarian engineer subunit. There was no guarantee that the engineer unit would be defended by U.S. soldiers armed to the teeth, as portrayed in Hungarian cartoons. Viktor Orbán, presenting his party's position, stated, "Maybe the Hungarian engineer unit will be defended by, say, Pakistani or Egyptian troops. Of course, I do not mean to offend either people." He said that the Independent Smallholders Party was wrong when it stated that Hungary should not risk sending its soldiers to participate in SFOR under conditions where they would be subject to uncertainties and that consequently Hungary should not participate in the mission at all. In the opinion of FIDESZ, if we decided to deploy troops and to contribute an engineer subunit, the responsible thing was for Hungary to do its best to ensure their protection as much as possible.

Over the course of the debate, some of the opposition parties were against any kind of participation. On the one hand, they were opposed to participation itself; on the other hand, they raised the question of compensation. Some representatives of the Hungarian Democratic Forum, the party that had led the previous government, stated that "the participation of the engineer unit is so insignificant that the risk involved in its deployment is far greater than what

Hungary can gain by participating in the mission."[10] In their view, the military risk was too great, partly because they believed that armed clashes could continue, and partly because, according to newspaper reports, there were huge quantities of mines in the region; therefore, the lives of the soldiers could be in danger. They pointed out that Hungarian troops were not fit to participate, as they did not have the skills required for the mission. They also considered the costs of participation to be too high. Their most important argument was that "if Hungarian soldiers cross the country's borders in whatever direction, they will always find themselves in territories where they face not only military and security risks but also the historical prejudices of neighboring peoples against us."[11]

It was evidence of the division within the party that other MPs saw participation as a means of shaking off historical preconceptions. "It is in our interest for psychological, political, and national reasons to take part in a successful mission and to be rid of political biases and resentments shared by us and held towards us by many of our neighbors."[12]

When presenting the position of his party, the president of the Independent Smallholders Party focused on the question of compensation. He pointed out that, in his party's view, Hungary would obtain nothing in return for taking the risks inherent in participation in the mission. He claimed that, while preparing to allow Hungarian participation in IFOR, the government had not put forward any claims that would improve the future situation of ethnic Hungarians living in the region. Hungary would take a risk by participating in the mission because its military capabilities were so lacking that "in its present condition, I doubt that our army could hold a military parade."[13]

Nevertheless, the negative views related above did not jeopardize the proposed participation in IFOR, as the government parties had a significant majority in the National Assembly. Part of the opposition also supported the participation of Hungarian troops in the IFOR mission. This was reflected in the final vote: the draft resolution was adopted by parliament with 281 votes for, 44 votes against, and 10 abstentions.

---

[10] Official Minutes of Parliament, No. 135, p. 15266.
[11] *Ibid.* Hungary is the only country in the region that is surrounded by Hungarian minorities living inside neighboring territory; neighboring governments are very sensitive about Hungary's historical military involvement in the region.
[12] *Ibid*, p. 15274.
[13] *Ibid*, p. 15270.

5. Military Preparation: The First Concepts

On 23 November 1995, the HDF learned that NATO would welcome the participation of a Hungarian subunit in a peacekeeping operation in Bosnia-Herzegovina. Through our liaison officer in Mons, Belgium, NATO also informed us that what the alliance had in mind was primarily an engineer subunit with a structure and potential similar to that of the Slovakian engineer battalion, which was already stationed in the region as a UN peacekeeping force. The battalion NATO requested should be capable of building and restoring both fixed and floating bridges, restoring destroyed roads, and maintaining roads that were hardly passable under winter conditions. Besides this, NATO requested that the unit also be capable of carrying out bomb demolitions and the removal of land mines. Secondly, NATO said medical subunits would also be considered.

As NATO continued its planning, Hungary also started preparing for its participation in the IFOR mission, and various options began to be elaborated. With the country's NATO membership in mind, representatives of the Ministry of Foreign Affairs did not exclude the possibility that Hungary might participate with combat units. In contrast, the military leadership was firmly opposed to this proposal and tried to limit military involvement to the lowest possible level. While planning the details of Hungary's participation, the country's political leaders were guided by two objectives: to spend as little as possible and to send a unit that would signal Hungary's intention to contribute yet would not strain bilateral relations with Serbia. Thus, especially in the early phases of planning, Hungary came up with the proposal that, in addition to the two logistical bases already established in the south of the country, only a medical team should represent Hungary in the mission.

The Hungarian leadership did not firmly believe in a quick conclusion to the war and feared that the forces stationed in Bosnia could be attacked despite the fact that NATO led the mission. Therefore, they also wanted to prevent Hungarian troops from being deployed in the mountains of Bosnia, where they would have been much more defenseless in the face of a possible attack. As had been expressed during the parliamentary debates, this anxiety was reinforced by the fear that the sort of atrocities people from both sides had committed against one another during the world wars could reoccur.

Thereafter, direct preparation started in Hungary. In the middle of December, a 24-hour operation center was established within the General Staff to coordinate these preparations. A few weeks earlier, at the beginning of December, work on the organizational structure of the engineer battalion had begun. Originally, two versions were prepared, one for a floating bridge battalion and the other for a road and bridge building battalion. At the same time, planners considered adopting the structure of a Slovakian battalion working within the framework of UNPROFOR, although such a structure was much larger than the Hungarian force according to preliminary plans. The costs of deploying a battalion of 800 soldiers were estimated at 5 billion forints, which equaled more than 5% of military expenditures at the time. Thus, cost effectiveness was the main factor in the compromise that was finally reached: a contingent of 400–500 people was to be gathered, in which the majority of the staff had to have more than one profession. In order to satisfy NATO requirements as well, its structure had to be designed in such a way that the battalion would be able to carry out a wide range of engineering tasks. Thanks to a good relationship with the Slovakian military leadership, there was considerable information at our disposal about the Slovakian engineer battalion, which consisted of about 400–700 people and had already been working on the scene for a longer time. Later, we began to carry out detailed consultations with the Slovaks. The information received during consultations with the Germans about the expertise of their engineer subunits in Somalia also turned out to be very useful. During these consultations, our German colleagues emphasized the importance of efficient recruitment, which was an influential factor in the success of such a task.

5.1. TECHNICAL CONSIDERATIONS

After the circumstances were studied, it became obvious that the main task of the battalion would be to secure free movement in the region, because more than 300 significant bridges in the region had been destroyed during the war. Many roads and railways were blocked, and the geographical conditions – mountains and forests – made free movement even more difficult. It was also well known that the opposing forces had hidden a lot of land mines. It was obvious that the transportation of technical equipment would be very complicated under winter conditions where the unit could encounter blizzards and slippery slopes. When considering the range of possible tasks to perform, the preparatory team came to the conclusion that the majority of the rivers had very unstable water levels; therefore, it was impossible to build bridges across them on low and fixed pedestals. The units were to be tasked primarily with the installation of floating bridges, along with the repair of ferry crossings and the restoration of fixed bridges. It was important to make clear what kind of technical equipment and machines were needed to accomplish such tasks and what requirements must be satisfied. Following the negotiations, specific subunits of the battalion were outlined. An engineer battalion was formed which:

1. Could technically scout out and secure all those areas, march lines, and riverbanks suitable for crossing where the Hungarian and other cooperating international subunits were moving about and carrying out their duties;

2. Could install and permanently maintain three ferry crossings (with two ferries in service at each) or a 220 linear meter floating bridge with a 60-ton weight-carrying capacity;

3. Could build bridges on different foundations and of various weight-bearing capacities on low pedestals up to five meters in water depth;

4. Could strengthen bridges or restore those that had been partially destroyed;

5. Should be supplied with all the technical equipment to support the building of a bridge (with a length of 40 linear meters, a weight-bearing capacity of 50 tons, and a water depth of 3.5 meters on fixed pedestals) at short notice;

6. Could install and maintain roads for military movement (40 – 45 kilometers) and ramps connected to ferry crossings even under snowy and icy conditions;

7. Could clean roads of snow and remove obstacles and wreckage using different explosive methods; and

8. Could perform the primary processing of timber (capacity: 20m^3/day) that would be used for accomplishing different tasks and preparing construction areas.

Thanks to such thorough analysis, the Hungarian engineer battalion stationed in Okucani was able to carry out all the aforementioned tasks from the very beginning of its deployment.

5.2. Elaboration of Logistical Support

A separate preparatory unit drew up a list of resources, equipment, and technical tools. The main objective was to select technical tools from the actual stock of the HDF and resort to purchase only under extraordinary circumstances (for instance, communication and computer devices and ambulances).

It was also important to planners that equipment come primarily from regular supplies on hand. It was a basic requirement to furnish soldiers with proper winter and waterproof clothes; bulletproof vests were, however, a new requirement. When elaborating the basis of the food supply, the main requirements were to meet international standards and to cater to Hungarian tastes.

On the basis of these calculations, the organizational structure of the logistics squadron within the contingent was elaborated; repair, supply, and camp-operations platoons were included. The ambulance station was staffed with extraordinary care so that the medical staff could attend to various fields of work at the same time and could also look after a multifunctional, permanent medical station of huge capacity.

There were more options to examine when planning the stationing of the soldiers. The experts considered four basic options. According to the first option, the whole contingent would have been lodged in a tent camp. Although this solution appeared to be inexpensive, heating costs were expected to be high; tents would be less comfortable, and the tent material could deteriorate quite quickly. The second option was to find accommodation in permanent buildings. This solution can be used in a war-stricken area only after significant restoration work has been done. Besides that, rental costs would have been considerable. Lodging in railway carriages seemed to be the least expensive solution. In this case, the drawback was that a huge track network would then be needed in the area. Local inspections proved that this requirement could not be satisfied. The fourth possibility was to follow the practice used by the UN troops and accommodate soldiers in containers. This unambiguously proved to be a cheap and civilized way to solve the problem. One of its main advantages was that the various pieces of container could remain in military stock for a long time.

Along with security considerations, a thorough economic examination preceded the selection of possible means for relocation. There were several possibilities to consider here as well. Relocation by road was the basic version. Mixed march was the second, and finally came the most expensive yet safest solution: relocation by train.

The preparatory work done by financial experts was also very comprehensive. Besides the terms of payment, a solution had to be found to such problems as customs clearance, life and accident insurance for the staff, indemnification, and, last but not least, taxation.

There were, however, some new and interesting questions that also emerged, such as how to run the canteen without violating duty regulations and which currency should be used – U.S. dollars, Croatian kuna, or Hungarian forints (a decision was ultimately made in favor of the use of cards). Only after consideration of all this information was it possible to work out a comprehensive system of logistical support and the final structure of the subunit. A Hungarian unit for logistics and supply was established to solve the aforementioned problems and to provide the Hungarian contingent with permanent supplies. This arrangement made it possible to estimate the approximate costs.

5.3. HUMAN RESOURCES AND LEGAL QUESTIONS

During the preparatory phase, it became obvious that successful participation would largely depend on the staff composition of the first contingent. It was also important to establish clear legal conditions by the departure deadline. One of the most important tasks of the military–legal experts and the specialists at the personnel department and recruiting centers was to thoroughly study the Hungarian constitution and the Law on National Defense. Finally, these experts came to the conclusion that already existing subunits could not be dispatched on a mission outside national borders, mainly because of the huge number of conscripts. After further study of the relevant legal regulations, it became clear that Hungarian soldiers could pursue military service abroad only on a voluntary basis and with the consent of parliament.

The recruitment policy and the rotation of the staff were worked out in accordance with the aforementioned requirements. Every Hungarian citizen (both men and women) could volunteer for the contingent, but every six months the entire staff had to be rotated back to Hungary (in two to three groups and within a month). This was the practice adopted within NATO forces. Basically, the soldiers who were the first to participate – all on a voluntary basis – were those who were performing their military service at that time; the staff of the contingent could have been composed entirely of either professionals or contract soldiers. The subunit commanders and field officers had to be recruited from the reservists sent to the professional and engineer troops. Soldiers who had re-enlisted, or those under contract, were recruited from the group of soldiers who were performing their military service at the time but had already completed basic training, or who were reservists under 35.

An important aspect of the recruitment policy was to select soldiers who were both physically and mentally healthy and who could endure physical challenges of long duration or unexpected stress situations. Obviously, basic requirements that applied mainly to officers included adequate military and professional knowledge, good commanding skills, and the knowledge of a foreign language. Experience in NATO-compatible operations and computer literacy were required of field officers, while subordinate soldiers had to have proper military experience and possibly more than one civilian profession.

5.4. SETTING UP THE TRAINING SYSTEM

Considering the facilities and the short time available to the defense forces, individual training and preparation had to be accomplished in two phases. In the first phase, the professional training of the subunits was carried out according a plan that included general knowledge of regular technical instruments; individual training of vehicle drivers and machine operators; driving lessons; complex practice of specific engineering tasks; and operation of technical machines in theory and practice.

In the second phase, personnel received general and specific training in combat and the use of weapons; target practice; first aid; recognition of the vehicles, military instruments, and helicopters of the countries involved; and the historical background of the Balkan conflict, including a short history of Croatia, Bosnia-Herzegovina, etc. Due to quick military planning, a detailed plan had been completed by 26 November, thus enabling the initiation of the actual military and political preparation.

5.5. CONSULTATION WITH NATO MILITARY LEADERS

On 29 November 1995, the military leadership consented to a skeleton plan for the participation of the Hungarian contingent. With a view to further coordination, a delegation traveled to the General Headquarters of the European Allied Forces of NATO, where they met Lieutenant-General Sir Jeremy MacKenzie, the Deputy Supreme Allied Commander, Europe, and those in charge of the planning division of the peacekeeping operation. The same evening, a meeting was held at the Ministry of Defense to coordinate the negotiation strategy. The Hungarian leadership agreed to offer first and foremost a medical unit. Second, they agreed on cooperation within the country. They also agreed upon the most important issues to be clarified.

The first meeting on the agenda was lunch at headquarters, where substantial work began. General MacKenzie stated that he found it significant that the Hungarian government was handling the issue so seriously. He went on to give a briefing on the actual situation and the basic considerations concerning future operations. He briefly outlined which countries had joined the operations so far and with what troops, and then discussed the possible ways for Hungary to participate, focusing on those tasks that would be the least dangerous and the most useful in the course of joint operations. He stressed that NATO primarily had engineer subunits in mind. The leader of the Hungarian delegation emphasized the Hungarian parliament's role in decision-making; he then expressed Hungary's firm intention to cooperate, yet asked NATO to take into consideration the country's geostrategic and economic situation as well as the common past that Hungary shared with states and peoples in the region. He reminded the Deputy SACEUR of the fact that there were large Hungarian minorities in neighboring countries to the south and stated that their interests must be considered when decisions were made.

Following the briefing, the Hungarian delegation explained how they thought cooperation was possible beyond the use of the military bases in Kaposvár and Taszár. They focused primarily on Hungarian medical facilities, although it soon became apparent that those countries contributing the main forces were already able to provide the necessary services through their hospitals established in the region. Therefore, the Hungarian medical team would work only as part of an international hospital. The Hungarian delegation then outlined their plan for providing engineer assistance (Version "B") but then concluded that U.S. troops already had the necessary means for a quick deployment.

The Hungarian delegation went on to explain what kind of engineer battalion (consisting of 500–600 people) they had in mind. They described in detail the structure, equipment, and potential of the Slovakian engineer battalion that was subordinate to UN peacekeepers (at that time, the Hungarian leadership did not yet know that Slovakia would not participate in IFOR). At this point, the leader of the Hungarian delegation asked for a break to carry out some consultations. The first thing to clarify was whether Version "A" (the original plan) in its present form could meet the requirements that had just been described. He acknowledged the report and attempted to call the Prime Minister and the Minister of Foreign Affairs, who were not available. He therefore consulted the Minister of Defense. The Minister asked what the opinions of the experts and officers were, and whether they could meet the requirements. When they reported that the HDF were capable of satisfying the aforementioned requirements, the negotiations began again. The leader of the delegation stressed that the Hungarian government intended to participate, but it was up to the parliament to make the final decision. Then he listed some requests the Hungarians wanted considered in the future, including the territory of deployment: we wanted our personnel to be as close as possible to the Hungarian border and asked for the camp to be situated in Croatia if possible. In this way, greater security and better provision of supplies could be guaranteed. He went on to pose some basic questions concerning the future role and activity of the Hungarian contingent, including subordination, the geographic boundaries of participation, and the location of the deployment site. The overall security of the battalion was also a discussion topic.

Thereafter, the deputy chief commander stressed how important it would be if the HDF could participate in IFOR because it was not only a military issue but a political one, as well. He then gave the answers to the questions we had posed. The Hungarian engineer battalion would be directly subordinate to the commander of the International Rapid Reaction Force, while Brigadier General Moore-Bick (British), the Chief Engineer of the corps, would be responsible for vocational guidance. The deployment area was to be primarily in the British and U.S. zones, to the south of Banja Luka, along the River Sava. The Hungarian engineer contingent, it was proposed, would be based in the district of Novska in Croatia, but the Hungarians should take the final decision on this matter. Defensive measures in the immediate vicinity were to be taken by the Hungarians, but the corps commander and the commander of the district where Hungarian subunits would carry out their duties would take charge of overall defense.

NATO planning officers asked us to inform them of our final decision by 5 December 1995, because they aimed to summarize the various national offers on that particular day. Moreover, they urged the Hungarians to send detailed information about the structure of the battalion as soon as possible.

5.6. CONSULTATIONS ABROAD

The officers from the planning section carried out the first consultations at NATO Headquarters in Mons right after parliamentary approval had been given. The delegation gave information about the capabilities of the battalion and announced that the Hungarian engineer contingent would be prepared to carry out duties by 22 January 1996.

NATO authorities called for the Hungarians to perform their duties in close cooperation with engineer battalions from Slovakia and Romania. It was emphasized that the Hungarians had caused some trouble through the designation of their area of deployment (south of the River Sava as far as the Banja-Luka – Doboj – Tuzla line, about 60 – 80 kilometers in depth from north to south). They described in detail the plans for the defense of the contingent. They stressed that the protection and defense of the camp should be independently organized. On the march, defensive measures in the immediate vicinity would also be the task of the contingent itself; moreover, marches should be announced at least 48 hours before they actually took place. NATO authorities also considered it important to have at least two Hungarian liaison officers with adequate military and professional skills and with a good command of English at the Allied Command Europe Rapid Reaction Corps (ARRC) headquarters.

Command hierarchy was also discussed. NATO authorities stressed that the contingent had to be subordinate to the corps commander, whose technical chief would be responsible for vocational guidance. In certain fields, however, national responsibility would remain unchanged. The most important tasks were military order and discipline, setting up camp, rotation, logistics and supply, permanent maintenance of technical instruments, and professional and safe mission execution.

The most important legal questions were also clarified, such as the question of responsibility in damage survey procedures as well as the investigation of accidents, the damage done, and persons injured. NATO authorities called attention to the fact that, in certain fields, in addition to a Status of Forces Agreement (SOFA), Hungarians would have to conclude special agreements and contracts with the Croatians. They provided detailed information about professional planning, the procurement of building materials, and the conclusion of different contracts. Finally, they emphasized the importance of individual and collective preparation and training of both soldiers and commanders. The NATO side announced that two inspection teams would visit Hungary during the time of preparation. The first team would check whether the staff and the equipment of the battalion met NATO requirements. The second team would want to see at what level the NATO training program had been carried out and to what extent rules and regulations had been adopted among the soldiers. They stressed how important it was for soldiers to become familiar with the rules of engagement (ROE) for weapons use. This consultation largely helped the planning officers to work out the final scope of duties and the time schedule. Officers in the preparatory planning group found it important to obtain useful information from their Slovakian colleagues who had been present in the region for several years (with an engineer battalion) as UN peacekeepers in UNPROFOR.

On 10 December 1995, a large delegation visited the General Staff of the Slovakian Armed Forces to carry out consultations in the following topics:

1. Communications: regular military use of signals and their application by professionally trained staff with special equipment, in order to provide necessary information to the military organization or international organizations.
2. Material and technical supply: arrangements for material and technical supply; special technical instruments and equipment; expected means and duration of use; local procurement and service facilities, as well as their reliability (water, sewage water, food, repair, etc).
3. Finances: opening of bank accounts; staff payments; arrangements for back pay; means of local procurement and utilization of services; terms of balancing bank accounts; customs clearance; life and accident insurance for the staff.
4. Technical tasks: special technical tasks occurring most frequently; requirements concerning camp installation and set-up; opportunities for procuring building materials (wood, stone, gravel, etc.); the use of special equipment; frequency of occurrence and characteristic locations of abandoned ammunition, land mines, and explosives; training and preparation in theater.

An important phase in the consultative process involved a visit to a potential operation area in Croatia. The aim of this visit was threefold: to specify the main points of general cooperation with the General Staff of the Croatian Armed Forces; to survey the area for the first time and select the potential deployment site; and to enable the Hungarian planning group to gain practical experience in the camp of the Slovakian engineer battalion.

It was with the extraordinary assistance of the Croatian party that the proposed deployment site was viewed, although in the Croats' opinion, Novska was not suitable for stationing soldiers. It was stressed many times that the Hungarians had to pay for everything, from the site itself to water and waste dumping, as well as for the use of buildings, should that be the case. They called the Hungarians' attention to the fact that there were many land mines and unexploded ordnance in the area. They also emphasized several times that the River Sava formed the borderline.

5.7. THE STAFF

It was only after the organizational problems had been solved that vacancies were advertised and the staff was selected. In theory, there should have been more soldiers with technical qualifications than were needed, but an anomaly caused by the downsizing and personal resentment largely limited the pool of potential peacekeepers. While there was a surplus of officers, there was a slight shortage of NCOs. At the same time, low wages in Hungary and an unemployment rate of almost 10% caused an increase in the number of applicants.

On 10 December 1995, the selection of the staff for the Hungarian contingent began. This was the day that the conditions for application were published, which authorized soldiers serving in the armed forces to apply for the engineer subunit without the permission of their commanders. Later, unfortunately, this turned out to be very disadvantageous for a certain part of the professional staff. Due to the reorganization of the military, commanders at home did not guarantee a place for those who had left to work in the contingent, and when they returned, they were often not given an assignment. Due to this practice, a huge number of officers and NCOs with international experience were compelled to leave the army.

There were seven times more applicants than expected. More than 50% of the applicants (1,417 people) were reservists, of whom 25 were women. Seventy per cent of the total number of applicants had families with two to three children; 50% had vocational training; and about 20–30% were unemployed. Their motivation to take a job abroad was primarily monetary, as 90% of them considered this to be an important factor. The majority of the officers in the battalion (61 people) already had international experience, and some of them had already attended various NATO courses.

After the applications had been handed in, the staff was selected in three phases on the basis of professional, medical, and psychological criteria. Before the final staff was selected, a personal interview was conducted with each potential participant. Only after this was it possible to start the professional and general preparation and the gradual departure of the staff, which was scheduled to begin in the middle of January 1996.

On 3 February 1996, 416 soldiers participated in the official ceremony, after which the battalion officially became part of IFOR. There were 67 officers, 179 warrant officers, and 170 NCOs. There were 245 contract soldiers, out of which 68 had applied as conscripts. The age of the group ranged from 18–60; 211 out of the total staff were single and 204 married. 149 people had two children; 78 people had three; one person had four children, and had five. Sixty-six people had university degrees; 132 had finished secondary school; 179 had vocational training; and 38 had attended only elementary school.

Before departure, the Hungarian contingent's security considerations once again caused some political debates in parliament. As a result, 21 additional staff members and 6 armored vehicles (BTR-80 type) without ammunition were added to the Hungarian contingent, despite the British promise to ensure the protection of the Hungarian contingent. 169 containers were installed in Okucani, which provided accommodation and service facilities for the staff. 76 containers were used for quartering purposes; usually six people were lodged in a container. 20 containers were used for washing and cleaning, and 18 were used for cooking and eating. A surgeon, a dentist, and a psychologist also worked in the camp.

After 3 February 1996, problems related to the Hungarian engineer contingent were no longer the focus of political and public attention. The activity of the battalion was characterized by the construction of bridges, restoration work, and high-level visits. Regular staff rotation occurred; those who returned took up their previous jobs, whether in the armed forces or in civilian life. Nobody paid any particular attention to the experiences that had been gained, but some individual experiences infiltrated the everyday life of the armed forces and played an important role in preparation for NATO accession.

6. Conclusion

Since 1996, more than 1,000 Hungarian soldiers have served in IFOR/SFOR. As of this writing, the Hungarian engineer contingent has completed nearly 200 tasks of varying character and magnitude during these missions. These tasks include building and operating 28 bridges of different types and sizes and laying 65 kilometers of railway track. Twenty-seven kilometers of roadway have been restored. In addition, the contingent has performed tasks involving snow and ice removal, minesweeping, water search, and underwater reconnaissance. Hungarian divers have made 1,700 dives. Hungarian experts have carried out mine clearance over an area of 102,000 square meters.

For Hungary, participation in IFOR/SFOR was designed not only to help the parties implement a peace accord to which they had freely agreed, but also to help prepare Hungary for NATO membership. The opportunity to work with NATO soldiers and use the alliance's Standardization Agreements (STANAGs) were a kind of preliminary training to help the Hungarian army become acquainted with NATO philosophy and military equipment, and to make progress towards interoperability and compatibility. It became possible for Hungarian soldiers to study and practice first-hand the decision-making processes used by NATO and, equally important, to practice indispensable English-language skills. During their everyday work, they adopted and started using NATO command procedures and documentation, thus increasing cooperative capabilities.

12. THE CASE OF BULGARIA

Valery RATCHEV and Yantsislav YANAKIEV

Outline:

1. INTRODUCTION [1]

1.1. BULGARIAN EXPERIENCE IN PEACEKEEPING OPERATIONS

Following the end of the Cold War, the Bulgarian Armed Forces began fulfilling a new mission: participating in United Nations (UN) peacekeeping forces. In this context, the National Concept for the Participation of the Republic of Bulgaria in Peacekeeping Operations was elaborated in 1994. It defines the goals, objectives, and terms and conditions for participation in peacekeeping operations (PKOs). The first PKO in which our country participated was the United Nations Transition Authority in Cambodia (UNTAC) in 1992 – 1993, where Bulgaria contributed one complete infantry battalion, staff officers, civilian and military policemen, and UN military observers.

Bulgaria has supported UN operations in Tajikistan and Angola. Several Bulgarian officers have served as UN military observers, as well. In late 1996, the Republic of Bulgaria joined peacekeeping efforts to settle the conflict in Bosnia and Herzegovina (BiH) within the UN-mandated NATO-led Stabilization Force (SFOR). Our contribution to the BiH operation presently includes one engineer platoon within the Netherlands contingent and one transport platoon within the BELUGA[2] logistical support group.

1.2. POLITICAL MOTIVATION TO JOIN THE SFOR OPERATION FROM THE BULGARIAN PERSPECTIVE

The new kinds of conflicts after the end of the Cold War and the situation in the Balkans today require Bulgaria to take a new approach to participation in peacekeeping and other crisis management operations. That is why our country has conducted an extremely active foreign policy toward pacifying the Balkans. This policy is the most important part of the strategy for the preventive defense of Bulgarian interests. According to the National Security Concept, Bulgaria's security is determined by the extent to which the country is able to provide security for its neighbors. Together with its regional initiatives for increasing mutual trust in the political and military sphere, the country

---

[1] We would like to express our deep thanks to the servicemen from the Bulgarian engineer and transport platoons that participated in the SFOR operation (June 1998–January 1999) for their collaboration in the course of the survey.

[2] Participating countries were Belgium, Luxembourg, Greece, and Austria.

assists the strengthening of security and stability in the Balkans.[3] Bulgaria strictly adheres to a policy of multilateral and bilateral cooperation, especially in the military sphere, to develop adequate armed forces for participation in PKOs. The Military Doctrine of the Republic of Bulgaria states that participation in PKOs is one of the main missions of the Bulgarian Armed Forces.[4] The military policy of our country supports the efforts of the UN and the Organization for Security and Cooperation in Europe (OSCE) in the field of arms control, conflict prevention, and the restoration of peace. The Republic of Bulgaria considers its participation with specially trained military, police, and other formations in PKOs and humanitarian missions to be a long-term investment to guarantee its own security.

The National Program for Preparation and Accession of the Republic of Bulgaria into NATO emphasized the participation of our country in the Combined Joint Task Forces (CJTF) created by NATO to implement PKOs. Bulgaria and the Bulgarian Armed Forces are taking part in the Multinational Peace Force in South Eastern Europe (MPFSEE). Bulgaria is a host country of the multinational HQ in the city of Plovdiv, as well.[5] In the context of the security and defense policy of the Republic of Bulgaria, our participation in the SFOR operation is a continuation of Bulgaria's international commitments to guarantee security and stability in the Balkans. We expected the following results:

• First, participation in this mission was seen as a test of our military's readiness to serve in NATO-led multinational forces. This experience will be valuable in the establishment and activation of the MPFSEE, as well as of other multinational formations in the Balkan region.

• Second, the lessons learned in the operation will be valuable for the implementation of programs concerning restructuring, modernization, and interoperability with the armed forces of NATO partners.

• In addition, during the SFOR operation, our military has gained new experience. Participation in PKOs has changed the Bulgarian armed forces' culture. The military now largely accepts the fact that their tasks are no longer focused solely on the management of violence; it is now widely acknowledged that military tasks in today's rapidly changing security environment

---

[3]   *The National Security Concept of the Republic of Bulgaria* (approved by the XXXVIII National Assembly on 16 April 1998).

[4]   *The Military Doctrine of the Republic of Bulgaria* (approved by the XXXVIII National Assembly on 8 April 1999).

[5]   Velizar M. Shalamanov, "Multinational Peace Force South-Eastern Europe – Regional Development of the CJTF Concept," Presentation at the 8th Multinational Peace Force South-Eastern Europe Meeting, Plovdiv, 26–29 April 1999; available at http:/www.md.govern.bg/news (2 May 1999).

also include the management of mediation, conciliation, and interagency processes.

• Finally, Bulgaria's participation in SFOR is another practical manifestation of our readiness to contribute to PKOs carried out by the UN, EU, and NATO in order to enhance stability in South Eastern Europe.

1.3. MAIN FOCUS

This chapter focuses on the Bulgarian experience concerning points of tension during the SFOR operation, the lessons learned, and perspectives for future Bulgarian participation in PKOs. Our analysis focuses on the tensions that arose within Bulgarian units and between our units and the contingents of other nations. Our country's level of involvement in the SFOR operation, in fact, generally excluded military relationships with international organizations, mass media, and non-governmental organizations (NGOs). As far as relations with the local population and the local authorities are concerned, there were some limited contacts, which will be discussed.

1.4. RESEARCH METHODS AND EMPIRICAL DATA

We have used both quantitative (questionnaire surveys) and qualitative (focus groups and consultations with experts) methods in our study. The analysis in this paper is based on data from the following empirical surveys:

• A longitudinal survey on motivation, cohesion, and morale of the Bulgarian contingent taking part in SFOR. In view of the limited number of members of the contingent (50), the survey was thorough. The fieldwork was done in two stages: in June–July 1998 immediately prior to the departure of the platoons for Bosnia, and in December–January 1999 immediately after the rotation. [6]

• A representative public opinion poll of the Bulgarian military on the attitudes towards the new missions of the Bulgarian Armed Forces, conducted by the Sociological Research Center of the Ministry of Defense (MoD) in April 1998. (A self-administered questionnaire was used as a method of data collection, N=1563.) [7]

• A nation-wide representative public opinion poll on attitudes towards participation of the Bulgarian Armed Forces in PKOs, conducted by the NOEMA

---

[6]   Yantsislav V. Yanakiev, *Motivation and Attitudes of Bulgarian Servicemen to Serve in Multinational Peacekeeping Forces*, available at http:/www.md.govern.bg/publications (15 May 1999).

[7]   Christo I. Domozetov and Yantsislav V. Yanakiev, "The New Security Risks and the New Missions of the Armed Forces: View Points of the Military and the Citizen," in Stephan E. Nikolov and Yantsislav Y. Yanakiev (Eds.), *The Armed Forces in a Democratic Society* (Sofia: Publishing House of the MoD and Hanns Seidel Foundation, 1999).

Private Agency for Social and Marketing Research in October 1998. (An individual home interview was used as a method of data collection, N=1240.) [8]

- A survey of experts on the topic of "Participation of the Bulgarian Armed Forces in PKOs: Problems and Perspectives," conducted by the Sociological Research Center of the MoD in April 1999 among experts from the General Staff, services, Rapid Reaction Forces, and officers who have participated in PKOs as UN military observers, staff officers, or commanders of armed contingents (N= 28). [9]

2. POINTS OF TENSION ON THE LEVEL OF THE BULGARIAN CONTINGENT

In this section, we will analyze the most important sources of tension that appeared within the Bulgarian national contingent taking part in the SFOR operation. First of all, we should point out that our conclusions are only valid for the servicemen from the engineer and the transport platoons that participated in the SFOR operation from June 1998 to January 1999. We will focus on the following issues: force selection and configuration, assessment of the pre-deployment training, perceptions of the acceptable risks and expected problems during the mission, confidence in the leadership, definition of success, and satisfaction with the mission.

2.1. SOCIAL PROFILE OF THE SERVICEMEN

As we have already pointed out, Bulgaria contributed two platoons – an engineer and a transportation platoon – to the SFOR operation. These platoons were composed of NCOs and commissioned officers on active duty. All of them volunteered for this mission. The selection of the servicemen was made on the basis of their professional records, physical fitness, and psychological test results. The average age of the servicemen was 35 years, with an average time of service in the armed forces of 11 years and four months. All of them were men. There were no representatives of ethnic minorities. The overwhelming majority of the servicemen were married, and only four of them were single. As far as education is concerned, 88% of servicemen were secondary school graduates; 6% had higher education, and 6% had military academy plus staff college, defense college, or equivalent education. The share of servicemen with prior UN experience was comparatively small. About 14% of the servicemen had previous experience in UN peacekeeping missions as UN military observers or as servicemen in the Bulgarian military contingent in Cambodia.

---

[8]   Unpublished paper. The results are cited with the permission of the NOEMA Private Agency
       for Social and Marketing Research.
[9]   Unpublished paper. The results are cited with the permission of the Bulgarian MoD.

Both platoons underwent special pre-deployment training in Bulgaria. In addition, the transport platoon underwent five weeks of training in the Netherlands.

2.2. SELF-ASSESSMENT OF PRE-DEPLOYMENT TRAINING

The servicemen from the Bulgarian contingent were asked to assess their platoon's level of preparedness to fulfill the mission in Bosnia, as well as the level of their personal proficiency, both before departure to and after return from Bosnia. The data received unquestionably show a substantial divergence between preliminary expectations about the preparedness of the personnel and the reality of the actual mission. More significant are the differences as far as the assessments of officers' proficiency are concerned.

Analysis of the survey data leads to the conclusion that members of the Bulgarian contingent in SFOR departed for Bosnia with the expectation that no serious surprises awaited them. This is probably a result of what they had learned during their pre-deployment training courses. At the same time, attention should be paid to the divergence registered between expectations and reality. The majority of servicemen departed with false ideas and a significantly heightened self-assessment of their own expertise. This fact should be taken into account when selecting and training future contingents because it could easily become a stress factor that could affect the morale of the personnel and hence the execution of tasks during the mission. It is necessary to create expectations that are as close as possible to reality about what is to come and what difficulties these people can encounter. To this end, it would be very useful to include the participation of servicemen who have already participated in such a mission in the training phase of future contingents.

2.3. ASSESSMENT OF ACCEPTABLE RISKS AND EXPECTED PROBLEMS DURING THE MISSION

Before departing for Bosnia, members of the Bulgarian contingent did not expect to face any threat to their lives, to fall seriously ill, to suffer a breakdown of morale, or to encounter any family problems resulting from their absence from home. The majority (58%) believed that there was a "very small" or "small" danger of losing their lives. Another 30% assessed such a risk as "medium likely." The rest (12%) believed that there was "a great possibility" of facing a threat to their lives.

Some two-thirds (68%) were of the opinion that there was minimum risk of permanent harm to their health because of injury or serious illness. Every fifth person (22%) assessed such a risk as "medium likely." Every tenth person believed that there was a great risk of permanent damage to health during the mission. Three-fourths of the members of the Bulgarian contingent (74%) did not expect any problems with their morale. Another 16% assessed the possibility that their morale would be damaged as "medium likely." Again, every tenth person assessed such a risk as "very likely." The predominant part of the surveyed personnel (80%) did not expect serious family problems to be a result of their absence from home. Every fifth person expected such problems as "medium likely."

Expectations of the servicemen from the Bulgarian SFOR contingent were generally optimistic in terms of problems and difficulties during the mission in Bosnia. This applies both to private life (overcoming the separation from one's family) and to one's professional career (mastering and performing new functions and duties in a multinational environment). Now let us see what changes occurred in the opinions of surveyed personnel, and to what extent their preliminary expectations overlapped with reality.

Among the more difficult problems that the participants in the Bulgarian contingent faced in the course of the mission were homesickness and the fact that they were away from their families. These problems were expected, but the expectations did not fully comply with the reality. We have registered a significant difference between preliminary expectations about being separated from relatives as a problem and the reality assessed upon return from the mission. This indicates to us that, during the preparation of servicemen for future missions, more attention should be paid to problems such as separation from family and to changes from everyday life in Bulgaria to which the servicemen are accustomed. These soldiers and officers will have to perform new duties in a new environment; when servicemen are not prepared to meet these challenges, tensions can result, not only among the soldiers but also between commanders and subordinates. Therefore, it is important to put special emphasis on these issues in pre-deployment training, so that the stress impact of these factors is reduced.

2.4. CONFIDENCE IN LEADERSHIP, COHESION, AND MORALE

The indicators we used to measure confidence in leadership, cohesion, and morale of the platoons were as follows:
- Assessment of the relations between commanders and subordinates;
- Assessment of the relations among colleagues;
- Confidence in colleagues and commanders;
- Satisfaction with the living and labor conditions over the course of the mission.

2.5. ASSESSMENT OF HIERARCHICAL RELATIONS AND RELATIONS AMONG COLLEAGUES

Analysis of the data received from the pre-deployment survey shows that the servicemen from both platoons of the Bulgarian contingent experienced a high level of cohesion and confidence. The majority said that in a risk situation in the course of the mission they would fully rely on their colleagues. There was not a single serviceman who left for the mission with the belief that he could not rely on the person next to him. More than 90% of the participants in the Bulgarian contingent assessed the relations among colleagues before leaving Bosnia as "good." When assessing the hierarchical relations before the mission, we arrived at the conclusion that high confidence in the leadership was prevalent. More than three-fourths of the servicemen assessed their relations with commanders as "good." Yet another 14% assessed these relations as "satisfactory." Three-fourths of those participating in the study stated that they could "fully" rely on their commanders, while the other one-fourth said that they could rely "to a certain extent" on them. Data from the follow-up survey show a decrease in confidence both in commanders as well as in their colleagues. Only one-fourth of the servicemen said that in the course of the mission they "fully" trusted their commanders. Almost half of them stated that in the course of the mission they trusted their commanders "to a certain extent." Another fourth frankly said that in Bosnia they "could not rely" on the command of the platoons.

When analyzing the data from the pre-deployment and post-rotation surveys, we can notice a significant change in assessments of both relations among equals as well as hierarchical relations before and after the mission. This fact calls for special attention, because it poses a question about the quality of pre-deployment selection of servicemen, and especially of commanders. In addition, this change of assessment should be taken into account when considering possible points of tension resulting from a lack of confidence among colleagues and a lack of trust in commanders. This situation can easily affect the morale and cohesion of the troops and, consequently, their performance during the mission.

2.6. SATISFACTION WITH MISSION PARTICIPATION AND ACHIEVE-MENT OF MISSION GOALS

About two-thirds of the participants in the Bulgarian contingent assessed the participation of their platoon in SFOR as "successful." However, another one-fourth thought their work was "more or less successful." Every tenth participant considered it poor, believing that the participation of his contingent in SFOR was a "failure." As far as personal participation in the mission is concerned, the majority of the servicemen (83%) thought that it contributed to their self-realization as experts in the military field. In addition, three-fourths stated that service in Bosnia has contributed to the realization of their personal plans. Half of the servicemen thought that they had fully achieved the goals they assigned themselves before leaving, while another half pointed out that they partially achieved their goals.

The most important sources of tension were related to lack of information, the lack of possibilities for communication with their families, poor equipment, and low pay. Servicemen were least satisfied with the information they received about life in Bulgaria. What they were missing in practice were the usual information sources (newspapers, magazines, and video films). Mail came with great delays, and not regularly, which contributed to a great extent to dissatisfaction with communications with families and relatives in Bulgaria. The fact that they were highly dissatisfied with their salaries is not a surprise. Before leaving for Bosnia, almost one-third of the servicemen stated that they did not approve of the contract they had signed in terms of salary. Yet another fifth was hesitant about whether to answer that question. Almost half of the participants in the Bulgarian contingent expressed dissatisfaction with the proposed salary. A second problem related to salaries was that everyone received an equal amount of foreign currency, without taking into account their military rank and position. According to the servicemen, it was expected that this would result in tensions between commanders and subordinates.

Attention should be paid to the relatively low satisfaction of the servicemen with the relations between the MoD and the General Staff (GS). The explanation could be found in the feeling that Bulgaria did not show enough interest in the Bulgarian contingent and demonstrated a lack of concern about and interest in their families.

3. RELATIONS BETWEEN THE BULGARIAN AND OTHER CONTINGENTS

When comparing the experience of the Bulgarian military in two PKOs (in Cambodia and Bosnia), we find several important differences between the two operations in terms of military-to-military relations:

- This is the first PKO in which the Bulgarian military participated in cooperation with NATO countries.
- SFOR is the first PKO where the Bulgarian military was integrated into a multinational, battalion-sized, mission-tailored command structure under the operational leadership of a non-Bulgarian commanding officer.
- Unlike UNTAC, the Bulgarian contingent in SFOR is not involved in combat activities. Its duties are logistics and construction.

In short, the Bulgarian contingent faced new challenges and gained new experience as a result of its contribution to the SFOR operation. These challenges were connected, on the one hand, with the need to integrate into a different military and organizational culture and, on the other hand, with the implementation of the new role of peacekeepers.

3.1. TRADITIONAL MILITARY CULTURE AND CHANGING MISSIONS OF THE BULGARIAN ARMED FORCES: BUILDING THE NEW PEACEKEEPER IDENTITY

The participation of the Bulgarian Armed Forces in PKOs puts forward a number of questions. First we must consider the extent to which these activities coincide with our national interests. At the same time we must consider the extent to which they support and develop the training of forces to work in real-life situations. This is connected with the legitimization of our participation in multinational PKOs as a new mission of the Bulgarian armed forces, and with the motivation of servicemen to volunteer for PKOs.

During the post-Cold War period, we have observed a process of gradual change in the traditional military culture towards the adoption of new roles and missions. This is a process of transition from the traditional role of warrior toward the new role of peacekeeper. In order to describe this process, we will analyze and compare the perceptions and attitudes of our military on three levels:

- First, we will analyze the mass attitudes of Bulgarian officers and NCOs towards the participation of the Bulgarian Armed Forces in military operations other than war (MOOTW).
- Second, we will examine the attitudes of experts towards the participation of the Bulgarian Armed Forces in such operations.
- Third, we will evaluate the perceptions and attitudes of the servicemen who were involved in the SFOR operation.

The data presented in Table 1 give us the opportunity to compare the attitudes of Bulgarian officers and NCOs toward the traditional military mission (the protection and defense of the national territory) and the new mission (participation in MOOTW). We can see in Table 1 that the traditional mission of the army – the protection and defense of the national territory – remains the priority task for Bulgarian officers and NCOs. The idea of being deployed to give assistance in case of civil disasters at home is also a mission widely accepted by both categories of servicemen. Given the rapid rise of criminality in the country after 1989, it is not surprising that there is broad agreement about the fulfillment of so-called police tasks, such as "struggle against organized crime and drug trafficking" and "struggle against international terrorism." The other point of total agreement between officers and NCOs is the low rating of "replacement of civilian workers in case of strike." This task is absolutely unacceptable to both categories. There is broad agreement among the surveyed personnel about deployment in an international theater. "Participation in peace-

Table 1: Approval of Some Probable Tasks of the Bulgarian Armed Forces by the Military (Representative public opinion survey among Bulgarian officers and NCOs in November 1999, N=1563. Tasks pertaining to PKOs are shaded, in order to facilitate comparisons between attitudes toward PKOs and other, more traditional military tasks and other MOOTW.)

N	Probable Tasks of the Bulgarian Armed Forces/ Level of Approval by Servicemen	Officers and NCOs (Mean scores on a scale of minimal approval=5, maximum approval=1)
1	Protection and defense of national territory	1.13
2	Assistance in case of civil disasters inside the country	1.22
3	Humanitarian missions	1.49
4	Protection of the environment	1.59
5	Struggle against international terrorism	1.64
6	Assistance in case of civil disasters abroad	1.66
7	Internal control of Bulgarian territory	1.68
8	Struggle against organized crime and drug trafficking	1.69
9	International arms control missions	1.72
10	Peacekeeping operations in cooperation with other countries	1.75
11	Peacekeeping operations under UN flag	1.77
12	Assistance in policing state borders (especially in case of mass immigration)	1.99
13	Ceremonial functions	2.35
14	Building civil infrastructure	2.35
15	Military actions under the supreme command of the UN	2.40
16	Peace enforcement based on UN resolutions	2.71
17	Replacement of civilian workers in case of strikes	3.33

keeping forces under the UN flag" is the most acceptable among all PKOs. This may also be said about the task "participation in peacekeeping operations in cooperation with other states." The approval rate falls when respondents are asked to rate tasks like "military actions under the supreme command of the

UN" and "military enforcement of UN resolutions." Analysis of these data on attitudes toward the future tasks of the Bulgarian Armed Forces leads to the conclusion that, as a whole, participation in PKOs is not a common task and is therefore not yet widely accepted by the Bulgarian military.

Comparing these results with the attitudes of the experts, we can find considerable differences. With regard to such tasks as "participation of Bulgarian servicemen in PKOs under the aegis of the UN," "international missions for control over armaments," and "humanitarian operations," we register absolute expert support. The experts' degree of approval of tasks like "joint operations with the forces of NATO member states and Partnership for Peace (PfP) countries in peace enforcement operations" and "operations without UN mandate" is comparatively smaller (although these operations are supported by the majority of experts). Experts are much more aware of the fact that Bulgarian military participation in PKOs contributes to the acquisition of new skills and knowledge and helps train forces for work in realistic situations. They think that our participation in multinational PKOs is directly associated with the realization of Bulgarian foreign policy priorities, including the rapid integration of Bulgaria into Euro-Atlantic security structures. According to the experts, the participation of the Bulgarian Armed Forces in this type of operation is precisely the sort of activity that will lead to the kind of experience shared by NATO member states. Moreover, participation in PKOs will help us to achieve a high degree of interoperability with these same NATO states. Finally, as a result of participation in PKOs, experts believe that the national security of Bulgaria will be enhanced.

The differences between experts' attitudes and the attitudes of Bulgarian officers and NCOs that we have just described can be explained by a lack of traditions and by a lack of knowledge about the new missions of the armed forces among those serving in the Bulgarian military. In both cases, further efforts should be made on the part of experts to devise a strategy to increase public support for Bulgarian military participation in MOOTW, because there is a problem with the legitimacy of Bulgarian participation in these operations. The problems of legitimacy and public support become particularly topical when considering the new type of PKOs in which Bulgarian servicemen are most likely to take part.

The attitudes of servicemen from the Bulgarian SFOR contingent toward Bulgarian military participation in MOOTW are close to those of the experts. This result can be explained when one considers the duties that they performed in BiH and their experiences in such operations.

Let us now shed some more light on the attitudes of Bulgarian servicemen towards the new role of a peacekeeper. The following items were included in our questionnaire to measure these attitudes:

- The performance of functions and duties with minimum use of force and arms;
- Impartiality to each of the belligerent parties;
- Service under a foreign (non-national) command;
- The performance of new functions and duties in multinational forces.

3.2. USE OF FORCE

One of the basic principles of "traditional peacekeeping" is that of minimal use of force, applied only when necessary for self-defense. [10] Although the SFOR mission is not a traditional PKO, it is important to know to what extent servicemen in the Bulgarian contingent have internalized this principle. Prior to deployment, about 62% of those surveyed said, "It is no problem at all to execute duties without the use of arms and force." Almost one-fourth (24%) said it would be a "small problem." The rest (12%) expected that obeying the principle of minimal use of force would be "a moderate problem" for them. There was no NCO or officer from the Bulgarian contingent who expected to have difficulties or to experience problems in fulfilling his duties without the use of force and arms.

3.3. IMPARTIALITY

Another important peacekeeping norm is impartiality. Prior to deployment, we asked our respondents whether they could "maintain complete impartiality to the parties in the conflict." Again, two-thirds (66%) said, "It would not be a problem at all." Almost one-fifth (18%) declared, "It would be a small problem." Roughly the same number (16%) said, "It would be a moderate problem." Not one of the surveyed servicemen expected to have problems following the principle of impartiality.

3.4. SERVING UNDER NON-BULGARIAN COMMAND AND PERFORMING DUTIES IN MULTINATIONAL UNITS

The SFOR operation is a real challenge for the Bulgarian military because subordination to foreign (not national) command, although only operational, is still somewhat unusual for our servicemen. In spite of that fact, for many of the participants in the poll, this was not a problem. The survey data bear this out. Service under a non-national chain of command was "not a problem" for 40% of those queried before departure to Bosnia. About one-third (34%) expected this to be "a small problem," and almost one-fourth (26%) thought it could be a "moderate problem."

---

[10] *UN Charter*, Ch. VI.

A comparison of the results from the pre-deployment and follow-up surveys leads to the conclusion that the surveyed personnel have shown they have
the knowledge and willingness to comply with the basic principles of peacekeeping. We can say that these principles are understood and adopted by the
members of the Bulgarian contingent, and that they believe that these principles posed no problems for them during the mission. When comparing the
perceptions given prior to departure for Bosnia and after the mission was completed, we can see that expectations and reality overlap to a great extent.

The successful accomplishment of a multinational PKO is strongly dependent on relations with colleagues of other nationalities. In this respect, it is important to bear in mind what sort of image the Bulgarian SFOR contingent had
of servicemen of other nationalities. The data from the pre-deployment survey
showed that the members of the Bulgarian contingent left for the mission with
optimistic expectations about their relations with their colleagues from other
countries (the Dutch and Greeks). The majority of them (90%) expected relations to be friendly, while just 8% expected relations to be formal. Only one
person among both platoons' personnel stated no opinion on the matter.

The fact that the expectations of the servicemen were fully confirmed after the end of the mission is a positive result. The majority of the servicemen (91%) who took part in the poll said that relations with their colleagues
from other countries were friendly. Only two people defined these relations
as "formal" and two other defined them as "reticent." In addition, we should
point out that Bulgarian servicemen reported high satisfaction with the recognition of their professional skills by their colleagues from the Netherlands and
Greece. In accordance with the results from the follow-up survey, we came to
the conclusion that the most serious problem for our servicemen in relations
with colleagues from other contingents over the course of the mission was an
insufficient level of English language knowledge.

3.5. ANALYSIS OF THE MOTIVES OF BULGARIAN SERVICEMEN TO VOLUNTEER FOR SFOR

The rating of servicemen's motives to join SFOR was calculated on the basis of
a number of possible reasons, which were rated by each respondent according
to a 5-point scale beginning with 1 ("insignificant reason") and ending with
5 ("very important reason"). Our approach in terms of items and scales was
close to the methodology applied by Franz Kernic for the Austrian chapter. [11]

---

[11]   Franz Kernic, "Peace Angels Versus Warriors for Peace," Paper presented to the International Sociological World Congress, Montreal, 1998.

Multidimensional analysis of the data shows that there are four major motivational factors that explain the decision of Bulgarian contingent members to volunteer for SFOR:

- The first factor accounted for 36.9% of the variance and combines such motives as "promote Bulgaria's prestige," "speed up integration into Euro-Atlantic security structures," "preserve peace and security in South Eastern Europe," and "enhance Bulgaria's national security." We termed this factor "normative motivation."

- The second factor, accounting for 17.5% of the variance, is totally dominated by the motive "this is an honest way to earn money that will help me solve my financial problems." We termed this factor "instrumental motivation."

- The third factor accounted for 13.5% of the variance; it includes such motives as "master new skills that are necessary for a military career," "better achievement in life upon return," and "desire to test oneself in a difficult situation."

- Finally, the fourth factor was dominated by the motive "participation in the mission is an opportunity to divert myself for a while from the problems of everyday life."

Outlined in this way, the structure of Bulgarian servicemen's motives to take part in the operation in Bosnia shows that they were driven both by "internal" motivational factors (such as the expectation to contribute to the promotion of Bulgaria's international prestige) and by "external" factors, such as monetary reward. A characteristic of these people is that they are not trying to evade personal problems at home or delay their solution. Another characteristic is that they are not adventure-seekers, and they do not perceive themselves to be "Rambo-like" heroes. We can summarize that the motivation patterns of Bulgarian servicemen to volunteer for the SFOR operation are, as a whole, close to the motivation patterns of other NATO and PfP countries' contingents. We therefore should not expect any serious points of tension based on different motivations. These conclusions can be incorporated into the pre-deployment selection and motivation of future contingents as well as the media policy of the MoD, in order to gain public support for Bulgarian military participation in multinational PKOs in the future.

3.6. PERCEPTIONS OF DIFFERENT STANDARDS AND RELATIVE DEPRIVATION

An important factor for the existence of tension when participating in multinational PKOs is the way people perceive different attitudes toward different nationalities. That is why we asked the participants in the Bulgarian contingent to make an assessment of whether in the course of the mission they had the feeling that different standards were applied to them in comparison to their Dutch and Greek colleagues. The data are presented in Table 2.

Table 2: Responses of the surveyed personnel to the question: "In the course of the mission, did you have the feeling that different standards were applied to the different nationalities as far as the following conditions and activities are concerned?"

N	Activities and conditions	Yes	No
4	Health care	19%	81%
2	Payment for one and the same job	95%	5%
1	Armament and equipment	63%	37%
5	Better paid or less risky job	61%	39%
7	Recreation conditions	49%	51%
3	Living and working conditions	29%	71%
6	Food and supply	19%	81%

Analysis of the data shows that the majority of participants in the study felt that different standards were applied in terms of payment for one and the same job. Around two-thirds think their armament and equipment is not equal to that of their Dutch and Greek colleagues. Almost two-thirds think they were sometimes given the less paid or the more risky job. In discussions, servicemen from the engineer platoon were unanimous in their opinion that comparisons they made with Dutch equipment made them uncomfortable and made them feel like "second-class people."

We believe that the way the different people understand the application of different standards to the representatives of different nations in multinational PKOs could easily evolve into a serious source of tension and undermine the achievement of the mission's tasks. Therefore, in missions to come, equipment and armament should be provided on a basis of equality, sufficient for the accomplishment of the mission. Moreover, all nationalities that serve together should receive equal salaries and have comparable living standards.

4. RELATIONS WITH THE LOCAL POPULATION AND LOCAL AUTHORITIES

Bearing in mind the level of involvement of Bulgarian servicemen in the SFOR operation, we will analyze everyday relations between our military and the local population in Bosnia. First of all, we should point out that we have regis-

tered differences between expectations prior to deployment and evaluations after the rotation, as far as the relations of our military with the local population
are concerned. The attitudes of our servicemen towards the local population
changed in a positive direction. The results from the pre-deployment survey
show that the percentage of servicemen who expected their relations with the
local population to be formal (47%) was higher than those who expected to be
received in a friendly manner (41%). Every eighth serviceman (12%) found it
difficult to define his expectations for relations with the local population.

Six months later we had a substantially changed picture. More than half of
the officers and NCOs (54%) defined their relations with the local population
in Bosnia as "friendly." Every eighth man (12%) considered these relations
to be "formal," and around one-third (34%) assessed their relations with the
population in Bosnia as "reticent."

The nature of duties performed (construction of roads, as well as the construction and reconstruction of public buildings) is probably one reason for the
positive image of our servicemen in the eyes of the local population. These
attitudes are reciprocal. After returning from Bosnia, Bulgarian servicemen
reported that they were highly satisfied with the recognition of their contributions on the part of the local population. Another reason good relations were
established between Bulgarian servicemen and the local population is probably the fact that our customs, culture, and traditions are close to those of the
local population. The same is true concerning the Serbo-Croatian language,
which could be understood by Bulgarians without great difficulties. This made
communication between our servicemen and the representatives of local population much easier. It is important to point out that, according to reports of our
servicemen, all ethnic groups in the area of service accepted them on an equal
basis. The same is true as far as the attitudes of Bulgarian servicemen toward
the local people in Bosnia were concerned. Finally, our servicemen were aware
of the political and economic situation in Bosnia, which helped them to better
understand the essence of the conflict.

One thing our servicemen really missed in their relations with the local
authorities and the local population in Bosnia was the lack of knowledge about
how to collaborate with civil organizations. They also reported insufficient
knowledge about the main principles of international humanitarian law. We
believe that it is appropriate to broaden the briefings on these topics in future
pre-deployment training.

5. PUBLIC SUPPORT FOR PARTICIPATION OF THE BULGARIAN MILITARY IN PKOs

5.1. ATTITUDES OF BULGARIAN CITIZENS TOWARD PARTICIPATION IN PKOs

The public's assessment of the Bulgarian military's readiness to take part in the SFOR operation was predominantly positive. More than one-third of them (35%) thought that the preparedness of the Bulgarian Armed Forces to take part in PKOs was "excellent" or "good." In addition, 16% believed it was "satisfactory." Less than 10% of the surveyed citizens were of the opinion that the readiness of Bulgaria's army to participate in PKOs was "not satisfactory." It is important to emphasize that a considerably high percentage (40%) of respondents did not have an opinion on this issue.

The following questions gave more precise information about the attitudes of citizens towards Bulgarian military participation in PKOs:
- What would be your reaction if some of your close relations decided to volunteer for peacekeeping operations like SFOR in BiH?
- Would you approve of raising military expenditures in connection with Bulgarian military participation in peacekeeping operations like SFOR in BiH?

Data show that most citizens (57%) would not interfere if one of their close relations decided to volunteer for a PKO. Less than one-third (27%) would be against this decision, while about 15% would approve of the decision of their relative. Public opinion is split almost equally about the financial dimension of Bulgarian participation in PKOs. Slightly more than a quarter (28%) declared readiness to pay more taxes for the military budget, while slightly less than one-third (32%) were unwilling to do so. Again, more than one-third (40%) declared that they had no opinion on the question. These results lead to the conclusion that an understanding of PKOs, as a new mission of the Bulgarian Armed Forces, was not yet common among Bulgarian citizens. For this reason, they had a comparatively low level of acceptance.

5.2. THE IMAGE OF THE BULGARIAN SERVICEMEN TAKING PART IN SFOR AMONG BULGARIAN CITIZENS

Referring to the data from public opinion surveys, we can say that the public image of the Bulgarian servicemen taking part in SFOR was positive. Most often, citizens characterized them as people who "work to promote Bulgaria's prestige and speed up the integration of Bulgaria into Euro-Atlantic security structures." The citizenry considered the participation of Bulgarian servicemen in the SFOR operation as a way "to preserve peace and security in South Eastern Europe" and "to enhance Bulgaria's national security." There is little public support for the notions that Bulgarian servicemen taking part in PKOs "are people who want to divert themselves from everyday problems in the country," or that they are "adventurers who want to test themselves in a difficult situation."

It is important to point out that, as a whole, both public and military assessments about the image of the servicemen participating in the SFOR operation coincided to a great extent. These assessments were predominantly positive and differ considerably from the attitudes toward the Bulgarian military contingent that took part in the UNTAC operation in Cambodia. [12] This is a good basis for improving and building upon the new image of the Bulgarian soldier-peacekeeper.

6. LESSONS LEARNED AND RECOMMENDATIONS

On the basis of the analyses made thus far, we will summarize what we have learned and what should be done as far as the future of Bulgarian participation in multinational PKOs is concerned. We hope that our conclusions might be taken into consideration by policy-makers and military commanders participating in PKOs in the future.

6.1. IMPROVEMENT OF THE LEGAL BASIS AND ORGANIZATION OF BULGARIAN PARTICIPATION IN PKOS

In our opinion, the concept of the Republic of Bulgaria for participation in PKOs must be redefined to take into account the requirements of the new Law on Bulgarian Armed Forces and the new Military Doctrine of Bulgaria. It is necessary to create a "Concept for Participation of Bulgarian Armed Forces in MOOTW." The vision of the Bulgarian Armed Forces' participation in PKOs should be clearly defined. Moreover, the new concept should differentiate between the two types of operations – classical peacekeeping and "second-generation" PKOs. The emphasis should be put on Bulgarian military participation in PKOs within NATO and WEU-led forces.

A much broader and positively oriented campaign in the Bulgarian mass media is also necessary for the attainment of wider social support for the participation of Bulgarian servicemen in PKOs. This will help increase the military's motivation. At the same time, the increasing popularity of participation in PKOs among Bulgarian servicemen can be used to inform the society about the new missions of the armed forces.

It is also very important to procure equipment, armament, and salaries for participants in future PKOs that correspond to the tasks and that are on an

---

[12]   Angel I. Velichkov, "Bulgarian Blue Helmets in Cambodia and the Public Reaction to their Mission," Paper presented at ERGOMAS Interim Meeting of the Working Group "Public Opinion, Mass Media, and the Military," Breda, 1996.

equal level with the other nationalities with which the Bulgarian peacekeepers jointly serve. If not, the perception of differing standards can easily grow into a serious source of tension. Finally, we think that it is obligatory to solve such problems as the provision of information, organization of leisure time activities, and assurance of support for the relatives and families of participants in PKOs. This will contribute to an improvement in communications and help to overcome problems related to this stress factor.

6.2. SELECTION PROCEDURES AND PRE-DEPLOYMENT TRAINING FOR PKOS

First of all, the military academies should lay the groundwork for Bulgarian officer participation in PKOs. This should start with the basic principles of peacekeeping. In addition, cadets should be familiar with NATO's Standardization Agreements (STANAGs) and should incorporate the experience of PfP exercises. For this reason, we deem it necessary to institute a systematic feedback program to analyze the experience gained from Bulgarian military participation in PKOs, to publish it, and to use it in the education of cadets and officers in the Higher Military Schools and the Defense College.

Training of Bulgarian servicemen for participation in PKOs should be conducted in a specialized center within the framework of the Rapid Reaction Forces of the Bulgarian Army, or be directly subordinated to the GS. Troops should undergo general training for participation in PKOs in this center, and, after receiving the operational order, they should start well-considered preparation for the tasks the peacekeepers will be expected to perform in accordance with the mission mandate.

The primary emphasis in pre-deployment training should be put on instruction in independent decision-making and task performance in realistic situations. Enhancing personal traits and skills such as psychological resistance, ways to cope with stress, teamwork, and communication capabilities are very important for participants in PKOs. Other important issues in the pre-deployment curriculum should include knowledge of the essence of the conflict, the political situation, the geographical features in the region of the mission, the traditions and customs of the population, and the norms of international humanitarian law. Finally, servicemen who will participate in PKOs should be very well instructed in how to handle the mass media, NGOs, and the local authorities in the region of the mission.

6.3. WORKING WITH SERVICEMEN DURING THE MISSION

First of all, it is very important to give the troops as much information as possible about their tasks (in accordance with the mission mandate) and the risks they may face during the mission. It is also necessary to incorporate an interdisciplinary team of competent specialists in the contingent to ensure constant observation of the psycho-physiological state of the participants and to help provide psychological support and stress management during the mission.

Commanders should bear in mind the necessity of a timely rotation and alternation of the more difficult with the easier activities and regions. One of the main stress factors during the SFOR operation was the lack of regular information about life in Bulgaria and about the families of those in the Bulgarian contingent. Therefore, the provision of constant and good communications with relations, family support activities, and the creation of a feeling of security are of great importance for keeping the troops' morale high and promoting their best performance.

6.4. POST-DEPLOYMENT REQUIREMENTS

At least three main issues should be faced in working with servicemen after the PKO ends. First, a system should be developed to provide servicemen with psychological help, re-adaptation assistance, and specialized medical observation after returning from the mission. Second, a system should be established to maintain experience achieved through participation in PKOs and perfect its maintenance, which should be further developed in future operations. To this end, organized periodic training must take place that will create a contingent of servicemen who are ready to participate in other missions. Third, preferences should be given to veterans of PKOs. Service in PKOs should be one of the most important advancement criteria for the career of every commissioned officer and NCO. Preferences for promotion should be given to veterans who participated in PKOs.

7. CONCLUSIONS

As we stated in the beginning of this chapter, the global security architecture and the security environment changed dramatically after the end of the Cold War. New security risks and new types of conflicts arose, which posed many questions about the adequacy of Cold War doctrines and concepts about the use of the military to cope with these new risks. We face a challenging and demanding situation. Intra-state conflicts and the destabilization of neighboring countries characterize the Balkan region. Traditional PKOs are no longer applicable to the new types of conflicts arising after the end of the Cold War. This situation requires the active involvement of Bulgaria in peace processes and a new approach to participation in PKOs. Under these circumstances, peacekeeping, as a non-traditional mission of the Bulgarian armed forces, has become a real challenge to military professionals. The lessons learned from the participation of Bulgarian militaries in the SFOR operation will be valuable in this respect.

To summarize, we found out that the main problems and points of tension with respect to participation of Bulgarian servicemen in the SFOR operation have appeared most often within our national contingent and rarely in the relations of our servicemen with other military contingents.

Examples of the most important points of tension within the Bulgarian contingent included:

- Instances when the discipline and personal conduct of commanders did not meet regulatory requirements;
- Bad organization and poor leadership, leading to uneven distribution of tasks performed by the different groups;
- Inadequate pre-deployment selection and training as far as social competence, psychological resistance, and language background of the servicemen were concerned;
- Insufficient sensitivity and attention toward the participants in the operation and their families on the part of the MoD and the GS, resulting in low salaries, lack of information about life in Bulgaria, and extremely insufficient opportunities for communication with their relations.

As far as relations between our contingent and the military contingents from other countries were concerned, points of tension usually appeared due to:

- Lack of equal treatment of representatives of different countries, leading to perceptions of relative deprivation that found expression in the underestimation of Bulgarian servicemen, the inappropriate assignment of tasks, as well as unequal salaries and equipment;
- Poor knowledge of the English language, leading to difficulties in communication between the contingents;
- Insufficient experience in PKOs and different levels of social competence among our servicemen as far as the implementation of the role of peacekeeper was concerned.

In conclusion, we should say that, despite all the difficulties that our country has experienced in the transition period, Bulgaria will, as a reliable partner, contribute more substantially to early warning and rapid reaction in crisis management. In this respect, our participation in MPFSEE is another practical step toward guaranteeing the security and stability of the Balkans. Bulgaria's international commitments, ranging from Cambodia to Kosovo, fully comply with our national interests – to keep and promote peace and security on a regional, continental, and global scale. We consider our participation in PKOs to be a long-term investment in strengthening our national security, as well as an important element of Bulgaria's integration into NATO and the WEU. This is the best way to achieve interoperability with our partners from NATO member states.

13. PEACEKEEPING IN A NEIGHBORING COUNTRY: THE ROMANIAN EXPERIENCE IN BOSNIA-HERZEGOVINA

Ionel Nicu SAVA [1]

Outline:
1. Introduction
2. Changing Organizational Culture and Training for a New Mission: Peacekeeping
3. Romanian Armed Forces before1990
4. First Romanian Experiences in Peacekeeping
5. Motivation for Participation in the Bosnia Mission
6. Accomplishing the Mission in a Complex Cultural Environment
7. Tensions Resulting from the Nature of the Mission
8. Comparison with Other Contingents
9. Cooperation with Other Contingents
10. Public Perceptions of Domestic and International Media Coverage
11. Relations with the Local Population
12. Relations with International Non-Governmental Organizations
13. Conclusions

1. INTRODUCTION

This chapter synthesizes one of the most important experiences the Romanian Armed Forces has had over the past few years: the war in Yugoslavia in general and the peacekeeping missions in Bosnia-Herzegovina, in particular. It focuses mainly on the Romanian experience, from its engagement in the IFOR/SFOR mission in Bosnia to selecting, training, and deploying personnel, and includes some conclusions about this mission. The approach is a sociological one, attempting to analyze the way in which the Romanian contingent succeeded in accomplishing its mission in spite of its lack of experience, minimal pre-deployment training, and a diverse and complex cultural environment.

This study includes the following points:

---

[1]   The views and conclusions of this study reflect the personal opinions of the author; they are not necessarily the views of the Romanian Ministry of National Defense.

- The creation of a peacekeeping culture and the training of Romanian military personnel for the Bosnia mission;
- The motivation for such a mission;
- The identification of cultural tensions, with an emphasis on the military's ability to accomplish the mission in a complex cultural environment;
- Lessons learned after the mission and their impact on the Romanian Armed Forces.

This is, therefore, a synthesis of the Romanian experience in Bosnia as it was seen by the participants and analyzed by the author.

The method used is that of the opinion poll, based on a questionnaire submitted to a sample of 182 military personnel who came back from Bosnia over the past three years. The sample is representative for the whole contingent that volunteered for Bosnia. Deeper analysis, based on interviews conducted with 24 military service members who had served in key positions during the mission (especially public relations officers) was also carried out, along with the use of data from research conducted prior to the Bosnia mission (on other peacekeeping missions).

Participation of Romanian armed forces in peacekeeping missions represents one of the changes that occurred just after the end of the Cold War. This is certainly important, since it has led to changes within Romanian society and its armed forces. The peacekeeping culture, almost nonexistent before 1990 in the Romanian public and military mind, has become a specific and natural element of the defense culture of the country. The public is of the opinion that it is natural and necessary to participate in peacekeeping missions as a way to contribute to the preservation of peace and democracy worldwide. Moreover, Romania's engagement in the Bosnia-Herzegovina mission was also connected with its wish to contribute to an end to the conflict in the former Yugoslavia. As a neighboring country, Romania has been adversely affected by the war, both politically and economically. [2] Romania shares mutual historical traditions with this war-torn region, which has been devastated by a civil war and by interethnic conflicts. The political decision to send a Romanian military contingent to participate in the Bosnia-Herzegovina peacekeeping mission thus acquired a particular significance.

Two aspects should be considered here: from a political point of view, there is a feeling of responsibility for the security and stability of the region; from a military and security point of view, there is the professional goal of acquiring the capability to perform a new military mission, i.e., peacekeeping, as well

---

[2] From an economic point of view, by 2000, government statistics show that Romania had lost around $7.5 billion since the beginning of the war in the former Yugoslavia.

as the goal of contributing to cooperation and integration with Euro-Atlantic structures (NATO and EU).

2. CHANGING ORGANIZATIONAL CULTURE AND TRAINING FOR A NEW MISSION: PEACEKEEPING

In 1990, previous experience in peacekeeping for many armed forces in Central and Eastern Europe was almost nonexistent or was seen in a rather negative light. On the one hand, people were not aware of the main peacekeeping concepts and procedures, as they had been developed within the UN after WWII; on the other hand, the actions of UN "blue helmet" troops in different conflict areas in the world were interpreted from an ideological point of view.

Many who had served with the former Soviet military were indoctrinated during their training to see peacekeeping as an operation similar to the Russian invasion of Afghanistan. This confusion was also shared at the senior political and military level in most of the former communist states.

3. ROMANIAN ARMED FORCES BEFORE 1990

The main attitudes and organizational habits of the Romanian armed forces before the country's first engagement in an international UN-mandated mission are issues worth mentioning in this chapter. Were there any favorable precedents to reflect the development of new types of missions for the armed forces? Certain data prove that there have not. An answer to this question is important for Romania, because such an answer would show the beginning and end points in peacekeeping missions, especially after the Bosnia-Herzegovina mission. Although existing studies are not explicit enough in this respect, from an organizational point of view, we could take into account at least three indices, set on a scale as follows (Romanian Armed Forces, pre-1990):

- *Collectivism – Corporatism* (organizational scale);
- *Orientation toward Task/Action according to Directives* (scale of bureaucracy);
- *Political Control – Democratic Control* (professionalization scale).

Without going into too much detail, according to all these scales, collectivist orientations dominated in the pre-1990 Romanian armed forces. These forces tended to have a bureaucratic approach to mission accomplishment. Politically, the armed forces generally subordinated military objectives to the former leading party. In the past, traditional military culture would generally discourage a subordinate from contradicting someone hierarchically superior, even when the mission or task would have required it. Following orders was important, whereas personal initiative was discouraged; major professional objectives were also subordinated to political objectives.

However, international peacekeeping missions with multinational participation and supra-national command slightly contradicted the purely national doctrine of engagement and use of force, as the use of the country's armed forces outside the national area had been banned.

In a nutshell, traditional military culture was isolationist, collectivist, bureaucratic, and "ideologized," qualities that contradict the prevailing peacekeeping culture, which is characterized by an internationalist orientation that is individualistic, task-oriented, and, most important of all, not ideologized or politicized. Further research carried out within the Armed Forces Section for Social Studies in 1990–1991 empirically confirms some of these observations. [3]

4. FIRST ROMANIAN EXPERIENCES IN PEACEKEEPING

Before 1990, Romania took part in no peacekeeping operation (PKO) in the classical sense of such a mission, as described in UN documents. The first international mission under UN mandate in which Romania participated was in Kuwait (1991); Romania also sent military observers as part of the international group of observers (UNIKOM) and sent a field hospital to participate in Operation DESERT STORM. Although small in relative numbers and taking place over a short period of time (two months), the Kuwait mission was significant, as it inaugurated Romania's membership in the international community of states that provide peacekeeping forces for UN missions.

After 1991, the Ministry of National Defense (MoD) took measures to create peacekeeping units and to train personnel for such missions. From 1992–1995, the General Staff created four peacekeeping battalions, whose main task was to participate in multinational peacekeeping missions. Other subunits were also made available for international missions, especially under the auspices of NATO and Partnership for Peace.

Many officers and civilian officials from the MoD and other national bodies (Defense Committees, the Supreme Defense Council) participated in peacekeeping training courses, in countries such as Canada, which offer extensive experience and background in the field. [4] Mandatory training courses were in-

---

[3] This is a series of sociological research projects conducted in 1990–1991 by the Armed Forces Social Studies Section in various fields such as the troops' morale, political attitudes, and professional orientations. The author took part in some of these research projects.

[4] The first to mention here is the Lester B. Pearson Canadian International Peacekeeping Training Center. According to Romanian records, this center trained over 60 officers and civilians from Romania. Subsequently, most of them led peacekeeping units or subunits at various levels.

troduced in the military academies and defense colleges, while all personnel received elementary training in peacekeeping. Cooperation with countries experienced in peacekeeping assisted in the transfer of skills and know-how, so that the Romanian military could more easily take its first steps in the field.

The opportunity to test the Romanian military's ability to participate in international PKOs under UN mandate came with the missions in Somalia (UNOSOM, 1993) and Angola (UNAVEM III, 1995).

Most of the military personnel for the contingents deployed before the Bosnia operations came from units that the MoD had designated over the past few years for such missions. It is well known that, in order for peacekeeping missions to be successful, pre-deployment training is vital. Unfortunately, most who took part in these first missions as peacekeepers did not even have several weeks of training, much less several months.

When questioned later about which conditions contributed to the success of their missions in Angola, a sample of military service members offered the following hierarchy of answers:
- General military training: 53%;
- Psychological training: 25.5%;
- Support of comrades: 10%;
- Commanders' leadership: 9%;
- Other: 5.5%. [5]

To a certain extent, the Romanian military participated in early PKOs without having a sufficient understanding of and proper training for the mission's requirements. Trained to defend their nation and remain faithful to the country's political leadership, most of these soldiers found themselves transformed overnight into soldiers who had been volunteered for international missions that required them to obey orders from a multinational command, to face unexpected situations, and to fight a less visible enemy who did not directly threaten their country but rather peace in general. [6]

Obviously, previous experience from Kuwait and then Somalia and Angola was extremely useful for the Bosnia-Herzegovina mission, but only a small number inside the military had participated in these operations, so the effects of

---

[5]   These data were taken from a study published in the *Gândirea Militară* (Military Mind) journal by researchers from the General Staff (Psychological Unit). M. Mitea and G. Spiridonescu, "Motivatia participarii militarilor la operatiunile de mentinere a pacii" (Motivation for participating in peacekeeping missions), *Gândirea Militară* 3, 1996, pp. 27 – 30. (Note on statistical breakout: a few respondents cited more than one condition that contributed to the success of their mission.)

[6]   For example, during the mission in Somalia, the Romanian military did not know that there were sharks in the waters off the shore of Mogadishu where the Romanian camp had been set up. Some of them lost their arms or legs in the waters off Somalia. In Angola, the main enemy was malaria: two Romanian military servicemen died there.

this experience were limited. In a way, one could say that soldiers participated in peacekeeping missions before they were trained or acquired the doctrine, main concepts, procedures, and rules of engagement. Practice came first; only after the military actually engaged in missions did theory or an understanding of the reasons for such missions develop.

In 1995, shortly before the Bosnia-Herzegovina mission, over 85% of the military members of the 26th Battalion "Neagoe Basarab" (that was destined for deployment on peacekeeping missions) had never participated in an international mission or exercise. [7] The situation was different in 1997, two years later, when over 71% of the servicemen in the battalion had already participated in at least one PKO. Over one third (34%) of them had participated in at least two missions. (Taking into account the experiences in Angola and Somalia, the maximum service abroad in PKOs was set at six months. After this period, service members must return home for at least six months.)

To a certain extent, a peacekeeping culture began to develop within the Romanian armed forces just after 1990, somewhere between 1992 – 1996. Only after the end of the first term of the mission in Bosnia, by mid-1996, could one say that the Romanian military had "been initiated" in peacekeeping as a military operation. Nevertheless, exaggerations exist about the military effectiveness of the troops destined to serve in international missions, but these are of a political nature. [8]

If we were to draw a sociological portrait of the Romanian peacekeeper during the early years, it might look like the following: his average age was 25, he was visibly inexperienced, rather poorly trained but well-intentioned, and eager to participate in a mission to which he adapted with difficulty but accom-

---

[7]   Data drawn from a study of military service members participating in the "Alba" mission during the civil unrest in Albania, after they had come back from the mission.

[8]   The establishment of a peacekeeping culture and the training of the first troops were not exhaustive or complete. It was part of the general modernization program of the armed forces. There are still drawbacks, both in doctrine and training. In order to bridge these gaps, there is a strange tendency toward exaggerating the military effectiveness of the troops sent on international missions, a phenomenon obvious at the top of the political and military hierarchy. Senior officers are tempted to report that the Romanian military in general is ready at any time to join NATO, for example. The gap between political will and reality at the level of troops is bridged by the too rich imaginations of these senior representatives of the MoD. An explanation could be that most of them have not had classical military careers and that almost all of them come from the former propaganda apparatus that existed before 1990 (the temptation to keep ideology alive is very great in this case). After 1996, the entire team of the civilian minister Victor Babiuc was actually made up of former party activists, who were well known for their belief in ideals and lack of realism. This issue is presented in this note due to its relevance for the tension existing between the military heads from Bucharest (who are motivated by political interests) and the military in the barracks, including those who have served in Bosnia (who have to face everyday challenges).

plished rather well, since he was looking for prestige domestically as well as internationally. In this respect, Bosnia-Herzegovina proved to be useful. Without exaggerating, the Romanian peacekeeper was born in Bosnia-Herzegovina.

5. MOTIVATION FOR PARTICIPATING IN THE BOSNIA MISSION

From the very creation of peacekeeping battalions, people showed a high interest in enrolling in these units. Their attractiveness was due mainly to their resources, which allowed advanced training and educational standards, higher wages than in other units, the possibility to travel abroad, and the opportunity for an easier career. Moreover, unemployment in civilian life pushed many young people who had completed their compulsory military service to volunteer for the Bosnia mission and conclude contracts with the military. Professional officers and NCOs were mainly motivated by wages, the opportunity to gain international experience, and career interests.

As for the Bosnia-Herzegovina contingent, they were mainly motivated to volunteer because of the potential for financial gain. Listed below are the top reasons that the 182 military personnel surveyed in our study cited as incentives for participation in peacekeeping missions (see also Table 1):

• Money: 74%;
• Curiosity, travel, risk and adventure: 12%;
• Professional training and career: 9%;
• Prestige: 3%;
• Other: 2%.

When asked to cite a second reason that motivated them participate in the mission in Bosnia, those surveyed almost always invoked another factor that had weighed very heavily in their decisions. This proves that there was usually a complex set of reasons for participating in the mission. The main reason was that of money (over 70% of those questioned), but this was usually linked to a second motivation, ranging from the spirit of adventure (32%) to the increased potential for (career) promotion (28%), prestige (21%), or even discontent with everyday life and/or boredom at home (16%). Volunteering for the mission in Bosnia was therefore linked not only to money, but also to adventure and career as well as personal and national prestige.

Having stated that the decision to join the mission in Bosnia was determined by the need for substantial financial gain, it is important to note that this reason determined only the servicemen's decision to participate and not his behavior during the mission, which remained under the influence of traditional military values: adventure ("Rambo" model), professional career, prestige, or even boredom during long intervals of peace.

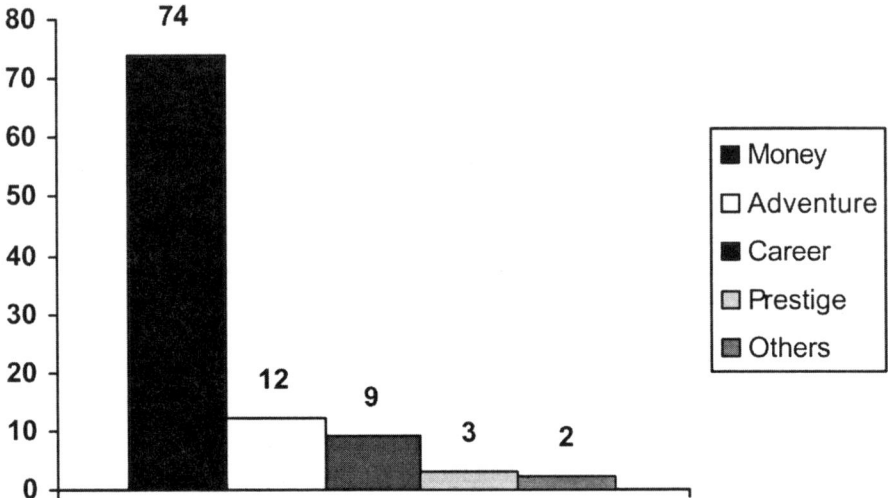

Table 1: Reasons for Joining the Mission (Question: What is the main reason you decided to join the mission in Bosnia? Responses in percent)

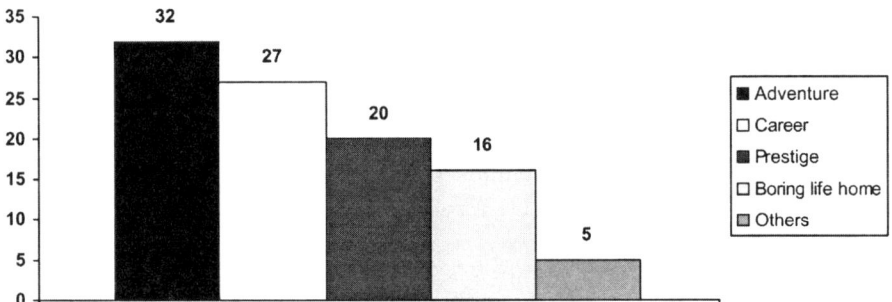

Table 2: Reasons for Joining the Mission (Question: What additional factor made you decide to join the mission in Bosnia? Responses in percent) (N=182)

Naturally, not all expectations connected with the reason for joining the mission were met. When asked upon their return from the mission whether conditions in Bosnia had been as expected, some servicemen (23%) said "no." Wages, for instance, had been as agreed upon at home, yet they turned out to be inferior to the wages of other contingents; in addition, the spirit of adventure had been far from what some of them thought it would be. [9]

---

[9]   Those who associated the mission in Bosnia with a spirit of adventure had in view the possibility of actually engaging in "peace-enforcing" operations; they dreamed about becoming sort of "supercops" who would defend law and order. Their discontent was to come, first of all, as a result of the fact that the Romanian 96th Engineer Battalion did not receive missions of the police type, but rather missions related to rebuilding infrastructure; their only armed military missions were those connected to guarding and defending their quarters and work site.

After six months of service in Bosnia – the maximum time allowed – motivation decreased significantly. Over 55% of respondents declared that, compared to the pre-deployment phase, they would be less interested in participating in a new peacekeeping mission during the next 12 months, at least as far as Bosnia was concerned. Was this a matter of unmet expectations for some of them? My opinion is that a lack of experience in past missions created, in some people, a very high level of expectations that actually proved to be a lack of realism. The higher the original expectations were, the greater was the disappointment. However, the percentage of those who declared themselves to be totally unsatisfied with the mission in Bosnia was nevertheless fairly low – below 14%, which was similar to those who had very high expectations. In other words, those who had been unrealistic had been dissatisfied as well.

The dissatisfaction associated with less realistic expectations was obvious, especially during the first deployments of the mission (1996). During the deployments that followed, realistic expectations became increasingly evident.

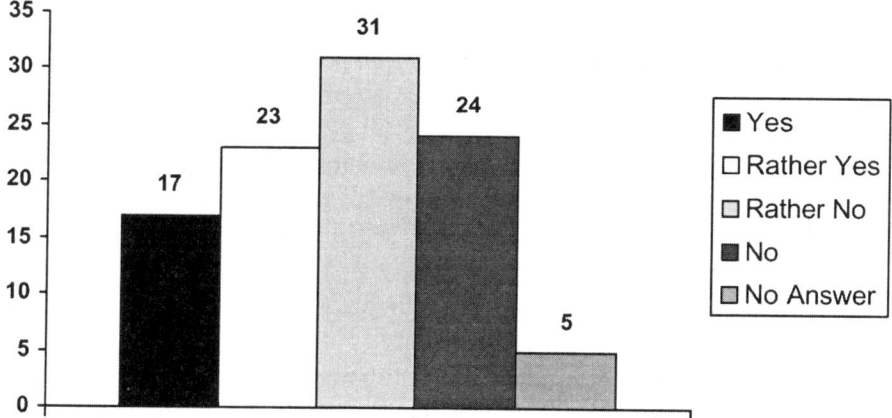

Table 3: General Interest in a Second Term in Bosnia (percent expressing interest). (N=182)

Through the peacekeepers' acquisition of first-hand experience and their subsequent adaptation to reality on the ground (especially after the first military contingent departed at the end of 1996), we found more realistic expectations about peacekeeping missions among those serving in the Romanian armed forces, which resulted in more reality-based motivations for wanting to participate in the peacekeeping mission in Bosnia. During the Bosnia mission, soldiers' perceptions evolved from enthusiasm to realism; in other words, the Romanian peacekeeper passed one of his first exams.

The difficulties of service in Bosnia, to which were added communication problems with the families and friends at home and extremely rare visits and periods of leave in Romania, contributed to a negative attitude toward a second term of service in Bosnia. Life as a peacekeeper is not so much dangerous as it is stressful.

6. ACCOMPLISHING THE MISSION IN A COMPLEX CULTURAL ENVIRONMENT

Mission accomplishment by the Romanian contingent has depended on two main elements: the nature of the mission established by the UN within IFOR/SFOR and the ability to contribute to peace building by cooperating with the other contingents, the local population, and the domestic or international organizations in the area. Indeed, the mission's success has depended not only on the current tasks, but also on the Romanian contingent's ability to actually contribute to peace in a complex cultural environment.

Following the request of the UN, Romania contributed an engineer battalion to the Bosnia-Herzegovina mission. [10] The 96th Engineer Battalion was quartered in Zenica in the American sector but was directly subordinate to SFOR in Sarajevo. The permanent battalion was composed of about 200 people, with few variations. The personnel rotation period was set at six months. [11] Shortly before deployment, a reconnaissance unit was sent ahead in order to select the site for their quarters, in an old plant destroyed during the war.

The Romanian engineer battalion was structured according to the specific tasks required by the mission: rebuilding means of communications, bridges, highways, and roads; demining activities; and reconstruction of certain public facilities. The battalion consisted of a company for rebuilding roads and bridges; a demining platoon; a logistics platoon; a guard platoon; and a signal platoon.

The tensions arising from the nature of the mission established, the tasks to be performed, and the challenges of daily life are of particular significance.

7. TENSIONS RESULTING FROM THE NATURE OF THE MISSION

The main task of the Romanian battalion was not peacekeeping or peace enforcement in the classical sense, through the specific UN rules of engagement,

---

[10]   Initially, the 96th Battalion belonged to the Allied Rapid Reaction Corps (ARRC), led by the British general John Moore-Bick. Starting in June 1998, it was subordinated to LAND-CENT, the NATO land force that replaced ARRC.

[11]   Zenica is to the northwest of Bosnia, about 100 kilometers from Sarajevo. After the mission was announced, the 96th Engineer Battalion was renamed in honor of Joseph Kruetzel, the U.S. State Department official who died in an accident in Bosnia. The initiative to give this name to the battalion came from Gheorghe Tinca, the Romanian Minister of Defense at that time.

but rather peace support operations that reestablish infrastructure and normal conditions of life for civilian populations after the fighting has ended. Peace support operations are much more specific to Bosnia.

To rebuild infrastructure is a part of the effort to build peace, and although it is a task of a civilian nature, it had to be accomplished with military means. Repairing a railway could hardly be called a peacekeeping mission, much less a "fighting" mission. Therefore, it was obvious from the very beginning that this was not a classical peacekeeping mission, but rather a peace support or peace-building operation. These facts led to the first tension resulting from the gap between what was expected and what was actually to be done.

Taking into account the specificity of the mission, selection of personnel for the Romanian contingent was made mainly according to the ability to run the contingent's bulldozers, cranes, trucks, and other equipment. The soldiers for peace thus became soldiers of "labor." Actually, over 70% of the personnel worked in such positions. That is why it is more proper to speak of "working conditions" instead of "fighting conditions" when referring to Bosnia. The specifics of the mission therefore had a deep impact on all other elements: selection of personnel, tasks to accomplish during the mission, procurement, and cooperation with the other contingents and with the civil population.

This reality also created tension and psychological discomfort for the military, whose expectations were connected to a spirit of adventure and to the need to assert themselves and serve with distinction. The "Rambo"-type soldier, a role many of them thought they could play in Bosnia, was replaced in their minds by the "slave" of bulldozers and cranes, fighting against debris and destroyed bridges, and having to secure the civilians' and the local government's cooperation in order to accomplish the mission.

The contingent's working environment featured extremely difficult conditions, very tight schedules, long hours (sometimes over ten hours a day), stress and strain, and unsafe surroundings. These conditions affected those soldiers and officers who had previously hoped to see Bosnia as the unique and exciting experience of a lifetime. Expectations before the mission did not match the reality on site. Tensions resulted from the difference between the high expectations during pre-deployment and on-site reality; this did not hamper the mission but did influence the soldiers' morale.

8. COMPARISON WITH OTHER CONTINGENTS

The nature of the mission also created tensions insofar as comparison with other contingents was concerned, both in the area of Zenica and throughout all of Bosnia. Many other contingents' missions were much closer to peacekeeping. Although not seen entirely as degrading, the peace support mission was

considered "inferior" to other ones, such as peace enforcement or even classical peacekeeping missions. The Romanian contingent occasionally felt "relative inferiority" to other contingents in a number of respects: soldiers were
particularly sensitive to the differences between their own facilities and those
of other contingents; the amount of wages, leave, and contact with families;
and some contingents' shorter terms of deployment.

However, when compared only to Romanian soldiers' own expectations
and not to the other contingents, most of the other conditions in Bosnia (except for the nature of the Romanian mission) could be seen as meeting average initial expectations. Seventy-two per cent of those questioned experienced
their accommodations, food, relations with other contingents, and freedom of
movement in their spare time largely as they had expected. Leave opportunities occurred less often than had been expected. Officers were given leave more
often than NCOs or soldiers who could leave the Zenica camp for only a few
days every six months.

In principle, soldiers were allowed to visit their families during their six
months of service in Bosnia, but leave was granted mostly to those with good
reasons for taking it. [12] The average age of the contingent was 25, and more
than 70% of servicemen were unmarried; this implies that their family obligations were minimal, generally only to parents, brothers, and sisters. Due to
the nature of the mission, women were not included in this contingent. For
most members of the Romanian contingent, telephones were the most efficient
means of maintaining contact with their families. Romanian soldiers and officers were ensured a free long-distance call once every ten days.

9. COOPERATION WITH OTHER CONTINGENTS

Due to the specifics of the mission, very complex reconstruction operations had
to be performed that required cooperation with other contingents. This was,
for example, the case with the rebuilding operations for the Visoko Bridge,
which could only be accomplished as a result of our close cooperation with
the German contingent in the area. [13]

This specific element of the mission in Bosnia – integration in a multinational structure and the need for cooperation in order to accomplish the mission – required not only language and communication skills, but also the ability
to work with partners from the other contingents. When asked about their pref-

---

[12] Serbian territory had to be crossed in order to get home, so after the NATO bombing over
       Kosovo started in March 1999 the route was changed to go through Macedonia and Bulgaria.
[13] The Mabey & Johnson-type bridge was built by Romanian and German engineers and was
       opened at Visoko on 21 April 1996, in the presence of IFOR, local government representa-
       tives, and the media.

erences for working with other military contingents, the Romanian military's most preferred partners were the Americans, followed by the Turkish, German, Dutch, French, and Hungarian contingents.

It is no secret that U.S. troops held a particular attraction for the Romanian military, since they have a clear admiration for the professionalism, living conditions, and facilities that the U.S. contingent offered to other contingents. More than that, the Americans were appreciated for their openness, friendliness, simplicity, and lack of sophistication. Sometimes people would mock the extreme seriousness of the U.S. leadership when dealing with even the simplest challenges. Many Romanian military men also noted that the U.S. contingent had the possibility to speak on mobile phones with their loved ones at home.

Less pleasant events also took place between the Romanian contingent and other contingents, or even the IFOR/SFOR authorities, but these were largely communication problems rather than differences in the vision for the mission or the tasks to be accomplished. One such event involved the Romanian Minister of Defense, Victor Babiuc. Babiuc was traveling to visit the Romanian contingent just before Christmas of 1998, when his plane was refused landing in Sarajevo – where the Romanian contingent was waiting for him in cars – and had to be redirected to Zagreb. This produced tensions at that time between the leadership of the Romanian contingent and the IFOR authorities. Later on, it proved to have been a misunderstanding caused by communication problems, as the flight and the visit had not previously received permission from SFOR. This was perceived by SFOR as a non-observance of procedures and not as an indication of ill will.

10. PUBLIC PERCEPTIONS OF DOMESTIC AND INTERNATIONAL MEDIA COVERAGE

Public opinion supported the mission of the Romanian battalion in Bosnia. The domestic media presented long commentaries about the situation of "our boys" in Bosnia. From this point of view, the public was kept informed about events in Bosnia as they were reflected in the Romanian contingent's activity. Radio and television stations, newspapers, and magazines presented news from Bosnia at least once a week. PRO TV, a private TV channel from Bucharest, made several live broadcasts from Bosnia in which the Romanian military in Zenica could speak directly to the public back home or even to their loved ones. Similarly, every Monday at midnight, the radio station CONTACT would play two hours of live communication with Bosnia, enabling the entire country to hear these messages. Radio CONTACT was very popular among Romanian soldiers in Bosnia; the usual response when asked about Radio CONTACT was "It makes you feel like home."

The concern shown by Romanian media demonstrated the extent to which the domestic authorities and population supported the mission in Bosnia. This support created a feeling of "security" and encouragement for the military, which was very advantageous for the accomplishment of their mission. Together with the clear support expressed for the mission in Bosnia, the national media was perceived as having a balanced and unbiased view of events in the former Yugoslavia.

Romanian perceptions of the international media were not the same. Over 63% of those questioned thought that the international press and television networks (such as CNN) were not always impartial. Certain events were presented from a partisan point of view, in favor of one of the parties involved in the conflict. Forty-eight per cent of the Romanian military thought that the Serbs from Bosnia-Herzegovina were generally presented in a worse light than they deserved. Half of them (about a quarter of the sample) were aware of the disastrous Sarajevo market bombing, an event for which the Serbs had been blamed, although later on questions were raised as to whether or not initial reports had been accurate.

According to those surveyed, the international media was seen as less credible than the national media. This means that media consumption is a cultural matter, too. However, when asked if they could give a particular example in which the international media presented an event from a biased point of view, only 11% could identify a specific incident; even so, they were unable to name the paper or radio/TV station that had "incorrectly" covered the event. The media from Western countries were generally perceived as anti-Serbian, whilst the Russian ones were seen as pro-Serbian. The phenomenon of bias in the international media was therefore a general perception that rarely involving the specific naming of events, papers, or radio/TV stations. There was one exception – CNN. Most of the time, this American television channel was identified as being biased.

11. RELATIONS WITH THE LOCAL POPULATION

Although they were on a peacekeeping mission that required the ability to work more than the ability to fight, most Romanian personnel did not assess service in Bosnia as inherently difficult. Rather, for them the mission was characterized by a demanding environment, uncertainty, isolation from home, stress, and a foreign cultural environment full of conflict. Even though basic personnel selection was made according to military criteria (evaluations were strictly based on an individual's ability to accomplish the military mission, i.e., health, military preparedness, and motivation), certain civilian abilities such as language competence, communication skills, and negotiating abilities were also taken into consideration. Although the mission was of a military nature, the Romanian contingent in Bosnia found themselves in the midst of a civil population with whom they had to cooperate and negotiate in order to accomplish their mission. A minimum of intercultural competence was therefore required; as this was not taught in any previous training, each soldier and officer had to acquire this competence on-site. Some of them succeeded, while others did not; this obviously led to tensions and dissatisfaction for those who could not adjust well. From a formal point of view, the task of cooperating with the civilian population fell to the leadership of the battalion and to the PR officers. The latter were particularly successful in what they accomplished.

The majority of Zenica's population is of Muslim origin, while nearly all members of the Romanian military contingent were Orthodox Christians. Although this combination certainly held the potential for tensions, this did not turn out to be the case. When asked to name with whom, of all the parties in conflict in Bosnia, they felt closer in mind and heart, the Romanian respondents ranked the Muslim population first and then the Serbs.

Sympathy towards the Muslims cannot be explained on religious or ethnic grounds; it was instead a social factor, directed towards the weakest group, in the sense that the Muslim community was perceived as being clearly disadvantaged in terms of living conditions and international support. Sympathy toward the Serbs, the second most preferred group, seems to have been based on mutual cultural elements, including shared history, religion, and traditions.

Due to their ability to communicate with the Muslims and Serbs, the Romanian military built bridges between the two communities as well as between these communities and the IFOR/SFOR authorities. When communicating with the Serbs, for example, the Romanian peacekeepers proved to be good go-betweens for the Americans. From a sociological point of view, the "go-between" helps to diminish tensions between groups; in Bosnia, this represented a vital step in creating and preserving stability and balance among the divergent interests of the Serbs, Croats, and Muslims. This communication advantage with the Serbs gradually diminished, especially after the Kosovo crisis began, after which the Romanians were perceived by the Serbs to have joined the "enemy."

12. RELATIONS WITH INTERNATIONAL AND NON-GOVERNMENTAL ORGANIZATIONS

In this field, there was little variation in the Romanian contingent's opinions. The activities of international and non-governmental organizations were considered to be "good" and "very good." Despite the difficult conditions, these organizations were viewed as having managed to achieve their goals. The difficulty was that the means at their disposal, and especially the results they achieved, were not in proportion to the needs in Bosnia. This led to tensions within the civilian population, who placed a high priority on humanitarian aid and medical assistance. The most disadvantaged population was the Muslims, especially because they were deprived of an extremely important "sponsor," an advantage both the Croats and Serbs already had. Even if there had been dis-crimination – probably impossible to avoid in the context of Bosnia – interna-tional organizations were perceived in general to be doing their jobs honestly.

13. CONCLUSIONS

PKOs that (a) must deal with a very difficult situation on the ground (including conflict) and (b) are characterized by the participation of a great diversity of national contingents (in terms of size, culture, rules of engagement, equipment, and daily duties) can give birth to a complex of tensions that in turn have a cer-tain impact upon the mission and the military itself. The operations in Bosnia seem to have involved a "melting pot" of factors that have helped to create a new type of military that must act in a less stable international environment and legitimize itself in a new, non-traditional way.

Romanian servicemen's motivations to volunteer for Bosnia were studied on an individual basis in a sample that is statistically representative for the whole contingent. Our study revealed a structure of motivation that ranked money first (74%) and included adventure and curiosity (12%), professional gains (9%), prestige (3%), and others (2%). One could say that the decision to join the mission in Bosnia was usually motivated by the need for substan-tial financial gain, but, according to our data, this reason determined only the decision to volunteer and not the soldiers' behavior during the mission. Atti-tudes and behavior during the mission itself were influenced by peacekeepers' attitudes toward traditional military values and experiences: risk and adventure ("Rambo" model); professional career; prestige; or even boredom with life at home.

In Bosnia, accomplishing the mission depended on two main elements: the nature of the mission itself and the need to cooperate with the other contingents and the local population in order to perform daily tasks. The shift from classical PKOs to peace support operations created a kind of discomfort and therefore a tension between pre-deployment expectations and realities in the field. Instead of performing typical soldiers' duties, those in the Romanian contingent had to work with bulldozers and cranes; this kind of work can hardly be categorized as a "fighting" mission. Comparisons with other contingents also created a kind of tension in terms of the relative deprivation perceived by the Romanian con-tingent when compared with other contingents' facilities; wages; contact with loved ones at home; length of deployment; and opportunities for home leave. Other tensions that appeared during the mission were found in relationships with the local population, non-governmental organizations, and the media, but these tensions were all properly managed.

The peacekeeping mission in Bosnia-Herzegovina, one of the longest deployments abroad for the Romanian military since the end of the Cold War, has acquired a particular significance both internationally and domestically. Romania, through its participation, joined the international community of states contributing to the preservation of peace and stability in the Euro-Atlantic area. Participating in a peacekeeping mission in a neighboring country also made Romania feel responsible for security in the area of South Eastern Europe. Along with contributing to peacekeeping, Romania sees itself as a contributor to security among the other states in the region.

Domestically, the experience in the Bosnia-Herzegovina peacekeeping mission proved to be very valuable, as well. A culture of peacekeeping, almost non-existent before 1990, has become a natural part of the defense and political culture of the country in recent years. To a certain extent, peacekeeping also influenced the process of changing the organizational culture and modernizing the armed forces. The move seems to be from an isolationist and bureaucratic military culture to a culture of professionalism, cooperation, and integration. Training courses in peacekeeping, which teach procedures and new rules of engagement, are now part of the educational system of the Romanian military. International experience, in general, and peacekeeping, in particular, have both become increasingly important to a professional military career. As an incentive, participation in PKOs is a good qualification for promotion and recognition. Many former peacekeepers are now in positions that require international experience, foreign language skills, and other peacekeeping-related skills (for instance, the Chief of Operations in the General Staff was a former peacekeeper). Since over 2,000 service members in the Romanian military have served in PKOs, their influence inside the armed forces should increase.

14. RUSSIAN PEACEKEEPERS IN THE FORMER YUGOSLAVIA: POLITICAL TENSIONS AROUND MILITARY COOPERATION

Alexander I. NIKITIN

Outline:

1. POLITICAL BACKGROUND

The participation of a Russian military contingent in the peacekeeping operations in the former Yugoslavia could be analyzed from different angles. Those who consider conflict resolution in Bosnia to be simply a normal continuation of the various UN-mandated operations everywhere in the world may say that Moscow's participation in the operations in the former Yugoslavia was not anything special. During the last few decades, the Soviet Union tradition- ally participated in UN-mandated missions on various continents. The size and strength of the Russian contingent in the former Yugoslavia (varying from 900 men in 1992 to 1,500 in 1994 and 1,340 in 1996) were, though significant, far from decisive for the international mission as a whole (as land-based SFOR forces exceeded 33,400 men).

At the same time, if one looks at the Bosnian case as a unique example of a new generation of international political/military operations, where NATO, rather than the UN, led a wide international coalition of countries representing different political orientations, then the involvement of Russia in this opera- tion meant an important breakthrough. For Moscow, as well for Washington and Brussels, the assignment of a Russian brigade to Bosnia was not only an operational decision within the context of the Yugoslavian conflict, but also a very serious political test within the general framework of relations between the Great Powers in the post-Cold War era.

First, it set a unique precedent of political and military cooperation be- tween yesterday's adversaries – Moscow and NATO – and was the first joint mission of Russian and Western contingents that, for decades, had trained to fight against each other.

Second, the mainly Slavic nation Russia, instead of playing a nationalis- tic card against NATO and taking the side of Slavic Serbs, took a balanced position of participation in the mission based on "unbiased disengagement." Of course, some preferences remained, but the partial unofficial pro-Serbian orientation of Russia in this conflict served as a counterweight to the partial, unofficial pro-Croatian (or anti-Serbian) orientation of some NATO nations and thus contributed to the relatively balanced character of the mission as a whole.

Third, Russia sent its contingent far abroad to the center of Europe at a historic moment, while several other regional conflicts with Russian military involvement were burning on the territory of Russia itself (Chechnya) and in neighboring CIS states (Georgia, Moldova, and Tajikistan). The military, eco- nomic, and diplomatic resources of Russia were insufficiently split in different directions; in the absence of domestic consensus, the concentration of efforts on the former Yugoslavia required the reallocation of resources by the Kremlin from other theaters.

Fourth, cooperation between Russia and NATO on peacekeeping in Bosnia overlapped with and was influenced by severe disagreements between Moscow and Brussels on the issue of NATO enlargement and the approaching crisis in NATO–Russian relations, which later exploded in connection with another NATO operation in the former Yugoslavia: Kosovo.

All these factors require an in-depth analysis of the broader domestic and international context of Russian participation in the operation in Bosnia.

1.1. THE RUSSIANS ARE COMING!

Units and subunits of the Russian Federation Airborne Forces were first used in peace support missions in the former Yugoslavia as early as 1992. No specially trained peacekeeping contingents existed in Russia at that time (except for a group of former Soviet military observers with mainly non-combat experience in UN missions). Therefore, a separate Russian infantry battalion was formed, drawn from the Airborne Forces, based on the Russian Federation's governmental decree, "On the Deployment of a Russian Contingent to Yugoslavia for Participation in UN Peacekeeping Operations" and on the Directive (26 February 1992) of the Commander of the Combined Forces of the CIS.[1]

Battalion strength was established at 900. Six weeks were spent assembling and training the battalion. The Table of Organization and Equipment (TOE) structure was as follows: a headquarters and headquarters company, and five rifle companies, each with three platoons. The initial estimate of required armaments called for 15 BTR-Ds, light arms, and approximately 150 vehicles.

The traditional simple structure of the contingent, the short period of unspecified training, and the light armaments profile all show that the Russians initially entered Yugoslavia with inadequate experience in operations of this type and the misperception that this was going to be classical UN peacekeeping, where arms were not really used except for demonstrations of force. The actual tasks under UNPROFOR, however, even before IFOR/SFOR, forced a change in the TOE structure and an increase in combat power. A mortar platoon and a support platoon were added soon thereafter. The battalion requested and received 54 more modern BTR-80s; 82 mm mortars; mobile anti-tank rocket launchers; and portable anti-aircraft missile systems from Russia. In 1994, the 554th Separate Infantry Battalion was reinforced by the 629th Sep-

---

[1] The Combined Forces of the CIS were a transitory structure and never accomplished the goals leading to their formation. The initial plan was to avoid a real division over the disposition of the united Soviet military infrastructure and to coordinate political mandates from the newly independent states for the collective use of "allied" or rather "combined" CIS forces. Marshall Ye. Shaposhnikov was nominated as the Commander-in-Chief of the Combined Forces, and it was he who ordered the first Russian military contingents to Yugoslavia. Soon after this, the majority of the newly created states (former republics) demanded that a portion of the military infrastructure be put at their full disposal and proclaimed the creation of separate national military forces; thus, the model of the combined CIS forces ceased to exist.

arate Infantry Battalion and the total number of Russian troops in the former Yugoslavia reached 1,500, with 200 trucks and 95 armored vehicles.

Soon after 15 December 1995, when UN Security Council Resolution 1031 was adopted, the Russian contingent attained a new legal status and changed its structure and size. Less than three weeks after the new UN Security Council mandate, on 5 January 1996, the Russian Parliament approved the use of a Russian military contingent as part of the multinational force in Yugoslavia. [2] Parliamentary approval of the country's participation in international peace-keeping was a new procedure undertaken in accordance with the new Russian law of 1995 regulating the use of national military contingents and civilian personnel in peace support activities.

In mid-February 1996, Russian President Boris Yeltsin issued a special decree establishing the strength of the Russian contingent for Yugoslavia at 1,600 men. [3] A year later, the personnel ceiling for the Russian contingent was decreased to 1,400 men; [4] the actual size of the Russian brigade in 1997 – 1998 was kept at 1,340.

Under SFOR, the Russian brigade was incorporated into the Multinational Division North [MND(N)]. The immediate "neighbors" of the Russian soldiers were the U.S. brigade, the Turkish brigade, and the combined "Nordic" brigade consisting of contingents provided by Sweden, Denmark, Norway, Finland, and Poland.

The Russian brigade was responsible for the control of a 1,750 square kilometer zone, with a 275 kilometer line separating the conflicting sides. The brigade's staff was located in Uglevik, while the 1st Separate Airborne Battalion was located in the Priboy area and the 2nd Separate Airborne Battalion was assigned to Simin-Khan.

As was the case with many former communist national contingents sent to Bosnia, the proportion of officers was much higher than is customary in regular national forces: 1,029 Russian soldiers/sergeants served under the command and leadership of 209 warrant officers and 102 commissioned officers. Twenty more Russian officers were assigned to command units of the MND(N).

Over time, the armaments of the Russian brigade were increased in comparison to the 1992 – 1995 period and reached 118 armored vehicles, including modern 2C9s and 1B119s in addition to special Airborne Armored Vehicles, BTRs, and 284 cars.

[2]   Federation Council, Federal Assembly of the Russian Federation (RF),*Resolution No. 772 – 1 SF*, 5 January 1996.
[3]   RF Presidential Administration, *Decree No. 195* of the President of the Russian Federation, 14 February 1996.
[4]   RF Presidential Administration, *Decree No. 365* of the President of the Russian Federation, 16 April 1997.

The Russian brigade was responsible for five permanent checkpoints for road control, the patrol of numerous routes in the zone of responsibility, as well as reconnaissance, search, and security checks. The diversity and large number of parallel functions forced the brigade to create eight special combined groups for *ad hoc* emergency tasks.

During the entire IFOR/SFOR mission, the Russian brigade did not participate in any conflicts with massive use of force. Casualties (four soldiers dead and 11 injured) occurred mainly as a result of mine explosions.

The general estimation of the Russian contingent by the command of the international peacekeeping force was high, demonstrating the military professionalism, good internal organization, and discipline of the Russian brigade.

1.2. RUSSIAN SOLDIERS UNDER NATO COMMAND?

One of the most difficult issues for the Russian side in IFOR/SFOR was the organizational structure and chain of command. The military command of the operation in Bosnia was almost completely NATO-centered, with the staff structure of SHAPE fully involved in planning and performing the operation. From Moscow's point of view, it was quite a contrast to other UN-mandated operations. First of all, in previous UN-mandated operations, commanders represented various countries, often neutral ones, in rotation. Second, commanders were chosen and approved by the UN, where Russia has a strong voice. Finally, the military side of the operation was subordinated to a UN political representative. None of these parameters were present in the case of the operation in Bosnia.

In the early stages of planning the operation, the initial command structure called for the Russian brigade to be built into the regular NATO vertical chain of command. In Moscow, that was considered in to be an unnecessary precedent. Some critical articles appeared in the Russian media exploiting topics like "Russian soldiers under the command of NATO generals." To avoid "ideological" complications, Russian military diplomacy insisted on a structural novelty that appeared to be illogical from an operational point of view but was useful to Moscow in both a diplomatic and psychological sense: the commander of the Russian brigade, General L. Shevtsov, was subordinated directly to the SACEUR and received the title of Deputy Commander for the period of the operation.

Shevtsov's office (officially called the "Operational Group of the Russian Ministry of Defense at the Supreme Headquarters Allied Powers Europe") consisted of five officers who were located with the general directly within SHAPE itself. Each Russian delegation (governmental or non-governmental) visiting SHAPE was shown a slide with the general structure of command, where the Russian brigade was separated from other coalition contingents and connected by thick red line directly with the SACEUR through the Russian Deputy Commander.

Russian command units also included 13 Russian officers and soldiers assigned to the MND(N) command group in Tuzla and ten officers and six commissioned officers in Vukosavzi in the brigade's staff unit.

This Russian liaison group in the MND(N) Staff participated in the division planning and was responsible for continuous tactical command over the Russian contingent. At the same time, the Commander of the MND(N) was fully responsible for the entire division's zone of responsibility, including the Russian brigade's zone of responsibility. In practice, such a trilateral command structure meant that orders and instructions from the Commander of the MND(N) were transmitted to Russian soldiers and officers only through the liaison group in the staff, which first coordinated and rechecked these orders (two levels up) with the Russian command group in SHAPE and only then passed the orders (one level down) to the contingent for implementation.

The operational group of the Russian Ministry of Defense at SHAPE participated in orientation and planning for the entire SFOR operation, prepared suggestions about the use of the Russian military contingent, and evaluated its operational abilities and the results of actions. It is important to note that the tasks formally assigned to the Russian command group in SHAPE included tasks not only of a military but also of a clearly political–diplomatic character. Among them were "Coordination of the issues of appropriate implementation of the peace agreement with the Bosnian political–military leadership" and "Organize and conduct sessions of joint conciliatory commissions consisting of representatives of Bosnian and SFOR leadership." Additionally, the Russian Ministry of Defense assigned the group the task of studying and analyzing the peacekeeping experience of the other countries' contingents.

The Russian military mission was not the only non-NATO mission established at SHAPE; military representatives of other countries that had never been interoperable with NATO before (for example, Egypt) were also invited to locate their small units at SHAPE. It was a vital lesson in interoperability that lasted until March of 1999, when the Russian contingent was ordered to withdraw from under the NATO general command as a result of the political implications of the crisis over Kosovo.

Participants in the interaction between Russian and international command units at all levels bear witness that the interaction went quite smoothly, with no major problems. The most difficult aspects of both the early stage of Russian involvement in Bosnia and Russian participation in IFOR/SFOR were not technical or military. They were political, and they resulted from the significant change in the doctrinal approach of Russia towards cooperation with NATO in peacekeeping and conflict resolution, as well as from the generally contradictory approach to Bosnian conflict resolution in Russian political circles.

1.3. MIXED MOTIVATIONS DEFINING RUSSIAN ATTITUDES TOWARDS THE OPERATION IN BOSNIA

There was a certain degree of egocentrism in Russian perceptions of NATO in the Soviet era, which has been partially incorporated into Russian perceptions of the Alliance. NATO is seen as a mechanism whose entire existence and actions rotate around Moscow and Russian military power. All NATO moves (even, say, discussions with Malta on ending its participation in "Partnership for Peace") are interpreted by many Russian policymakers as aimed, directly or indirectly, either at cooperation or confrontation with Russia.

It is obvious, for example, that very few politicians in Moscow judge relations between Brussels and the Central European capitals who joined NATO through the prism of European integration and the internal political dynamics of Central European societies. The actions and intentions of both NATO and its new members are mostly seen as an indirect assault or pressure on Russia. The same is true for the perception of NATO involvement in peace support missions in the former Yugoslavia, namely in Bosnia. Rarely do Russian politicians see them from the point of view of the internal logic of developments in the Balkans. More often, NATO involvement was interpreted either as a "rehearsal" for intervention in conflict resolution in the CIS or as biased support of Muslims against Slavs (Serbs), again indirectly targeted against Russia as the leading Slavic nation.

Such self-referential tendencies were cultivated during the Cold War by decades of the bipolar "zero-sum game" logic, when all international relations in the Northern hemisphere – and even worldwide – were interpreted (and not only by Moscow and its proxies, but by Washington and its allies too) as merely the projection of the juxtaposition of superpowers: good against evil, us versus them. This is why, even today, aspects of NATO transformation, such as broadening the scope of missions and shifting the emphasis to non-Article V missions (i.e., missions not connected with the collective defense of NATO nations against massive aggression from open adversaries), are not well understood and not appreciated by Russian policymakers. Obviously, Russian public opinion underestimates the importance of such "internal missions" of NATO in deterring European powers from the renationalization of defense, cooling down mutual political (though not economic) claims, and stabilizing relations among Alliance members. A manifestation of these functions that is a little bit more understood and appreciated by Russia is the component of keeping "giant Germany" tied down by common security arrangements. Nevertheless, in general, NATO is still perceived by the majority of Russians (and not only by the uneducated public but also by sophisticated politicians) as, first and fore-most, a unified Western military machine designed to wage land, sea, and air battles.

The peacekeeping and peace enforcement functions performed relatively successfully by NATO in Bosnia received a dubious reception in Russia. From one side, this new mission was perceived as correlating much more with the requirements of the time than, for example, military exercises in Northern seas aimed at tracing Russian nuclear submarines. In many articles by Russian authors and in political statements by Russian parliamentarians, the shift of NATO to peacekeeping is recognized as a sign of real and positive change. From the other side, however, the example of involvement in Bosnia was far from praised by most Russians. There were several reasons for this.

First of all, NATO's actions are viewed as biased. There is more or less open distrust between NATO and the Serbs, multiplied by the more or less open historic ties between the Serbs and Russia. It might be said, with only a certain degree of overstatement, that the Russians and NATO feel themselves to be on different sides of the Yugoslavian conflict (with the obvious comment that while this statement is true for public attitudes, on the level of official statements, everybody was on nobody's side in this conflict).

Second, many Russians believe that NATO violated its international mandate when, at some stage in the action, it undertook bombing and overused force.

Third, as in many peace enforcement operations everywhere in the world (the UN has long records of this), NATO was more effective in accomplishing the forceful part of the task but proved unable to supplement and cement it with a political settlement. This demonstrates, in Russian public perception, that even while conducting non-article V missions, NATO shows its warrior qualities and is best at performing mainly violent tasks.

1.4. Russian-NATO Relations in the Mirror of Peacekeeping

Dr. Sergej Kortunov, deputy chief of administration of the Defense Council in the period of IFOR/SFOR, explains why Russian political circles remained somewhat critical towards NATO's involvement in peacekeeping: "Currently, the military structures of NATO have been created and adapted for the conduct of broad-based military operations – in an Eastern direction, what is more. The military potential of peacekeeping that is being created is not substituting for but complementing these structures." [5]

---

[5] Sergej V. Kortunov, "Treaty Couldn't Compensate for Enlargement," *Nezavisimaya Gazeta,* 13 February 1997, p. 5. See also Sergej V. Kortunov, "A Treaty Cannot be a Fee for Enlargement: Moscow Must Consider Itself Deceived," FBIS On-Line Document ID #

One of the main expectations of Russian policymakers concerning NATO transformation was a conversion of NATO from a collective defense to a collective security organization. Such a formula might not sound like a radical change to those who are acquainted with the history of European security institutions. In fact, however, changing one word ("defense" to "security") requires a quite radical change in missions, structure, and the whole essence of an organization. Collective defense means that an organization concentrates on effective functioning in times of potential war and subordinates its peacetime activities and structures to military readiness. Collective security functions require that an organization shift its emphasis to conflict prevention and political means of conflict resolution. Military force becomes simply a tool of last resort in the conflict management arsenal.

Is NATO transforming itself in the direction of elaborating an arsenal of measures for conflict monitoring, political conflict prevention, and conflict resolution? In part, yes; NATO moved in this direction by establishing links with former adversaries, by creating a category of partner nations and inviting them into joint political forums like NACC, and by performing peacekeeping and peace enforcement functions in one concrete conflict area in Europe.

Is this transformation towards becoming a collective security organization full and complete? Far from it. And not because of shortness of time, but because NATO has no intention to fully depart from collective defense functions and change to a collective security forum, which requires a quite different organizational profile. Why? The answer lies, in part, with the selective character of membership (in contrast to the OSCE, NATO is not an all-European structure). Moreover, because of NATO's unwillingness to interfere in domestic conflicts (even if they have international spillover) that could be sensitive to its members, NATO is not ready, for example, to invest efforts in a settlement on Cyprus or in Northern Ireland. NATO is definitely not ready to become a "fire brigade" that is automatically summoned for any further ethnic conflicts of the Yugoslavian type. NATO has internal skeptics who question the continued use of its resources for out-of-area peacekeeping.

1.5. WHO ACTS ON BEHALF OF THE INTERNATIONAL COMMUNITY: DEBATES REGARDING AN APPROPRIATE MANDATE

Why has Russia cooperated with NATO in Bosnia but criticized NATO severely for its involvement in Kosovo? Both cases of the use of a NATO-led coalition (on behalf of the UN in Bosnia and NATO air strikes against the territory of the Federal Republic of Yugoslavia in the spring of 1999) were undertaken without a UN mandate, which raised numerous debates in Russia as

FTS19979395991172, 13 February 1997.

well as in the West. The main issues, which might at first look be quite academic, are: who has the right to act on behalf of the international community, when is it time to intercede, and what are the limits to intervention?

The UN Charter prohibits the use of military force in relations between nations except in two cases: 1) when necessary for self-defense (Chapter 51), and 2) in case of use of military force by the UN itself or by UN regional structures on the basis of a Security Council resolution (Chapter 39). In the latter case, the use of force is permitted against the state that challenged peace or created the threat for international peace.

Basically, during the period of their creation, both NATO and the Warsaw Pact, as well as the collective security system of the Commonwealth of Independent States (based upon the CIS Collective Security Treaty of 1992, renewed in 1999) referred to the right of a group of states to act in collective self-defense.

In recent times, some countries, primarily the U.S., have interpreted the right to self-defense in a very broad sense. It is interesting to note that Russia in the 1990s took the same approach as the U.S. in this respect. In June of 1993, when the U.S. referred to the right to self-defense and undertook a missile strike against Baghdad in response to Iraq's attempt to arrange a terrorist act against President Bush, Russia approved of the actions of Washington. [6] Russia herself used references to the extended right of self-defense when, on 1–4 December 1995, Russian border guard contingents on the Tajik–Afghan border struck against military groupings on Afghan territory, in response to their artillery/missile strikes. The statement made by the Russian Foreign Ministry declared that the motivation for Russian strikes against the territory of the other state was based upon an extension of the right to self-defense. [7]

NATO, however, refused to employ "extended self-defense" rhetoric when explaining its actions in the former Yugoslavia. The mission in Bosnia was clearly defined as "non-Article V" and "out-of-area." Therefore, the only other way to justify and legitimize it was to stress that the mission was undertaken, not on behalf of NATO, but on behalf of the UN as UN-mandated peacekeeping.

1.6. UN, NATO, AND THE AD HOC DAYTON AGREEMENT

NATO's cooperation with the UN is a breakthrough in several respects. There was a growing distrust of the UN in the U.S. (both among the public and within the government) in the 1980s and early 1990s; a decade ago, very few analysts

---

[6]   Ministry of Foreign Affairs of the Russian Federation, *Statement of the MFA RF*, *Diplomatichesky Vestnik*, No. 13 – 14, 1993, p. 40.

[7]   Ministry of Foreign Affairs of the Russian Federation, *Statement of the MFA RF*, 5 December 1995, *Diplomatichesky Vestnik*, No. 1, 1996.

could imagine that, using U.S. influence in NATO, Washington would encourage operational overlap between NATO and the UN. During the same period, the Soviet Union actively backed the UN. Russia has continued to promote very active ties with the UN; therefore Moscow naturally was surprised when, in the absence of other relevant resources, the UN turned to NATO for help in Yugoslavia.

It goes without saying that Moscow took notice when, in 1992, NATO first took the decision to undertake operations under OSCE mandate and, only six months later, when Brussels extended its offer to do the same under UN auspices.

Acting on behalf of the UN has, to some degree, positively influenced the image of NATO in the eyes of part of the Russian public. But NATO's "no double key" demand (meaning that, after receiving the political mandate of the UN, NATO did not want its military chain of command to be operationally subordinated to the UN) received many negative comments in the Russian media. Some commentators said that NATO just used the UN mandate as a *carte blanche* to maintain its own interests in the Balkan region under the "cover" of the UN.

It is obvious that, because of limited resources and the excessive burden of more than a dozen simultaneous operations continuing in different regions of the world, the UN needs help from NATO (or any other organization or coalition) in implementing the most difficult peace support functions. The question is: to what degree will NATO need the UN in the future after the Bosnian experience of cooperation? Many international organizations united their efforts and worked for peace in Yugoslavia; these organizations include the UN, the OSCE, NATO, the Red Cross, and the Council of Europe, as well as not less than 400 non-governmental organizations. This was a unique demonstration of the ability of the international community to work in very complicated situations; this level of cooperation should not be underestimated. At the same time, Bosnia teaches lessons that cannot be ignored. Even when united by general goals, each organization and group of states was, to some degree, promoting its own separate interests through the Bosnian peace process.

The Dayton Agreement on peace implementation in Bosnia was reached under the leadership and strong influence of the U.S. The political supervision of the process was given not to the UN but to the *ad hoc* institution – created in Dayton – of the High Representative, who for this mission was separated from UN structures (this was one more manifestation of the lasting distrust between the U.S. leadership and the UN). Only four months after the beginning of the implementation of the Dayton Agreement and the arrival of the High Representative in Bosnia, more or less regular coordination meetings began between regional representatives of the whole group of structures involved in peace implementation. While operating under UN mandate, NATO forces in IFOR (later SFOR) expected more progress in the political settlement, not from UN political structures but from the separately created and administered mechanism created by the Dayton Agreement.

Inside NATO itself, a conclusion seems to have been drawn that the first UNPROFOR stage of NATO action under a very limited UN mandate and in the role of limited supporter was relatively unsuccessful. "Mission crippled" put the whole future of cooperation between NATO and the UN under a big question mark. Only during the IFOR stage, when NATO's hands were untied and NATO virtually took full military control over planning and implementing the operation, were the disengagement tasks accomplished. Of course, these were military tasks, while the second half of the mission – the political settlement and the establishment of a stable civil balance allowing the international military forces to leave – was considered in NATO circles to be "not our direct responsibility."

This brings one to the conclusion that further deepening of interoperability between NATO and the UN is probably not high on the current NATO agenda for the transformation of the Alliance. There would be no automatic approval for providing NATO resources for new UN operations. Relations between NATO and the UN were upgraded to a higher level by years of cooperation on actions in the former Yugoslavia, then broken in an early stage of the Kosovo crisis and reestablished again in mid-1999. But the times are gone when the Alliance sought any new mission after its old enemies disappeared. UN authority again remains respected but has become less vital for the transformed Alliance. As of this writing, current mainstream thought on NATO transformation does not aim to bringing NATO closer to the UN than it already is.

1.7. Russia's Attitude to the OSCE's Role in Conflict Resolution in Bosnia

Moscow's vision of the preferred model of conflict resolution for Bosnia was OSCE-centered, not NATO-centered. As a compromise version, Moscow was expecting a transformation of the Alliance from a collective defense organization into an organization of collective security that dealt with regional conflict prevention and conflict resolution and advanced political means of action before military functions. Some Russian analysts suggested that the ideal combination would be "OSCE diplomacy with NATO's muscles."

The Organization (formerly Conference) on Security and Cooperation in Europe (OSCE) was Moscow's "old love," since the Soviet Union was one of the "founding fathers" of the CSCE in 1975. And – in contrast to NATO or even the Council of Europe or the European Parliament – in the OSCE, Russia feels like an equal partner, not like a newcomer or alien. Russia constantly stresses the importance of the OSCE and the impossibility of promoting NATO into the position of the leading European security structure as long as the OSCE is alive and functioning.

After all, the OSCE, in contrast to NATO, provides universal political representation for all – new and old, big and small – European states plus the U.S. and Canada. And, again in contrast to NATO, the OSCE consciously orients itself toward political conflict resolution – exactly the function that Russia (with a half dozen regional conflicts on its borders) considers to be key for the new security environment.

This does not mean that the obvious weaknesses of the OSCE are not seen by Moscow. Most of them (such as the absence of mechanisms for the obligatory implementation of decisions; overload with more than 50 countries; financial and organizational amorphousness; the inability to directly undertake peacekeeping operations, etc.) are clearly recognized by Russian side. But who said that the "transformation of the OSCE" would be easier than the "transformation of NATO"? Russia agrees that, in its current form, the OSCE cannot sufficiently play the role of collective security guarantor; however, in its current form, NATO cannot play such a role, either. It is supposed that NATO and the OSCE should find an appropriate correlation of functions and responsibilities. It is not in the interests of Russia for the more or less internationally recognized political security authority of the OSCE (where Russia's role is obvious and equal) to be taken over in significant part by NATO (where Russia's role is close to alien).

The existence of the OSCE (even with a very limited role in Bosnian conflict resolution) and Russia's emphasis on its legitimacy as a security actor in the region foreshadow a definite limit to the absorption of European collective security and peacekeeping functions by NATO.

1.8. RUSSIA'S CAUTIOUSNESS CONCERNING NATO OUT-OF-AREA OPERATIONS

For most of its existence, NATO was quite attentive to the notion of "zone of responsibility." It was a natural way to behave in a bipolar world where between superpowers there was no "no man's land." Any step, any out-of-area action was immediately considered by "the other side" to be an assault on its interests or as a provocation.

The Gulf War, NATO peace support actions in the former Yugoslavia, and Russian peace support operations on the territory of other CIS states – these realities of the post-Cold War world changed perceptions of zones of responsibility. A clear division of spheres of influence in Europe (the "iron curtain") is gone. But still, in the same way that NATO is very attentive to Russian military and diplomatic moves in the "Near Abroad," Russia feels some sensitivity about NATO's growing readiness to conduct out-of-area operations.

How far out-of-area is NATO ready to go? Under which circumstances? Are there any limitations or exceptions? Is it a doctrinal change or is each out-of-area step a matter for *ad hoc* decisions? These questions are inevitably posed by Russian analysts when studying the lessons of NATO's involvement in the former Yugoslavia.

Of course, the area of geopolitical interests of any Great Power or coalition is larger than its immediate geographical territory. The U.S. has a long record of proclaiming this or that area far from its shores a region of "U.S. vital interests," for example, because some sea lines of communications important for the U.S. economy go through this region. Russia also considers some neighboring areas geopolitically vital for its security and survival. At the time of the Bosnian crisis in 1996, the real threat of Taliban insurgence from Afghan territory into Tajikistan and Uzbekistan motivated Russia to issue joint statements of warning, together with Central Asian CIS states. These statements declared Russian interests to be endangered[8] and directed additional measures of military protection along southern CIS borders. This region was considered by Russia to be vital for its own security because of forecasted flows of refugees, small arms transfers, and a possible break of regional economic ties and trade flows. These examples stress once more that the projection of interests out-of-immediate-area is not a new challenge – for either NATO or Russia. A problem might arise, however, when protection or projection of these interests takes the form of military operations with the involvement of armed forces.

The decision to undertake massive military operations on the territory of non-NATO countries (in the divided geopolitical space of the former Yugoslavia) was not an easy decision for NATO. But after the precedent was created, it started a chain of further steps violating old international "taboos." NATO proceeded from an air-only operation to the involvement of ground forces. Heavy military traffic related to the operation went through the territory of non-NATO countries like Hungary (of course with the country's permission); the use of non-NATO countries' airfields by NATO aviation became another "novelty." During the course of Bosnian operations, including NATO "surgical" air strikes and the real (i.e., not in exercises) use of armed forces in urban civilian surroundings, NATO crossed many thresholds for the first time. A particularly important line was crossed when NATO forces, in accordance

8   Council of Defense Ministers of the CIS, *Statement on the Situation on the Tajik–Afghan border*, Almaty, Kazakhstan, 16 September 1996.

with their UN mandate, proceeded from peacekeeping to elements of peace enforcement.

These first-time experiences of NATO were observed with cautiousness by the Russian government, which was dubious about many of these actions. As a member of the UN Security Council, Russia voted to support a peace enforcement operation and sent a brigade as a contribution to the international coalition. But from the other side, clear "ideological" dissatisfaction was expressed by some members of the Russian State Duma[9] who objected to the fact that the international mandate motivated and legalized NATO's evolution towards more and more broad and deep out-of-area military actions.

More than once in the Russian media, discussions artificially took NATO's out-of-area involvement to the extreme and frightened the public with statements of the following kind: if NATO got the skills and acquired a "taste" for military action in conflict areas outside the borders of its members, doesn't that mean that there are no longer any doctrinal or political barriers preventing NATO from showing up in conflict areas of the CIS (like Moldova or the Caucasus) under the umbrella of international peacekeeping? By the way, these quite artificial public fears were inflamed by some commentaries from the side of Moldovan and Georgian authorities: both at certain stages considered it possible, if not desirable, to invite NATO to provide disengagement contingents to help to stop conflicts on their territories. Thus, the shift of NATO in the direction of creating precedents for active out-of-area military operations and breaking former "taboos" in this respect was interpreted mostly negatively in Russia. UN "blessing" for such missions was perceived to be almost a "mistake" and the Russian government was more than once criticized by various representatives of the internal political opposition for taking a passive stand on the Yugoslavian issue, which enabled NATO "to impose its interests" in this conflict region.

1.9. DOCTRINAL BACKGROUND OF RUSSIA'S PARTICIPATION IN PEACEKEEPING

The crisis of the Communist regime, the collapse of the Soviet Union, and the division of its infrastructure between the new independent states in the early 1990s all had a dramatically negative effect on the status and public image of the former Soviet military. Obviously, Russia inherited the biggest and most powerful part of the former Soviet military infrastructure, but inside Russian society, the role and place of the military was seriously undermined, at least in

---

[9] These included the Chairman of the CIS Affairs Committee at that time, Konstantin Zatulin, the leader of the "Anti-NATO Commission," the Deputy Chairman of the Duma, Sergej Baburin, and others.

the first half of the 1990s, when the very necessity of the further existence of the oversized military machine came seriously into question.

Various *ad hoc* steps in the direction of reform of the Russian military sphere in the period of 1992–1996 led, among other changes, to a redefinition of the aims and purposes of Russian military power. Tasks designed to prepare for a massive war against an external threat (the U.S. and NATO) or to militarily support third world proxy regimes (Afghanistan), both of which formerly had ideological support, were now no longer seen to be relevant as a result of the political changes in the post-Cold War world. At the same time, the collapse of the former Soviet Union gave way to numerous regional conflicts as well as to domestic internal instabilities (interethnic and social conflicts) in Russia itself. Adapting to these challenges, the current Military Doctrine of Russia introduced novel possible tasks such as the use of military forces inside the country in case of internal instabilities. This doctrinal point was soon employed in practice when not only police contingents but also mainframe heavy military forces were used in domestic conflicts in Ossetia/Ingushetia and Chechnya. Both the Military Doctrine and the National Security Concept of Russia postulated further that the use of military force in the course of regional conflict resolution had become a first-priority purpose for the existence of adequately armed, trained, and ready military forces.

One of the most important doctrinal foundations for Russian participation in international peacekeeping is to be found in the "Federal Law of the Russian Federation on the procedure of RF military and civilian personnel assignment for participation in operations aimed at the maintenance and restoration of international peace and security and other peacekeeping activities," adopted by the Russian Parliament in late 1994 and signed by the RF President in early 1995. This law established (in Article 1) that Russia may send peacekeepers abroad in two cases: to implement UN requirements (in UN-mandated operations) and to implement Russia's obligations under bilateral or multilateral treaties and agreements. Thus, sending Russian peacekeepers to Bosnia and sending Russian contingents to CIS conflict spots under bilateral agreements with other CIS heads of state are both defined by this law as comparable cases of peacekeeping activities.

While the size, structure, and rules of engagement (ROE) for Russian peacekeepers abroad are, by law, defined by the President and the government (first of all, by the Ministries of Foreign Affairs and Defense), political approval "to send or not to send" is required from the Parliament – namely from its upper chamber, the Federation Council (Chapter 4 of the law).

Some legal and political aspects of participation in international peacekeeping are regulated by the collective CIS documents drafted under the strong influence of Russia, like the "Treaty on the Collective Security of the CIS States," [10] the "Concept of Collective Security of the States-Participants of the Treaty on Collective Security," [11] the Memorandum of the CIS States "On the Support of Peace and Security in the Commonwealth of the Independent States," [12] and the Concept of Prevention and Settlement of Conflicts on the Territory of the CIS States. [13]

2. THE GEOGRAPHY OF RUSSIAN PEACEKEEPING: ON A PARALLEL TRACK WITH BOSNIA

Russia's participation in peacekeeping in Bosnia took place in a historic moment when Russia was involved in four other conflict resolution operations that Moscow also considered peacekeeping missions. Russian politicians and media alike presented the deployment of Russian peacekeepers to Bosnia as a continuation and further development of Russian peacekeeping involvement in the CIS, namely in Tajikistan, Georgia, and Moldova – parts of Eurasia that remain some of the most conflict-rich areas in the world. Between 1988 and the turn of the century, military force was used or martial law was implemented 28 times, on the territory of both the Russian Federation and the newly independent states. Long-lasting conflicts occurred or continue to burn on the territories of Tajikistan, South Ossetia/Georgia, Abkhazia/Georgia, North Ossetia/Ingushetia, Moldova/Transdniester, and Chechnya. Several of these conflicts have become an arena for multilateral "peacekeeping-like" operations modeled after UN peacekeeping practices, but initiated and implemented by Russia jointly with groups of CIS countries. These operations took place in parallel with Russian participation in Bosnian conflict resolution. They should be taken into consideration while analyzing Russian participation in Bosnia, because, at least in the Russian domestic political context, they are perceived to be "in one basket" with Bosnia. The resources, efforts, and contingents, which Russia was ready to send to Bosnia, were constrained by the need to share resources with the other four active peacekeeping cases in the CIS. Commanders and some contracted officers came to Bosnia after (or before) rotation

---

[10] This treaty was signed on 15 May 1992 in Tashkent by six states (Russia, Armenia, Uzbekistan, Kazakhstan, Kyrgyzstan, and Tajikistan). Later, Belarus, Georgia, and Azerbaijan joined the Treaty. In the process of renewal of the Treaty in 1999, Uzbekistan, Georgia, and Azerbaidjan did not confirm their participation, thus again leaving the number of participating states at six.

[11] The "Collective Security Concept" was adopted on 10 February 1995 in Almaty by a decision of the CIS Collective Security Council.

[12] Adopted in Almaty on 10 February 1995.

[13] The "Concept on the Prevention and Settlement of Conflicts" was adopted in Moscow at the CIS summit on 19 January 1996.

from CIS operations; Russian peacekeepers found that their experience from CIS conflicts (dealing with secessionist trends, refugees, unauthorized military groupings, etc.) was very much in keeping with their experiences in the former Yugoslavia.

2.1. THE CIS EXPERIMENT WITH MULTINATIONAL PEACEKEEPING: THE CASE OF TAJIKISTAN

The full-scale international peace support operation in Tajikistan started in October 1993, after the completion of the most bloody stage of the domestic civil war in this region, which brought a new leadership to power in the capital city of Dushanbe. Many months of armed hostilities between the different clans and ethnic groups took tens of thousands of human lives.

Reacting to formal appeals for help from the Dushanbe authorities, the heads of state of the CIS countries adopted joint statements on the situation in Tajikistan (in October 1992 and January 1993) and an agreement on the creation of the Multilateral CIS Peacekeeping Force for Tajikistan. This agreement was concluded on 24 September 1993 after a serious sharpening of tensions inside Tajikistan and at the Tajik-Afghan border.

Initially it was decided that military contingents from Russia, Kazakhstan, Kyrgyzstan, Uzbekistan, and Tajik governmental forces would make up the Peacekeeping Force. Several months later, Tajik forces were excluded from the international contingent for being too biased. The decisive part of the force was provided by Russia: around 6,000 troops from the 201st Motorized Infantry Division (situated in the area since Soviet times) were reinforced by specially relocated and rotating contingents and means of support. Small contingents were provided by Uzbekistan and Kazakhstan, while the Kyrgyz Parliament objected to the participation of their soldiers in operations outside national borders. Less than 10,000 troops were involved in these operations (in contrast to the approved but unrealized plans to increase troop strength to 25,000). While these forces were performing disengagement and disarmament tasks, the separate but most important task of sealing the border between Tajikistan and Afghanistan was performed by Russian Border Guard troops on the basis of a formal request of the Tajik government.

Peace negotiations and the peace accords signed in 1997 proved that the settlement in Tajikistan was not a settlement between any visible "sides" of the conflict but rather a multilateral balance of power between numerous mutually hostile, amorphous armed groupings under the constant influence of the border war.

UN observers served in the area following the CIS actions. In 1995, the presidents of the five CIS states, including Russia, Tajikistan, Kazakhstan, and others, formally appealed to the UN Secretary General to initiate a full-scale,

UN-mandated peacekeeping operation for Tajikistan. This request was refused; neither the UN nor any other international organization outside the CIS expressed any readiness to undertake collective efforts to stabilize the situation and reestablish peace in this Central Asian area. Under such circumstances, the CIS peacekeeping operation played an important stabilizing role.

2.2. PREVENTING SEPARATISM: RUSSIANS IN SOUTH OSSETIA/GEORGIA

South Ossetian autonomy on the territory of Georgia became an arena for the revitalization of historic frictions between Ossetians and Georgians in 1992, after South Ossetian authorities expressed the intention to secede from Georgia. The situation was very much complicated by the involvement of numerous armed volunteers from North Ossetia (territory belonging to the Russian Federation), who actively supported their "southern compatriots" under the slogan of "reunited Ossetia." Negotiations between the Russian and Georgian sides were arranged in Dagomys near Sochi and ended with the "Dagomys Agreements on the Georgian-Ossetian Conflict settlement," dated 24 June 1992.

The task of stabilizing the existing situation was compromised by the respective sides. Joint peacekeeping or "patrolling" forces were created on a trilateral basis, including Russian as well as Georgian and Ossetian patrol contingents. Initially, the Russian part of the force was composed of an airborne regiment from the 76th Airborne Division.

Political representatives of the three sides formed a Consultative Commission working in Tskhinvali, the capital of South Ossetia. The trilateral military contingent was subordinated to the Commission as the civilian political organ generally responsible for settlement of the conflict and for providing a working interface with the governments of Georgia, Russia, and the authorities of South Ossetia itself. Since the beginning of trilateral patrolling, the cease-fire has been mostly preserved and the operation was considered a reasonably successful case of international peacekeeping.

2.3. THE STALEMATE IN ABKHAZIA/GEORGIA

Although armed hostilities on the autonomous territory of Abkhazia within the territory of the Georgian state were under way for three years, no formal peacekeeping involvement started until the Georgian–Abkhazian agreement on a cease-fire and disengagement was achieved on 14 May 1994. The agreement corrected the situation when a more or less stable area of disengagement between Georgian and Abkhazian forces was formed along the Inguri River. The mandate negotiated between Georgia, Abkhazia, and Russia envisaged the creation, with the help of Russian troops, of a 12-kilometer wide "security zone" along the river running the whole length of disposition of the armed forces of the respective sides, as well as patrolling in the Kodor valley after the withdrawal of Georgian troops from there. An additional important task for the forces was the protection of the numerous returning refugees (especially in the Galsky district) who left the Abkhazian area during previous active stages of the civil war.

Around 1,100 Russian military personnel were located in the area for the whole duration of hostilities with the narrow mission of protecting military installations and sources of humanitarian supplies without interfering in the rivalry between the parties in conflict.

In contrast to the Ossetian case, the operation in Abkhazia did not assure stable peace, partly because of an inability to resolve the problem of refugees, and partly because of attempts by both the Georgian and Abkhazian sides to impose onto peacekeepers tasks incompatible with unbiased mediator status. At the same time, various peacekeeping tasks contributed to the stabilization of the region:

- 5,000 tons of humanitarian assistance from the UN and OSCE were escorted into the area and distributed to the population, as well as 200,000 tons of economic and humanitarian assistance from Russia and Georgia;
- 9,000 refugees returned to native areas;
- 92 pieces of armored vehicles and heavy military equipment with 5,000 pieces of munitions were confiscated from the warring parties;
- About 70 unauthorized military groupings disarmed, with up to 1,000 small arms confiscated;
- More than 800 factories, schools, hospitals, and public sites on the territory of 2,500 square kilometers were checked for mines or cleared of mines.

2.4. LIMITED SUCCESS: TRILATERAL OPERATION IN MOLDOVA/ TRANSDNIESTER

The roots of another conflict on the territory of the CIS states where multilateral forces were involved date back to 1992, when the Transdniester area (populated mainly with Russians) of the former Soviet Republic of Moldova rejected subordination to the government of the independent state of Moldova created after the collapse of the Soviet Union. A separate Moldovan Republic of Transdniester was proclaimed in the region.

Tensions exploded in summer of 1992 with mass armed violence between the supporters of the central authorities in Kishinev and the proponents of Transdniestrian separatism. As the chain reaction of uncontrolled mass clashes spread, civilians were killed. Under these circumstances, a trilateral preliminary political agreement was reached between Russian, Moldovan, and Transdniestrian leaders on 21 July 1992; a basic document; "Agreements on the principles of peaceful settlement of the armed conflict in the Transdniester region of the Republic of Moldova," was signed by President Boris Yeltsin of Russia and President Mircea Snegur of Moldova. The third non-state signatory was Transdniestrian leader Igor Smirnov. This agreement provided a mandate for a quick operation separating the sides by Russian troops, which was followed by a substantive de-escalation enabled by trilateral patrols of the area to prevent unauthorized use of arms or population clashes. It is important to stress that locally involved and biased military contingents of the former 14th Soviet Army, which had been stationed in Moldova for decades, were not used in the disengagement phase. Instead, battalions of the 45th Motorized Division of the Leningrad Military District and the106th Airborne Division were relocated to the area to perform the task.

After the disengagement and cease-fire implementation, the trilateral peacekeeping forces were composed of four Russian battalions (around 1,800 men) plus three Moldovan and three Transdniestrian battalions supplied by the conflicting sides themselves.

The United Control Commission was created as the main multilateral political organ responsible for supervising peace support efforts, for further diplomatic negotiations, and for the peaceful settlement of the crisis. Formally, all military authorities involved in the peacekeeping mission came under the jurisdiction of the Commission. Though full political settlement of Transdniestrian separatism has not been negotiated yet, both sides still fulfilled their responsibilities of disengagement and the peacekeeping phases of the operation; there were no significant reported cases of armed violence in the region after the trilateral military contingent started patrolling of the area.

3. TRENDS IN MODERN PEACEKEEPING:

3.1. COMPARING THE BOSNIAN AND CIS EXPERIENCES

Within CIS administration circles in Minsk and in the Moscow-based Staff for CIS Military Cooperation, the following distinctions are usually applied. Only the multilateral operation in Tajikistan is considered to be a full-scale CIS peacekeeping operation, while the operation in Abkhazia/Georgia (while approved by the CIS *de jure*) remains *de facto* almost purely Russian. The operation in Tajikistan has a clear CIS mandate, signed by the heads of all the CIS states (all of whom participated in the Tashkent treaty at the moment of decision about involvement in the Tajik conflict). It is the only operation where the command is directly subordinate to the CIS collective bodies – i.e., to the Council of Heads of State and the Councils of Foreign Affairs and Defense Ministers. The operation is administered not by national ministries of defense but by the international Staff for CIS Military Cooperation, which nominates commanders on a rotation basis. From their point of view, this operation alone has the legal right to be considered a CIS regional peacekeeping operation. Other cases on the territories of Georgia (in South Ossetia) and Moldova (in Transdniester) are trilateral operations based on interstate agreements.

Operations performed completely internally based upon a decision of the Russian authorities and with the use of Russian forces on the territory of the Russian Federation (in North Ossetia/Ingushetia in 1992 and in Chechnya in 1994 and 1999) are formal domestic police-type operations reestablishing internal civil order and territorial integrity. These actions do not have an international, interstate character. They are neither peacekeeping nor peace enforcement by definition or content. Most of the operations with Russian military involvement on the territory of the CIS have several important features in common. Some of these features differentiate peacekeeping in the CIS from the Bosnian case, while some others are largely common to both the Bosnian and the CIS conflict resolution experiences.

1. Operations in Bosnia were undertaken on the basis of UN Security Council resolutions. In contrast to the Bosnian case, the NATO operation in the former Yugoslavia was started in March 1999 in the absence of a UN Security Council mandate. Russia's criticism of this operation is well known. At the same time, UN Security Council decisions concerning conflict cases on the territory of the CIS states are absent as well.

   It is important to mention that CIS states, including Russia, argue for the internationalization of conflict resolution in the CIS if there should be readiness for this from the side of the UN or OSCE. The UN was constantly informed about the status of the operations in Tajikistan, Georgia, and Moldova. In 1995, Russia requested, with the support of four other former Soviet states, that the UN conduct a full-scale, UN-guided international peacekeeping operation for Tajikistan. There were also OSCE statements concerning conflicts and calling for peacekeeping operations in Nagorny Karabakh and Georgia/Abkhazia.

   Many in UN circles expressed great doubts about UN readiness to initiate involvement in formal international peacekeeping on the territory of the newly independent states in any form other than observer missions. The OCSE, even after the previously mentioned decision to undertake an OSCE-led operation in Karabakh, acquired no infrastructure to conduct international operations with the use of armed forces.

   Thus, in the absence of a UN mandate, the lower-level agreements were used as a mandate for the operations in the CIS. Such mandates were represented by the decision of CIS heads of state in the case of Tajikistan; by OSCE decisions concerning Karabakh; by OSCE and CIS decisions backed by Georgian/Abkhazian/Russian agreement on Abkhazia; and by interstate agreements (with additional non-state signatories) for South Ossetia and Transdniester.

2. According to the acting Constitution of the Russian Federation, the presence and use of any Russian contingents outside national borders should be legitimized by decisions of the Federation Council (the upper chamber of the Russian Parliament) in each and every case. [14] A legal collision has now been created by the fact that, in 1992 – 1993, Russian armed contingents began to be involved in all operations in the conflict areas discussed in this article, while the new Constitution was adopted in December 1993. In 1994, the Federation Council vetoed for a significant period the participation of Russian troops in the operation planned for Abkhazia. This case has shown that legitimization of the presence and use of the Russian forces in other conflict areas could be a subject for serious domestic opposition and debate. Since that time, none of the mandates for other CIS conflict regions have been brought up in the agenda of the Russian Parliament. At the same time, Russian participation in Bosnia (in the "Far Abroad") was considered to be "too international" to undertake without parliamentary approval. The Bosnian case has been brought to the Federation Council several times; [15] Russian military participation in Bosnia has received (together with approval to send a contingent to Abkhazia) support from the Russian Federal Assembly.

3. A recognized common problem of operations in the CIS is the absence of the necessary political (civilian) control, both national and international, over the actions of the military in the conflict regions of the CIS. A positive and not fully appreciated feature, especially outside Russia, is the presence of multinational political commissions composed of representatives of the parties in conflict and involved nations inside the conflict areas (Tajikistan, South Ossetia, Abkhazia, Transdniester). These commissions are subordinated to national governments (and to CIS collective bodies in the case of Tajikistan) and provide civilian political control over the course of military actions. At the same time, a negative feature is the absence of an appropriate connection between these political commissions and international organizations (the UN, the OCSE, and in some cases the CIS).

National parliaments are also typically informed about the course of the operations only indirectly and in very general terms. For example, during

---

[14] This requirement is confirmed in Article 4 of the "Federal Law of the Russian Federation on the procedure of the RF military and civilian personnel assignment for participation in operations aimed at maintenance and restoration of international peace and security and other peacekeeping activities," signed by the RF President in 1995.

[15] Federation Council, Federal Assembly of the Russian Federation, *Resolution of the Federation Council N772 – 1 SF* of 5 January 1996 and *Resolution N33-SF* of 12 February 1997.

its entire term, the current Russian Parliament never received a direct report from the military commanders of the Russian contingents participating
in several operations on the territory of the CIS and in Bosnia. There was
also no formal discussion of the conditions facing Russian civilian and military personnel participating in conflict resolution activities outside Russian
borders.

4. According to the standards of the international peacekeeping community,
   mediators and peacekeepers should not be representatives of countries or
   forces that have their own interests in the region of conflict. That is the reason why, for example, peacekeepers from Scandinavia, Canada, or Japan
   are willingly used for operations in Africa or other regions, where their
   countries do not have any direct current interests or historic record of involvement. From the point of view of this preferable rule, all operations in
   the CIS are violations of this tradition, as the operation in Tajikistan is performed by countries of the same Central Asian region. Russia is involved
   in all operations mentioned here, while at the same time having both vested
   interests and a historic record of involvement in Georgia, Tajikistan, and
   Moldova.

   At the same time, the experience of UN operations in recent decades shows
   that use of the forces from the same region is *de facto* becoming more and
   more acceptable. As operations are becoming more numerous, "pure" contingents, which can serve in the region over an extended period of time,
   are harder and harder to provide in necessary proportions. As a comparable example, one could refer to the composition of the international peacekeeping forces for Rwanda, which, besides the Canadian and Bangladesh
   contingents, included representatives from Nigeria. One can also look to
   the example of Bosnia, where all the major European states surrounding
   the Balkans or having historic records of involvement there (including, say,
   Germany) were represented in the international force.

5. An innovation in Russian conflict resolution practices is the involvement
   of representatives of the conflicting parties in the peacekeeping processes,
   including military contingents supplied by these parties. As described in
   the case of South Ossetia, both Georgian and South Ossetian military patrol
   battalions patrolled the area jointly with Russian troops. In Transdniester,
   three Moldovan and four Transdniestrian battalions made up the trilateral
   peacekeeping force, along with four battalions supplied by Russia. Practical
   reports show the high efficiency of local joint patrolling with the participation of military representatives of both parties in the conflict. In the early
   stages, however, it took significant efforts from all parts of the multinational
   contingent supplied by the conflicting sides to adjust to each other.

6. From a military–technical point of view, both the Russian-led operations in the CIS and the NATO-led operation in Bosnia are often criticized for the use of heavy weapons and warlike tactics, as well as the use of regular soldiers in sensitive operations in civilian surroundings instead of specially trained and equipped purely "peacekeeping" contingents. This was especially true in the CIS before the first rotation, when there was a visible lack of specifically trained soldiers and officers.

After late 1993–early 1994, the situation started to change: special training camps and sites were organized on the base of the 27th Motorized Infantry Division of Russia, which has been designated by the Russian General Staff as a special "peacekeeping oriented" contingent. Peacekeeping training centers in Russia were established in Gorokhovetz and Totskoye, with training courses of 3 – 6 months in length. Staff officers undergo a two-month peacekeeping training program organized on the base of the First Higher Officers' Courses "Vystrel" in Solnechnogorsk.

Russian conscripts are no longer sent to conflict areas outside the country. All Russian military peacekeepers are now recruited on the basis of voluntary contracts and undergo appropriate training. As of mid-1999, there were approximately 150,000 military service members under contract in the Russian armed forces; this provided a sufficient quantity of contracted professionals for the Bosnian mission.

7. As for tactical and technical characteristics, operations in Bosnia and the CIS show either the same or very similar features. Changes in modern international operations in conflict areas are so significant that the notion of "second-generation peacekeeping" was coined to stress the semi-enforcement character of these new practices. [16] As, for example, the American analyst John F. Hillen has written in his analysis of the NATO peacekeeping experience in Bosnia,

> the basic distinction between peacekeeping and enforcement action ... has been blurred .... In recent missions, the rules of engagement have been substantially expanded to allow peacekeepers to impose a solution on the local parties through the use of force. Recognizable political dividends have yet to be harvested from the concept of "peacekeeping with teeth." [17]

---

[16] J. Chopra, *Second Generation Peacekeeping* (J. T. Watson Institute Report, Washington, D.C., October 1993).

[17] John F. Hillen III, *UN Collective Security: Chapter Six and a Half* (U.S. Army War College, Carlisle Barracks, 1994, p. 3).

3.2. COMMON CHANGES IN PEACEKEEPING PRACTICES OB-SERVED BY THE RUSSIAN MILITARY IN BOSNIA AND THE CIS

These changes can be summarized briefly as follows:

- There has been a shift toward earlier involvement (even if not all precon-ditions are observed) in an attempt to prevent mass violence, rather than [seeking to] stabilize the situation after blood has been shed.
- Disengagement often starts before a cease-fire is achieved, thus demand-ing warlike tactics from the disengaging contingents (Somalia and Bosnia provided numerous examples).
- The use of force occurs not only for the self-defense of the peacekeeping troops but also to put serious pressure (though with attempts to minimize force) on the opposing sides to clear the area, obey a cease-fire, give up weaponry, and other missions.
- Advanced structural composition and more heavy weapons are used for peace support purposes (including tanks, artillery, air force support, ra-dio frequency jamming, technical reconnaissance, etc.), thereby providing peacekeeping forces not only with "diplomatic" resources, but also with real combat capabilities.

The practical side of the NATO-led operation in Bosnia and of the Russian-led operations in the CIS, irrespective of the obvious legal and political dif-ferences, demonstrates significant similarities in the trends and problems of modern peacekeeping in ethnically motivated conflicts.

15. Ukrainian Participation in Peacekeeping: The Yugoslavian Experience

Volodymyr CHUMAK and Alexandr RAZUMTSEV

Outline:
1. Background
2. Main Goals of this Study
3. Legal Basis for Ukrainian Participation in Peacekeeping Operations
4. Tasks for the Ukrainian Contingent under SFOR
5. Organization and Training of the Deployed Contingent
6. Motivation for Participation in Peacekeeping Operations
7. Cooperation with other Contingents
8. Cooperation with the Local Population
9. Problems and Challenges in Peacekeeping Operations
ANNEX: *Database for this study*

1. Background

The history of Ukrainian participation in contemporary peacekeeping operations began almost at the same time as the adoption of the nation's declaration of independence in 1992. It was at that time that the country proposed to the United Nations that it give Ukraine a military role in the UN peacekeeping forces that participated in the peacekeeping operations on the territory of the former Yugoslavia.

Today, Ukrainian peacekeepers have significant experience in executing peacekeeping missions under UN authority. In all, 9,000 Ukrainian servicemen have performed peacekeeping duties in Eastern Slavonia, Bosnia and Herzegovina, Macedonia, Angola, Abkhazia, Guatemala, and Tajikistan. During those actions, 17 Ukrainian servicemen died, and 60 were injured or wounded. The level of Ukrainian commitment to participation in global peacekeeping efforts is demonstrated by the fact that, in terms of the number of servicemen involved in peacekeeping operations, Ukraine is as of this writing one of the top 25 countries out of 80. As the special Ukrainian experience in peacekeeping efforts requires special analysis, its bilateral cooperation with Poland and

Romania should also be mentioned. There is a joint Ukrainian–Polish peace-keeping battalion, and a Ukrainian–Romanian peacekeeping unit is being created.

A group of Ukrainian policemen were deployed to Bosnia and Herzegovina as a part of the Special International UN Police Forces; there were also military personnel, staff officers, military police, and military observers at the temporary UN administration in Eastern Slavonia (Croatia), as well as military observers and a group of civil policemen in Macedonia and a group of UN military observers in Prevlaka (Croatia).

Despite such solid practical experience in peacekeeping, there has been almost no reflection of these operations in research publications. As a matter of fact, this sort of information has thus far accumulated only in the corresponding departments of the Ministry of Defense, and although these data are not classified most researchers find that there are some difficulties in getting access to such data. Unfortunately, as of this writing, we have had only a few publications dedicated to this issue, such as "The Report of a Workshop on Ukrainian Security," held in Washington, D.C., in April 1998, [1] and an article by Eugene Sharov.

However, both of these publications concentrated first of all on providing an overview of the political and military aspects of the problem and did not limit themselves to the Balkans alone. The humanitarian dimension of peacekeeping activity was not discussed at all. Therefore, Eugene Sharov was correct in his statement:

> In order to draw full benefit from the Bosnia experience and build on it for future operations, NATO and Ukraine need to undertake an honest and candid assessment of the strengths and weaknesses of the Ukrainian contribution. Improvement in Ukraine's ability to contribute to peacekeeping and other joint operations will derive most directly from identification of problems and weaknesses in Bosnia. There is a strong mutual interest in confronting and eventually eliminating such shortcomings. [2]

Thus, this chapter can be considered pioneering research in the area of Ukrainian peacekeeping, focusing mainly on the analysis of its humanitarian role in this mission.

Data from a sociological survey, "Involvement of Ukrainian Servicemen in Peacekeeping Missions," were used as the basis for this research. This survey

---

[1] "Fulfilling the Promise: Building an Enduring Security Partnership Between Ukraine and NATO," Report of a Workshop sponsored by the Harvard Project on Ukrainian Security and the Stanford–Harvard Preventive Defense Project, Washington, D.C., 89 April 1998.

[2] Eugene Sharov, "Ukrainian Policy in the Field of Peacekeeping and Possible Means for its Participation in the Settlement of the Georgian-Abkhazian Conflict," *The Vector: Belorusian Journal of International Politics* 2, 1997, pp. 20–23.

was conducted during March–May 1999 by the National Institute of Strategic Studies at the National Security and Defense Council in cooperation with a non-governmental organization, the Association of the Veterans of Peacekeeping Operations of Ukraine. 98 persons who responded to this survey, about 60% of whom were involved in peacekeeping operations in the Balkans.

2. MAIN GOALS OF THIS STUDY

The main goals of this study are:

- To understand how well servicemen were informed of the country's tasks, and the importance of their personal duties in the peacekeeping operation;
- To discover the basic motivations of servicemen who took part in the international peacekeeping operation;
- To study the psychological problems that appeared as a result of communication between the Ukrainian peacekeepers and the peacekeepers who are representatives of other countries;
- To find out what kind of humanitarian problems occurred as a result of personal contacts between the peacekeepers and the local population;
- To outline the everyday problems connected to the organization and logistics related to the peacekeepers' daily lives and the peacekeeping units' performance of duties.

The questionnaire and its statistical analysis are given in Table 1 at the end of this chapter.

3. LEGAL BASIS FOR UKRAINIAN PARTICIPATION IN PEACEKEEPING OPERATIONS

The most important responsibility that faces the serviceman of any country conducting his duties outside of his nation's territory is making sure that the tasks he carries out have a national legal basis and are in agreement with the strategy of the country and its foreign and military policies.

On 3 June 1992, the *Verkhovna Rada* (Ukrainian Parliament) passed a bill "On the Participation of a Battalion of the Ukrainian Armed Forces as a Part of the UN Peacekeeping Forces in the Zones of Conflict on the Territory of the Former Yugoslavia." On 19 September 1993, taking into consideration the UN Secretary-General's inquiry about increasing the number of Ukrainian troops involved, and the Ukraine's responsibilities according to the UN decisions referring to the country's execution of the Security Council's decisions (for example, providing armed troops for UN missions), the *Verkhovna Rada* passed Resolution #3626-XII. This particular decision instituted a limit of 1,220 servicemen to be sent off as part of the UN forces. The resolution also tasked the

Ministry of Internal Affairs with providing 20 men to be possibly used as a part of the UN Civilian Police Forces.

Those decisions were absolutely in accord with the resolution, "Main Directions of Ukrainian Foreign Policy," which was confirmed with corresponding legislation by the *Verkhovna Rada* on 2 June 1993. This document announced, "further, Ukraine will cooperate with the UN in providing global and regional security by means of taking part in operations to uphold peace and will always stand for raising the effectiveness of UN sanctions' mechanisms."

It is worth noting that Ukrainian participation in the peacekeeping efforts of the world community is not regarded as merely a contribution to the national obligations that it took upon itself as a member of UN. The Ukrainian National and Regional Security Concept (Guidelines for State Politics) regards armed conflicts as well as military and political instability in neighboring countries as outside threats to national security; this was confirmed by the Parliament in the beginning of 1997. Therefore, Ukrainian Military Doctrine (confirmed by the *Verkhovna Rada* on 19 September 1993) states:

> Ukraine stands for the establishment of comprehensive systems of universal and all-European security and considers taking part in those matters an important component of its national security. Keeping a neutral nation's status, Ukraine favors the creation of reliable international mechanisms and an all-European security structure on the bilateral, regional, and global levels with the goal of strengthening trust and partnership.

The document also points out that Ukrainian military security can be achieved only through "active collective actions to resolve conflicts that appear."

Finally, at the end of March 1999, the Parliament passed a bill entitled "On Ukrainian Participation in Peacekeeping Operations." It states, "Ukraine looks upon participation in peacekeeping operations as an important part of its foreign policy." This law determines legislative, organizational, and financial regulations of Ukrainian participation in international peacekeeping efforts, and also defines how Ukrainian servicemen and civilians can be used in international contingents, as well as the organization of their professional training and logistics.

The law defines the peacekeeping operations in which Ukraine participates as international actions or measures that

> are carried out under a decision of UN Security Council, the European Security Council, and other regional organizations that are responsible for the support of international peace and security according to Paragraph VIII of the UN Charter, and all actions and measures conducted by multinational forces that are created with the permission of the UN Security Council and that are conducted under the full control of the UNSC.

According to the Ukrainian Constitution (Article 85, Item 23), any decision about sending peacekeeping troops or peacekeeping personnel that will represent Ukraine in an international peacekeeping operation is to be made by the President of Ukraine with the simultaneous initiation of a draft law for the *Verkhovna Rada*'s approval of that action.

The law specifies that Ukrainian citizens can be included in peacekeeping contingents or serve as peacekeeping personnel only on voluntary basis. Enlisted personnel of the Ukrainian peacekeeping contingent receive preliminary training at special training centers.

Expenses connected with Ukrainian participation in international peacekeeping operations are financed by the Ukrainian national budget, based upon an agreement that the expenses will be reimbursed with funds from the UN or any other regional organization that finances peacekeeping operations, if other conditions were not stated by the *Verkhovna Rada* at the time the issue was being considered. Thus, it can be said that Ukraine has developed a strong legal basis that determines the basic regulations, goals, tasks, and conditions of the country's participation in international peacekeeping efforts.

4. TASKS OF THE UKRAINIAN CONTINGENT UNDER SFOR

In the Balkan operations, Ukraine was represented by the 240th Separate Peacekeeping Battalion (400 servicemen), which was located near the city of Mostar. The battalion was part of Multinational Brigade headquarters, which were located in a western suburb of Sarajevo. This brigade was part of the SFOR Multinational Division South East (whose headquarters are located on the territory of Mostar airport). The battalion was tasked with the following:

- In cooperation with the International Police, to ensure free movement of the civilian residents and SFOR units in the battalion's area of responsibility (50 kilometers north to south, and 78 kilometers east to west);
- To control the demilitarized status of the zone of separation of different ethnic groups;
- In case of necessity and according to the decisions of the SFOR commander, to supplement the division's units with the Ukrainian battalion's own assets;
- To conduct periodic controlled separation of forces of both sides (troops and heavy armament once a month, and military infrastructure once every two months);
- To implement constant surveillance in the area of responsibility for timely discovery of armed units and heavy armament locations that are not officially permitted;

- To observe the condition of the relationships between groups of local residents and their moods, and to reveal zones of tensions;
- To execute humanitarian missions as ordered by the brigade commander (such as distributing humanitarian assistance, etc.);
- To provide settlement of refugees and control the places of their dislocation in the area of the battalion's responsibility; and
- To guard the bridge over the Neretva River.

The supporting battalion's logistics activity was conducted on a common basis and was executed according to common norms through the "Center" of the multinational brigade headquarters. The only exceptions, which were supplied by Ukraine itself, were uniforms, financial provisions, and fuel and lubricating materials for automobiles and armored vehicles. Through a mutual agreement with the French command, the battalion used standard living modules, as well as sanitary and feeding modules. Therefore, in that sense, the living conditions of Ukrainian peacekeepers were on the same level as those of the representatives of other nations.

5. Organization and Training of the Deployed Contingent

The battalion's personnel performed its tasks as an integral part of SFOR forces for a term of six months, after which the battalion became subject to rotation. It was replaced by a full battalion, which had already been trained for peacekeeping operations at the special Training Center for the Peacekeeping Forces of the Ukrainian Armed Forces. One other specialized training center was created for the preparation of a Ukrainian air mobile battalion, which was designated as a reserve unit for UN forces.

The peacekeeping battalion spent two months at the training center. Special attention was paid to combat training; learning the legal code of the country where they would be deployed; the rights of the members of peacekeeping missions; and the warrior code of behavior.

The peacekeeping battalion was manned on a purely voluntary basis. Privates and NCOs were included in the force under contract and under the condition that they continue their service in the armed forces after the conclusion of their peacekeeping mission. For the vast majority of Ukrainian peacekeepers, a second deployment in the battalion in the Balkans was not allowed, although according to the research data, practically all peacekeeping veterans would agree go again in any position.

The national experience in peacekeeping has proven to require strong coordination in the activities of key government agencies (such the Ministry of Defense, Ministry of Foreign Affairs, and the Ministry of Internal Affairs) and constant communication with the multinational forces command. That is why, in 1997, a liaison agency was created in the Ukrainian Armed Forces' General Staff: the Department for the Coordination of Cooperation in the Framework of the "Partnership for Peace" Program and of Peacekeeping Operations. Besides providing oversight of the tasks at hand, this department must also conduct constant monitoring of Ukrainian servicemen participating in peacekeeping operations, and participates in the process of choosing and training the peacekeeping contingents. Research results have shown that this structure is quite effective. None of the respondents negatively evaluated the way in which the preparation and accomplishment of these missions was organized. This was demonstrated in responses to questions concerning the level of logistics; quality of specific preliminary training; peacekeepers' professional combat preparation; and service organization in the zone of responsibility.

6. MOTIVATION FOR PARTICIPATION IN PEACEKEEPING OPERATIONS

The survey results demonstrate Ukrainian peacekeepers' full support of the policies of the state military and political leadership. Soldiers and officers took part in these missions without any hesitations for a variety of reasons. In particular, they believed that the participation of Ukrainian troops in peace support efforts raises Ukrainian authority in the world (more than 90%); provides financial resources for the national budget (50%); and helps to improve their level of professionalism (more than 45%). Almost a third of those surveyed believed that participation in peacekeeping operations in the Balkans would help maintain Ukrainian influence in the region. [3]

Research shows that the main reasons identified by servicemen for participation in peacekeeping operations were the desire to take part in the socially important act of keeping peace and to improve their own professional qualifications; [4] at the same time, however, today's servicemen did admit to seeing participation in peacekeeping operations as a way to improve problems with financial and material status.

According to this survey, almost 69% of the respondents had to make significant efforts to be admitted to the peacekeeping forces, while nearly 27.6% were chosen and sent by their command since they did not mind serving in this operation. Only 3.4% of the respondents felt they had to put out relatively little effort to become part of the peacekeeping force; they simply expressed a desire to their command leadership and were later chosen to serve in the force. [5]

---

[3] For more detailed information, see Table 1, question 7.
[4] For more detailed information, see Table 1, question 5.
[5] For more detailed information, see Table 1, question 4.

The leading motivation for the officers of the units was a desire to take part in a socially important action and to raise their level of professionalism. The privates, on the other hand, were motivated by a desire to experience the feeling of being at risk. For privates and sergeants serving on contracts, a desire to raise their level of professionalism and see new places and countries played a significantly important role (20%) in making their decision to be a peacekeeper. A desire to meet new people and experience a new culture was a motivation for only a small number of officers, who served as military observers (perhaps because officers believed they would have more opportunities for these experiences than did the enlisted men serving in the units).

Interestingly enough, there was a noticeable difference in the leading motivations for participation in peacekeeping between the Ukrainian servicemen and their Russian colleagues. After questioning the soldiers of the Russian peacekeeping battalion, Russian journalists reported that the main reason service in the Balkans was attractive to Russian peacekeepers was because participation in these operations offered them an opportunity to solve their financial problems. [6]

7. COOPERATION WITH OTHER CONTINGENTS

As stated above, financial factors were important for Russian servicemen in Bosnia. For example, they heard that U.S. soldiers in Tuzla were paid $4,000 a month. At the end of their service, these Americans returned home and were respected as veterans of war. This did not happen in the Russian Federation; nevertheless, Russians were more diligent in trying to become peacekeepers than Americans. A Russian private was paid around $1,070 per month, and a Russian brigade commander earned about $1,400 per month. Those in the Russian brigade located in Uglevik found service there to be an "American dream," since half a year of duty there helped solve a lot of financial problems for a Russian peacekeeper. In addition, it was no secret that many of Russian peacekeepers gained their positions only due to family or friendship connections. [7]

Ukrainian servicemen have daily and financial problems that are similar to those of their Russian colleagues. According to the Ukrainian members of the peacekeeping mission on the Balkans, they get almost the lowest salary of all deployed there; even compared with Russian servicemen, Ukrainian salaries were, on average, $200 – 250 lower. Nevertheless, the data show that, for the Ukrainian soldiers, the financial side of the affair, although important, wasn't the decisive factor in making the decision to take part in the peacekeeping

---

[6]   Gennady Sysoyev, "Come in!" *Kommersant Vlast'*, No. 8 (309), 2 March 1999, pp. 31 – 33.
[7]   *Ibid.*

force. In addition, unlike their Russian colleagues, almost one third of the veterans responding made no special personal efforts to be included in the peacekeeping forces.

It is improbable that the above-mentioned differences in motivations are completely incorrect or that they are the result of a desire on the part of Ukrainian respondents to create a more attractive image of Ukrainian peacekeepers, since the poll was conducted anonymously, usually at different times and in different places, personally, and over quite a long time period. Therefore, insincerity on the part of the Ukrainian respondents and consultations between them can almost certainly be ruled out.

The survey of Ukrainian peacekeepers shows that commanders at all levels as well as enlisted personnel were satisfied with the organization of command of the peacekeeping mission in the Balkans, and with the tasks they had to perform. At the same time, servicemen said they never had a feeling of inequality or of being "secondary" in relation to the representatives of other nations. The respondents also did not mention anything about language difficulties: they said that, on a daily basis and for all intents and purposes, a language barrier did not exist, as there were always regular interpreters available for interaction and coordination between battalion commanders and the brigade command.

The fact that the high- and mid-level commands of peacekeeping forces were filled by officers from NATO member states was absolutely accepted by Ukrainian peacekeepers. As a matter of fact, there were no complaints voiced about this situation. Apparently this reflects to a certain degree the belief that the general leadership of an operation should be assigned to countries that have significantly greater experience in peacekeeping activities. This belief is confirmed by veterans' full certainty that Ukraine should continue to take part in peacekeeping operations (despite the human losses), since such participation is felt to demonstrate and enhance a nation's level of authority. There were no comments or complaints regarding the scale of involvement or representation of the state in the area. Respondents stated that the only area of disparity that made them feel moral discomfort was the significant differences in salaries, which was in turn reflected in different capacities for financing rest and recreation activities. But this, in any case, was a national problem, since the financial provisions for the peacekeepers were defined by Ukraine itself.

Evidently, this relatively united and satisfied position arose due to three main factors: (a) the Ukrainian contingent's strict adherence to the officially declared policy of neutrality with respect to all sides involved in the conflict while on peacekeeping missions in a conflict zone; (b) professional conditions of Ukrainian peacekeepers; and finally (c) a feeling of equality with and lack of pre-conceived attitudes towards the representatives of other nations. (This last factor, for example, differs substantially from the attitudes of Russians towards Americans. This can be seen in the article mentioned above by G. Sysoyev, which reveals considerable sarcasm and ill-will towards U.S. peace-keepers, a sentiment that was apparently broadly shared by Russian peacekeeping forces and the Serbian population.) Therefore, it is no wonder that most of the Ukrainian servicemen established friendly and partner-like relations with the members of other nations' forces.

8. COOPERATION WITH THE LOCAL POPULATION

A similar picture can be observed in the case of Ukrainian attitudes towards the local population: with only a few exceptions, all of them – leaders as well as regular servicemen – attempted to establish friendly relations with the civilian population in their area of responsibility. Despite the fact that there is a special Public Relations service in the battalion, which is responsible for relations with the locals, a risk to soldiers' lives nevertheless was always present.

Two-thirds of respondents encountered risky situations during their deployment. Military police officers and military observers were the groups that encountered situations of risk most often, while staff officers mentioned danger less frequently. When considering situations that presented real risks to peacekeepers' lives, about a third of those surveyed believed most were a consequence of problems related to communication and cooperation with the local population. Another third attributed these life-threatening situations to mistakes made by other countries' contingents, while about a quarter attributed these dangers to force of circumstance. [8]

Those surveyed in the Ukrainian contingent about the general attitude of the local population towards their unit believed that the local people's attitudes were generally positive. This is especially true concerning the servicemen who served in the peacekeeping forces in Eastern Slavonia and Angola, and the group of military observers on Prevlaka Island. [9]

9. PROBLEMS AND CHALLENGES IN PEACEKEEPING OPERATIONS

The veterans of peacekeeping operations gave the lowest evaluation to the organization of communications with their relatives and family, and to the level of concern with their humanitarian needs. [10] A good example of this is the fact that more than 70% of the respondents had to rely on their own efforts to or-

---

[8] For more detailed information, see Table 1, question 9.
[9] For more detailed information, see Table 1, question 10.
[10] For more detailed information, see Table 1, questions 29 – 33.

ganize rest and recreation opportunities. In 1999, however, a remarkable event took place that, it seems, had no precedent in the multinational contingent of the peacekeeping forces in the Balkans: the parents of deployed Ukrainian troops visited their sons; they were accompanied by the Minister of Defense, who inspected the Ukrainian battalion. It is hard to tell whether these actions will take place in the future, but the servicemen confirmed that, despite the importance of such strong moral "empowerment," there is no substitute for the ability to communicate regularly with family members.

Despite the close-to-combat conditions, Ukrainian peacekeeping units were regularly supplied with everything necessary for routine service. Special attention was paid to service organization and combat training. [11] Respondents gave the organization of professional and humanitarian preparation a slightly lower evaluation. [12] Living conditions received the lowest evaluation; however, these low marks must be understood in relation to the generally high marks received by all other categories, since half of the respondents evaluated living conditions as "good," and more than 42% evaluated them as "fairly good." [13] There was a noticeable difference between officers on the one hand and non-commissioned officers and privates on the other regarding the evaluation of living conditions. Most of the first group considered their living conditions to be "good," while the second group mostly evaluated them as "fairly good." Evidently, a simple comparison factor took place here, since living standards for officers were generally a bit more comfortable.

These differences did not have an impact on the attitudes of subordinates towards their commanders or on the relations between them. On the contrary, the servicemen of the peacekeeping battalion were mostly satisfied with the personal relations between themselves and their commanders: there were no negative responses on this issue. [14]

The importance of this aspect deserves special attention. Unfortunately, at home, in the Ukrainian National Army, relationships between the contingents of different draft years are often still problematic. Hazing and other bullying behaviors, including abusive disrespect and frequently physical abuse of younger servicemen by older ones, are still serious concerns. In contrast, veterans of peacekeeping missions return home from duty abroad and bring with them their experiences with other countries' armed forces, who have very different traditions, attitudes, and relationships in the line of duty. The positive experiences that Ukrainian peacekeepers bring home are extremely important

---

[11] For more detailed information, see Table 1, questions 15 and 16.
[12] For more detailed information, see Table 1, questions 17 and 18.
[13] For more detailed information, see Table 1, question 19.
[14] For more detailed information, see Table 1, questions 26, 27, and 28.

and necessary for implementing a new set of morals for the armed forces of a young and still developing country.

ANNEX: DATABASE FOR THIS STUDY

Table 1. Responses to Survey of Ukrainian Peacekeepers

No.	Questions and Options	% of all*	% of respondents**
1	*Which particular peacekeeping mission did you take part in?*		
1	UN Mission in Eastern Slavonia	10.34	10.34
2	UN Mission in Angola	6.9	6.9
3	UN Mission in Tajikistan	6.9	6.9
4	Military observers' mission on Prevlaka Island	3.45	3.45
5	UN Mission in Guatemala	3.45	3.45
6	Stabilization Forces in Bosnia and Herzegovina	48.28	48.28
7	Other	27.59	27.59
2	*What was your position?*		
1	An officer in a unit	13.79	13.79
2	Non-commissioned officer in a unit	0	0
3	Private (sergeant) on mandatory service in a unit	6.9	6.9
4	Private (sergeant) under contract service in a unit	34.48	34.48
5	Officer in headquarters	10.34	10.34
6	Military police officer	6.9	6.9
7	Military observer	20.69	20.69
8	UN civilian police officer	0	0
9	Officer of UN Civilian Administration	0	0
10	Other	10.34	10.34

*This column refers to the percentage of answers by all respondents who took part in the case study, whether they gave an answer to the question or not.
**This column shows the correlation between the answers of only those respondents who answered each concrete question; some respondents did not answer all questions.

3	What was the term of your service as a part of a peacekeeping force?		
1	Less than 1 month	6.9	6.9
2	1 to 3 months	6.9	6.9
3	3 to 6 months	58.62	58.62
4	6 to 9 months	0	0
5	9 to 12 months	31.03	31.03
6	More than 1year	0	0
4	Did you have to have to make any special efforts to become a part of the peacekeeping forces?		
1	Yes, and some significant ones	68.97	68.97
2	Yes, but insignificant ones, only expressing desire to the leadership	3.45	3.45
3	No, chosen and sent by the command, since I did not mind	27.59	27.59
4	No, chosen and sent by the command, although I did mind	0	0
5	If you had to put forth a significant effort to become part of the peacekeeping forces, what was your motivation?		
1	A desire to improve my financial status, make some money	13.79	14.81
2	A desire to raise my level of experience as a serviceman	37.93	40.74
3	A desire to see new places, new countries	10.34	11.11
4	A desire to experience the feeling of being at risk	13.79	14.81
5	A desire to take part in the socially important matter of peacekeeping	68.97	74.07
6	A desire to meet new people and experience a new culture	3.45	3.7
7	A desire for a rest from the problems of my daily life	0	0
8	Other	0	0

6	Do you think ukraine should take part in peacekeeping missions, even though sometimes it means sacrificing its citizens' lives?		
1	Yes, it should	100	100
2	No, it should not	0	0
3	Other	0	0
7	If you think that Ukraine should take part in peacekeeping missions, why?		
1	PKOs raise Ukraine's level of authority	89.66	92.86
2	PKOs help promote Ukrainian influence in the region where the operation takes place	31.03	32.14
3	PKOs help contribute funds to the national budget	48.28	50
4	PKOs help raise the professionalism of servicemen who take part in the operations	44.83	46.43
5	Other	0	0
8	Did you personally encounter any situations that put your life at risk?		
1	Yes, I did	68.97	68.97
2	No, I did not	31.03	31.03
3	Other	0	0
9	What was the reason for that situation?		
1	Mistakes made by your command	3.45	5.26
2	Your own mistakes	0	0
3	Incorrect actions or mistakes of subordinates	0	0
4	Mistakes of servicemen from the forces of other nations	20.69	31.58
5	Force of circumstances	17.24	26.32
6	Communication and cooperation problems with the local residents	20.69	31.58
7	Other	13.79	21.05

10	As a whole, what was the attitude of the local residents?		
1	Always friendly	34.48	34.48
2	Always suspicious	24.14	24.14
3	Always hostile	0	0
4	First friendly, then hostile	10.34	10.34
5	First hostile, then friendly	10.34	10.34
6	Other	20.69	20.69
11	Did your leadership, and you in partic- ular, try to establish friendly relations with the local residents?		
1	Yes	93.1	93.1
2	No	0	0
3	Hard to tell	6.9	6.9
12	If friendly relations were established, at what level were they established?		
1	On a day-to-day level	27.59	50
2	On a level of wide cooperation	10.34	18.75
3	On a level of cooperation during the execution of special tasks	6.9	12.5
4	On a leadership level	3.45	6.25
5	Based on the cooperation of the mid- level leadership	6.9	12.5
13	Were friendly relations established with representatives of other nations' forces?		
1	Yes	86.21	89.29
2	No	3.45	3.57
3	Hard to tell	6.9	7.14
14	If friendly relations were established, at what level were they established?		
1	On a wide level	48.28	93.33
2	On the leadership level	3.45	6.67

	If you served as part of a unit, how would you evaluate the following aspects of your service:		
15	*Service Organization*		
1	Good	65.52	73.08
2	Fairly good	24.14	26.92
3	Fairly bad	0	0
4	Bad	0	0
16	*Organization of Combat Training*		
1	Good	65.52	73.08
2	Fairly good	24.14	26.92
3	Fairly bad	0	0
4	Bad	0	0
17	*Professional Training*		
1	Good	62.07	69.23
2	Fairly good	27.59	30.77
3	Fairly bad	0	0
4	Bad	0	0
18	*Humanitarian Preparation and Information*		
1	Good	65.52	73.08
2	Fairly good	20.69	23.08
3	Fairly bad	3.45	3.85
4	Bad	0	0
19	*Logistics and Accommodations*		
1	Good	51.72	57.69
2	Fairly good	37.93	42.31
3	Fairly bad	0	0
4	Bad	0	0

	How satisfied were you with the following aspects of life:		
20	*Financial provisions:*		
1	Very satisfied	55.17	59.26
2	Fairly satisfied	37.93	40.74
3	Fairly unsatisfied	0	0
4	Unsatisfied	0	0
21	*Systematic manner of payment*		
1	Very satisfied	62.07	66.67
2	Fairly satisfied	31.03	33.33
3	Fairly unsatisfied	0	0
4	Unsatisfied	0	0
22	*Quality/Quantity of food*		
1	Very satisfied	55.17	59.26
2	Fairly satisfied	37.93	40.74
3	Fairly unsatisfied	0	0
4	Unsatisfied	0	0
23	*Organization of meals and serving of food*		
1	Very satisfied	51.72	55.56
2	Fairly satisfied	41.38	44.44
3	Fairly unsatisfied	0	0
4	Unsatisfied	0	0
24	*Material provisions*		
1	Very satisfied	41.38	44.44
2	Fairly satisfied	51.72	55.56
3	Fairly unsatisfied	0	0
4	Unsatisfied	0	0
25	*Organization of material provisions*		
1	Very satisfied	37.93	40.74
2	Fairly satisfied	55.17	59.26
3	Fairly unsatisfied	0	0
4	Unsatisfied	0	0

26	Relations between you and your subordinates, if you had any		
1	Very satisfied	58.62	65.38
2	Fairly satisfied	31.03	34.62
3	Fairly unsatisfied	0	0
4	Unsatisfied	0	0
27	Relations with your commanders, if you had any		
1	Very satisfied	68.97	74.07
2	Fairly satisfied	24.14	25.93
3	Fairly unsatisfied	0	0
4	Unsatisfied	0	0
28	Relations with your fellow servicemen		
1	Very satisfied	72.41	77.78
2	Fairly satisfied	20.69	22.22
3	Fairly unsatisfied	0	0
4	Unsatisfied	0	0
29	Organization of communications with your family and relatives		
1	Very satisfied	20.69	22.22
2	Fairly satisfied	65.52	70.37
3	Fairly unsatisfied	6.9	7.41
4	Unsatisfied	0	0
30	Opportunities for intellectual relaxation		
1	Very satisfied	62.07	66.67
2	Fairly satisfied	24.14	25.93
3	Fairly unsatisfied	6.9	7.41
4	Unsatisfied	0	0

31	Opportunities for physical fitness		
1	Very satisfied	62.07	66.67
2	Fairly satisfied	27.59	29.63
3	Fairly unsatisfied	3.45	3.7
4	Unsatisfied	0	0
32	Organization of rest & relaxation (R&R) facilities		
1	Very satisfied	34.48	38.46
2	Fairly satisfied	55.17	61.54
3	Fairly unsatisfied	0	0
4	Unsatisfied	0	0
33	What did you personally do in your free time?		
1	Communicated with people	3.45	14.29
2	Rested	3.45	14.29
3	Played sports, read, or watched TV	17.24	71.43
34	Last Question: If you had the chance, would you take part in a peacekeeping mission again?		
1	Yes	96.55	100
2	No	0	0
3	Hard to tell	0	0
4	Other	0	0

PART III

LESSONS LEARNED FROM MULTINATIONAL INTERCULTURAL PEACEKEEPING IN BOSNIA-HERZEGOVINA

16. WARRIORS IN PEACEKEEPING: AN OVERVIEW OF THEMES AND ISSUES

Bernard BOËNE, Jean CALLAGHAN, and Christopher DANDEKER

Outline:

1. Introduction
2. History and Strategic Context of International Participation in the Peace Operations in the Former Yugoslavia
3. Internal Dynamics of National Armed Forces
4. Inter-Military Dynamics: Points of Tension Among National Contingents
5. Points of Tension in Relations between Military and Non-Military Actors
6. National Military Contingents and the Local Populations
7. Emerging Problems, Solutions, and Further Research Questions
8. A Note on Methodology

1. INTRODUCTION

It is fair to characterize the past decade as a rather uncertain era of "violent peace," when compared with the bipolar Cold War. However, it is nonetheless relatively safe to assume that one of the major missions of the future, and for some states probably the main one, will be peacekeeping operations of either the classical or more strategic type that evolved (although not exclusively) in the former Yugoslavia. This volume makes a modest contribution to the learning process that is required in order to maximize the benefits and avoid some of the pitfalls that have emerged in the complex, multinational, and multifunctional operations that have been the subject of this project.

For all the personnel involved, a key theme in their experience of these operations was that these operations could be characterized by what we term a series of "complex cultural encounters." These encounters occurred as a result of a variety of relations with their own military organizations – including the historical traditions of their own national civil-military relations – as well as with other national contingents, a variety of non-military actors, and the conflicting parties themselves. When referring to cultural encounters, we do not mean that these relationships were organized exclusively on the basis of symbols and meanings, but rather that culture provided one dimension – indeed a pervasive one – of the multifaceted relations of power and interest connecting military and non-military actors.

In this chapter, we review the key themes and lessons that have been learned from this collaborative investigation into the experiences of a variety of armed forces personnel in the successive military operations in the former Yugoslavia, namely UNPROFOR, IFOR, and SFOR. We draw on the conceptual framework and research design that informed each of the individual country studies in order to identify common themes and significant contrasts among individual states as well as groups of states. In analyzing these relationships, we turn first to the historical and strategic context of the individual national contingents, then to their internal military dynamics, before examining their relationships with other national military participants, a variety of non-military actors, and the conflicting parties. In the conclusion, we identify some of the key challenges that have arisen for those who participated in these operations. We also indicate some of the ways in which these problems might be addressed by those who will be responsible for ensuring that service personnel are as well-prepared and well-equipped as possible for such missions in the future.

2. History and Strategic Context of International Participation in Peace Operations in the Former Yugoslavia

Each of the national participants in the peace operations in this region had different historical experiences of peacekeeping, especially those conducted under the auspices of the UN. They also had different motives for contributing to one or more of the phases of UNPROFOR, IFOR, and SFOR. Some countries have a long-standing and distinguished record of achievement in the traditional forms of UN peacekeeping. In the cases of Sweden, Austria, and Ireland, for example, peacekeeping has been an expression of these countries' foreign policy positions of, on the one hand, non-alignment in peace and neutrality in war, and, on the other, their commitment to the UN as a vehicle of international peace and security. All three view peacekeeping as a way that they, as small neutral states, can help provide a context for the further development of a worldwide, deep commitment to the values of international law, non-aggression, and tolerance along with respect for the rights of small states. Canada, another traditional peacekeeping country, sees participation in these operations as a way to increase Canadian "soft power," which allows the country to "punch above their weight" in the UN and other international fora; this same phenomenon also applies to all three of the European neutral states included in this study.

Like most other countries, these European neutral states have had to redefine their security and defense policies in the post-Cold War context. They all joined the Partnership for Peace (PfP) in the 1990s, are members of the EU, and have served as active observers in the WEU. Through participation in the peace operations in the former Yugoslavia, they were able to work more closely with NATO as well as its EU partners, thus establishing a stronger presence in Euro-Atlantic security structures.

Other Western European powers shared with these states humanitarian and strategic concerns that "something must be done" about the violent conflict in the former Yugoslavia and agreed on the need to try and build a lasting peace in the region. Given the experience of ethnic cleansing and worse in World War II, it was difficult to tolerate its recurrence on the fringes of the EU. Moreover, for powers like France and the U.K., which have seats on the UN Security Council, it would have been impossible to ignore the responsibilities that go along with such positions of influence when conflicts of this kind emerge, let alone bloody conflicts on their very doorstep. [1] Along with other powers in NATO and the EU, participation in the operations in the former Yugoslavia provided larger European powers like France (as well as the U.K. and Germany) with the means of refocusing on Euro-Atlantic security structures as well as influencing the evolution of that process, including, for example, the building of a European Security and Defense Policy and managing the linkages between the U.S. and European members of NATO. (This was to lead to tensions between the U.S. and France, for example, as has become apparent in recent debates over the relationship between the so-called "European Army"/EU Rapid Reaction Force and NATO.)

Other NATO European powers, which (like France) had previously had a relatively low-key role in UN peacekeeping operations, became drawn into operations in the former Yugoslavia. One example was the Netherlands, a country that became able to become much more involved in peacekeeping operations after 1989, when the barriers on major powers playing such a role were removed. Of particular note was the dilemma faced by Germany, a central land power likely to be at the forefront of any NATO war in Europe. The initial question of whether Germany should become more involved in peacekeeping operations raised further questions about whether its forces should be allowed to operate outside NATO, as well as more specific concerns about flexing its military might in the sensitive area of the Balkans, where memories of the *Wehrmacht*'s activities in World War II were still very much alive. Meanwhile,

---

[1] Although the results of this research project do not include chapters on the United Kingdom and Germany, the experiences of these countries will be included in this chapter when they are germane to this discussion.

France had its own problems, caused by the perception that it was pro-Serb, which reflected its World War I and interwar security policy in the region.

Across the ocean, the former Yugoslavia presented a problem to the United States for several reasons. President Clinton was forced to admit the failure of the Europeans to deal effectively with a major regional security problem. He took a more liberal internationalist and interventionist view of security and defense policy than the Republicans did, believing (as did the Blair government in the U.K.) that decisions about the Yugoslav conflicts had to be based upon a fusion of humanitarian concerns, absolute values, and the idea of a peaceful international order under the rule of law; Clinton's government asserted that these tenets provide the basis of not just a good society but also a prosperous one. Moreover, they argued that there was little point in redesigning and expanding NATO as the major instrument or organization of global peace and security (in which the U.S. plays the leading role) if it was going to be seen as a failure in one of the most serious crises of the post-Cold War era. Finally, President Clinton had specifically said he would do more for Bosnia during his election campaign; he could not walk back on this campaign promise without adversely affecting the domestic legitimacy of his presidency.

In playing a leading role in global security organizations, especially NATO, the United States sought to ensure that its interests in Europe were preserved while at the same time breaking with its long-standing hostility to, or lack of interest in, peacekeeping operations, especially under the Powell-Weinberger doctrine. (This was not a smooth process and also not without internal political and military tensions within U.S. security and defense policy circles!) This also led to some tensions with other participants, as we shall see later. Yet for countries with an imperial past like France and the U.K., such operations did not constitute a serious challenge to either their strategic or their military cultures.

In any case, all powers – small and large – have a material interest in preserving the international order of states that provides the framework for peace and security as well as the economic intercourse from which prosperity derives. Failure to "do something" in the former Yugoslavia would have established a dangerous precedent in Europe and also encouraged instability not only in the region but also further afield as a result of movements of refugee populations.

Several post-communist countries, such as Romania, Bulgaria, Hungary, and the Czech Republic, also recognized that, in addition to their own regional interests in the area of the former Yugoslavia, their future security depended upon closer relations with Euro-Atlantic structures of the EU and NATO, including their ability to participate in peace operations sponsored by these institutions. Indeed, for Hungary, the very decision to participate was an expression of its newfound sovereignty and freedom from Soviet control. Yet with these states' new sovereign independence came (as was the case to a greater or lesser degree with the European non-aligned countries) the recognition that their individual security rested on participation in global security organizations, of which the Euro-Atlantic structures of NATO and the EU are pivotal players. [2] In so doing, these countries had to break with the Soviet and communist ideologies, which held UN peacekeeping operations in suspicion during the period between 1945 and 1989. Thus, for example, the Czechs had only had sporadic participation in peacekeeping up to 1989. Meanwhile, Russia was not particularly happy with the NATO phase of operations in the former Yugoslavia. Russia is reasonably content when it perceives NATO as acting on behalf of and accountable to the UN, but becomes much more suspicious and hostile when it perceives NATO as an autonomous "sub-contractor" that rejects direct control from its UN chain of command; this became a major point of contention between the U.S. and Russia in the NATO phase of operations in the former Yugoslavia. Russia's fear of NATO domination was palpable; it would certainly have preferred a UN or OSCE focus, organizations in which Russia has a greater role. This concern led to specially designed arrangements for preserving Russia's status during its participation in the NATO sub-contracted peace operations after the difficulties experienced in the UNPROFOR phase.

Not surprisingly, given their differing amounts of power in the international system and the extent to which they wished to influence the evolution of the operations as well as the security organizations that provided the framework for their actions, countries varied in the size and composition of the military units they sent. The U.S., for example, was clearly the largest and most powerful element in IFOR and SFOR, starting with 2,600 in Bosnia and Croatia in December 1995, then building to approximately 30,000 participating troops in IFOR as a result of the Dayton negotiations. In contrast, as a former superpower, the Russian contingent peaked at 1,500 (in 1994), making up about 5% of the multinational force as a whole. France, the U.K., and Germany also contributed significant forces, with a variety of approximately battalion-sized components from other countries.

At first, under UNPROFOR, the Russians were rather lightly armed, but then quickly became aware of the non-classical peacekeeping texture of the operations. Like other countries post-UNPROFOR, they recognized the need for mechanized infantry and a more robust stance for this particular "muscular"

---

[2] This is not meant to detract from the significance that these countries attached to participating in UN-sponsored operations in other parts of the globe as an expression of their commitment to the international order.

peace operation. All contributing countries recognized the critical importance of logistics and engineers, not just front-line fighting arms, and, as the French discovered, later learned to respect even more the value and importance of these combat support and service support components to the overall success of the mission. This was not only because of the way in which dispersed small-scale units have to perform their duties, as basic infantry units have traditionally conducted operations, irrespective of branch, but also because so much of the mission itself depended upon effective logistical support. This is true not just for core military tasks but also in key areas such as assisting in rebuilding infrastructure, upon which peace-building depends.

There was variation not only in the size and technical composition of the contingents, but also in the mix of conscript and volunteer components. For those countries deploying conscripts, the norm was that they should volunteer and not be obliged to serve in missions where defense of national territory was not involved. For example, 70% of the 2,700 German peacekeepers were regulars. The remainder of the contingent was comprised of conscripts drawn from a pool, of which 10% had expressed a willingness to go.[3] Sweden and Austria also sent volunteer conscripts. Sweden became concerned about the professionalization of peacekeeping to such an extent that it decided to require conscripts to spend a year away from an operation before being allowed to volunteer again.[4]

In all cases, despite the participation of conscripts, who, with proper training, have done very well in these operations, it has become apparent that these operations have vindicated the general move to smaller, more flexible, and professional forces able to operate with other countries. Furthermore, such operations, which require rapid reaction on the part of participating nations, are likely to lead to the continued attenuation of conscription and thus the end of the mass armed force in Europe as a whole. Thus, the dramatic changes in manning the armed forces, which has occurred in France, the Netherlands, Belgium, Spain, and Italy, are likely to continue to spread. This will pose problems of adjustment for some of the participants (e.g., the Czech Republic and Bulgaria) because of the expensive start-up costs in a post-communist context. Although it might be costly to make this transition, new NATO countries and other countries with aspirations to NATO membership will need to reconsider fundamental armed forces personnel issues if they are to cooperate effectively, at least on a military basis, with Euro-Atlantic security structures in the future.

It is more and more difficult for states to commit their armed forces to mis-

---

[3]   Reinhard Panian, "Warriors in Peacekeeping: The German Experience," background paper prepared for this research project, Winter 1999.

[4]   These points arose in a discussion with Alise Weibull.

sions without being confident of the support of significant sections of public opinion, especially as the public has access to near real-time and often strikingly visual information about the crises to which these missions relate (or more correctly, those crises upon which media organizations choose to focus). The country studies in this volume shed a good deal of light on recent debates about the relationship between military missions and public opinion, not least the so-called "zero-casualties hypothesis." In the face of casualties, it is difficult for a state to commit its forces to missions – particularly ones where it is difficult to identify a clear threat to vital national territorial or strategic interests – and still retain the support of the public, which is more or less influenced by the media, especially television. This phenomenon is perhaps especially pronounced in the case of ground troops but applies as well to aircrews, with consequent effects on how airpower is used, e.g., the heights at which weapons are released. This thesis has been especially prevalent in the U.S., but some have supposed that it may be a generic feature of modern democracies: missions in pursuit of liberal interventionism are acceptable – even enthusiastically supported – as long as the casualties are "theirs," not "ours." [5]

In the case of the U.S., the zero-casualties hypothesis has achieved a near mythic status. However, in recent years, opinion poll data and skillful analysis by a number of scholars have shed serious doubt on the validity of this hypothesis, even in the country where it is supposed to apply most – the U.S. itself. [6] Notwithstanding this critique, the hypothesis has entered into the discourse and assumptions of sections of the political and military elite; they assume that the public thinks as the hypothesis suggests and act accordingly. As a recent study by the Triangle Institute for Security Studies (TISS) [7] reveals, political elites fear that casualties will undermine the public's willingness to support its interventionist missions, especially after the experience of Somalia. [8] And because military leaders perceive that political leaders, in particular, think this way, then these military leaders also assume that they should only conduct missions, especially of this kind (i.e., operations other than war where no sharp victories can be achieved) that are likely to produce zero losses, especially when they are in command. This is what is known as the zero-defect mentality, which is associated with the "absolutizing" of force protection as a component of the

5   Michael Ignatieff, *Virtual War: Kosovo and Beyond* (New York: Henry Holt, 2000), pp. 161–215.
6   See, for example, James Burk, "Public Support for Peacekeeping Operations in Lebanon and Somalia," *Political Science Quarterly* 114, Spring, 1999, 53–78.
7   Now published as Peter D. Feaver and Richard H. Kohn (eds.), *Soldiers and Civilians: The Civil–Military Gap and American National Security* (Cambridge, MA: MIT Press, 2001).
8   Lecture by Peter D. Feaver on "Key TISS Findings," delivered at the French Military Academy at St. Cyr, 20 October 2000.

mission; some military personnel have even come to see force protection as a substitute for the mission itself.

National contingents were sent by states with varying degrees of domestic public support for the operation. In the case of the United States, the data show that we must continue to doubt the zero-casualties hypothesis. Studies have shown that the public's aversion to loss of life is less a reflection of a decline in tolerance of casualties and more a questioning of the merits of the operations in which they arise. It seems that the public weighs the risks and costs associated with a particular mission. A reluctance to accept what are perceived to be futile losses in a mission that is popularly viewed as pointless or less likely to achieve success is quite a different proposition from a demand for zero casualties or a decline in toleration of losses *per se*. The perceived futility or level of unacceptable risk is also sensitive to the confidence with which a President holds to a policy line and, by implication, convinces the public that it is the right course of action and one that, even at the cost of losses, will produce an effective result. If true, such findings raise questions about those who interpret modern political leadership as needing to rely on a detailed understanding (e.g., via focus groups) of what the public wants rather than offering leadership based upon conviction. Indecisive positions lead to a warier public. Thus, decisive leadership need not be stymied by what may appear to be trends towards a risk-averse culture in society at large and not just in the field of military affairs.

3. INTERNAL DYNAMICS OF NATIONAL ARMED FORCES

National contingents varied in the nature and size of the forces deployed. In addition, these forces had contrasting social profiles. Thus, while the British, Irish, and U.S. forces were drawn from longstanding all-volunteer systems, most other contingents had conscript forces, with some states having recently made a transition to an all-volunteer format (such as the Netherlands) and others in the process of doing so (such as France, which will have completed the process by the end of 2002). While officers from some countries (for instance, those from Denmark) could be ordered to deploy, others (e.g., Austrian and Swedish officers) had the choice of whether or not to volunteer – although not volunteering could, or so it was perceived by the personnel involved, lead to limited future career prospects. Conscripts in all national contingents volunteered for peacekeeping service; in some cases, such as Hungary, the consent of Parliament was also required. National contingents tended to rely on various combinations of volunteer, experienced conscripts and professional offi-

cers and NCOs (with the Russian contingent including a far higher representation of officers).

In the case of Sweden, male applicants who were not already regular or
reserve officers were selected on the basis of a completed term of national
service with a good service record. The skills required varied from specific
military skills to types of civilian expertise that were needed for some of the
more technical tasks, such as medical care, computing, carpentry, and so on.
That said, Sweden (as well as Ireland and Austria) has experienced difficulties
in finding sufficient numbers of mission-relevant personnel due to the smaller
number of those doing national service. This will become a serious problem
if the recruitment pool declines further, especially if the technical standard of
current peacekeeping personnel is to be maintained. Austria and Ireland, the
other two traditionally neutral, non-aligned countries included in this project,
also relied upon volunteers for this particular mission. Similarly, there have
been discussions in both countries about the potential need for the military to
be allowed to order soldiers and officers to serve on peace missions, abandon-
ing the long-standing practice of sending only volunteers on such operations.

Small numbers of female personnel were present in many national contingents, including those of Sweden, the U.S., Ireland, and the Czech Republic, with most performing tasks in medical, administrative, communications,
and observer roles. That said, as with the armed forces generally, the great
majority of personnel were male, young (e.g., the average age of Romanian
peacekeepers was 25), and– it must be said in this particular case – inexperienced although well intentioned. The average age of Bulgarian peacekeepers
was higher (35), while Swedish peacekeepers, like the Romanians, were particularly young, with over 50% between the ages of 20 – 25.

All contingents ensured that their troops received training before deployment. For example, Swedish peacekeepers received special training at the
Swedish Armed Forces International Center (SWEDINT), the Irish contingent
attended the United Nations Training School Ireland (UNTSI), and Austrian
and Czech personnel were trained at their own peacekeeping training centers.
Many contingents received training in leadership under combat stress conditions; responding to hostage-taking situations; the principles and objectives of
the Dayton accords; and complex ethical situations likely to arise in UN operations. Some countries' contingents were able to take advantage of international training facilities; for example, the Romanians attended both the Canadian peacekeeping center as well as their own domestically provided training
program.

The U.S. military also invested heavily in pre-deployment training, not
least because they were in the process of making a cultural transformation from

a more or less exclusive focus on clearly demarcated war-fighting scenarios to the somewhat murkier and operationally fluid missions of peace support operations. In this context, the war-fighting, military goals of attack, defend, and delay have to be supplanted by the peacekeeping goals of securing, protecting, and supplying populations, as well as the peace enforcement goals of establishing zones of separation and working on joint military commissions with non-military elements, such as political and religious leaders. The U.S. Army Peacekeeping Institute at the U.S. Army War College, established in 1993, is a central source for training in these non-war-fighting skills, although the degree of the specialized training it provides, especially in cultural awareness skills, is not yet as extensive as would be desirable.

Once trained, national contingents performed different missions based upon the division of labor of the multinational force in which they participated. These included separating the warring parties; transferring weapons to international supervision; liquidating minefields; creating local institutions; serving as the police force for the peacekeeping mission itself; monitoring the military and political situation within a sector; securing conditions for the successful operation of humanitarian and other NGOs; and assisting in the holding of elections, as in the Republika Srpska and Bosnia-Herzegovina in 1996–1997. The Hungarians and Romanians were tasked with securing free movement by restoring bridges and telephone lines and disposing of landmines, often in difficult winter conditions. Meanwhile, Ukrainian troops were tasked with providing free movement for SFOR troops as well as civilian residents; controlling buffer zones separating ethnic groups; periodic control of impounded assets of belligerent parties; surveillance and gathering of intelligence; as well as humanitarian assistance and providing refugees with settlements. The Swedes' mission changed with the participation of NATO: apart from protecting the population from assault and calming conflicting parties, they were charged with maintaining zones of separation and securing freedom of movement for humanitarian organizations as well as the peacekeeping troops themselves. Meanwhile, other contingents, such as the Russian one, were responsible for permanent roadblocks, reconnaissance, and patrolling. While they were not involved in any exchanges of fire, they did (along with other contingents) suffer casualties due to mines. Some troops, such as the Romanians, were somewhat disappointed that they were tasked mostly with engineer and infrastructure jobs in contrast to the more operational roles performed by contingents such as those from the Netherlands, France, the U.K., and the U.S.

National contingents had contrasting expectations about the mission on which they were being sent and differing motives for their participation. The Swedes, who were surveyed before their deployment to IFOR, had mixed views. Some had very high expectations, believing that the mission would provide a vehicle for them to express altruism by helping those in need. Others expected that the mission would present an opportunity to find out more about themselves and develop personally. Those with greater UN peacekeeping experience adopted a more pragmatic view, expecting opportunities to meet old friends and colleagues and earn useful extra pay. These experienced peacekeepers expected that the mission would provide opportunities to carry out important humanitarian work, while those with less experience looked forward to the task of performing well in a realistic, challenging environment. There was a tendency for Swedish veterans to warn newcomers not to have exaggerated expectations; this was connected with a more general shift in the structure of motives from an emphasis on altruism and humanitarian achievements to a stress on factors such as personal and professional excitement. Such a shift to more pragmatic motives was bound up with soldiers' realization that the prospects of bringing an end to the conflict by the end of their six-month tour were remote.

As is often the case, the motivations of the other "traditional peacekeepers" from Canada, Ireland, and Austria were similar to those of the Swedes, and equally pragmatic. Strong arguments for service on peacekeeping missions for soldiers and officers from these countries included the relatively high pay (for Austria, this was clearly the top motivating factor); the wish to experience something new and exciting; and the prospect of experiencing friendship and military comradeship. More and more, regular NCOs and officers from these countries find that successful participation in this sort of international mission is becoming not just an advantage for their careers, but also, in some cases, a requirement for promotion.

Some troops, for example, those from Bulgaria, had high expectations of their own expertise as well as that of their peers and superiors. In addition, they expected that few problems would arise from implementing doctrinal principles such as minimal use of force and impartiality; furthermore, they expected that their unit would work effectively with the other contingents in the multinational force. The Czechs were driven not only by instrumental values such as extra pay and anxieties about civilian unemployment but also by the importance of the mission to their own country as well as to the recipients of the humanitarian aid and security provided by the peacekeepers. For the Hungarians, the opportunity to make additional money appeared to be the most important motivating factor.

Motives also varied according to military background; for example, Danish conscripts focused on an exciting challenge while their senior officers (who were ordered to deploy rather than volunteering) stressed professional motives such as the challenge of the mission or the tasks. Romanian volunteer peace-keepers were attracted by monetary rewards, the possibility to use advanced equipment and to benefit from training and education, and the opportunities to travel abroad and enhance their career opportunities. Meanwhile, Ukrainian personnel emphasized the opportunities to participate in an important mission, to improve their own professional and financial status, to travel, and to experience adventure.

The motives and expectations of personnel – including their attitudes toward future missions and their own participation – were affected by the realities of their service. The Swedes were not alone in having some of their initial humanitarian hopes and enthusiasm tempered by the somber facts on the ground. Thus, for Romanians, there were significant feelings of disillusionment and disappointment, which were magnified by high and unrealistic initial expectations. However, as with other contingents, expectations became more realistic with an accumulation of experience, albeit at the expense of enthusiasm for the mission, especially after 1996. To take another example, German troops had to contend with the emotional strain of feeling unable to do more to help the local populations because, as they perceived it, higher military and political objectives meant that cases of injustice had to be tolerated. Canadians also commented on their dismay at corruption and abuses witnessed during the peacekeeping operation, noting with frustration and dismay that other contingents were active in black market activities and the provision of prostitutes to UN forces. Such unethical behavior was contrary to Canadian military and civilian norms; frustration with the lack of action against these abuses was noted frequently in the Canadian Ethics Survey. Many contingents also felt the public at home did not sufficiently appreciate the nature of the peacekeeping role being performed and the importance of their countries' contribution to crisis management overseas, although the flip side of this coin is that military personnel expressed corresponding appreciation when media reports demonstrated to their home countries that peacekeepers' jobs had indeed been well done.

As Romanian personnel perceptively reported, the peacekeeper's operational life is stressful rather than dangerous. All national contingents reported a variety of factors that led to stress during the operations. The most important ones were: feelings resulting from being exposed to danger or potential danger; homesickness; equipment difficulties; and feelings of isolation, particularly in dispersed detached units, as was noted by the Czechs. Difficulties were most pronounced at the beginning of the mission, when personnel had to adapt to novel conditions, no matter how well trained they had been. (These difficulties were worse for first-timers compared with more experienced personnel). Some just could not get used to the mission, which was more complicated and arduous than expected; these problems could then be compounded by family and separation problems.

The key concerns of the Bulgarian troops were homesickness; separation from families (which was more pronounced than among other national contingents); lack of information about current affairs in Bulgaria; and – significantly – concern about poor pay and equipment, especially in comparison with other contingents. Issues of relative deprivation are likely to be a persistent problem in future multinational operations. The U.S. (which invested heavily not only in pre-deployment training but also in monitoring stress prior to, during, and after deployment) found interesting results in surveys of troops prior to IFOR deployment that focused on stress factors. U.S. troops expected stress from the following factors, in descending order: the need to complete personal business; loss of educational opportunities; imminent separation from families and friends; concern about how the rear detachments would deal with their families; and lack of opportunities for job advancement as a result of being deployed. Troops were also surveyed during deployment and the initial stressors were found to be: having to leave family just before Christmas; isolation once deployed; high operational tempo; fatigue and sleep deprivation; and spartan living conditions in what was one of the hardest winters seen for many years in-theater. During the second and third months, significant and persistent stressors were isolation; uncertainty; confusion about the nature of the mission; lack of knowledge about the wider unit mission; distance from home; lack of means of communicating with home and loved ones; and a 7-day workweek.

In general, national contingents experienced a diffuse feeling of disappointment that arose from having had to endure a good deal of privation despite having pursued what they felt was a worthwhile mission. Many felt that their sacrifices in Bosnia would lead to only fleeting benefits; further, the fact that the citizens of their own countries did not understand what was being done or achieved did not help matters. The U.S. Army has attempted to deal with the most important stressors, especially by promoting a sense of mission (why are we here); working to reduce the sense of isolation; giving recognition to superior performance; and improvements in rear detachment functions. While due recognition should be given to these stress factors, one should also note countervailing sources of satisfaction mentioned by the peacekeepers in IFOR and SFOR including achievement personal achievement and professional development; the sober and realistic assessment of mitigating some of the worst of the humanitarian disasters, which could have been far worse had troops not deployed at all; and the sheer technical achievements performed by logistics and engineer units in building bridges and rebuilding significant components of the infrastructure of a conflict-torn society.

While all troops value pre-deployment training, many felt that improvements could and should be made, especially in the areas of local culture and customs, the political context of the conflict, and basic training in the local languages. The Bulgarians reported the need to make pre-deployment training more realistic and the value of making greater use of recently returned veterans in the process. German troops indicated that they were given insufficient psychological preparation for the stresses and strains that they would face on operational tours. [9]

Troops from a number of the countries studied valued surveys of personnel and the use to which data collected in this way could be used to improve conditions, e.g., by providing effective social-psychological support not only for those deployed but also for their families. Some contingents expressed concern about the duration of and intervals between tours. For example, the Swedes linked the issue of tour intervals with what they considered to be the problem of an incipient professionalization of peacekeeping service, which could, in turn, lead to the development of a stressed and maladjusted military group at the margins of Swedish society. [10] Related concerns about professional burnout and the high personal price for frequent deployments were expressed by some of the other traditional peacekeepers in this study, including the Austrians, Canadians, and the Irish, who have had to maintain a similar high operational tempo in increasingly complex and difficult missions while still relying on all-volunteer peacekeeping contingents. In addition to the above stresses arising from deployments, national contingents also experienced problems related to working with their professional colleagues and superiors in the chain of command, as well as dealing with the challenges to their professional self-identity and ethos.

Peacekeeping operations, by their very nature, are characterized by a tendency for forces to be dispersed in relatively small units far away from their bases. This situation consequently requires lower-level commanders to have a degree of command autonomy, even though, for political-military reasons, there are pressures working in precisely the opposite direction. Given that the smallest tactical decision can have operational and even strategic consequences, there is always a tendency for higher-level commanders and politicians to use communications technology (especially when under pressure from

---

[9]   Panian, *Ibid.*

[10]   Bernard Boëne, Christopher Dandeker, Jürgen Kuhlmann, and Jan Van Der Meulen, "Armed Forces, State, and Society in Sweden: A View from a Wider European Perspective," in Jürgen Kuhlmann and Alise Weibull (eds.), *Facing Uncertainty*, Vol. 2 (Karlstad, Sweden: Swedish National Defense College, 2000).

media reportage of events) to claw back some of the autonomy that military necessity requires them to give to lower levels of command. [11] Examples of the
attendant problems arising from these tensions between local autonomy and
centralization – which can be termed the "dialectic of control" – are neatly
demonstrated by the Dutch experience. The Dutch found that dispersal required quite junior personnel – lieutenants or sergeants – to respond to serious local problems, such as human rights abuses. These problems could be
magnified if there was a need for rapid response in situations where no clearly
defined and appropriate courses of action were laid down in the procedures;
in this context, higher-level commanders had to trust their subordinate commanders to assess the situations correctly and then take appropriate action – a
nice example of the implementation of the principle of mission command in a
peacekeeping context. The Dutch found that, with the first rotation of troops
to IFOR, their commanders had high degrees of autonomy; in many respects,
they had to find out for themselves the best way of operating – despite the fact
that they had to work within what they had found to be rather restrictive regulations. The Swedes experienced restrictions in UNPROFOR, stemming not
just from lack of consent from warring parties but also from the political level,
a problem that persisted during NATO period.

For other contingents, there was a need to deploy professionally able commanders. The Hungarians discovered that their deployments coincided with a
50% reduction in the professional component of their armed forces. It was not
until 1995 that a group of officers emerged who were capable, in a peacekeeping context, of commanding large contingents. The Romanians, too, acquired
significant peacekeeping experience in Bosnia-Herzegovina, thus adding to the
command potential of their forces; some 2,000 of their troops gained peacekeeping experience through their participation in these operations, including
their chief of operations on the General Staff. Military command issues were
also connected with problems of coordination between the armed forces and
other national agencies, such as departments of foreign and internal affairs.

Quite apart from problems connected with cooperating effectively with
other national contingents, national armed forces also had to deal with issues
of internal coordination (on which senior officers of the Danish contingent
spent just over half of their time) and, at times, rivalry between one or more of
their force elements. The Dutch contingent had to deal with significant rivalries between different branches. For example, during the IFOR deployment,
a conventional infantry battalion was deployed (minus one company) along

---

[11]   For a general discussion, see also Christopher Dandeker and Bernard Boëne, "Post-Cold
War Challenges and Leadership Strategies in West European Military Institutions," in Gwyn
Harries Jenkins (ed.), *Leadership for Change* (Centre for Research on Military Institutions
for the European Research Office of the U.S. Army Research Institute, 1999).

with a tank squadron and military engineer and medical units. The units were divided into three teams, one led by a cavalry major and the other two by infantry majors. In 1996, this structure for deploying in peace support operations was not well known; thus, a team commander had under his command a unit that he did not know how to use effectively. In one case, after the demilitarization of warring factions, local mayors had asked IFOR not to use their tanks anymore. Team commanders then had to think creatively about how best to use their cavalry soldiers in this new tactical context. This was not too difficult for the cavalry officers, but the infantrymen had more problems responding to this situation. There were also conflicts between engineers and the team commander, for example, on how quickly roads could be cleared of mines. The team commander would press for more speed so as to make roads available for patrols while the engineers were, understandably, more cautious. The Dutch found that inter-branch tensions were higher during the SFOR phase than during IFOR. For example, maneuver units felt that they performed operational – and thus relatively high-risk – tasks, compared with others, such as repair and medical personnel, who did not leave the base camp. This led to something approaching a division between "real soldiers" and the "nine to fivers."

Such a division within the contingents themselves raises more general questions about military ethos and identity according to how different national contingents experienced the peacekeeping mission. In recent years, the question of what effect peacekeeping has had on military ethos, especially that of the war-fighter, has become a significant theme in the literature. It is well known, for example, that in the British doctrinal tradition, the best peacekeepers, especially in the complex and uncertain world of strategic peacekeeping, are those well versed in the practicalities of high-intensity war-fighting. In short, while war-fighters can (with appropriate training) adjust to peacekeeping, it is not easy for troops to adjust the other way. It is for this reason that, shortly before his retirement, Sir Charles Guthrie (former Chief of Defense Staff) expressed (like his predecessors) a concern that British soldiers must be assured adequate resources and time to train in war-fighting so that they do not become transformed into a peacekeeping or a *gendarmerie* force, ill-equipped in terms of materiel, psychology, and ethos for the business of war. [12] As noted above, while the U.K. is content with having its soldiers continue to take part in peacekeeping operations so long as their war-fighting ethos is not damaged, the U.S. is still in the process of managing a shift to such a posture.

The Swedes provide a fascinating case of a culture of classical peacekeeping, confronting and adjusting to the demands of the more muscular forms of

---

[12] General Sir Charles Guthrie, speech at the Royal United Services Institute (RUSI) on 22 December 2000.

peace operations to be found in Bosnia-Herzegovina, especially in the shift from UNPROFOR to IFOR and SFOR and their cooperation with NATO. Survey data show the emergence of two distinct types of peacekeeper. The first holds a traditional or "classical" view of peacekeeping, consistent with Sweden's longstanding contribution to the UN. For those identifying with this role, being part of a contingent of heavily armed troops with the capability of adopting a robust strategic approach to conflicting parties is anathema. In contrast, the second viewpoint embraces a more warrior-like role, consistent with a strategic approach to peacekeeping, while also including the requirement for diplomatic skills – a diplomat in combat gear, as it were. Whichever of these identities is finally adopted by the Swedes, both types emphasized the need for in-depth training in the culture and traditions of local warring factions.

Although all the Danish senior officers surveyed regarded themselves as military professionals, 80% mentioned the significance of the role of mediator and ambassador and just over half mentioned the role of humanitarian worker, indicating a shift in self-identity from the Cold War era. The Irish and Austrian militaries also seem to be adjusting well to the prospect of participating in more robust peacekeeping operations. Participants from both countries remarked that they were pleased – despite their countries' declaratory policies on neutrality – to be included in the NATO operations in the former Yugoslavia. This is true on the governmental level, as well; the Irish *Dáil* has adopted legislation allowing Irish participation in more muscular peace enforcement operations, adapting to changing peacekeeping requirements. Anecdotal evidence appears to support the claim that those serving in the military in both countries seem eager to move beyond traditional peacekeeping toward more robust capabilities – even advocating changes and modernization of equipment to allow for better capabilities in these operations.

Germany's peacekeepers, meanwhile, discovered that while, for historical reasons, they could not – and perhaps should not – model themselves on the expeditionary concept of military operations characteristic of their French and British allies, they could operate successfully and with some pride in a complex multinational peace support operation. [13] For former members of the Warsaw Pact, such as the Czech Republic, participation in the Bosnia-Herzegovina operations provided evidence of their capacity to operate professionally in a modern multinational operation, thus demonstrating their capability of being a competent member of the NATO alliance. An additional consequence of their participation was that the professionally competent performance of the Czechs also raised the prestige of the armed forces domestically. Somewhat in contrast, the conduct and attitudes of Romanian military personnel during the op-

---

[13]   Panian, *Ibid.*

eration indicated the persistence of traditional military values and a slowness in adopting key elements of peacekeeping culture.

Meanwhile, for the U.S. (as for the U.K.), participation in these operations led to serious concerns about an erosion of the capacity of the armed forces to maintain its war-fighting ethos – a concern that is connected with the broader problems of resource constraints or "overstretch." Quite simply, the United States – like the United Kingdom – was asking its diminished armed forces to conduct more and more missions with decreased resources.

The data, however, indicate that one should be cautious about assuming that participation in peace support operations necessarily degrades the combat effectiveness of U.S. forces. The main concern of many leaders in the U.S. armed forces during the Bosnia operations was that if the U.S. had to be ready to fight two nearly simultaneous regional wars, then additional peace operations would blunt the sword of the U.S. military. Their reasoning was as follows:

1. Deployed units are unable to practice relevant war-fighting skills;
2. There are also negative consequences for supporting units, as well as the unit having just returned and the one preparing and training to deploy;
3. The brigade cannot train for combined arms combat operations because a subordinate armor or infantry unit has deployed to a peace operation; and
4. Such peace operations divert vital equipment from being used for combat training.

The U.S. chapter, however, suggests it is hard to infer a general deterioration of overall readiness from participation in peace operations. On the other hand, a specific "first [or second] to fight" division's readiness might suffer in this way. Survey data of the next generation of senior officers indicate that they are concerned about this relationship between peace operations and combat effectiveness. On the other hand, other data indicate a reverse relationship, not least the idea that peace support operations can sharpen unit leadership and other skills. While more research is needed on this theme, it seems that much depends on which skills sets are being practiced in a peace support operation. Insofar as basic combat skills are not used in peace operations, then mechanized infantry, armored units, and heavy-equipment-dependent units are likely to suffer the most. This is in contrast to logistics, support, intelligence, and command and control branches. Again, what may well be the crucial factor is less the participation in peace support operations*per se* and more the provision of resources and training time for war-fighting training.

A far more serious issue for the U.S. (and a point of tension in its relations with other national contingents) is the emphasis the U.S. forces place upon force protection in comparison with the achievement of the mission, especially when compared with, for example, other large powers like either the French or British forces in-theater. There is some evidence to suggest that this is linked to casualty and risk aversion by senior military political leaders: military leaders do not want serious problems occurring on "their watch," not least because they perceive political leaders as extremely casualty-sensitive. In turn, both military and political leaders assume that the mass public shares their concerns, which is in the face of evidence that points in a contrary direction, as has been noted above. [14]

4. INTER-MILITARY DYNAMICS: POINTS OF TENSION AMONG NATIONAL CONTINGENTS

It is hardly surprising to find that, in a complex multinational operation engaged in a difficult mission, there will be conflicts and difficulties as well as relations of cooperation between one or more of the participating national contingents. These relationships should be placed in context, as inter-military connections formed only one nexus of a complex set of linkages between each military contingent and a variety of other non-military agencies. For example, in the Danish case, their military personnel were in regular contact with 19 different agencies, of which only a few were military: the Multinational Division North [MND(N)], the Nordic–Polish Brigade, and the Baltic and Danish soldiers within the Danish Battalion. It is also important to note that the mere existence of tensions should not lead one to assume that, in and of themselves, these would lead to inefficiencies or disintegrative consequences; as in other areas of life, such tensions can produce innovative solutions and increased co-operation – in short, they can lead to synergies. These tensions, which are derived from inequalities in the distribution of organizational power, language, and communications difficulties as well as broader contrasts in military culture or "ways of doing business," affected the contingents' interpretations of what the mission was and how best to achieve it.

Clearly, in operations of this kind, there is not only a division of labor but also a division of power, with a hierarchy stretching from the most powerful (the U.S., the non-European superpower) to the major western European powers, such as the U.K., France, Germany, the Netherlands, and so on, down to smaller players, including the former Warsaw Pact nations. Russia's unusual relationship to the NATO command structure at SHAPE and in MND(N) and its unconventional chain of command were both demonstrations of its former power and continuing influence, as well as an effort on the part of NATO to include Russia as an active participant in these important peace initiatives. One

---

[14]   See TISS study at http://www.unc.edu/depts/tiss/RESEARCH/CIVMIL.htm and Burk, *Ibid*.

of the arguments for maintaining a capability of providing a major component to such a multinational operation is that this also provides the means of influencing, if not co-leading, the coalition that underpins such operations. [15] The power of the U.S. in IFOR/SFOR was rooted in its occupancy of key positions (military commander of NATO, commander of SFOR, and within SFOR, commanding positions in intelligence operations, civil-military relations, and public information, as well as command of special operations and support). The U.S. so dominated the process of policy development and implementation that it often had decided upon courses of future action before headquarters had reached a decision. Officers of other nations (especially the Europeans) could understand why this was the case but still found U.S. supremacy, once the U.S. became actively involved, rather difficult to accept; this was particularly the case for the French.

Some tensions can arise even without the existence of major conflicts between different systems of values, as was apparent in the Nordic–Polish Brigade. Apart from obvious language difficulties, other problems arose due to differences in the lengths of tours; the fact that some officers volunteered for service (Norway) while others did not (Denmark); and the fact that some contingents had a different force mix in terms of the balance of conscripts, reservists, and regulars. There can also be significant cultural differences concerning attitudes towards the consumption of alcohol, power-distance relations between officers and men, and expectations of the extent to which soldiers should demonstrate initiative – as was evident, for example, with the Danes' views of Baltic soldiers. In addition, there were differences connected with conditions of service and "perks," such as the chance to bring one's spouse on tour, the quality of equipment such as personal computers and mobile phones, and differences in military procedures arising from NATO membership status. Furthermore, other things being equal, NATO membership also bestowed greater status and influence on a national contingent. It is interesting to note that while it was quite normal and acceptable to the Ukrainian contingent that a greater contribution normally led to greater influence in the multinational force, this was less the case among Russian soldiers. This was connected with the special political-military relations set up for integrating the Russians into the multinational command structure.

Not surprisingly, links between NATO and non-NATO contingents could lead to some difficulties. Thus, the Czechs experienced some problems between battalion and brigade commands in what was their first opportunity to work alongside NATO in IFOR/SFOR missions. There was insufficient famil-

---

[15] See RUSI *Whitehall Paper* 50, "Coalitions and the Future of UK Security Policy," International Centre for Security Analysis, 2000.

iarity with operating procedures and work at the headquarters level and also problems of compatibility between communications systems. All these difficulties created some tensions between the Czech command and higher command levels, although these problems were gradually resolved. This involved an important learning exercise and confirmed the need to improve the personnel's command of English as a working language (a point that applied also to the Bulgarians and the Romanians, who found that language difficulties could lead to misunderstandings and problems, even if no ill-intent had been involved). [16]

Also mentioned as issues of concern were: the need for respect for command structures; the requirement for the multinational command to coordinate the activities of national units, especially neighboring units; the necessity of ensuring cooperation with national forces in preparatory and training phases; and also, significantly, the need to share certain classified information. The frustration over lack of access to classified information was shared by other non-NATO members of the peacekeeping force, including to a certain extent the Irish, who, as native speakers of English, generally have had an easy working relationship with the U.S. and U.K. contingents, in particular. The Irish were able to successfully work around a lack of access to NATO-only classified information because of these good relations; however, frustration over lack of access to classified material was an issue that was brought up in a number of interviews and press accounts.

Command of language was also connected with other issues of power: this is why the French were concerned about using French (see below). More generally, all countries, and not just the French, saw command of the English language as a key advantage for the English-speaking powers (the U.S., U.K., Canada, and Ireland) in the multinational operation and a disadvantage for others (e.g., those from Southern, Eastern, and Central Europe). At meetings, the use of English argot could place contingents without a strong command of English at a distinct disadvantage, which some felt acutely.

As was to be expected, inter-military relations were not free from stereotypical cultural expectations, although these expectations were not immune to change in the light of experience. For example, after serving in Bosnia, the Dutch did not regard the soldiers of the U.K. and U.S. to be as outstanding as they had expected them to be, while the Russians turned out not to be as bad as some had feared. During their deployment, the Dutch found that their opinion of themselves, in comparison to their opinion of other contingents, became

---

[16] On the other hand, many members of these contingents were proud to report their belief that they were able to communicate better and more easily with the local population than members of other contingents, thanks to the similarities between their languages and social customs.

stronger, with a decreasing feeling that they were worse than others. On the other hand, the feeling that they were better than others (with the exception of the British) had to be adjusted downwards. At the end of the mission, the Dutch peacekeepers saw themselves as "less bad" in comparison with other contingents than they had expected. In the beginning, they had had a good deal of respect for the U.S. and British troops, but by the end of the mission, this attitude had disappeared. The Americans considered their allies to have less discipline, as reflected in appearance, promptness, adherence to chain of command, and after-hours behavior. Moreover, there was a perception that non-U.S. units "improved" in each of these categories within a short span of time and as a result of the example and expectations set by American troops. These judgments may well tell us as much about professional self-evaluation as they do about the objective performance of other contingents.

Meanwhile, it was not surprising to note that some ex-Warsaw pact countries were sensitive to the ways in which they appeared to be treated in comparison with other contingents. For example, the Bulgarians felt that, in comparison with other contingents, they were given riskier jobs and had inferior quality equipment; in general, they felt like second-class citizens. They were not the only contingent to experience a perception of relative deprivation; the Romanians reported that they felt they were "stuck with" inferior work while other contingents got on with the business of "real peacekeeping." However, the Ukrainians felt little such deprivation, although their pay was substantially less than that of the Russian, let alone the American, soldiers. (It should be noted that the more "warrior-style" soldiers did feel more uncomfortable about such pay differentials.)

Working with the Dutch, the Bulgarians noticed the divergence in wealth as well as equipment. Yet these cultural differences were associated with harmony rather than disharmony. This was because of the efforts the Dutch made to build good relations with their partners; small symbolic gestures included a welcome speech partly in phonetic Bulgarian, the production of a new badge for the binational unit, and acknowledgement of the craft skills displayed by the Bulgarians, who had made excellent use of limited and simple equipment. This acknowledgement of the Bulgarians' contributions by the Dutch leadership made a huge difference in binational working relations.

The Czech chapter pointed out the fact that the Czech contingent took full advantage of their participation in the multinational operation to compare their professional abilities with those of their partners. (This was true for most of the contingents, particularly those working with NATO for the first time.) The Czechs worked mainly with the U.K., Canada, and the U.S., but also with Jordan, Kenya, Indonesia, and Malaysia as well as Hungary, Poland, and Slovakia.

They regarded themselves as superior technically to the non-European forces and other post-Communist forces. They also saw little reason for a lack in self-confidence when comparing themselves with western European contingents. They saw their professional qualities as comparable with the French, British, and Canadians, while they viewed their equipment as superior to that of the Germans and the British. They even saw themselves as better disciplined than the Germans. Finally, they had the extra advantage over many other (particularly non-Slavic) contingents in that they were able to communicate effectively with the local populations.

As was mentioned briefly above, one of the most serious points of tension in inter-military relations was the emphasis that the U.S. placed on force protection. The U.S. country study details the reasons behind and the benefits of U.S. force protection efforts; it must be noted, however, that this issue created tensions both within the U.S. forces as well as in its relations with other national contingents, who perceived that this posture made it difficult to build effective relations with the local populations. The more relaxed attitude of the European contingents was palpable. For example, it is a well-known feature of British military culture that patrolling soldiers are willing and able to mingle with the local population in pursuit of their peace mission without the paraphernalia of force protection seen to be required by the U.S. who, from a European perspective, are overly fond of what night be termed a "siege mentality."

As the Danes remarked, U.S. officers up to the rank of lieutenant colonel often have a "zero defect mentality" and are not prepared to take even minor risks. Europeans view force protection to be the main U.S. army objective in Bosnia, whereas for the Europeans, it is merely one important consideration among others. On the other hand, the U.S. personnel found the European attitude insensitive to the special value that hostile parties attach to achieving a U.S. casualty; thus, they felt that an emphasis on force protection was not unreasonable when viewed in its wider context.

While tensions between the U.S. and European contingents was a significant feature in the reports of almost all of the contingents surveyed in this study, it is important not to lose sight of the other side of the coin: that a wide variety of relations characterized by effective cooperation were also established and that US–Russian cooperation was one of the great success stories of IFOR. U.S. troops worked closely with MND(N), the Nordic–Polish Brigade, and, as far as combat support branches were concerned, most of the other national contingents. Survey data indicated that U.S. officers with experience of higher command levels cited tensions more frequently, which is not surprising given that, at higher levels, divergences in national visions of the nature of the mission are most likely to be brought into sharp relief.

One of the most serious inter-military tensions occurred between Danish and U.S. personnel (although the numbers of Danish personnel involved in the survey must make one cautious about drawing too many firm conclusions). As far as the Danes were concerned, the most problematic relationship they had in their inter-military relations was with the U.S. at MND headquarters. There were three reasons for this tension: divergent national values and organizational principles, command and control problems, and, finally, daily working relationships.

Other countries had their own inter-military problems. For example, one can consider the Dutch experience in the multinational brigade headquarters, where their two units had to work with four French and four British units and fought successfully in Operation DELIBERATE FORCE against the Bosnian Serbs. Three key issues emerged. First, this multinational group operated more slowly than a wholly national unit because of the friction created by language difficulties, a process not helped by the insistence of French personnel on using bilingual translations at meetings when English would have sufficed. Second, confirming other studies from the business world, the national contingents had rather different management styles. [17] The Dutch and the British felt that an effective way of working was for staff to work out solutions and present them to the commander for decision in consultation with the staff. In contrast, when the French commander was presented with a problem, he would reflect and then provide a solution, which he would subsequently present to the staff for detailed elaboration and implementation. Similarly, the French commander was irritated to find that British subordinates were working on solutions to looming problems without consulting him, when, in fact, the British were only doing what came naturally to them, namely working out problems in advance in order to present options to the commander in an effort to expedite operations more effectively.

Differences in management style became very apparent when dealing with violent incidents. For example, the Dutch, who are used to devolved governance or mission command, were surprised to see that, although such models are popular in American management theory, they do not seem to be applied in the U.S. military, where heavy-handed micro-management seems to them to be the order of the day. This was a point often noted by the Swedes, too, who

---

[17] See Geert Hofstede, *Culture's Consequences: Comparing Values, Behaviors, Institutions and Organizations Across Nations*, 2nd Edition, (Thousand Oaks, CA: Sage Publications, 2001); "Country versus Sector Effects: Out with the Old, in with the New," IBCA, March 2002, www.bcaresearch.com; "Employee Satisfaction in the World's 10 Largest Economies: Globalisation or Diversity?" ISR International Survey Research, www.irsurveys.com.

had expected a NATO more attuned to mission command than was actually the case. At the same time, when confronted by high-risk situations, U.S. soldiers tended to behave like warriors, in contrast to the Europeans, who tended to opt for a mediating or supervisory role when faced with violent conflicts between the local parties. The other side of the coin of the Americans' "siege mentality" associated with force protection is over-reaction with force in high-risk situations: both sides of the coin point to the need for a more modulated approach to the use of force in peacekeeping.

Third, the rank and hierarchy of multinational headquarters tended to be too top-heavy. The French and British opted to send higher-ranking officers than was necessary in order to maximize their influence in the headquarters, a process of rank inflation (known as "Star Wars"!) that was seen as unnecessary and counter-productive by the Dutch, who are more relaxed about hierarchies. Yet the Dutch could afford to be more relaxed, because the French and British governments had more at stake in terms of their influence and the roles that both countries wished to play in the multinational operation as a whole. The French, British, and U.S. personnel formed national networks in the headquarters and elsewhere in various echelons in order to maximize their national influence in the structures of the multinational force as a whole.

5. POINTS OF TENSION IN RELATIONS BETWEEN MILITARY AND NON-MILITARY ACTORS

Strategic multinational peacekeeping operations of the kind witnessed in the IFOR and SFOR missions that succeeded UNPROFOR are marked by a remarkable complexity. One significant aspect of this complexity is the linkage between military components and a range of governmental and non-governmental actors other than those representing the warring parties. These include the national governments of the countries participating in the military operations, NATO, the UN, and a range of non-governmental organizations (NGOs); it is to the latter that particular attention is paid in the present discussion. As the U.S. experience indicates, the term "NGOs" embraces a diversity of actors. There are useful distinctions to be drawn (as they are in U.S. Joint Doctrine) between international organizations with "global influence, such as the United Nations and the International Committee of the Red Cross," NGOs, and "transnational organizations of private citizens that maintain a consultative status with the Economic and Social Council of the United Nations." John Garofano, the author of the U.S. case study, explains, "NGOs may be professional associations, foundations, or simply groups with a common interest in humanitarian assistance activities. NGO is a term normally used by non-U.S. organizations." Meanwhile, private voluntary organizations (PVOs) are described as "private, nonprofit humanitarian assistance organizations involved in development and relief activities. PVOs are normally United States based."

In the discussion of the U.S., the term NGO is used to refer to all three of the above. The U.S. experience is notable for a number of reasons. First, in addition to the participation of many different military contingents, the armed services had to deal with a bewildering number and variety of NGOs; Bosnia was little different from other operations, such as Somalia, in this regard.[18] Yet despite the demonstrated success of other countries in making links between the military and NGOs in peacekeeping missions, the U.S. has not devoted enough time to these issues. Until recently, Combined Joint Task Forces (CJTFs) have not made sufficient use of the expertise of NGOs. One of the reasons for this is the divergence in culture and leadership style of these two very different types of organizations. Working effectively with NGOs requires consensus-style decision-making, a degree of humility towards the local population that both sets of organizations are trying to assist, as well as a flexible attitude towards the value of non-military ways of doing business. Tensions can arise when NGOs see the military as overly bureaucratic, hierarchical, and inflexible while the military, in turn, regards NGO personnel as "children of the 1960s."

Yet both sets of organizations require the assistance of the other for overall success in the field of operations. This was evident in the Czech experience, where there was a realization that NGOs may often have greater local knowledge than the military contingents; these organizations can thus be extremely valuable rather than being an unwanted source of obstruction. That said, even when working relations are excellent, as seemed to be the case with the Danes and personnel from other traditional peacekeeping countries like the Swedes, Austrians, and Irish, the withholding of information could prove to be a source of tension. It goes without saying that most if not all NGOs understand that they need the military to provide order and security if they are themselves going to be successful in delivering humanitarian aid; therefore, cooperative and pragmatic attitudes on both sides are likely to produce effective results.

The Romanians, too, noted the value of NGOs and, despite some concerns about the discriminatory distribution of humanitarian aid, thought that without the NGOs, the local population would never have received effective help. German troops based their working relations with NGOs on a "complement, don't supplant" philosophy in order to avoid stirring NGO fears of unfair com-

---

[18]   At the start of U.S. participation in UNITAF (the United Nations International Task Force), there were 38,000 troops drawn from 21 nations as well as 49 UN organizations and NGOs; by the time the U.S. withdrew from the operation, the number of UN organizations and NGOs had increased to 90.

petition between them and the military in the "compassion market," and to decrease any tensions arising from clashes of divergent leadership styles.

Such pragmatic cooperation can provide the basis of more effective assistance to the local populations; the specialist role of reservists and regular specialists can be vital in this regard. However, one note of caution is that some peacekeepers, for example, the Czechs, regarded some NGOs less as disinterested parties in the conflict and more as representing the interests of one or the other of the contending parties. The U.S. is, however, learning the importance of making a success of these military-civilian linkages and thus the need for a well-staffed civil–military operations center (CIMIC); these have been the key lessons not only of Bosnia, but also of Somalia and Haiti.

As far as Bosnia was concerned, quite apart from paying insufficient attention to the task of integrating its plans with NATO or international partners by perhaps overly concentrating on enforcement issues, the U.S. did not plan sufficiently for difficult political tasks and did not do very well at integrating military support with civil implementation. One indicator of the attendant difficulties was that the NGOs did not know who was in charge of CIMIC activities. There were strategic vision difficulties as well, in that the military did not perceive itself (or perhaps desire) to have a nation-building mandate, while the political leadership assumed this was part of the mandate but did not do enough to make this explicit.

From these problems, three key lessons have been learned. First, the CINC needs to have a campaign plan that incorporates all the elements of national power. Second, there is a need to include the NGOs in theater and strategic planning by, for example, expanding the role and authority of the political advisor's office within the headquarters to facilitate planning and communication and, furthermore, to deploy a multi-agency support team of experts to join the Joint Task Force or Combatant Commander. Third, and finally, there needs to be an expanded civil affairs staff to develop and disseminate doctrine about these important issues.

6. NATIONAL MILITARY CONTINGENTS AND THE LOCAL POPULATIONS

The whole purpose of strategic multinational peacekeeping operations is, in the end, to improve the lot of the local populations by providing security and a basis for peace and reconstruction. Yet in addition to the tensions between the military and non-military actors that we have considered above, the relations between these actors and the local populations themselves are not always free of tension. Here we focus on the military strand of such tensions with the local parties.

Inherent in operations of this kind is the risk that the military contingent will be viewed as an army of occupation – or worse, be seen not as an impartial and helpful presence but as biased towards the interests of one or other of the parties in conflict. Of course, not all contingents were as closely involved with the local population as others. For example, in IFOR, the main task of the Dutch was peace implementation – a fundamentally military operation that, in consequence, restricted their contacts with the local population. In SFOR, their tasks were to ensure that the warring parties left the declared zones of separation and withdrew heavy weapons to barracks; to organize elections; and to return refugees to their homes. With SFOR's emphasis on controlling and stabilizing the situation in a more peaceful context, the Dutch had greater opportunities to make contacts with the local populations and to play a policing and humanitarian role. Here, the Dutch were seen by the locals more as helpers than as the occupiers they had been perceived to be some years before. In this process, the Dutch deployed a "tit for tat" system of reciprocity, in which aid was given in exchange for cooperation with the wishes of the military. That said, local attitudes towards the Dutch were influenced by the fact that The Hague is the location of the International War Crimes Tribunal; while good relations could assist the Dutch under IFOR/SFOR in the apprehension of alleged war criminals, not all local populations looked with favor upon this fact.

Taking the case of the Swedes, the 1st battalion came into contact with practically all the warring parties, while those in subsequent battalions had little or no contact with Serb civilians, the Bosnian Serb population, or the Croatian army. During the UNPROFOR period, there was evidence that the Swedes held negative views about the local populations and a perception that these feelings were mutual. However, during the NATO period, these sentiments became more positive, especially as far as the Bosnian Serb and Serb civilians were concerned. Despite the fact that, during the NATO phase, there were some feelings amongst the locals that the Swedes were too neutral and not on the side of either of the conflicting parties, in IFOR there was a greater sense amongst the locals of a more positive future with heavily armed peacekeepers as a firm basis for a stable cease-fire. Generally speaking, data consistently show more positive relations between the local populations and the peacekeepers in the NATO phase.

The Danes experienced friction with the local authorities at the outset of their involvement in the operations. Yet this friction declined over time, a process that was assisted by the Danes' reputation for impartiality, which was facilitated by their having units stationed on both sides of the local conflict. The Czechs discovered one unexpected factor that helped them to build good relations with the local population; this was the skill base of their troops, especially in connection with performing house repairs and other construction tasks. Their skills in mine liquidation and the provision of medical aid were also appreciated. In building good relations with the local population, the U.S. was not alone in recognizing the need for their mid-level officers to have relevant skills in negotiation and confidence building, known as "grunt diplomacy." The U.S. discovered that its other national partners could serve as a useful bridge with the local population, as was the case, for example, with the Romanian contingent; the Romanians could, in any case, serve as a bridge between Serbs and Muslims on their own account.

Despite problems cooperating with local populations, such as military perceptions of the untrustworthiness of one or more of the local parties, and the stresses caused by acts of aggression between the parties in the presence of peacekeepers, the military contingents recognized that the mission would not be successful without such cooperation. In this connection, it is critical to maintain a robust stance and a reputation for impartiality and to cultivate friendly and constructive relations with the locals, which should be informed by an appreciation of the political and cultural context. If, as the Bulgarians and Czechs discovered, both cultural awareness and helpful skills can be combined, then so much the better.

However, maintaining a reputation for impartiality is never easy; despite the best intentions, relationships can become tricky, for example, when – as was the case with the Czechs – a contingent is based in an area with a high concentration of alleged war criminals. Even though the Czechs were regarded as pro-Serb by other parties, this was no guarantee that the Serbs themselves would not be hostile, as the Czech military presence was seen as an obstacle to their designs on "solving" the "Muslim problem" in Bosnia-Herzegovina.

7. Emerging Problems, Solutions, and Further Research Questions

Strategic multinational peacekeeping operations are likely to be a key feature of the future international security landscape. Thus, it is important that we do as much as we can to learn from the lessons of the past in order to improve the effectiveness of future operations. This study has identified a number of such lessons and raised some issues that warrant further detailed inquiries.

Not surprisingly, as a result of participating in operations of this kind, soldiers change their views of the capabilities of the other contingents with which they have worked. After the excitement of the early phase of a mission, there can be something of a culture shock when contingents have to deal with other national partners and overcome cultural differences in the way each does business. At the same time, stereotypical expectations and judgments can be eroded by the facts revealed through experience. The process can be assisted by more effective means of inter-cultural management. This does not involve removing cultural differences; rather, it calls for sharpening the recognition of what problems need to be overcome as well as what, despite the differences, each country shares, contributes, and can build upon to make the operation a success. Here there are some important issues to be resolved, not least the need to ensure that the more powerful and minor players work effectively together and that smaller powers do not feel excluded or view themselves as "bit part players" in a show managed and planned by the powerful, with little regard for their own interests and sensitivities. The case of rank inflation and national power games cited by the Dutch in multinational headquarters provides some indication of the difficulties to be resolved here. Attention must be paid to the problem of ensuring that contingents have a working knowledge of and a willingness to use English as the means of communication during these operations. At the same time, the gap between NATO and non-NATO members in terms of rules of procedure and information-sharing as well as fundamental equipment issues needs to be addressed. In addition, the question of unit organization must be examined. Mixing units could help to improve inter-cultural understandings among national contingents; on the other hand, this form of organization may well lead to friction and clumsiness in operations in contrast with separate national units, which, as we have seen, are easier to manage and reduce the chances of internal confusion caused by a Tower of Babel of different languages and management styles.

Quite apart from such basic issues as the distribution of power and status in multinational operations of this kind, other important issues requiring further attention include perceptions and experiences of relative deprivation with regard to the standard of equipment, pay, and conditions; distribution of tasks; effectiveness and quality of links with families and home; quality, variety, and amount of food; provision of training; and psychological support. As we have seen with regard to the U.S. case, there is a good deal of debate on the extent to which participation in peace support operations undermines the combat effectiveness of armed forces in terms of their readiness to engage in war-fighting.

Other than the points raised in the earlier part of this discussion, it is important to note that too much of the data are based upon self-assessment; there is a need for more objective indices of the supposed effects of peace support operations on military units or on the larger organizations from which they are drawn. More important is the fact the U.S. has spent a decade in slowly becoming used to the idea that, in addition to being prepared for war-fighting, it must expect to lead and participate in a range of peace support operations in the future.

To do this, the U.S. military needs more assistance from its friends and allies, both materiel – i.e., the ability to deploy, operate, and supply other forces in order to ensure that they can operate on a more equal footing with the U.S. – and doctrinal. Under the Bush administration, one of the key themes in defense policy will be how best to configure the U.S. military so as to equip it to fight major wars as well as to play a significant role in the kind of peace operations discussed in this book. While some suggest that it would be appropriate to establish a division of labor between the U.S. and its allies and friends – with the U.S. focusing on war and the others on peacekeeping and associated tasks of nation-building – political and military constraints are likely to make it difficult to develop this posture in any clear-cut fashion.

That said, whether we focus on war or peace operations, the events of "9/11" have made it imperative that the U.S. and European Union countries do even more to build agile, flexible forces. These forces will need to be well equipped materially and culturally for multinational operations as the security conditions of the 21st century require the armed services of the U.S. and other countries to be deployed increasingly in coalitions.

One of the key lessons learned from this study is that all national contingents recognize the importance of family support for the health and morale of their peacekeepers. The Czechs, for example, found that the extent of satisfaction with peacekeeping duties is closely related to the degree of support they receive from their families; their worries about their own families increased when they saw the superior communications resources that western forces had. While participation in peacekeeping could adversely affect families and even lead to divorce as a result of separation and a high operational tempo, closer inspection shows that in most cases when marriages of peacekeepers end in divorce, the marriage was already facing difficulties before deployment. When one looks at partners who had already developed strong bonds, participation in a mission could strengthen the marriage.

It is also apparent that troops from all countries expected to receive help in dealing with the stresses inherent in missions of this kind, in addition to the best training that can be developed. Investing in training and psychological support for deployed personnel and returning veterans is a key priority for those planning missions of this kind in the future. (Peacekeeping veterans, especially immediately after repatriation, are a key source of first-hand "lessons learned" that should be – and in some countries like Sweden and Ireland, already are – recycled back into peacekeeper training.) There may well be legal-related costs for defense ministries that fail to make sufficient provision of this kind of professional care for their returning service personnel.

Finally, all contingents were aware of the crowded nature of the theater of operations. In this regard, the success of the operation depends upon effective working relations with NGOs as a means of helping the local populations. Moreover, peacekeepers must understand and expect that an effective working relationship with the media is necessary for the success of the mission, primarily because peacekeepers' work is scrutinized closely by the media, whose support – as well as that of their domestic populations – is crucial in sustaining their morale and thus their will to continue the mission.

8. A NOTE ON METHODOLOGY

Although all but one [19] of the participating members of the research team used the same basic instrument – the six-section questionnaire that served as the research framework – there were individual variations in how the data were collected. Some data sources were of high quality, yet based on quite small numbers. For example, the Danish study was based on interviews with all but one of 30 Danish senior officers during the period 1996 – 1999, supplemented by interviews with soldiers in March 1999 and a detailed literature survey. Meanwhile, the Dutch study focused heavily on operational infantry, cavalry, and engineer units from January 1996 through June 1999, using interview transcripts of 25 personnel from IFOR and SFOR, along with secondary analysis of 13 journals, written by Dutch military participants, that detailed Dutch participation. The Swedes have a long and distinguished record of UN peacekeeping but have only recently begun to conduct detailed and in-depth scientific analysis of this experience. The questionnaire used by the Swedish author surveys 10 mechanized infantry battalions during the UN and NATO periods; these surveys have proved an invaluable addition to our understanding of the subject. These questionnaires were distributed both before the battalions departed for deployment as well as after these units returned. The populations surveyed were quite large; at its peak, the battalion numbered 1,020 and later dropped to 405.

The Czechs based their study on official and press documents and a survey of IFOR/SFOR participants during the period 1996 – 1998 before operations (194), during operations (211), and after operations (518). This third stage in-

---

[19] The Russian study was added later in the course of the research project, and although it covered many of the points in the agreed framework, it also analyzed other key issues related to peacekeeping in both Bosnia and the CIS. Because of the value of this additional information, we did not require that the study be rewritten to conform to the general outline used by the other country study authors.

cluded an analysis of responses by soldiers' spouses to their partners' deployment abroad, which, as we have seen earlier, produced some fascinating and policy-relevant data. The Austrian study was based upon extensive analysis of original fieldwork and questionnaires. The author of the Irish study made use of available scholarly literature on the subject, official and press documents, newspaper accounts, and Internet and database searches; most importantly, she conducted extensive interviews with Irish scholars and peacekeepers who have served in the former Yugoslavia. Like the Austrian author, the Canadian author conducted much of her research in the field, interviewing peacekeepers on the ground; she also made extensive use of Canadian research on this peacekeeping mission, in particular the *Ethics Survey*.

The Bulgarians used questionnaire surveys with control groups and supplemented their work with data garnered from focus groups and interviews with experts. The Romanian research team administered the questionnaire to 182 soldiers returning from Bosnia, which was a representative sample of those deployed there), together with post-questionnaire interviews with 24 soldiers who had held key positions during the mission (especially Public Relations officers). The Ukrainian study was based upon a government-sponsored sociological survey of former peacekeepers. Finally, the U.S. study was based mainly on secondary sources, many of which were based on first-hand experience, together with interviews and results from two after-action conferences held at the U.S. Army War College in 1996 – 1997.

APPENDIX

17. Appendix: Major Issues and Guiding Questions for Country Studies

1. Area I: Background

The introduction should include (but is not limited to):

- A brief history of the country's experience in peacekeeping operations (PKOs);
- A general statement about the particular national political motivations for sending a contingent to Bosnia;
- An answer to the question why military personnel volunteer for the PKO in Bosnia (if applicable) (For professional soldiers and units deployed without volunteers: what are motivations and attitudes toward participation for those in unit?);
- Time frame of the country's participation in this operation;
- Statement about the research methods applied and the main focus of your country paper.

2. Area II: Internal Military Dimension

This section of the paper should focus on points of tension that are internal to the military organization involved in this PKO. Such points of tension might be related to:

- Different perceptions of meaning, value, and effectiveness of the mission;
- Different perceptions of the adequacy of material, human, and organizational resources allotted to the PKO;
- The confidence or lack of confidence that the operation's conduct generates in all levels of leadership (tactical, operational, strategic, political);
- The degree of relative deprivation as perceived by different units or in other parts of the theater with regard to discrepancies in material or symbolic resource allocation as well as organizational doctrine, structure, and process;
- The credit or discredit the PKO brings upon those involved and the military as a whole.

  Questions to consider for your country could include:

- How is the PKO in Bosnia compatible with your country's national security strategy and military doctrine?

- Force selection and configuration: How are soldiers chosen for service in Bosnia (professional-volunteer draftee mix; whole units vs. mix and match, active duty vs. reserve, skill mix adequate to task)?
- Are the people experienced in peace support operations, and does that make a difference?
- Is their training (language skills, social and cultural competence) adequate to the mission?
- What is your country's mission in this PKO?
- Rules of engagement (ROE): differing regulatory status depending on location and situation? Is your contingent satisfied with this?
- Perception of acceptable risk? (Likely to change over time with changes in national public opinion.)
- Perception of value/meaning of mission – definition of "success"?
- Mission momentum?
- Confidence in political–military leadership?
- Valuable for individual?
- Useful for soldiers?
- Useful for career?
- Opportunities/attitudes to contact with local population?
- Is the mission valuable for individual and career interests? Unit? Country?
- Any differences in gender roles depending on theater?
- Are tensions between men and women in military exacerbated, reduced, or not affected by deployment?
- Branch rivalry (infantry/airborne disdain for intelligence or support units)?

3. AREA III: MILITARY – MILITARY DIMENSION

This section of the paper should focus on points of tension in military–military relations in the PKO. In this context, the following questions/issues should be discussed:

- *The power politics of the PKO*: Different militaries will have differing abilities to influence the mission and differing abilities to place people in important positions in Headquarters. This might be directly related to the country's level of participation in the operations in the FRY. The level of contribution may affect a state's ability to influence the decision-making process. How does such a "big game" affect the country's military units in the area of operations?
- *The level of NATO, WEU, and Warsaw Pact experience for each military contingent.* How does this experience – or lack of it – affect the national military unit's ability to work with other military contingents?

- *Language skills, communication problems, and, in particular, command of English.* Please detail whether and how fluency in English (or any other language) benefited your contingent's performance and/or how language barriers affected the performance of your contingent. If there were language barriers, were your troops able to work around them, and if so, how?
- *Differences between contingents.*
  - Do soldiers notice differences with respect to military culture between the different contingents?
  - Is there any common "peacekeeper" identity or common view of peacekeeping?
  - What are the major differences between the national contingents with respect to equipment, training, doctrine, etc.?
- *The image of the military.*
  - How does/did the local population perceive the military?
  - Is the mission supported at home by the national population and national government?
  - Does this affect morale?
  - What is the self-image of the soldiers?
  - What is their image/stereotype of the other contingents?
- *Differences between time frame and rotation methods among various countries.*
  - Do whole units rotate at once or just a small number of personnel at a time?
  - Do different military contingents have different tasks, with some being more exposed to danger than others?
  - How do soldiers of your country perceive the time frame and rotation methods with respect to the accomplishment of the mission?

4. AREA IV: MILITARY RELATIONS TO GOVERNMENT AND TO INTERNATIONAL GOVERNMENTAL ORGANIZATIONS

This section of the paper should focus on points of tension that result from the interaction between the military and governmental or international (governmental) organizations, including an analysis of the relationship between the military and the acting Bosnian and non-Bosnian governmental institutions/international organizations in Bosnia.

How does your military contingent interact with the "international community," i.e., with:

- The Peace Implementation Council (PIC);

- NATO (in particular SHAPE);
- OHR (Office of the High Representative for Bosnia);
- OSCE (Organization for Security and Cooperation in Europe);
- Other international organizations (or sub-institutions) like UNMIB (UN Mission in Bosnia) and the ICRC (International Committee of the Red Cross/Crescent);
- The acting Bosnian parties (governments, i.e., the independent Bosnia-Herzegovina government, including "Republika Srpska" and "Federation") in the theater as well as all local authorities (Opstina);
- At what level do military commanders and civilian governmental institutions interact (i.e., explore the potential gap between the military commander's SFOR task and his country's mission in Bosnia)?

5. AREA V: MILITARY RELATIONS TO NON-GOVERNMENTAL ORGANIZATIONS (NGOS), PRIVATE VOLUNTARY ORGANIZATIONS (PVOS), MEDIA, AND LOCAL POPULATION

This section of the paper should shed light on the relationship between the military and NGOs, PVOs, media, and local population. This might include an analysis of:

- *The differences between the military and NGOs and PVOs with regard to the tasks they have to accomplish.*
  - How does each group – military, NGO, PVO, and media – define success and view its mission?
  - How does the fact that each group has different tasks and responsibilities cause tensions between the groups and affect the accomplishment of the mission?
- *The complexity of the PKO results from the fact that a large number of organizations and parties are involved.*
  - How important are smooth and positive civil–military relations for the successful outcome of the PKO?
  - What is your country's military's experience with the media during the time of the PKO (on both levels, i.e., with regard to national media representatives as well as the international media)?
- *Intensity of relationships between NGOs/PVOs and the military.*
  - How much did the intensity of the relationships vary over time?
  - How was the relationship formalized?
  - Were liaison officers exchanged?

  – Were periodic meetings of all PVOs and NGOs in a given sector con-
    ducted with the leaders of the military contingent in the area?
  – How did public affairs officers (PAOs) conduct their mission with the
    media?
- *The military's relationship with the local population. Frequently, national
  contingents become sympathetic to the ethnic group with which they have
  the most frequent contact.*
  – Is this true for your country's units?
  – What is the military's view of NGOs, PVOs, the media, or local popula-
    tion, and vice versa?

18. AUTHORS

Prof. Dr. Bernard BOËNE, Director General for Academic Affairs, École Speciale Militaire de Saint-Cyr, Coëtquidan, France

Dr. Hans BORN, *formerly*: Royal Netherlands Military Academy, Breda, *now:* Center for Democratic Control of Armed Forces (DCAF), Geneva, Switzerland

Dr. Tessa op den BUIJS, Faculty of Military Sciences and Management, Royal Military Academy, Breda, Netherlands

Jean CALLAGHAN, M.A., Deputy Director, Research Programs, George C. Marshall European Center for Security Studies, Garmisch-Partenkirchen, Germany

Dr. Volodymyr CHUMAK, National Institute of Strategic Studies, NISS, Kiev, Ukraine, *now:* Counselor, Embassy of Ukraine, Washington, DC

Prof. Dr. Christopher DANDEKER, Head, Department of War Studies, Kings College, London, Great Britain

Prof. Dr. John GAROFANO, *formerly:* U.S. Army War College, Carlisle Barracks, *now:* Harvard University, USA

Dr. Eva JOHANSSON, Senior researcher at the National Defense College, Department of Leadership, Karlstad, Sweden

Dr. Franz KERNIC, Colonel, Austrian National Defense Academy, Vienna, Austria and Universität der Bundeswehr, Neubiberg, Germany

Dr. Alexander NIKITIN, Director, Center for Political and International Studies, and Professor, Moscow State Institute of International Relations, Moscow, Russian Federation

Colonel Valery RATCHEV, Center for National Security, Bulgarian Ministry of Defense, Sofia, Bulgaria

Dr. Alexandr RAZUMTSEV, National Institute of Strategic Studies, NISS, Kiev

Dr. Stefan SARVAS, *formerly:* Research Department, Ministry of Defense, Prague, Czech Republic,*now:* Philip Morris International in Lausanne (Switzerland) as Manager, Market Research

Dr. Ionel Nicu SAVA, *formerly:* Office for International Information, Ministry of Defense, *now:* Director, Omega Publishing House, Bucharest, Romania

Dr. Mathias SCHÖNBORN, Director, Research Programs, George C. Marshall European Center for Security Studies, Garmisch-Partenkirchen, Germany

Dr. Henning SOERENSEN, Director, Institute for Sociological Research, Copenhagen, Denmark

Dr. Laszlo SZABO, *formerly* Deputy Director Institute for Strategic and Defense Studies, Budapest, Hungary, *now:* Defense Attaché at Embassy of Hungary in Canada.

Dr. Marie VLACHOVA, *formerly:* Head, of Research Department, Ministry of Defense, Prague, *now:* Center for Democratic Control of Armed Forces (DCAF), Geneva, Switzerland

Dr. Ad VOGELAAR, Faculty of Military Sciences and Management, Royal Military Academy, Breda, The Netherlands

Prof. Dr. Donna WINSLOW, Department of Anthropology, Vrije Universiteit, Amsterdam, The Netherlands

Dr. Yantsislav YANAKIEV, Center for National Security, Ministry of Defense, Sofia, Bulgaria